Speech Communication and Human Interaction

Scott, Foresman's Consulting Editor in Speech Communication

Douglas Ehninger
The University of Iowa

Speech Communication and Human Interaction

Thomas M. Scheidel
University of Wisconsin

Scott, Foresman and Company
Glenview, Illinois   *London*

Dedicated to My Parents

Library of Congress Catalog Card No. 70-190717

PICTURE CREDITS

Cover   Collection of John Mayahara
Page 2   (top) Ron Sherman/Nancy Palmer Photo Agency; (bottom) Photograph by Ken Heyman
Page 3   (top) Wide World; (middle) Photograph by Ken Heyman; (bottom) Photograph by Laurence Fink
Page 8   (top) Photograph by Marion Bernstein; (bottom) Photograph by Paul Conklin
Page 9   (top left) Kenneth Murray/Nancy Palmer Photo Agency; (top right) Cornell Capa/Magnum; (bottom) Photograph by Ken Heyman
Page 10   (top) Photograph by Marion Bernstein; (middle and bottom) Photographs by Charles Gatewood
Page 11   Business Committee for the Arts. Photo courtesy of The Advertising Council, Inc.
Page 13   (left) Susan Feinberg/D.P.I.; (right) Don Wong/D.P.I.
Page 15   Courtesy of United Artists Corporation
Page 20   (top) Photograph by John W. Moore; (bottom) Photograph by Marion Bernstein
Page 21   Historical Pictures Service, Chicago
Page 22   (top) United Press International; (bottom) Chicago Tribune Photo
Pages 24–25   Photographs by Rusty Culp
Page 27   (top left) Alinari/Art Reference Bureau; (top right) United Press International; (bottom) Wayne Miller/Magnum
Page 39   Rona Beame/D.P.I.
Page 52   (top) Leonard Freed/Magnum; (middle) John Bryson/Rapho Guillumette; (bottom) Bettye Lane/Photo Researchers
Page 53   (top) Constantine Manos/Magnum; (bottom) Raimondo Borea/Photo Researchers
Page 65   (all) Wide World
Page 68   (both) Photographs by James L. Ballard
Page 70   Pioneer Press Photo by William Tiernan
Page 77   (top) Photograph by Hal A. Franklin; (bottom) Leonard Freed/Magnum
Page 88   Photographs by Laurence Fink
Page 89   (top left) Photograph by Ken Heyman; (top right) Photograph by Paul Sequeira; (bottom) Wide World
Page 99   United Press International
Page 100   Sue Kellogg/Black Star
Page 102   Fred Ward/Black Star
Page 107   Chicago Tribune Photo
Page 108   (left) United Press International; (right) Photograph by Joe Molnar
Page 112   (top) Photograph by Paul Sequeira; (middle left) Photograph by Paul Conklin; (middle right) Photograph by Marion Bernstein; (bottom) Photograph by Ken Heyman

Preface

This textbook is intended for a first-level college course in speech communication. Its aims are twofold: to develop an understanding of basic concepts and principles operating in the speech communication setting and to provide a sequential set of materials and structured experiences leading to improved comprehension and performance by the reader. These two aims are interrelated and integrated as cogently and completely as possible. Throughout, the focus is upon speech communication as a *process*—an ongoing, multidimensional phenomenon in which many variables are acting and interacting.

The major elements of the speech communication process are (1) *agents* who (2) *interact* (3) in a *context*. The situation in which two persons converse is suggested as the archetype of all oral communication contexts; the principles which apply there are also applicable and may be extended and generalized to all other settings.

Approximately one half of the book (Parts I, III, and IV) is devoted to the exposition of principles and the explication of constructs. The basic variables operating in the speech communication process are surveyed; the wide-ranging purposes served by the speech process are examined, as are the many effects produced by it; and the development of rhetorical propositions is traced from initial environmental sensation to complex decision making.

The other half of the book (Parts II and V) presents a sequence of exploratory, experiential, and instructional materials and study probes intended to assist the reader in improving his analytical and performative capabilities in "live" speech communication situations. Based upon the central, archetypal context of two persons conversing to achieve maximally productive feedback and interaction, the participatory/performative chapters (3, 8, 9, and 10) progress from interpersonal communication to small group communication to speech making appropriate for the public platform and the mass media.

Appearing at numerous junctures in the ten successive chapters are *study probes* which are closely interwoven with the fabric of the text where the reader's exposure to and completion of them will be most meaningful. Sometimes they serve to initiate and direct thinking about a new concept or problem of communication; at other times they exemplify or elaborate upon points previously introduced or steps previously taken; always they are designed to clarify, expand, and reinforce the reader's understanding of an essential idea or a key construct. Lists of carefully chosen *suggested readings* are located at the conclusion of various chapters to encourage him to expand his knowledge of the subject and to make possible further explorations of it. Textual illustrations, of both a photographic and diagrammatic nature, are employed to illuminate or vivify various facets of the textual content. The use of a second color is intended to add a special dimension, emphasis, and visual appeal to the printed commentary and to certain graphic presentations which are an integral part of it. Appendices include *a model speech* for referential comparisons and analyses and a number of *self-assessment scales* and *evaluative guides* to assist the reader in analyzing his own communicative expectations, interactive capacities, and performative achievements as well as those of his fellow communicators in speech communication contexts.

Many persons have contributed substantially to the development of this textbook. Verne Powers, editor of speech and theatre publications, Scott, Foresman and Company, provided invaluable editorial assistance. I owe him a great deal. Professor Carroll C. Arnold of the Pennsylvania State University examined the entire manuscript, recommending numerous additions and improvements and providing a wealth of suggestions for strengthening the organization and presentation of the materials. Professors Douglas Ehninger and Donovan J. Ochs of the University of Iowa contributed significantly to Chapters 6 and 10, respectively; and I deeply appreciate their assistance. Numerous others, including past and present colleagues and students, offered help, advice, and encouragement at various times and in various forms in the creation and completion of this volume. I am grateful to all.

T.M.S.

Overview

Contents

Part III
Speech Communication: Identifying Purposes and Assessing Effects   86

Part IV
Deriving Speech Substance, Advancing Propositions, and Making Decisions   156

Part V
Speech Communication in Action: Advanced Concerns   236

Speech Communication and Human Interaction

Part I

The Nature of Speech Communication

For it is by this one gift that we are most distinguished from brute animals, that we converse together, and can express our thoughts by speech. . . . What other power could either have assembled mankind, when dispersed, into one place, or have brought them from wild and savage life to the present humane and civilized state of society? . . . Go on, therefore, as you are doing, young men, and apply earnestly to the study in which you are engaged, that you may be an honour to yourselves, an advantage to your friends, and a benefit to the republic.

These ageless views of Cicero, voiced twenty centuries ago by the great Roman statesman, orator, and rhetorician, suggest certain basic assumptions which will be echoed in this contemporary textbook on speech communication.

The first of these assumptions is that those factors which combine to produce the act of speech may be considered to be the defining elements of *man,* and that they represent his distinctiveness from all other animals. If the essential character of man is indeed revealed in the speech act, then the study of that act requires no other justification. Accordingly, one major concern of this introductory textbook will be an investigation of the available contemporary knowledge about speech behavior: What brings speech into being? What are its antecedents? What are the elements of the oral communication process? How does it develop? What are the purposes of speaking? What are the potential influences and consequences? What do we know now, and what are the major gaps in our knowledge of speech? In sum, we will explore speech communication as a distinctive form of human behavior.

A second assumption, consistent with the view of Cicero and that of both classical and contemporary teachers of rhetoric in general, is that any human being possessed of normal wits and inclination can improve his speaking ability by study and training, by practice and guidance. While some unquestionably are endowed with greater natural gifts than others, in any society, practically everyone—regardless of his inherent advantages or limitations—will come to use oral utterance throughout his life as his most frequent and most direct means of communication. Underlying this book, therefore, is the conviction that special instruction and training in communicative interaction can enhance any person's natural abilities and increase his capacities to learn from meaningful experience.

Finally, a third postulate fundamental to this work is that a sound and healthy society will be made up of citizens who are active, involved, and who will exercise their voices in the maintenance and conduct of that society. For this reason, every man in a free society has both the privilege and the *duty* to gain the knowledge and experience necessary to acquit himself with effectiveness in interacting constructively with his fellowman. As Aristotle argued in his *Rhetoric:*

> *It is absurd to hold that a man ought to be ashamed of being unable to defend himself with his limbs, but not of being unable to defend himself with speech and reason, when the use of rational speech is more distinctive of a human being than the use of his limbs. And if it be objected that one who uses such power of speech unjustly might do great harm, that is a charge which may be made in common against all good things except virtue, and above all against the things that are most useful, as strength, health, wealth, generalship. A man can confer the greatest of benefits by a right use of these, and inflict the greatest of injuries by using them wrongly.*

Because of these beliefs and assumptions, the author's pervasive purpose in this textbook will be to identify those communicative behaviors unique to humankind; to consider and evaluate the effects, extensions, and probable consequences of the communicative process in such a way as to encourage present and future citizens of our society to participate actively, sensitively, and sensibly in the determination of their destinies; and—to this end—to proffer those principles and practices which can assist those seriously interested in improving their communicative skills.

Chapter 1

Speech Communication: Concept and Challenge

Speech communication
is a socially learned process,
occurring when two or more persons
are interacting by transmitting
and receiving auditory and visual stimuli
which are treated as symbolic cues
to which meaning is attached.

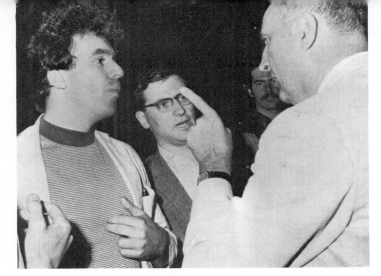

The pollution of the environment is one of the chief concerns of our time. In the past, the indiscriminate disposal of wastes into the earth, water, and air was considered by many to be "the inevitable price of progress." Now we are finding that pollution in many areas is approaching dangerous levels. The current opinion of numerous responsible persons is that we have unintentionally created environmental problems of great severity, the solutions to which must be promptly conceived and effected if mankind is to survive.

Swift and far-reaching control of pollution exemplifies that type of significant social problem confronting our populous and mushrooming society with increasing and disturbing frequency—a problem demanding assiduous searching for and sifting of information, serious and unselfish thinking, and skillful speech communication. Such problems are too complex and interrelated to be solved easily by any single individual. They must be approached with an understanding that comes only from accurate information filtered through sober reflection. Solutions to such problems demand prompt social cooperation and united action of unprecedented proportions.

Clearly, human interaction through speech communication is the primary means by which individuals are brought to cooperative effort. And the cooperation of a sufficient number of concerned citizens *can* produce dramatic results. In *The Unclean Sky,* for example, Louis Battan describes one such success in the treatment of air pollution:

> An almost miraculous change was brought about in Pittsburgh. In a matter of four years it was transformed from a dramatic example of how bad a city can get with too little planning and too much smoke, to a city that is the pride of its residents and the whole state. It is taller, cleaner, and has a shinier future. Industry has profited, the people have profited, and the country has, too.
>
> There was an important lesson to be learned from the scrubbing up of The Smoky City. It showed that even the most industrialized community can be changed, and in short order. But it was necessary, first, for the leading citizens to understand the problems and to want to change them.[1]

Note especially the significance of the words *understand* and *want to*. One can easily imagine the many conversations, arguments, investigations, meetings, discussions, and persuasive appeals that were necessary to unite the Pittsburgh community forces in effecting this "almost miraculous change." Even a quick analysis of the case dramatically demonstrates the functions—and accomplishments—of speech communication in contemporary society.

The Pervasiveness and Permanence of Speech Communication

Always man's task is to meet and solve the dilemmas of his day. Many of our social problems, including environmental pollution, have been with us for a long time, occurring and recurring in one form or another.[2] As the times change,

---

[1] Louis J. Battan, *The Unclean Sky* (Garden City, N.Y.: Doubleday & Company, Inc., Anchor Books, 1966), p. 120.

[2] See, for example, Thomas R. Detwyler, *Man's Impact on Environment* (New York: McGraw-Hill Book Company, 1971).

of course, so do the manifestations, dimensions, and urgencies of the problems. The need for new solutions and united action, therefore, is with us always. We have to recognize the difficulties, discuss probable causes, identify possible solutions, weigh alternatives, and ultimately decide upon what we hope will be a desirable and generally agreed-upon course of action. Hence the need for speech communication exists in every age and at every time. In fact, throughout man's recorded history we can readily discern that speech has been our universal, primary, and most frequently used means of communication. Note, for example, how Professor George Kennedy has vividly described the prominent role played by oral interaction in early Greek society:

> *Both the mechanics of ancient civilization and its primary expression remained oral. The political system, for example, operated through the direct speech of the citizens among themselves and to their magistrates, and of the magistrates to their administrative assistants. Writing was used to record a vote, a law, a resolution, but rarely to achieve it in the first place. Political agitation was usually accomplished or defeated by word of mouth. The judicial system was similarly oral: verbal complaints were brought before magistrates, who held hearings; then the litigants pleaded their own cases in public before a jury of citizens. Documents were few. There were written business contracts, but they were negotiated and enforced by face-to-face arguments rather than any prolonged correspondence. There were no newspapers, magazines, handbills, or circulars; information was spread orally. Entertainment was provided only to a limited extent by reading; informal conversation, the legitimate stage, or the sound of the human voice in some form constituted the commonest form of diversion. All literature was written to be heard, and even when reading to himself a Greek read aloud.*[3]

With such an emphasis upon the speech act, it should not be surprising that the leading scholars of the time focused attention on it. The moralistic Plato criticized the speaking in Athenian society, and in the *Phaedrus* outlined what he deemed an ideal rhetoric. Aristotle, taking a somewhat more dispassionate view, developed his *Rhetoric,* which still influences the writing of speech textbooks today. And so it has been through generation after generation. Cicero, Quintilian, St. Augustine, Machiavelli, George Campbell, Richard Whately, James Rush, Adolf Hitler, James Winans, and countless others have contributed to an ever-enlarging body of knowledge and thinking about speaking.*

In our own day we can find on all sides concern for various aspects of speech communication. College speech departments have long and typically offered courses in the history of rhetorical theory and practice, and have made available to students courses which explore the principles and performative elements of public speaking, group discussion, argumentation and persuasion, speech and hearing science, and phonetics, as well as speech training in theater, radio, and television. Further, depending upon their own special interests, stu-

[3] George Kennedy, *The Art of Persuasion in Greece* (Princeton, N.J.: Princeton University Press, 1963), p. 4. This source is listed for suggested reading at the conclusion of this chapter.

* Students interested in the history of rhetoric will find at the conclusion of this chapter a number of annotated references providing background information of this kind.

dents will find that nearly every basic textbook in the fields of psychology, sociology, anthropology, and linguistics will treat or touch upon some phase or aspect of the speech communication process. Readily observable, too, is an increasing interest in and emphasis upon training in speech throughout all the years of the students' formal education. Beyond the classroom and the home, our business community is keenly aware of the vital role of communication in commercial and industrial endeavors, and seminars in speech are frequently offered to both management and employees for the purpose of facilitating and extending their functions. The same is true in the broader political and economic sphere, with speech communication specialists offering training and theoretical advice to various groups from foreign countries who come to study in the United States. The need for effective speech communication generally in society—in education, in business, in politics, in race relations, in counseling and psychiatry—is increasingly becoming recognized.

Defining Speech Communication

On first thought, because speech communication is so fundamental to relating our own lives to the lives of others, we might conclude that we already understand what the term means. After all, we have been involved with the process from a very early age; all of us have had considerable first-hand experience both as senders and receivers of oral messages; almost every day we have observed its successes and its failures. Such a conclusion, however, might be misleading.

As a test of whether we truly understand what speech communication is, let's try to devise a satisfactory *definition* of it.

STUDY PROBE 1
Exploring a Definition

Take a pencil and a sheet of paper and write your own definition of *speech communication.* Consider carefully what this term means to you. When you are satisfied, tentatively at least, with what you have written, resume reading the chapter and compare your definition with those provided in the ensuing paragraphs. When you have concluded your comparison and have finished reading the chapter, return to *your* definition. Examine it critically and determine in which respects, if any, you would want to alter it. Why? By which *means* or *techniques* did you choose to define the term in the first place?

If you compare your definition of speech communication with others written by the class, very probably you will discover that no two of the definitions are identical. The author's previous experience with the Study Probe has produced the following descriptions which might be regarded as typical:

> Speech Communication is *the process of transferring one's ideas, facts, or theories through the use of language, gestures, and vocal intonation to another person or group of persons.*

Speech Communication is *the meaningful exchange of thoughts, feelings, ideas, emotions, etc., through verbal stimuli, with production by one person (or more) and received by one or more others.*

Speech Communication is *the process by which thinking beings are able to convey their thoughts and emotions to others.*

These are adequate definitions. They compare favorably with many found in published works on communication. Consider, for example, the following:

Communication is the verbal interchange of thought or idea.[4]

Communication: the transmission of information, ideas, emotions, skills, etc., by the use of symbols—words, pictures, figures, graphs, etc. It is the act *or process of transmission that is usually called communication.*[5]

Every communication act is viewed as a transmission of information, consisting of discriminative stimuli, from a source to a recipient.[6]

There are distinctions, of course, to be noted among these definitions. Some speak of "transferring," and others of "transmitting." Some call it "act," and some refer to "process." The elements included differ from example to example. Our real question becomes: Do these distinctions make any difference? By defining speech communication in a slightly different way, will we understand our subject any differently? The answer is, of course, a decided *yes.* The act of defining lies at the core of *understanding shared meanings.* And understanding shared meanings, in turn, lies at the heart of effective speech communication. Without this understanding, we cannot hope to interact intelligently and constructively with others. What, then, are the specific purposes which we should hold in mind when we define a term—*any* term—and what are the means by which we can accomplish those purposes?

Purposes and Procedures for Defining Terms

Quite simply, we define a term so that we and others can know what *our* meaning of the term is. We must clothe the term in a fair amount of "mutual" meaning in order that our listeners may know how we are *using* the term. Only in this way can we hope to be able to employ it usefully in communicative interactions. As interactants, certainly, we must first reach an understanding of the requisite terms before we can hope to proceed to an understanding at any higher level.

There are at least three important ways of defining any term, and all of them are useful to the communicator. We may define (1) *by example,* (2) *by genus* and *difference,* or (3) *by stipulation.*

---

[4] John B. Hoben, "English Communication at Colgate Re-Examined," *Journal of Communication,* IV (1954): 77.

[5] Bernard Berelson and Gary A. Steiner, *Human Behavior: An Inventory of Scientific Findings* (New York: Harcourt Brace Jovanovich, Inc., 1964), p. 254.

[6] Theodore M. Newcomb, "An Approach to the Study of Communication Acts," *Communication and Culture,* ed. Alfred G. Smith (New York: Holt, Rinehart & Winston, Inc., 1966), p. 66. This anthology, listed at the conclusion of this chapter, is recommended for exploratory reading.

Definition by Example

Definition by example, the illustrative definition, is very common. This is probably the way most children learn labeling and definitions: "This is a ball." "This is not a ball. This is a block." The label and the object are presented side by side. We can also define more complex concepts by exemplifying them. Note, for instance, how we might define *speech communication* by a series of examples. Visualize the late Martin Luther King, Jr., standing before the Lincoln Memorial in Washington, D.C., presenting his speech "I Have a Dream." Imagine a small group of adults gathering during an evening for a "Great Books" discussion. Think of a situation in a Sears store where a salesman is pointing out the merits of a particular washing machine to a prospective buyer. Call to mind the scene of three elderly men sitting on a park bench discussing today's youth, or the sight of a small group of children deciding what game to play. Envision lovers discussing their future. Or consider a student-instructor exchange in your own college classroom. These are all *examples* of speech communication. The photographs shown here also provide illustrative examples of this kind of definition. Each exemplifies a kind or a phase of the speech communication process.

EXAMPLES OF SPEECH COMMUNICATION
Each of the photos in this series provides an example of speech communication, and taken together the situations depicted encompass a wide range—from one person engaging in speech to interpersonal situations of varying purposes and varying degrees of speaker-listener interaction.

10

While the examples of speech communication seen in these photos are interesting and of value in our attempts to define speech communication, any number of examples can do no more than provide a potpourri of impressions. What ties them all together and furnishes a basis for regarding them as illustrative of the process we call "speech communication"?

Here, of course, communication is occurring only on the part of some of the persons present.

While defining by example affords certain advantages, the technique is not without its drawbacks. Suppose the situation in which a man, on going to bed at night, accidentally collides with the bed frame in the darkness and stubs his toe. "Damn you!" he mutters to the frame. Since there can be no interaction between the object and the man, this would not be an example of "speech communication" according to the view of this textbook. And this points up a weakness of definition by example: While it may help our understanding to be shown actual cases to which a label applies, the *reasons* for the definition are not made clear. That is, we are not told *why* the label does or does not apply.

Definition by Genus and Difference

As a second means of defining, we may cite genus and difference and thus formulate an analytical definition. Here the object, concept, or idea to be defined is analyzed in terms of classes and subclasses. We can, for instance, define a triangle as a three-sided polygon, saying that it is one of a *class* of polygons. Triangles can be then divided into three *subclasses:* scalene, isosceles, and equilateral. In much the same manner, speech communication may be considered as a subdivision of a larger topic: *communication.* S. S. Stevens has defined communication as "the discriminatory response of an organism to a stimulus."[7] By this definition, a man swearing at a bed frame or a dog baying at the moon might be considered an instance of communication. This type of broad and general definition for a very inclusive term is helpful, for it provides both a useful starting point for intercommunication, and an umbrella label under which persons with related interests can be united. Under this definition, a person interested in the baying of dogs could be said to be interested in communication. So could a computer programmer who is adjusting his program to the specifications of his computer.

Hockett limits communication further than Stevens by defining it as "those acts by which one organism triggers another."[8] This definition restricts the study to those situations in which only two organisms are involved and would rule out from consideration the cases mentioned. Under Hockett's definition, a person seeking a communication code among dolphins, or in the dancing act of bees, would be making a study of communication. By adding "speech" to communication, we further narrow and specify the scope and limits of our concern, thus ruling out as instances of speech communication the examples in this paragraph. When speech communication is defined as a special class of communication, however, you cannot yet be positive of just how the term is being used.

Definition by Stipulation

A third means of defining a term is by stipulation. In the famous communicative interchange between Alice and Humpty Dumpty, we have a clear-cut instance of definition by stipulation:

"There's glory for you!"

"I don't know what you mean by 'glory,' " Alice said.

Humpty Dumpty smiled contemptuously. "Of course you don't—til I tell you. I meant 'there's a nice knock-down argument for you!' "

"But 'glory' doesn't mean 'a nice knock-down argument,' " Alice objected.

"When I use a word," Humpty Dumpty said, in a rather scornful tone, "it means just what I choose it to mean—neither more nor less."

"The question is," said Alice, "whether you can make words mean so many different things."

"The question is," said Humpty Dumpty, "which is to be master—that's all."[9]

In those cases where a single term may have different meanings for different persons, it may be most helpful for clarity and mutual understanding to define by stipulation—to specify what the term means to you, and how you intend to use it.

[7] S. S. Stevens, "A Definition of Communication," *Journal of the Acoustical Society of America,* XXII (1950): 689.

[8] C. F. Hockett, *A Course in Modern Linguistics* (New York: Crowell Collier and Macmillan, Inc., 1958), p. 573.

[9] Lewis Carroll, *Through the Looking-Glass* (New York: Random House, Inc., Modern Library ed., undated), pp. 246–247.

Defining Speech Communication by Stipulation

Let us stipulate and explain what speech communication will be considered to mean in this textbook:

> **Speech Communication is the socially learned process occurring when two or more persons are interacting by transmitting and receiving visual and auditory stimuli which are treated as symbolic cues to which meaning is attached.**

This stipulated definition is lengthy and includes many concepts which themselves need defining. Our hope is that a fuller understanding of speech communication will result from an explication and analysis of this definition.

Speech Communication: A Socially Learned Process

Speech does not just happen. It *develops* and *is* developed. It is not innate or instinctive, but rather develops out of social contact. Whereas all human behavior can be said to come from the individual, speech behavior requires a social setting if it is to develop in the individual.

The Development of Speech

The development of speech in children progresses in general and overlapping stages.[10] The first few weeks of a child's life constitute the prelingual or *crying* stage. During this period the baby's crying is wholly emotional and reflexive, indicating general unpleasant feelings. At about the end of the first month, the child's cries become somewhat differentiated. A mother can often tell from her baby's cry whether he is hungry, wet, frightened, uncomfortable, or becoming restless and sleepy. These cries are still reflexive, but each indicates a different internal state, and the differentiation shows the process of maturation occurring in the child's nervous system.

[10] See Giles W. Gray and Claude M. Wise, *The Bases of Speech,* 3rd ed. (New York: Harper & Row, Publishers, 1959), Chapter 8, "The Genetic Basis of Speech." This source is listed for suggested reading at the conclusion of this chapter.

In infants, speech development normally progresses from the crying phase (below, left) through a babbling phase and into a stage of imitation (right photo), where auditory stimulus by another person elicits the child's response to and repetition of sounds.

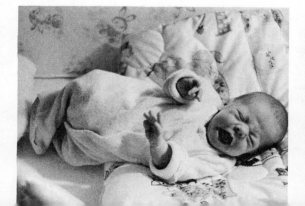
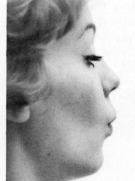

Some time later, at about the sixth month, a very significant second stage begins to overlap with the first. This is the *babbling* stage. The child now engages in vocal play, producing most of the vowel and consonant sounds of which man is physiologically capable. The child usually produces this "nonsense" speech as an indication of a pleasant mood and reverts to crying when he is unhappy. During this period the *ear-voice circular response* can be noted. The babbling not only seems pleasurable, but the sounds produced stimulate the child to further babbling. So a child at this stage can be heard repeating "da-da-da" and other seemingly meaningless sounds for long periods. The significance of hearing becomes obvious in this stage of speech development. As a child begins to make syllabic utterances, sounds that he hears himself produce reinforce his learning and thereby further his progress. The speech development of a congenitally deaf child will progress into this babbling stage, but then it is arrested. Without hearing ability, normal speech development is impossible because the gratifications that encourage further progress are not fully attainable.

In the next stage of speech development the social stimulus becomes significant. The ear-voice circular-response stage gradually leads to the stage of *imitation*. In the former, the child is stimulated by his own voice and repeats the sounds which he hears. In the imitative stage, the auditory stimulus is provided by another person. The child now responds to and repeats sounds produced by others to the extent that those sounds are reasonably similar to sounds the child has already made by himself. He will repeat the sound that he hears or something like it. This stage, which begins when the child is about one year old, represents the onset of articulate utterance, for he will now be repeating and learning the sounds, words, syntax, and grammar of his society. And this language development will occur because of stimulation by other persons.

The Social Influence of Speech

In an effort to substantiate the assertion that speech communication can only be developed in a social setting, it might be meaningful to consider the rare examples of children who, through accident, neglect, or circumstance, have been raised in relative isolation from other people.[11] The few available reports of such children, usually termed feral children, point to a single striking conclusion: the feral child appears to be "unhuman." His behavior seems more that of animal than of man. His "speech" consists largely of grunts and isolated sounds. Although one cannot conclude too much on the basis of these reports, they do provide some insight into the profound and far-reaching effects which "others" have upon us. Some contemporary existentialists tell us that, because of man's nature, each of us is aware of himself as *subject* but of others as *object*. We cannot easily put ourselves in another's shoes. For this reason we are often well aware of our communicative influence on others; but because our own reactions to communication seem so natural and self-determined, we tend to discount in large measure the influence exerted on us by other men.

George Herbert Mead has suggested that, in addition to these essential human qualities, each of us develops his concept of *self* as a result of his inter-

[11] If interested in this topic, you could begin your reading with Susanne K. Langer, *Philosophy in a New Key* (New York: The New American Library, Inc. Mentor Books, 1948), pp. 97–99.

A celebrated case of a feral child was that of Victor, the "wild boy of Aveyron," reported to have been found in the forest by French peasants when he was about 10 or 11 years old. Attempts by Jean-Marc Itard to educate and civilize the boy were promising at first, but Victor was never able to learn more than a few words or communicate except in the most rudimentary way. This photo of Jean-Pierre Cargol in the title role of *The Wild Child* is from François Truffaut's film version of the story.

action with others in society, largely in the speech communication setting.[12] As children we become aware of the perceptions others have of us and of their expectations from us. Through the subtleties of their communication, we learn the image they have of us, and we then are psychologically punished if we do not conform to that image. If it is "expected" that we be the butt of others' jokes, we may tend to play the clown. If we "will be a scholar," then we may spend more time in study and, if for no other reason, do better in our classwork. We discover the roles that others assign to us, and often we play those roles. As that role-playing becomes habit, it internalizes to form a part of our self-concept, a subject to which we will devote further attention in Chapter 4.

STUDY PROBE 2
Discovering a Concept of Self

On a sheet of paper write what you consider to be your image of "self." How do you see yourself? What image do you believe you project to others? What "type" of person do they see you to be? Do their typical reactions to you present any consistent pattern which might reveal how they think of you? Try to recall interaction with your parents, relatives, siblings, and peers when you were a child. How do you perceive that you were perceived? What seemed to be expected of you? Can you make any connections between your self-image now and roles and behaviors expected of you when you were a child?

---

[12] George Herbert Mead, *Mind, Self, and Society: From the Standpoint of a Social Behaviorist,* ed. Charles W. Morris (Chicago: University of Chicago Press, 1934). See especially Part III on "Self."

Speech communication is a necessary and profound part of the development of humanness and selfness in every individual. It is the significance of this social influence that Aristotle and Cicero are asserting when they refer to speech as the defining element of man.

The Need for Training in Speech

Academic training in speech communication has been considered by some persons to be unnecessary and even frivolous. "We don't take courses in school about how to walk," they say, "but we all do learn to walk. So why not the same with speech?" Edward Sapir refuted this position some years ago when he wrote:

> In a very real sense the normal human being is predestined to walk, not because his elders will assist him to learn the art, but because his organism is prepared from birth, or even from the moment of conception, to take on all those expenditures of nervous energy and all those muscular adaptations that result in walking. To put it concisely, walking is an inherent, biological function of man.
>
> Not so language. It is of course true that in a certain sense the individual is predestined to talk, but that is due entirely to the circumstance that he is born not merely in nature, but in the lap of a society that is certain, reasonably certain, to lead him to its traditions. Eliminate society and there is every reason to believe that he will learn to walk, if, indeed, he survives at all. But it is just as certain that he will never learn to talk, *that is, to communicate ideas according to the traditional system of a particular society.*[13] [*Emphasis added*]

Since speech is socially learned, it can be poorly learned. But also, as we can readily observe, relearning is possible.

Speech communication behavior arises out of an interacting society. It provides the individual with the means for gaining self-impression and self-expression. It is also society's binding and dynamic force. This is the meaning of the first part of our definition of speech communication: *a socially learned process.*

Speech Communication: Personal Interaction

This portion of our definition delimits the scope of our interest, and highlights the transactional element in speech communication. Broad definitions of communication, such as "the discriminatory response of an organism to a stimulus," were cited earlier. These definitions would allow us to consider as communication a situation such as that in which a man arises and goes to work when the sun comes up. Using the broad definition given above, it could be said that the sun communicated by "telling" the man to get up. Similarly, we could categorize as communication the examples previously cited—the man who stubs his toe against a bed frame and speaks angrily at it, and the computer programmer who "writes messages" to his machine. In each of these instances we have one human

[13] Edward Sapir, *Language* (New York: Harcourt Brace Jovanovich, Inc., 1921), pp. 3–4.

agent responding to some nonhuman element in his environment in a way that involves communication in a broad sense of the term.

We must consider also the possibility of man speaking to himself. Perhaps that is basically what happened in the "damning" of the bed frame. Obviously, the "damner" is not intending to establish a communicative bond with the bed frame by his exclamation. Rather, he is releasing tension and comforting himself. Just as he may exclaim "Oh, that's too bad" to comfort his daughter when she has stubbed her toe, his comment—ostensibly to the bed frame—is actually self-comforting. It is because oral activity usually has a public quality about it, even if spoken without other auditors present, that this man can be thought of as publicly proclaiming support and sympathy for himself.

While the general reactions of man to nonhuman stimuli and the topic of intrapersonal communication are interesting in their own right, our primary concern will be *inter*personal communication. It should be noted, however, that to some degree all speech acts are addressed to the self and serve to provide a measure of self-satisfaction. To this extent, therefore, all speech acts are intrapersonal. It will be necessary to discuss intrapersonal communication in a few appropriate places in this textbook, but the emphasis will be upon speech communication among conjoined persons. Thus the criterion of our definition is *joint participation*. While face-to-face communication will serve as our ideal case and our model, we will not exclude communication via the mass media. A television speaker and the television viewer, for example, can be considered conjoined and participating jointly in the communication process, even though they are not in direct confrontation.

The choice to limit our special concern to communication between persons places a focus directly upon the process of human interaction and transaction. Psychiatrist Joost Meerloo defines communication as:

> *a cluster of transactional functions whereby a state of body and mind is conveyed from one person to another, and responses evoked. Both sender and receiver are supposed to take part in the rhetorical operation.*[14]

This definition highlights the transactional activity in speech communication. Another psychiatrist, Jurgen Ruesch, approaches this essential element in communication in a slightly different manner, speaking of *the perception of perception* as the key:

> *The perception of the perception, as we might call this phenomenon, is the sign that a silent agreement has been reached by the participants, to the effect that mutual influence is to be expected.*[15]

Sociologist Erving Goffman comments from yet another frame of reference:

> *In any society, whenever the physical possibility of spoken interaction arises, it seems that a system of practices, conventions and procedural rules comes into play, which functions as a means of guiding and organizing the flow of messages. An understanding will prevail as to when and where it will be*

---

[14] Joost A. M. Meerloo, "Contributions of Psychiatry to the Study of Human Communication," *Human Communication Theory,* ed. Frank E. X. Dance (New York: Holt, Rinehart & Winston, Inc., 1967), p. 131.

[15] Jurgen Ruesch and Gregory Bateson, *Communication: The Social Matrix of Psychiatry* (New York: W. W. Norton & Co., Inc., 1951), p. 23.

permissible to initiate talk, among whom, and by means of what topics of conversation. . . . When this process of reciprocal ratification occurs, the persons so ratified are in what might be called a state of talk—*that is, they have declared themselves officially open to one another for purposes of spoken communication and guarantee together to maintain a flow of words.*[16]

The open interaction between two or more persons who expect and exert mutual influence is the heart of the speech communication process, and it is to this concept that the major focus of our attention will be directed.

Speech Communication: Transmitting and Receiving Stimuli

One of the student definitions listed earlier presented speech communication as the process of "transferring one's ideas, facts, or theories." Communication occasionally is defined as a process of *transfer*. But the word "transfer" too often implies the conveying of an image or idea intact from one person to another. In this author's view, one cannot exercise any direct control over the receipt of the messages he sends out. One cannot say that the ideas, images, impressions, and information that he holds and speaks about will be the same ideas, images, impressions, and information held by the listener following the speech communication. Thus the word "transfer" may distort our view of what occurs during the speech process.

The word *transmit,* with the implication of "sending out," will be used here in place of transfer. Our position is that all a speaker can do is to transmit, to send out stimuli. The speaker may very well take the nature of his listener into account as he speaks, and he may attempt to adapt his material to that specific listener. But once he has sent a message out, a speaker can do no more with it. At best, he can adapt it further and send it out again.

The process of receiving is the province of the listener. We are reminded here of the old question of the tree in the forest: If a tree falls in a forest and no living being is present to hear it, is there any sound? The answer obviously depends upon the definition of "sound." If the creation and transmission of sound waves is accepted as the definition, then in this case there is sound. But we wish to focus on those instances in which at least two persons are conjoined—in which sender and receiver are present. Given this orientation, if one person shouts in a forest and no other person is present to hear, speech communication does not occur. Transmitting by speaker and receiving by listener are complementary processes, and both are necessary for the speech communication act as we have defined it.

We have said that a speaker can only transmit and that a receiver is necessary for speech communication. But what is transmitted and what is received? Contrary to some of the definitions cited earlier, we must assert that ideas, facts, theories, images, impressions, and information are *not* what is transmitted or sent out by a speaker. Images, impressions, and information are qualities existing *within persons*. These elements do not exist in the channels which link persons during the communication act. A speaker transmits *only* visible and auditory

[16] Erving Goffman, *Interaction Ritual* (Garden City, N.Y.: Doubleday & Company, Inc., Anchor Books, 1967), pp. 33–34.

stimuli. He can do no more than send out audible sounds in combination with factors of vocal quality and inflection, as well as visible postures, gestures, and facial expressions. Since, as listeners, we can only receive patterns of audible sound and visual appearances, we can perceive only the *sounds* and the *sights* of communication.

Speech Communication: Attaching Meaning to Symbolic Cues

If only sounds and sights are transmitted during the communication process, then how do we gain ideas, impressions, and information from that experience? This portion of our definition focuses on the manner in which a listener attaches meaning to the audible and visible stimuli he receives.

Language is often described as a code. The visible and audible stimuli of speech communication are somewhat like the dots and dashes of the Morse code. These marks or sounds are quite meaningless in themselves and to someone unfamiliar with the code would represent nothing more than a series of dots and dashes or audible dit-dahs. But the person who knows the Morse system recognizes the dots and dashes as signs or symbolic cues, and he attaches meaning to them.

Some communication specialists make use of the terms "encoding" and "decoding." A speaker is said to encode a message when he transforms his idea into words and gestures to be transmitted to another; that is, the changing of an idea into visible and auditory stimuli by a speaker is labeled the process of *en*coding. As a listener perceives the transmitted stimuli and attaches his own meaning to them, he is employing the *de*coding process.

Comparing the use of the Morse code to the communication process furnishes a simple illustration of the process of transforming thoughts into transmittable signs and back again into thoughts. But the analogy can be misleading. A code is limited and highly structured, and likening it to the process of speech communication might lead one to oversimplify the communication process. To go from a letter of the alphabet (s), to a sign (. . .) and back to a letter of the alphabet (s) is a fairly simple, straightforward procedure. In the speech communication process, however, the idea of the speaker does not lead so easily to a simple sign that can be readily and predictably decoded by means of a highly structured previous agreement between sender and receiver. In speech communication, the idea held by the speaker and the idea formulated by the listener are not necessarily the same; the "idea" represents the meaning each has attached to the symbolic cues transmitted and received during the communication process. The thoughts behind a speaker's statement and the thoughts of a listener as he interprets that statement can never be identical. This fact again emphasizes why we should not think of speech communication as a process of transferring ideas. The linkage between speaker and listener simply is not that direct and mechanical, nor is the relation between signs and meanings wholly predictable. As Colin Cherry writes, "If I push a man into the lake, he inevitably goes in; if I tell him to jump in, he may do one of a thousand things."[17]

[17] Colin Cherry, *On Human Communication* (New York: John Wiley & Sons, Inc., 1961), p. 220.

Many of the concepts and definitions briefly presented here will be developed more fully in later chapters. The aim of this preliminary examination has been simply to provide some substance to our definition, so that we can conduct the ensuing dialogue on speech communication with a common point of view. This explication should enable you to attach new and fuller meanings to the idea of speech communication as a socially learned process, occurring when two or more persons are interacting by transmitting and receiving auditory and visual stimuli which are treated as symbolic cues to which meaning is attached.

STUDY PROBE 3
Analyzing the Sights and Sounds of Speech Communication

In the speech communication setting, consider some of the sights and sounds to which you attach fairly consistent meanings. Beyond the literal meaning of the words spoken, what additional interpretations would you generally associate with the following communicative situations: (1) Someone with whom you are conversing avoids looking you in the eye; (2) a person converses in a consistent monotone; (3) a participant in a small group discussion frequently interrupts others; (4) a public speaker slumps across the lectern while speaking.

If you were in the audience of the speaker at left, what meanings would you attach to his somewhat languid, world-weary presentation? Quite possibly that he had good reason to feel a detachment toward his message (= boring) and the part he is playing in the interactive process (= hardly worth anyone's while). Either on a conscious or subconscious level, you would likely react to the visual stimuli in ways manifested by the audience in the picture below.

Speech Communication: A Charge and a Challenge

 I urge on college-bred men, that, as a class, they fail in republican duty when they allow others to lead in the agitation of the great social questions which stir and educate the age. Agitation is an old word with a new meaning. Sir Robert Peel, the first English leader who felt himself its tool, defined it to be "marshalling the conscience of a nation to mould its laws." Its means are reason and argument—no appeal to arms. Wait patiently for the growth of public opinion. That secured, then every step taken is taken forever. An abuse once removed never reappears in history. The freer a nation becomes, the more utterly democratic in its form, the more need of this outside agitation. Parties and sects laden with the burden of securing their own success cannot afford to risk new ideas. "Predominant opinions," said Disraeli, "are the opinions of a class that is vanishing." The agitator must stand outside of organizations, with no bread to earn, no candidate to elect, no party to save, no object but truth—to tear a question open and riddle it with light. In all modern constitutional governments, agitation is the only peaceful method of progress.[18]

Wendell Phillips

The above admonition was presented about a century ago to the Phi Beta Kappa members at Harvard. It was delivered by Wendell Phillips, who was one of the most effective practitioners of speech communication in American history. Born to a socially prominent Boston family, he gave up the approval of his family and friends and turned his back on a promising legal career to become an agitator and speak out for social change. One of the most famous of the antislavery speakers, Phillips spoke also for the rights of other minority groups, for women's rights, for the rights of laborers, for prison reform and an end to capital punishment, and for temperance.

We emphasize that an agitator in Wendell Phillips' sense of the term uses speech communication to persuade; he does not resort to coercive actions. If one has the wit, he can gain attention without the use of four-letter words, and is likely to hold it longer. With reason, argument, and evidence in hand, a socially sensitive and adaptive speaker can be highly persuasive in molding public opinion. Many types of agitators are present in contemporary society. A few are noisy and do an especially effective job of alienating the very people they claim to want to persuade. Much like the man who curses the bed frame he has bumped, they are either insensitive to their audience or are, in fact, speaking only to themselves. We are more interested in that *other* type of agitator Phillips speaks of—the one who seeks social progress through persuasion, by establishing contact and interaction with others.

[18] Wendell Phillips, *Speeches, Lectures, and Letters* (Boston: Lee and Shepard, 1905), second series, pp. 349–350.

John Kerry of the Vietnam Veterans Against the War, appearing at a news conference (right photo), and the Kent State students waging a voter-registration campaign (lower photo) may serve to exemplify young agitators who —in the manner described by Wendell Phillips—are working constructively for social reform.

In a very real sense, today's college student is more of an agitator than the college student of the past few decades. Many students are now assuming a more active role in society. They are advocating changes in their local educational establishments as well as in the larger political structure. And their advocacy is effecting some important changes in those establishments. These changes are coming about more slowly than some would like; nevertheless, they are occurring and they are significant. Other students, however—possibly the majority— still are quiet and uninvolved. We direct Wendell Phillips's charge particularly to these students.

There are some who fear this involvement of the younger generation in social concerns. They place the highest value on stability and order in society. They decry all agitation and change. Thomas Jefferson, in his First Inaugural Address, spoke thus to those who hold this position:

If there be any among us who would wish to dissolve this Union or to change its republican form, let them stand undisturbed as monuments of the safety with which error of opinion may be tolerated where reason is left free to combat it.[19]

One motivation for writing this textbook is the belief that it is the duty of the citizen in a democratic society to inform himself on the issues of his day and to speak out effectively at every level of society. The goal of this book is to assist every interested reader to gain a better understanding of the speech communication process and the means for self-improvement in that process so that he may ever be an agitator in the very best sense of that word.

STUDY PROBE 4

Examining the Uses of Speech Communication

List the different uses you have made of speech communication in the past week. Have you inquired, informed, persuaded, pleaded, scolded, prayed, confessed, thanked? On what variety of topics? With what persons? Which of these uses have you found most gratifying? With which uses have you been most successful?

Suggested Readings

Donald L. Clark, *Rhetoric in Greco-Roman Education* (New York: Columbia University Press, 1957). This work presents an account of rhetorical training in Greece and Rome, and provides an overview of principles, as well as a description of the procedures then used for speech training. Chapter 4, "The Precepts of Rhetoric," is particularly helpful.

George Kennedy, *The Art of Persuasion in Greece* (Princeton, N.J.: Princeton University Press, 1963). Rhetorical theory and practice in Greece from the fifth to the first centuries B.C. are covered. The preeminent role of speech in Greek culture is made clear.

Giles W. Gray and Claude M. Wise, *The Bases of Speech,* 3rd ed. (New York: Harper & Row, Publishers, 1959). This excellent reference contains chapters on the social, physical, physiological, neurological, phonetic, linguistic, psychological, genetic, and semantic bases of speech.

Frank E. X. Dance, ed., *Human Communication Theory* (New York: Holt, Rinehart & Winston, Inc., 1967). This work contains chapters outlining the contributions of various disciplines to human communication theory.

Alfred G. Smith, ed., *Communication and Culture* (New York: Holt, Rinehart & Winston, 1966). This work contains many significant readings on speech communication. It touches on contributions made by mathematics, social psychology, and linguistics; and it ranges from intrapersonal to intercultural settings.

[19] *The Life and Selected Writings of Thomas Jefferson,* ed. Adrienne Koch and William Peden (New York: Random House, Inc., Modern Library ed., 1944), pp. 321–325.

Chapter 2
The Speech Communication Process

The simplest
and most accurate illustration
of the speech
communication situation
would be one in which we see
(1) *agents* who (2) *interact*
within (3) a *context*.

Most contemporary writers refer to speech communication as a "process." To view oral interaction in this way can add significantly to our understanding of the term as we defined and developed it in the preceding chapter. The concept of process implies a dynamic, changing, ongoingness; something which flows to and fro, which never stands still. Process implies an operation in which the elements are multidimensional; to view something as a process is to pay particular attention to the interrelatedness of its elements. In this chapter we will explore a number of these implications of viewing speech communication as a process, enlarging upon some of the ways in which it is dynamic, multidimensional, and interactive.

Speech Communication As a Dynamic Activity

Our understanding of the dynamic character of speech communication can be heightened by noting some contrasts between written communication and spoken communication. As instances, consider these three opinions:

1. Writing, you know, . . . has this strange quality about it, which makes it really like painting; the painter's products stand before us quite as though they were alive; but if you question them, they maintain a solemn silence. So, too, with written words: you might think they spoke as though they made sense, but if you ask them anything about what they are saying, if you wish an explanation, they go on telling you the same thing, over and over forever.

2. . . . all great, world-shaking events have been brought about, not by written matter, but by the spoken word . . . the speaker gets a continuous correction of his speech from the crowd he is addressing, since he can always see in the faces of his listeners to what extent they can follow his arguments . . . the writer does not know his readers at all. Therefore, to begin with, he will not aim at a definite mass before his eyes, but will keep his arguments entirely general. By this to a certain degree he loses psychological subtlety.

3. . . . in speech we tend to react to each situation that occurs, reacting in tone and gesture even to our own act of speaking. But writing tends to be a kind of separate or specialist action in which there is little opportunity or call for reaction.

Plato (left) with Aristotle

Adolf Hitler

Marshall McLuhan

The first statement comes from the Greek philosopher Plato. It appears in his dialogue *Phaedrus*,[1] which was written c. 370 B.C. and which deals in some detail with suggestions for speech communication. The second quotation is from Adolf Hitler's *Mein Kampf*,[2] written during the early 1920's. The work includes a number of comments revealing Hitler's emphasis on the value of the spoken word. The final quotation is from *Understanding Media*[3] by Professor Marshall McLuhan, one of the most influential contemporary spokesmen on the communication process. The differences between Plato, Hitler, and McLuhan can hardly be overstated. The ages in which they lived, their national origins, their languages, their political and ideological orientations, and their general circumstances of life reveal little in common. Yet the same thread of meaning connects their thoughts, expressed or implied, on the unique energizing nature of speech communication. Their common emphasis is upon the dynamic, changing, and adaptive process that is distinctive of speech.

What comes to mind when we think of a painting or a piece of writing? Probably we visualize a particular painting or call to mind a certain book we have read. We probably think of a *completed product,* a finished painting or a printed book or article or letter existing in a fixed and visible form. And if we

[1] Plato, *Phaedrus,* trans. W. G. Helmbold and W. G. Rabinowitz (Indianapolis: Liberal Arts Press, Inc., 1956), p. 69.

[2] Adolf Hitler, *Mein Kampf,* trans. Ralph Manheim (Boston: Houghton Mifflin Company, Sentry ed., 1943), p. 469.

[3] Marshall McLuhan, *Understanding Media: The Extensions of Man* (New York: McGraw-Hill Book Company, 1964), p. 79.

fail to understand the painting or writing, we can only go on looking at or reading the same material over and over again. We cannot expect the object of our study to change in order to adapt to *us* and our questions. By the time we view a painting, it has been finished. By the time we read a poem, it has been written. If we require understanding beyond that which can be gained from the completed object or material itself, we must go outside of or beyond that material for the understanding.

In contrast, speaking communicatively is an active, adaptive, and dynamic activity. When we listen to a person speak, we hear what *is happening* rather than what *has happened.* In this sense speech is a "happening" which involves us as active participants. An effective speaker will receive a continuous reaction from his listener, a reaction to which he will adapt. If the listener seems puzzled and unable to understand, the speaker can modify his presentation at that very moment. The speech situation does not bring together an audience and *an object,* as does the exhibition of a painting or the study of a piece of writing; the speech situation brings together a *speaker* and a *listener.* The mutual involvement and interaction of persons with one another, rather than the relation of persons to objects and materials, is the essential distinguishing characteristic of speech communication. This is a point we shall continue to emphasize.

Consider for a moment the Gettysburg Address, a beautiful expression of man, printed in thousands of books and now, in certain instances, even carved in granite or marble. The process view of speech communication will lead us to argue that the real Gettysburg Address existed only once, that the speech as we know it is a monument to the Gettysburg Address of November 19, 1863. For instance, Lincoln apparently had not planned to speak the phrase "under God," and had not written it in the copy held in his hands as he delivered the speech. But he did insert that phrase as he uttered the speech, and he included it in the later copies he wrote out. Another phrase, "our poor power," appears in all written copies of the speech. Although Lincoln seemingly intended to use this phrase, the evidence of a written transcript of his words on that occasion indicates that he *said* "our power" when actually delivering the speech.[4] Such adaptations characterize the communication process, and an awareness of them can increase our understanding of its dynamic aspect.

STUDY PROBE 1

Exploring the Dynamics of the Speech Process

Compare the recorded version of any speech with the printed manuscript version. Analyze the discrepancies word for word, giving possible reasons for the speaker's departure from the prepared text of the speech.

What comparisons can you make between the speaker's pauses in the recorded version and the commas, periods, and paragraphing in the printed account? Do you find any meaning in the speaker's inflections and emphases which are not accounted for in the written text?

---

[4] David C. Mearns, "Unknown at This Address," *Lincoln and the Gettysburg Address,* ed. Allan Nevins (Urbana, Ill.: University of Illinois Press, 1964), pp. 118–133.

Much more is involved, of course, than mere changes in word choice or the issue of what is "historically accurate." Valuable though printed transcripts may be for purposes of content analysis and rhetorical structures and strategies, they do not reveal much of the "life" of a speaking event: the actions and reactions of the moment, the fleetingly salient features in the speaking context, the interactions between speaker and listener. Transcripts of speaking—be they of interview sessions, group discussions, or formal speeches—are much like still photographs: They "freeze" parts of action and help preserve a portion of some of the records of an event. They are especially helpful because we can go back over them again and again in trying to analyze the event. But we must realize that they cannot include the dynamic interaction of all the important elements in the process. If we want to see and understand speech communication as the process it is, we must seek to see the *whole* of it and the *activity* in it.

Speech Communication As a Multidimensional Process with Interrelated Elements

Thus far in our considerations, we have emphasized that the speech communication process is energized flow that is multidirectional, mutually involving, and interactive. And by implication at least, we have taken recognition of the fact that in oral interaction, as in other processes, there are certain *elements* or dimensions which, when combined operationally, add up to a *multidimensionality* greater than the sum of the dimensions of its parts. Our conception of speech communication, then, implies multidimensionality and an ongoing activity in which various elements are *interrelated* and *interacting*.

Clearly, therefore, if we wish to gain a fuller understanding of what goes on in the speech communication process, we will have to bring to it a degree of *analysis*. Whether we are trying to be an independent observer or an active participant, such an analysis will require that we

A. Try to identify the constituent elements of speech communication and examine these elements and their dimensions in isolation.

B. Attempt to detect and depict in some useful way the *interrelationships* of these elements, one with another; for, in a scientific sense, without such interworking there can be no process.

C. Try to define the dimensions of the key elements individually, and to comprehend how interaction is affected by their total multidimensionality.

The first and second of these objectives will be the central focus of the remainder of this chapter; the third will be a continuing goal of this textbook as a whole.

Identifying the Constituent Elements

In the kind of analysis we will be doing, we will be looking at the "parts of the puzzle" individually before putting them together; we will be "taking the clock apart" before reassembling its components. Ultimately, of course, our overriding concern, both in this and the ensuing chapters, will be to put the elements back together, to *synthesize* the process of speech communication as a whole.

If you observe, even casually, a situation in which oral communication seems to be taking place, you will readily recognize some of the essential elements. Fundamentally, there will be:

    A speaker
    Some sounds (words or noises)
    One or more listeners

If you watch longer and a bit more critically, you will probably conclude that the word-sounds are supposed to constitute a "message" of some kind. And so you alter your list to read:

    Speaker
    Message
    Listener(s)

Now focus your attention for a time upon the third element, the listener. If he's a polite and attentive participant in the process, he probably isn't *saying* anything aloud; but he is, nonetheless, nonverbally telling the speaker what he is thinking and feeling about the speaker and/or about what he is saying. You, therefore, extend your list to include the essential element of:

    Listener feedback to speaker

As the communication process continues, direct your attention back to the speaker. Note that very probably he is sensing or becoming aware of his listener(s)' reactions. Perhaps he hesitates, or glances at his notes, or adjusts the frames of his glasses. Possibly he interrupts the flow of his words, or he may merely alter the pace of his utterance, adjust his vocal tone, raise or lower his pitch. But, perceptibly or imperceptibly, *he* changes; he modifies his mien and message because of the reaction of his listener(s), and by so doing he reveals still another element of the process:

    Speaker adaptation to listener feedback

Shift your observation to the listener again. How is *he* reacting to the speaker's reaction? Perhaps he's leaning forward; maybe his frown is gradually changing into a more agreeable expression; he may even be nodding affirmatively. And so you add to your list of elements:

    Listener adaptation to speaker feedback

But suppose that another listener—Listener No. 2—happens to disagree with the reaction of Listener No. 1 and that Listener No. 3 makes clear, either verbally or nonverbally, that he disagrees with the reaction of Listener No. 2. Better enlarge your list to include:

    Listener feedback to other listener(s)

In the final analysis, if the oral interaction goes on long enough, we will become increasingly aware of the significant ways in which and the vast extent to which this interaction and adjustment of speaker/message/listener—this *reciprocity of reaction*—determines the success or failure of a particular oral communication.

In the formal, public communication situation, of course, the roles of the speaker and the listener(s) are more or less arbitrarily defined. In less formal conversation and small group discussion, the roles are alternated; the speaker at one moment becomes the listener in the next. Indeed, the roles may shift back and forth so rapidly that the two become almost indistinguishable in terms of the process as a whole.

Thus far in our considerations, then, we have identified as constituents of the speech communication process the following elements:

Speaker
Message
Listener
Listener feedback to speaker
Speaker adaptation to listener feedback
Listener adaptation to speaker feedback
Listener feedback to other listener(s)
Continuing reciprocity of reaction until a conclusion or impasse is reached

Depicting Interrelationships of Speech Communication Elements

In the foregoing paragraphs, in our efforts to identify various elements we have necessarily made some attempt to depict—through verbal description—a notion of the way in which these elements interrelate, their "back-and-forthness/to-and-fro-ness," their interplay, their in-process modification. Let us now consider another way in which we might illustrate more fully and perhaps more strikingly how these elements act and *interact,* how we might depict their dimensions and functions more *graphically.*

Depicting Interrelationships by Models

One method frequently used by speech communication scholars is the *model* or illustrative abstraction. This method, you will find, has its limitations. The perfect model has not yet been devised, nor is it likely to be. A good one, however, can afford a more visual approach to analysis; it can help to identify readily the basic elements, to vivify their multidirectionality in the energized flow, and to emphasize the ongoing nature of the process. Our purpose here is not to build a case for or against models as such. Rather, it is to offer them as *one* means by which to gain further insights into productive oral interaction. With that intent in mind, let us look briefly at some of the earlier attempts to develop a workable model. At the same time we will note a few advantages and disadvantages of the method.

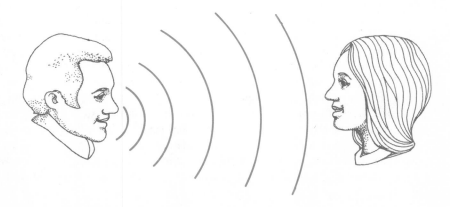

This diagram, intended to show how a speaker creates sound waves which then travel to a listener, identifies a *speaker, sound waves,* and a *listener* as the key elements in the process. Another illustration conceptualizing the process relies on a series of boxes and verbal labels:

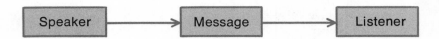

As scholars examined the communication process more fully, they recognized that the reactions of a listener are observed by a speaker who, in turn, reacts to those reactions. As we noted above, this reaction, transmitted from listener to speaker, they called "feedback," and they incorporated this concept into a graphic depiction that looked something like this:

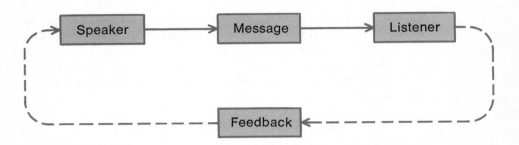

The speech communication process is, of course, much more highly complex than these drawings suggest; and as research has continued, new diagrams and models have been devised to reflect that complexity. These initial depictions have been amplified and expanded in various ways, and numerous writers have developed very complicated models from them. Later in these pages we will present a contemporary model especially designed to serve the major thrust of this book, but the examples shown here should suffice to suggest the methods and some of the advantages to be gained from looking at the process in this way.

Some Disadvantages Inherent in Models

A review of the purely verbal description of the speech communication process on pages 30–31 will reveal that the models shown do omit important information or mislead in certain significant ways. In the first place, these elementary models obscure the fact that in speech communication—throughout the process—the sender of a message also becomes a receiver, and the receiver also becomes a sender. These depictions convey an image of speech communication which separates too sharply the roles of speaker and listener. The distinction produces an impression of events that is too static. As we know, both parties to a communication send and receive messages *throughout* the process.

Whether a person is to be labeled sender or receiver is influenced by the viewpoint from which the labels are applied. For example, if you were ever to visit the St. Louis Zoo, you could throw peanuts to the gorilla, and you would see him "dutifully" slap his chest. You might tell a friend that the gorilla was "conditioned" to slap his chest for the reward of a peanut. You are the manipulator, and the gorilla is manipulated. But the gorilla, if he were to speak, might give a quite different explanation. He might point out that he is, in fact, well fed by his handlers, that the little peanut is hardly much of a reward, and that if you observed carefully you would see that he doesn't eat many of the peanuts anyway. Moreover, he might explain that zoos are really quite boring places—nice to visit but not much of a place to live. And so, to allay some of the boredom in his cell, he has taken to conditioning the humans who come by to look at him. He has only to slap his chest, and the viewers will "dutifully" produce grunts and grimaces and throw peanuts at him. He is the manipulator, and man is manipulated. Which viewpoint—which set of labels—is correct? Perhaps both.

In the same way, in the ongoing speech process, the roles of "sender" and "receiver" are neither static nor mutually exclusive. In conversation and group discussion, as we have said, the roles often are interchanged, and the sender of one moment becomes the receiver of the next. And, as we have tried to demonstrate, even in a public speaking setting one who acts as sender may be influenced by the reactions of his audience and therefore be simultaneously the sender (insofar as we consider what he says and does in the speech) *and* the receiver (insofar as we consider how audience reactions influence him).

Let us develop more fully how a single individual may play these roles simultaneously. The concept of feedback, which was mentioned above, may be defined as *the reception of stimuli that allow for correction and modification of behavior*. Put another way, feedback from a listener provides the means whereby the listener can influence the behavior of the speaker.

For our example, keep the public speaker in mind for a moment. As the speaker presents his speech, he follows a certain course of action. In some respects his actions have been consciously preplanned for the occasion, while in other ways his actions represent his usual and habitual manner of behaving. One of the goals of any speaker is to modify the immediate or future behavior of his audience. He may be asking for contributions to a charitable cause, hoping to see the contributions increase in number and amount. He may speak for the election of a certain candidate with the hope of influencing that election. He may present information about the dimensions of modern art in the hope of producing in his listener a greater appreciation for his subject.

As the speaker acts, his listener reacts. At some points, a listener may deliberately and overtly react to a speaker. But even his less deliberate reactions will nearly always be apparent: his posture, movement, and facial expressions will reveal his feelings to the speaker. And the speaker who hopes to influence the ultimate behavior of that listener must adapt to this immediate, reactive behavior. In every act of adapting to audience feedback, the speaker is—in effect —allowing the listener to communicate with him and to modify certain aspects of his own behavior. This adjustment to feedback is highly essential to effective communication, and it will be examined in depth in Chapter 3.

While we may consider the speaker and the listener as separate personalities, we must not let these terms become synonymous with sender and receiver, or with the influencer and the influenced. In genuine, interactive communication, the sender must also be the receiver, and the influencer must also be the influenced. We cannot emphasize too often that the actions and reactions of speaker and listener are *reciprocal*. Any graphic representation of the communication act which causes these roles to appear to be mutually exclusive, static, and separate will be misleading.

Still another misleading aspect of the elementary models presented above is their tendency to make the speech communication process appear as a straightforward, *linear* process. From the drawings, one could get the mistaken impression that a speaker sends out a message and stands back while the message floats along toward the receiver who finally absorbs it intact and sends his reaction back toward the speaker. Reality is quite otherwise. We must remember that both speaker and listener are *acting* and *reacting, sending* and *receiving,* and doing both *simultaneously* throughout the speech communication process.

Further, such illustrations make the listener appear as a *passive* participant influenced only by outside forces. The depictions obscure the fact that the listener himself determines to a large degree what he hears and what he accepts. The listener's whole past will influence what he hears, how he interprets what he hears, and the degree to which he will be influenced by it. Moreover, in a great many instances the listener's influence upon the speaker may begin a long time *before* that listener begins to generate feedback reactions to the speaker's words. The moment any individual decides to become a speaker, especially if the situation is to be a public one, he begins to ask himself: "Who will my listeners *be?* And how will they react to me and to what I want to communicate?" At that very moment, the influence of the listeners-to-be (real or imagined) begins to "work" on the speaker, providing a potential feedback which will help shape his decisions as to how he will behave and what he will say.

In sum, then, as students of speech communication we will want to remain alert to the possibility that analytic models, however simple or complex, have inherent in them certain flaws, among them:

Failure to reflect accurately the interchangeability of sender and receiver.

Failure to particularize the identity and viewpoint of the "labeler."

Failure to show that the speech communication process is not straightforward and linear.

A Contemporary Model of Speech Communication

What, then, would serve as an adequate, contemporary, graphic illustration of the speech-communication situation? Ideally, such an illustration should be as simple as possible without omitting any major elements, and as accurate as possible in depicting the essential elements and their interrelatedness. The simplest and most accurate illustration would be one in which we see (1) *agents* who (2) *interact* within (3) a *context*. Diagrammatically, our model of speech communication would look something like the one shown on the opposite page.

While there might be those who would argue that this model is not unique to communication situations—that there are other kinds of situations such as fist fights, riots, and wars that operate within a context similar to this one—in the broader view even those violent forms of social interaction can be seen as communicative (albeit destructive) efforts. Unlike the models depicted earlier in this chapter, the concept of *agents interacting within a context* does not impose

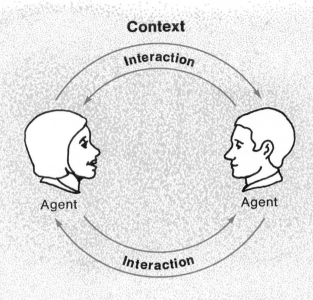

an artificial and absolute distinction between "sender" and "receiver." It does not imply a linear process, but attempts instead to point to simultaneous, multi-directional, and multidimensional activity. It focuses upon *interaction* as the central criterial aspect of the process. Although it is not, strictly speaking, a "scientific" model, it possesses as a representation of process the useful qualities of clarity, flexibility, and simplicity. The three constituent elements of this contemporary model—*context, agents, interaction*—merit closer scrutiny.

Context

Every communication act is bounded by a context: an *occasion,* a *place,* a *setting,* a *situation,* and a *time* in which that communication occurs. What may and what will occur during the act is constrained and limited by the immediate circumstances of context. And many possibilities provided by this context are there for use. In our illustration, context is shown as an "open" circle, revealing that it has influence in molding the act and yet is open and, in some respects, limitless. All contexts have certain *physical dimensions* and certain *psychological dimensions,* all of which are, in turn, influenced by and interrelated with a number of *social, temporal,* and *cultural* factors.

Physical Dimensions of Context

The physical size and seating arrangement in a lecture hall will influence what goes on there. This serves to reemphasize the point that speech communication is multidimensional and that the dimensions are interrelated. The audience's psychological frame of mind may be favorably disposed toward the speaker; but the barnlike size of the place, its draftiness, and the remoteness of the seats from the podium—the environmental factors—may alienate them from the speaker despite his prestige and best efforts. Thus we see that the *physical dimensions* and the *psychological dimensions* of the context can interact; that is, they can reinforce or they can nullify each other; their multidimensionality is interrelated and interactive.

Further, note that this interactive interrelationship extends to the communicative agent. Not only do the physical and psychological dimensions of the context affect the reactions of listeners; they also work upon the speaker, influencing his behavior, his choices of action, his communicative effectiveness. For example, almost any teacher will tell you that there are certain classrooms which have the "right feel" for him, a physical setting which seems to "work best" for him—one in which he can get his ideas across to his students, and in which the students readily communicate their "thinking" to him. These judgments are based upon the physical facts of the room as he sees them, and upon both his conscious and subconscious psychological reactions to those physical conditions.

STUDY PROBE 2
Considering Some Physical Dimensions of Context

Compare the various classrooms you use this semester, and try to assess their effects upon the communication which has taken place there. Consider all physical aspects of the rooms—size, shape, color, furnishings, view from the windows, etc. How do the settings separate the teacher from the students? Do these settings seem to facilitate or impede productive social interaction? In general, try to determine how the physical characteristics of each classroom can constrain and mold the speech communication which can occur there.

Other physical, nonverbal elements of context can also be highly influential in determining communicative outcomes. The vantage point from which we view other participants in the process and from which they view us—the sights of communication, if you will—can determine in a very large measure the nonverbal cues with which we can relate and to which we can react. We have already suggested the adaptability advantages of face-to-face, spoken communication over written communication. Part of this advantage stems from the fact that because of the immediacy of the situation and the proximity of the participants, each agent can perceive more cues and thereby gain more "information" from the speech communication event. By seeing what is "going on," he is able to add the meanings of nonverbal messages to the meaning of the verbal messages he receives. We should, therefore, take careful note of the placement of the participants within the communicative context.

In this regard, a number of studies have dealt with seating arrangements as factors in small-ground interactions.[5] Here again we can see the interrelatedness of the physical and psychological dimensions of context. With X representing a seated person, the following seating arrangements were used in the experiments:

[5] See, for example, Marvin E. Shaw, *Group Dynamics: The Psychology of Small Group Behavior* (New York: McGraw-Hill Book Company, 1971), pages 129–136. Also see Robert Sommer, "Further Studies of Small Group Ecology," *Sociometry,* XXVIII (1965): 337–348. The diagrams on pages 37 and 38 are based on those in Sommer's work; and the diagram on page 38 is a modification and combination of Figures 1 and 2, pages 342 and 345 respectively, in Sommer's study.

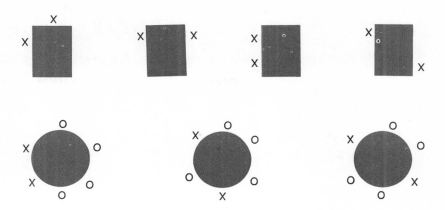

In the studies cited by Shaw, members of small group discussions had a strong tendency to communicate with persons facing them, rather than alongside them.

STUDY PROBE 3
Discovering the Effects of Spatial Factors on Interaction

Consider the seating arrangements pictured below. Using the numbers 1, 2, 3, 4, rank order the rectangular table positions in terms of the arrangements you would prefer if you were (a) *casually conversing with the other person,* (b) *cooperating with the other person,* and (c) *competing with the other person.* Do the same for the circular table positions, using the rank order 1, 2, and 3.

Choices	Conversation	Cooperation	Competition

Research on this topic revealed the following results:

Choices	Conversation	Cooperation	Competition
[seating diagram: X above, X at left of table]	2	3	4
[seating diagram: X at left, X at right of table]	1	2	1
[seating diagram: X, X both at left of table]	3	1	3
[seating diagram: X above, X at lower right of table]	4	4	2
[seating diagram: X, X at left; O, O at right of round table]	1	1	3
[seating diagram: X, O around round table]	3	3	2
[seating diagram: X, O, X around round table]	2	2	1

In general, we seem to prefer to speak with people close to us and with whom we can maintain easy eye contact. In one study, subjects were asked where they would seat themselves at a table if someone they disliked were already seated there. They tended to choose a seat at some distance from the person and not directly opposite him. From such studies we can conclude that physical spatial barriers can serve as psychological barriers and—therefore—as barriers to communication.

Psychological Dimensions of Context

Just as the physical aspects of the room or communicative scene are often significant influencing factors in the communication context, so too are the size and mind of the audience—the numbers of listeners and their predispositions, biases, and emotional states. Political speakers and evangelists, as well as demagogues, do not seek large, assembled throngs as audiences solely for the purpose of spreading their messages widely and efficiently; they recognize the possible contextual effects of a "mass" audience. While speech communication scholars are not in general agreement as to the psychology and operational validity of "mass mind" and "crowd effects," there are at least two aspects of the ideas which are useful to our considerations here: audience polarization and social facilitation.

Much has been written about these concepts of mass phenomena. *Polarization* is the common focusing of listener attention upon the same stimulus—the all-to-one relation in which the individuals of the audience respond to the single object of attention: the speaker. *Social facilitation* refers to the effects which the members of an audience have upon one another because of their physical and emotional proximity. For instance, when a few individuals begin to applaud, others in the audience tend to join in the applause. In *Mein Kampf* Hitler wrote of the effect of the atmosphere of the meeting hall and of the effect of the crowd upon the individual; he recommended night meetings because at night an audience will "succumb more easily to the dominating force of a stronger will."[6] In a large group all behavior is magnified, and the focus of our concern is drawn more strongly to factors outside our own person. In a sense, then, we can lose a measure of control-by-self in that psychological setting. Since the focus is drawn to gross behavior by the very size of the setting, we can well expect less subtle response. In the face of the human instinct for self-preservation, it is little wonder that those speakers who ask us to lay down our lives employ such crowd-unifying, nonverbal symbols as uniforms and robes, flags and medals, and music —using them as the central, environmental conditioners of large group activity.

[6] Adolf Hitler, *Mein Kampf,* trans. Ralph Manheim (Boston: Houghton Mifflin Company, Sentry ed., 1943), p. 475.

In this historic scene, with Adlai Stevenson at the rostrum of a national Democratic convention surrounded by enthusiastic admirers, we can clearly detect something of the contextual effects of a "mass" audience.

Social/Temporal/Cultural Influences on Context

Audience composition is a significant factor influencing the speech communication context. What listener or listeners will hear you when you speak? Who will *overhear* you? With parents present, teen-agers may feel constrained in what they say. If the parents leave the room, the subjects of conversation, the language used, the "tone" of voices may all change. As this case suggests, the alert and sensitive speaker will adjust not only to his hearers, but he will also make adjustments, as in the case just mentioned, to his overhearers if he knows they are likely to be within earshot. Some interesting studies could be made of speakers' adaptation to overhearers. Consider the way people speak in the presence of waitresses and taxicab drivers. Some carry on a conversation with their companions as if these overhearers did not exist. Others will draw the overhearers into conversation. Still others will sit in embarrassed silence, unable to reconcile what they interpret as their split role.

The factor of *time*—epochal time and durational time—like the space factor, must be catalogued among the other contextual influences bearing upon oral interaction. The durational dimensions of the communication act are diverse and can be extremely important to the outcome. They reflect the urgency of the message. If the speaker has elected to say too much in the time available, or if he feels that his role as speaker may be preempted too quickly, he may speak too hurriedly and thereby reduce the effectiveness of his communication. If he speaks too slowly or leisurely, the attention of his listeners may wander, or his words may be cut off by another.

The content and style of utterance of a message must be appropriate to its era. The oratorical majesty and the language used by Daniel Webster were undoubtedly powerful and proper for his time; in ours, they would quite probably seem old-fashioned and "out of phase."

Timing, another of the many facets of the time factor, is a crucial variable within a communication setting. What you may say, for instance, during the last five minutes of a half-hour's conversation with a comparative stranger may have been highly inappropriate during the *first* five minutes. A pause following a humorous comment or a joke must be timed with precision. If it is too brief, the "punch" of the jest may be lost or badly impaired; if it is too long, the speaker may lose some of his credibility.

To our catalog of contextual influences we must also add *cultural characteristics* and *social values,* for they, too, determine norms for physical-psychological patterns of communicative behavior. In certain cultures, for example, men stand closer together when conversing than they do in ours. Edward Hall, who has written with authority on these matters, describes the meeting of two men from cultures with different norms for what they regard as "proper" conversational distance.[7] The European takes a step forward to achieve what he deems the correct space. The American takes a step backward. And so it goes, with the American backing up the entire length of a corridor until he is finally cornered. Hall is, of course, exaggerating, but his implication is significant: such a contextual element may interrupt or even prevent communicative interaction without either agent realizing why he "just cannot seem to get on well conversing with that other fellow."

In sum, then, communicative acts must occur in a context having physical,

[7] Edward T. Hall, *The Silent Language* (New York: Fawcett World Library, 1969), p. 160.

psychological, and social dimensions. If we are to understand a specific communication act, we must be able to describe and explain the context in which it occurs; and we must be sensitive to the elements of that context which may be influencing the course and outcomes of that communicative interaction. Not only must we recognize the effects of the more obvious factors in the physical setting—such as place and space and numbers—but we must also seek to learn what we can of the psychological context and the possible influences exerted by the time, the culture, and the prevailing social values.

Agents

The agents in a communication act are the participating persons. These are the persons conjoined or engaged in the communicative process—mutually influencing and mutually influenced. The participants, by our definition of speech communication, are human; and it follows that everything we can know about human behavior will be important and will contribute to our understanding of the roles of agents in initiating, energizing, and propelling the speech communication process forward.

All actions in a communication setting come from the agents. We will want, therefore, to study what *action-choices* are available to a specific agent, what *constraints* limit and guide his action-choices, what *strategies* for action-choice are open to and appropriate for him. In this analysis we will see repeatedly the interdependency of context and agents, for the choices available to a communicator and the constraints which are operative are determined in part by context (as by social mores or even by physical arrangement of furniture in the room) and in part by agents themselves (as by their intellectual abilities and by experiential range). The strategies or typical patterns for choice making will come from the agents' respective backgrounds, their conscious application of acquired knowledge about themselves and others, their capabilities for creativity, their abilities to generate ideas and to organize and express them, and the totality of their outlook upon themselves, upon others, and upon their environment.

How does man learn, remember, solve problems, make choices, create? How does he use language to identify, abstract, generalize, and voice his thoughts? How are all these human abilities employed in the speech process? These are questions for which we need some of the answers if we are to comprehend the complexities of the speech communication act.

Answers to these questions come from many sources. In a general sense, all that you have read or can read about psychology, sociology, anthropology, history, political affairs, art, and music will be helpful. Contemporary studies by behavioral scientists can be enlightening. These materials are available in sources ranging from such esoteric professional publications as the *Journal of Personality and Social Psychology* to best sellers written for general readers, such as *The Naked Ape.* One may learn much from case studies such as Oscar Lewis's *La Vida,* an account of a Puerto Rican family living in poverty. Or from *The Autobiography of Malcolm X.* Libraries are filled with the accounts of perceptive and sensitive men who have written biographies, novels, plays, and poems about the human condition.[8] All of these sources are readily available to any interested

---

[8] An interesting comparison of literature and social science materials as paths to the understanding of human behavior can be found in Gordon W. Allport, *Personality and Social Encounter* (Boston: Beacon Press, 1960), pp. 3–15.

student who would understand how human abilities, capabilities, frailties, foibles, insights, foresights, and hindsights are employed in the social/oral interaction we call the speech communication act.

There is yet another important resource for the understanding of human behavior: you yourself. You should seek to know yourself; you should look to and within yourself. As a college student, you have lived for at least eighteen years and have met and known hundreds of people with widely ranging interests, sets of values, and life-styles. If you examine yourself and your life fairly, you probably will be surprised to discover the extensive information you already have about man's nature and the forces which motivate and shape his thinking and acting. Do not, therefore, neglect your own experience as a source for information about insights into human behavior.

In Chapter 3, as we begin to put our theoretical knowledge of the speech communication process into practice, you will encounter a set of Self-Assessment Scales. These scales offer a systematic means of analyzing yourself, your feelings, and behaviors in a variety of speaking contexts with a wide range of agents. A careful completion of the scales will enable you to enlarge your self-knowledge and thereby draw upon this valuable resource more discriminatively.

Of course, as students of speech behavior we must also look *beyond* ourselves to others. We must all constantly be attuned to studies and statements about man's behavior, for nearly any new, emergent knowledge of it is almost certain to have some application to our understanding of what goes on when we attempt to interact with one another. Obviously, of course, we cannot hope nor do we intend to cover broadly the very many facets of human behavior, but we will draw as widely as possible from what is known about the subject in order to illuminate this as well as subsequent discussions of interaction.

Interaction

Interaction, as we have emphasized, is the central concept—the core—of communication; and it is, therefore, the major concern of this text, directly or indirectly infusing each of the successive chapters. Only through interaction are human beings able by speech to make mutually satisfying contact with one another. For sheer survival, it must be a continuing and pervasive goal. Hence, here and elsewhere we will approach the concept from many different directions and in different ways in order to find out as much as we can about it.

Many terms other than *interaction* have been used to label this uniting of agents in the speech communication context. It has been called coupling, linkage, contact, transaction, human relatedness, and even togetherness. For our purposes here, however, *interaction* seems the most appropriate and useful word with which to label and identify the energized, multidirectional, multidimensional, mutualized flow that is oral communication.

How and in what particular ways does this energized communicative flow take place? What are the channels through which it travels to and fro? Review for a moment our definition of speech communication:

. . . *the socially learned process occurring when two or more persons are interacting by transmitting and receiving visual and auditory stimuli which are treated as symbolic cues to which meaning is attached.*

Now reexamine the somewhat altered version of our model of agents interacting within a context.

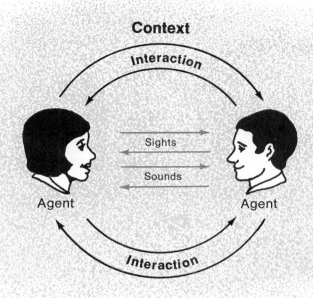

This time we have attempted to suggest that the channels which link the communicative agents are chiefly the senses of *sight* and *hearing*. Through these channels (primarily) the agents are sending and receiving visual and auditory stimuli; both are transforming these stimuli into symbolic cues; both are attaching *meaning* to these cues. They are linked or coupled by communicative channels while they transmit and receive stimuli over these channels. Through these channels and in this manner, the agents produce a meaningful interchange. Note in particular that coupling must be at least *a two-way event* before we can say that interaction has actually taken place: the agents must be *responding* to one another.

When, can we say, does the interaction start? *At what point does the interactive process begin?* For our considerations, we will accept as the threshold of interaction the standard established by Ruesch and Bateson and mentioned in Chapter 1—a standard which they term "the perception of perception," a situation in which the actions of one agent are perceived as responses by another agent. As they say:

> . . . *such exchange of communication begins with the moment in which the actions of the other individual are perceived as responses—that is, as evoked by the sender's message and therefore as comments upon that message, giving the sender an opportunity of judging what the message means to the receiver. Such communication about communication is no doubt difficult, because it is usually implicit rather than explicit, but it must be present if an exchange of message is to take place. The perception of the perception, as we might call this phenomenon, is the sign that a silent*

agreement has been reached by the participants, to the effect that mutual influence is to be expected.[9]

For our purposes, then, we will maintain that *communicative interaction begins with the recognition of and reaction to feedback*. Communicative interaction begins when the contextual "circuitry" of the participants is sparked, when the impulse or impetus to communicate is mutually recognized, and when the openness of the process flow is maintained to accommodate multidirectional stimulus and response. It begins when both agents are sending and receiving, interpreting and reacting to the stimuli from the other, and when *both are aware* that they are jointly participating in the communication act.

This mutual awareness and receptivity are of vast importance to speech communication. There can be no productive interaction unless there is mutual acceptance of the ground rules and conditions necessary to make the process operable. In this sense, communicative interaction is something like a game which can be played only if the players will accept and agree to abide by the ground rules. While one person may talk in a contextual vacuum, there can be no communicative interaction unless two or more persons "agree" to it. Just as people cannot play bridge or Monopoly or football without a commitment to interact in accordance with the rules, they cannot communicate unless they agree to try to understand and "hear each other out."

In evolving our contemporary model of speech communication, then, we have singled out as the essential elements *context, agents,* and *interaction.* Actually, of course, each of these element-labels serves to cover a cluster of sub-elements, thus:

CONTEXT
    Physical environment
        Place
        Space
        Occasion
        Setting
        Numbers
           . . . the *physical dimensions*

    Psychological environment
        Prevailing emotional states/feelings
        Sender/receiver expectations
        Conditioning and biases
        Polarization
        Social facilitation
        Audience composition (as influenced by)
            Hearers and overhearers
            Time/timing
            Cultural characteristics
            Social values
                . . . the *psychological dimensions*

[9] Jurgen Reusch and Gregory Bateson, *Communication: The Social Matrix of Psychiatry* (New York: W. W. Norton & Co., Inc., 1951), p. 23.

AGENTS (PARTICIPANTS IN THE PROCESS)
    Initiators/energizers
    Propellers
    Choice-makers
    Choice-discriminators
    Communication strategists
    Idea generators/organizers
    Stimuli senders
    Responders/reactors
    Problem posers/solvers
    Generalizers
    Abstractors
    Identifiers
    Self-recognizers
    Self-realizers
        . . . all by reason of
            Background
            Perceptual skills
            Creative capabilities
            Acquired knowledge
            Purposive inclinations

INTERACTION
    Uniting the agents in the speech communication context by means of
        Psychological coupling/linking
        Sense contacting and connecting
            (especially through sight and hearing)
        Human interrelating (togetherness)
        Transacting
        Transforming stimuli into symbolic cues
        Attaching meaning to symbolic cues
        Sensing mutual "perception of perception"
        Sustaining multidimensional, multidirectional stimulus/response flow
            . . . all dependent upon
                Participants' mutual
                acceptance of communicative
                "rules" and conditions

Such clustering of subelements serves to emphasize again the multidimensionality of the speech communication process, and restresses the interrelatedness of these elements and subelements, as suggested in our model. And only when these element clusters are interacting with a fair amount of effectiveness is genuine communication likely to occur.

A General Paradigm of Speech Communication

Thus far we have attempted through a number of different approaches to enlarge your comprehension of the speech communication process. Verbally, in Chapter 1, we defined the term by stipulation. Pictorially, we drew upon a series of photographs to show varied instances of "frozen" segments of oral interaction. Each of the instances pictured was *real,* and each was *unique.* In the present chapter, up to this point, we have developed the implications of viewing speech as an ongoing process. In order to amplify and illuminate our textual considerations, we have presented a number of graphic illustrations or "speech models" which attempt in abstract form to vivify the *central features* of the oral communication process.

Let us now try a concluding and somewhat different approach in which we combine the essential features of these abstractive illustrations with those of real people engaged in speech interchange: a general paradigm or "living" model which we might define as the one ideal "essentiality" which ought to characterize all human communication. Our "living model" is made up of people rather than drawings, boxes, or labels, although the personalities involved are abstracted and generalizable. For our paradigm you will have to visualize *two persons conversing.*

To Mark Hopkins, the American educator, has been attributed the observation that an ideal educational setting would consist of a teacher on one end of a log and a student on the other, both talking in close context. We can view the two-people-conversing form, similarly, as an ideal communicative context, for in it the essential elements of the process seem to be most pronounced. This general paradigm of speech communication is the simplest instance of speech in that it is comparatively easy to analyze context, agents, and interaction in this setting. It may be at the same time the most complex of speech forms, in the sense that the interchange resulting from this setting may produce more *feedback stimuli which, in turn, generate more response* than from larger group settings. Therefore, to better understand the speech communication process in all its phases and occurrences, we maintain that you should understand first the instance of two persons conversing. The principles discoverable in this paradigm will be seen to apply in all communication forms and settings.

STUDY PROBE 4

Exploring the Essentiality of Speech Communication

List what you consider to be the essential factors involved in effective speech communication in two-person settings. What facilitates good communicative interaction between two people? What impedes it? Now consider a public speaking setting. How well would the criteria you listed for the two-person setting apply to the one-to-many public communication setting? Explain.

That two persons conversing could be at once the simplest and the most complex speech form may seem a paradox. But perhaps the explanation lies with our most central concept: interaction. In saying that more feedback stimuli will be generating response in that setting, we mean that there is greater participant inter-action and involvement there. In research related to this question we have found some evidence that even in a discussion group of five or six persons, a discussant cannot interact with the entire group all at once, but seems rather to interact with only one person at a time.[10] Small group discussion appears to be made up largely of fragments of two persons interacting. One could make a good argument for the assertion that a man can establish maximal contact and meaningful interaction with only one other person at a time. This possibility could serve as the basis for some challenging studies of the public speaking setting where one speaker addresses an audience of many persons. To whom does he speak? To the entire group at once? To one individual, and then another, and another? Or to a generalized "other"?

Watch a few "soap operas" on afternoon television. Compare the number of speech encounters involving two persons with those involving three or more. Usually the movement of the program—here the interaction of characters rather than the unfolding of events—is carried by scenes of dialogue between only two actors; while three or four additional members of the cast may be present, their function seems mainly to provide transitions between scenes. In contrast, mystery and adventure programs, where dialogue serves not so much to reveal interaction between the characters as to reveal what is happening in the general plot progression, rely much less on speech and more on materials that are highly visual and "action-packed." But even there, many of the speech encounters which do occur will involve a one-to-one pattern.

The case of two persons conversing, fortunately, is a form of communication with which you and most other college students have had much experience and can also observe readily. At first thought, you may be inclined to consider your one-to-one speech experiences to be quite unlike participation in a group discussion, or the giving of a speech to a large audience, or participating in a television interview. If you think further about the matter, however, you will realize that since nearly everyone feels comfortable enough when conversing with a friend, there is no real and valid reason to become fearful, as if in a totally alien environment, when you find yourself conversing with a stranger, or taking part in a business meeting, or when giving a short speech to an assembled audience. After all, as we will maintain here and later develop quite fully in Part V, the differences between the converser, the discussant, and the public speaker are merely matters of degree, and no sharp dividing line can be drawn between them.

The question of when the converser becomes the public speaker has been commented upon with considerable discernment by the late James Winans of Cornell University. He said:

> Let us imagine all speeches and all memory of speech-making to be blotted out, so that there is no person in the world who remembers that he has ever made a speech, or heard one, or read one; and there is left no clue to this art. Is this the end of speech-making? Here comes a man who has seen a great race, or has been in a battle, or perhaps is excited about his new invention, or on fire with enthusiasm for a cause. He begins to talk with a friend on the street. Others join them, five, ten, twenty, a hundred. Interest grows. He lifts his voice that all may hear; but the crowd wishes to hear and see the speaker better. "Get up on this truck!" they cry; and he mounts the truck and goes on with his story or his plea.

---

[10] Thomas M. Scheidel and Laura Crowell, "Feedback in Small Group Communication," *Quarterly Journal of Speech*, LII (1966): 273–278.

When does the converser become a speech-maker? When ten persons gather? Fifty? Or is it when he gets on the truck? There is, of course, no point at which we can say the change has taken place. There is no change in the nature or the spirit of the act; *it is essentially the same throughout, a conversation adapted, as the speaker proceeds, to the growing number of his hearers. There may be a change, to be sure, if he becomes self-conscious; but assuming that interest in story or argument remains the dominant emotion, there is no essential change in his speaking. It is probable that with the increasing importance of his position and the increasing tension of feeling that comes with numbers, he gradually modifies his tone and his diction, and permits himself to launch into a bolder strain and a wider range of ideas and feelings than in ordinary conversation; but the change is in degree and not in kind. He is conversing with an audience.*[11]

There are obviously some typical situational differences between conversation and public speaking; but these, as we have said, should be viewed as differences of degree only. For example, one usually speaks more loudly in a public speech than in a conversation. But not always. A teacher, for instance, may speak much more loudly, carefully, and distinctly when conversing with an eighty-five-year-old neighbor than when lecturing to a class of twenty students. The general principle is that, in any speech context, one tries to speak loudly enough to be heard.

The same is true with other general principles of speech communication. One tries to speak in terms that will be clear and appropriate for his listener, to adapt his ends to the interests of his listener, to be in a position if possible to look at his listener, to react to his listener's reactions. These are desirable goals and behaviors in any speech setting. All that one tries to do in good conversation he tries also to do in a small group discussion or in a public speech.

In support of this view are the results of a recent study made of the perceptions and feelings students have toward participation in the speech activities of (1) conversation, (2) group discussion, and (3) public speaking.[12] The outcomes of this analysis strongly indicate how similar these activities were deemed to be by two groups of students: Group A having completed course work in speech communication, and Group B having had no such work. In diagrams shown below, representing the general conclusions reached by the two groups, the length of the lines between the concepts (C = conversation, GD = group discussion, PS = public speaking) indicates the extent of difference perceived between these respective speech settings by the students.

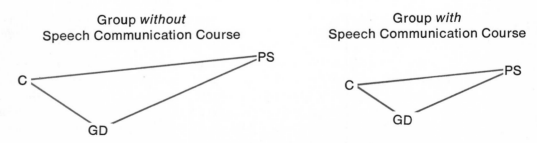

Group *without*
Speech Communication Course

Group *with*
Speech Communication Course

[11] From *Public Speaking*, Revised edition by James A. Winans. Reprinted by permission of Appleton-Century-Crofts, Educational Division, Meredith Corporation.

[12] This was a graduate-student project completed by Marylee Bradley Wallace.

Note that both groups gave similar *placement* to conversation, group discussion, and public speaking in relation to one another. The basic difference is that, following a speech communication course, students tended to see these different situational forms of speech as *much more closely related* and more alike.

The findings of this study further reinforce the position that these forms *are* alike in the essentials and come to be seen as such by persons with speech communication training. The study also stresses the point that you will progress more quickly in your speech training if you see the close relationships of these communication forms early in the course of your study rather than later in your work. All of your past experience in speech—primarily in the one-to-one setting —should be considered as something significantly and usefully related to what you are learning now.

In summary, the goal of this chapter has been to provide the foundation for our understanding of the essential elements in the speech communication process: agents, interaction, and context. We have emphasized the dynamism, multidimensionality, and interrelatedness of these elements. And, finally, we have suggested that you can usefully consider *two persons conversing* as the basic paradigm of all speech communication, as the useful archetype of all speech forms, and as the foundation for your future efforts toward learning to interact effectively through speech.

Suggested Readings

Theodore Clevenger, Jr., and Jack Matthews, *The Speech Communication Process* (Glenview, Ill.: Scott, Foresman and Company, 1971). This very helpful paperback text provides a clear and comprehensive overview of all the significant elements in the speech communication process, including a chapter which synthesizes the elements into a usefully detailed model.

Gardner Lindzey and Elliot Aronson, eds., *The Handbook of Social Psychology,* 2nd ed., Five volumes (Reading, Mass.: Addison-Wesley Publishing Co., Inc., 1969). These volumes contain the best summaries of recent studies in social psychology. A student interested in expanding his knowledge of the social aspects of the communication process could do no better than to turn to these volumes. The general contents are as follows:

   I Historical Introduction and Systematic Positions
  II Research Methods
 III The Individual in a Social Context
 IV Group Psychology and Phenomena of Interaction
  V Applied Social Psychology

Bruce Westley and Malcolm MacLean, Jr., "A Conceptual Model for Communication Research," *Interpersonal Communication,* ed. Dean C. Barnlund (Boston: Houghton Mifflin Company, 1968). This chapter provides an interesting system of concepts and explores theoretical and disciplinary differences reflected in speech communication models.

Part II

Speech Communication in Action: Preliminary Phases

Speech communication becomes necessary because people are psychologically isolated from one another. Human beings *need* other human beings; they are essentially interdependent. Speech communication, therefore, must *proclaim* mutuality as well as *create* mutuality. Kenneth Burke emphasizes this point when he writes:

> *If men were not apart from one another, there would be no need for the rhetorician to proclaim their unity. If men were wholly and truly of one substance, absolute communication would be of man's very essence. It would not be an ideal, as it now is, partly embodied in material conditions and partly frustrated by these same conditions; rather, it would be as natural, spontaneous, and total as with those ideal prototypes of communication, the theologian's angels or "messengers."* [1]

Although speech communication can and does bring men together, this juncture is possible only when the communicative condition is "right," only when the communication agents permit it. One individual may desire and seek communication; but if his or her counterpart—the prospective *other* agent—rejects the possibility, communication will not be achieved. One agent may initiate and try to control the act, but communicative interaction can occur only when the involved agents mutually *desire* it and *accept* the requisite conditions.

At the same time, we must strongly emphasize that even if mutual desire and acceptance do prevail, these conditions in and of themselves by no means guarantee that productive communication will result. Even if the conditions are met and some interaction does take place, we cannot expect that *cooperative action* will automatically and invariably follow that inter-

---

[1] Kenneth Burke, *A Grammar of Motives and a Rhetoric of Motives* (New York: World Publishing Company, 1962), p. 546.

action. Nor does oral interaction necessarily equal sweetness and light. Deeply imbedded in our cultural roots is the age-old myth that every failure in human relationships is a sign of "failure to communicate." This myth should be critically examined. We have to recognize that sometimes differing systems of government, different people, different values, and different ideas really *are* incompatible. And with such recognition we must admit the possibility that certain of these differences may actually be aggravated by open and full communication. One of the lessons to be learned by any person attempting to improve his communicative abilities is that there are times when he should remain silent—when communicative interaction ought to be avoided. As a basic principle we should be *discerning* in our use of it. We should recognize the high promise it holds, but we should not harbor unrealistic expectations.

Our basic aim in the ensuing section will be to examine this promise, to ascertain what we may realistically expect from speech interaction, and to determine what is essential if a speech communication act is to be deemed effective and productive. In the chapter which follows we will consider these important matters from the viewpoint of the communicating agent who is speaking: the *speaker*. That is to say, our discussion will be speaker-oriented;[2] and as a speaker you will be asked to view operationally and experientially the major components of the speech act as we have previously defined it for purposes of this textbook. *Self-assessment* will be a practical concern as we ask that you take some preliminary steps toward attaining a fuller understanding of yourself; and we will examine some of the ways in which that understanding can help you achieve a useful interaction between yourself and the other agents functioning within a communicative context.

[2] For a discussion of speaker-centered versus meaning-centered approaches, see Dean C. Barnlund, "Toward a Meaning-Centered Philosophy of Communication," *Journal of Communication,* XI (1962): 198–202.

Communicative interaction begins
with the agents' recognition of
and reaction to feedback.

Chapter 3
Initiating Effective Speech Communication

In almost any speech situation, certain general and major requirements would seem to apply. The speaker must:

1. Have something to communicate.

2. Desire to communicate with another agent regarding that "something."

3. Be aware of the elements of the communication process, as identified and explored in Chapter 2.

4. Somehow engage the "receptiveness" of the other agent—his willingness to receive stimuli and send back response.

5. Establish a mutual acceptance of the "rules" of communicative interchange.

6. Recognize the possibilities and limitations of oral interaction.

In sum, to be effective the speaker (a) *must know what the communication elements* are, and (b) *must know how to put these elements together in order to achieve meaningful communicative interaction.*

Enlarging Your Understanding of the Communication Elements

As a first requisite for communicating effectively, then, you must be aware of and sensitive to the major components of the speech process. These, you may recall, we have defined as (1) the Self as Agent, (2) the Other as Agent, and (3) the Communication Context.

Understanding How the Self Functions as an Agent

"Know thyself," admonishes the ancient adage, and this is sound advice. You should try to formulate a clear concept of yourself *as a speaker*. You should try to see yourself *as others see you* in the act of speaking, attempting self-assessment as if you were an impartial, outside observer. As a first step, you should endeavor to make *systematically* a careful, objective analysis of your feelings and behaviors in a number of speech communication *situations*.

Analyzing Your Feelings as a Speaker

One helpful approach to self-assessment is the accompanying set of Speech Communication Assessment Scales. Their purpose, primarily, is to help you tap your own feelings and predispositions about oral interaction with others. Glance at the titles of the Scales, and you will see that they are designed to probe the ways in which an individual feels differently when speaking with different persons and for different purposes. Note, too, that they attempt to specify the nature of some of those differences and to measure their degree. At the same time, these scales further emphasize the many, previously mentioned dimensions characterizing the speech communication act. We suggest that you take time now to respond to this succession of Assessment Scales and to make the recommended interpretations and comparisons.

SPEECH COMMUNICATION ASSESSMENT SCALES

The following scales are designed to help you assess your probable reactions in various speech communication settings. The desired method of marking the scales and the procedure by which to make your assessments are demonstrated in the sample scale immediately below and in the explanation which follows it.

SPEAKING WITH A SMALL CHILD

a.	Relaxed	⑦	6	5	4	3	2	1	Tense
b.	Pleasant	7	6	5	4	③	2	1	Unpleasant
c.	Informative	7	6	5	④	3	2	1	Not Informative
d.	Stimulating	7	6	⑤	4	3	2	1	Boring
e.	Self-fulfilling	7	6	5	4	3	②	1	Not Self-fulfilling

First, try to imagine yourself in the situation described in the title (in the sample scale, "Speaking with a Small Child"). Then, for each of the five listed responses (a, b, c, d, e) circle the number (7, 6, 5, 4, 3, 2, 1) in the response-continuum range which best describes how you think you would feel in the designated speech communication situation.

If, for example, the descriptive term at the left end of the scale (Relaxed) *describes your feelings completely*, then circle the number 7; if the descriptive term at the right end of the scale (Tense) describes your feelings most accurately, circle the number 1.

If one of the terms *describes your feelings fairly well*, but not completely, then circle the number 6 or 2, one scale position away from the term.

If one of the terms *describes your feelings only somewhat*, but better than does the other term, then circle the number 5 or 3, two scale positions away from the appropriate term.

If neither term at the ends of the response-continuum scale seems appropriate, or if both terms *describe your feelings equally*, then circle the number 4.

In the sample scale above, the respondent is describing his experience in speaking with a small child as completely relaxing, somewhat stimulating, somewhat unpleasant, for the most part not self-fulfilling, and neither especially informative nor especially uninformative.

Now try to imagine yourself in each of the twenty-four speech communication situations listed on pages 56–59. For each item (a, b, c, d, e) in each of the twenty-four situations, indicate on the response-continuum range (7, 6, 5, 4, 3, 2, 1) your numerical assessment, as explained above, of the feelings that you believe you would experience in the designated situation.

You will be using these scales four times in this chapter: twice here and twice later on. We suggest that you use four colored pencils—a different color for each time you mark the scales. Or use duplicate scales, pages 354–366.

There are no correct or incorrect responses. Try only to estimate in each instance how you believe you would feel in the given circumstance. After you have filled out these scales, you will score them on the basis of your numerical responses, and in accordance with the instructions on pages 60–63. From this score you will be able to appraise your expected performance in each of the areas covered. This can provide a positive first step toward "knowing yourself" as a communication agent.

SPEECH COMMUNICATION ASSESSMENT SCALES

1. TALKING WITH YOUR FATHER ABOUT YOUR FUTURE PLANS

a.	Relaxed	7	6	5	4	3	2	1	Tense
b.	Pleasant	7	6	5	4	3	2	1	Unpleasant
c.	Informative	7	6	5	4	3	2	1	Not Informative
d.	Stimulating	7	6	5	4	3	2	1	Boring
e.	Self-fulfilling	7	6	5	4	3	2	1	Not Self-fulfilling

2. RECEIVING A CRITICISM FROM YOUR MOTHER

a.	Relaxed	7	6	5	4	3	2	1	Tense
b.	Pleasant	7	6	5	4	3	2	1	Unpleasant
c.	Informative	7	6	5	4	3	2	1	Not Informative
d.	Stimulating	7	6	5	4	3	2	1	Boring
e.	Self-fulfilling	7	6	5	4	3	2	1	Not Self-fulfilling

3. DISCUSSING CURRENT WORLD EVENTS WITH A CLOSE FRIEND OF THE SAME SEX

a.	Relaxed	7	6	5	4	3	2	1	Tense
b.	Pleasant	7	6	5	4	3	2	1	Unpleasant
c.	Informative	7	6	5	4	3	2	1	Not Informative
d.	Stimulating	7	6	5	4	3	2	1	Boring
e.	Self-fulfilling	7	6	5	4	3	2	1	Not Self-fulfilling

4. CONVERSING AT A SOCIAL AFFAIR WITH A CLOSE FRIEND OF THE OPPOSITE SEX

a.	Relaxed	7	6	5	4	3	2	1	Tense
b.	Pleasant	7	6	5	4	3	2	1	Unpleasant
c.	Informative	7	6	5	4	3	2	1	Not Informative
d.	Stimulating	7	6	5	4	3	2	1	Boring
e.	Self-fulfilling	7	6	5	4	3	2	1	Not Self-fulfilling

5. TALKING ABOUT YOUR FUTURE PLANS WITH A CLOSE FRIEND OF THE OPPOSITE SEX

a.	Relaxed	7	6	5	4	3	2	1	Tense
b.	Pleasant	7	6	5	4	3	2	1	Unpleasant
c.	Informative	7	6	5	4	3	2	1	Not Informative
d.	Stimulating	7	6	5	4	3	2	1	Boring
e.	Self-fulfilling	7	6	5	4	3	2	1	Not Self-fulfilling

6. RECEIVING A CRITICISM FROM A CLOSE FRIEND OF THE OPPOSITE SEX

a.	Relaxed	7	6	5	4	3	2	1	Tense
b.	Pleasant	7	6	5	4	3	2	1	Unpleasant
c.	Informative	7	6	5	4	3	2	1	Not Informative
d.	Stimulating	7	6	5	4	3	2	1	Boring
e.	Self-fulfilling	7	6	5	4	3	2	1	Not Self-fulfilling

7. DISCUSSING CURRENT WORLD EVENTS WITH A JOB SUPERVISOR

a.	Relaxed	7	6	5	4	3	2	1	Tense
b.	Pleasant	7	6	5	4	3	2	1	Unpleasant
c.	Informative	7	6	5	4	3	2	1	Not Informative
d.	Stimulating	7	6	5	4	3	2	1	Boring
e.	Self-fulfilling	7	6	5	4	3	2	1	Not Self-fulfilling

8. CONVERSING AT A SOCIAL AFFAIR WITH A TEACHER

a.	Relaxed	7	6	5	4	3	2	1	Tense
b.	Pleasant	7	6	5	4	3	2	1	Unpleasant
c.	Informative	7	6	5	4	3	2	1	Not Informative
d.	Stimulating	7	6	5	4	3	2	1	Boring
e.	Self-fulfilling	7	6	5	4	3	2	1	Not Self-fulfilling

9. TALKING ABOUT YOUR FUTURE PLANS WITH YOUR MOTHER

a.	Relaxed	7	6	5	4	3	2	1	Tense
b.	Pleasant	7	6	5	4	3	2	1	Unpleasant
c.	Informative	7	6	5	4	3	2	1	Not Informative
d.	Stimulating	7	6	5	4	3	2	1	Boring
e.	Self-fulfilling	7	6	5	4	3	2	1	Not Self-fulfilling

10. RECEIVING A CRITICISM FROM A TEACHER

a.	Relaxed	7	6	5	4	3	2	1	Tense
b.	Pleasant	7	6	5	4	3	2	1	Unpleasant
c.	Informative	7	6	5	4	3	2	1	Not Informative
d.	Stimulating	7	6	5	4	3	2	1	Boring
e.	Self-fulfilling	7	6	5	4	3	2	1	Not Self-fulfilling

11. DISCUSSING CURRENT WORLD EVENTS WITH YOUR FATHER

a.	Relaxed	7	6	5	4	3	2	1	Tense
b.	Pleasant	7	6	5	4	3	2	1	Unpleasant
c.	Informative	7	6	5	4	3	2	1	Not Informative
d.	Stimulating	7	6	5	4	3	2	1	Boring
e.	Self-fulfilling	7	6	5	4	3	2	1	Not Self-fulfilling

12. CONVERSING WITH YOUR MOTHER AT A SOCIAL AFFAIR

a.	Relaxed	7	6	5	4	3	2	1	Tense
b.	Pleasant	7	6	5	4	3	2	1	Unpleasant
c.	Informative	7	6	5	4	3	2	1	Not Informative
d.	Stimulating	7	6	5	4	3	2	1	Boring
e.	Self-fulfilling	7	6	5	4	3	2	1	Not Self-fulfilling

SPEECH COMMUNICATION ASSESSMENT SCALES (Continued)

13. TALKING WITH A CLOSE FRIEND OF THE SAME SEX ABOUT YOUR FUTURE PLANS

a.	Relaxed	7	6	5	4	3	2	1	Tense
b.	Pleasant	7	6	5	4	3	2	1	Unpleasant
c.	Informative	7	6	5	4	3	2	1	Not Informative
d.	Stimulating	7	6	5	4	3	2	1	Boring
e.	Self-fulfilling	7	6	5	4	3	2	1	Not Self-fulfilling

14. RECEIVING A CRITICISM FROM YOUR FATHER

a.	Relaxed	7	6	5	4	3	2	1	Tense
b.	Pleasant	7	6	5	4	3	2	1	Unpleasant
c.	Informative	7	6	5	4	3	2	1	Not Informative
d.	Stimulating	7	6	5	4	3	2	1	Boring
e.	Self-fulfilling	7	6	5	4	3	2	1	Not Self-fulfilling

15. DISCUSSING CURRENT WORLD EVENTS WITH A TEACHER

a.	Relaxed	7	6	5	4	3	2	1	Tense
b.	Pleasant	7	6	5	4	3	2	1	Unpleasant
c.	Informative	7	6	5	4	3	2	1	Not Informative
d.	Stimulating	7	6	5	4	3	2	1	Boring
e.	Self-fulfilling	7	6	5	4	3	2	1	Not Self-fulfilling

16. CONVERSING WITH A CLOSE FRIEND OF THE SAME SEX AT A SOCIAL AFFAIR

a.	Relaxed	7	6	5	4	3	2	1	Tense
b.	Pleasant	7	6	5	4	3	2	1	Unpleasant
c.	Informative	7	6	5	4	3	2	1	Not Informative
d.	Stimulating	7	6	5	4	3	2	1	Boring
e.	Self-fulfilling	7	6	5	4	3	2	1	Not Self-fulfilling

17. TALKING WITH A JOB SUPERVISOR ABOUT YOUR FUTURE PLANS

a.	Relaxed	7	6	5	4	3	2	1	Tense
b.	Pleasant	7	6	5	4	3	2	1	Unpleasant
c.	Informative	7	6	5	4	3	2	1	Not Informative
d.	Stimulating	7	6	5	4	3	2	1	Boring
e.	Self-fulfilling	7	6	5	4	3	2	1	Not Self-fulfilling

18. RECEIVING A CRITICISM FROM A JOB SUPERVISOR

a.	Relaxed	7	6	5	4	3	2	1	Tense
b.	Pleasant	7	6	5	4	3	2	1	Unpleasant
c.	Informative	7	6	5	4	3	2	1	Not Informative
d.	Stimulating	7	6	5	4	3	2	1	Boring
e.	Self-fulfilling	7	6	5	4	3	2	1	Not Self-fulfilling

19. DISCUSSING CURRENT WORLD AFFAIRS WITH YOUR MOTHER

a.	Relaxed	7	6	5	4	3	2	1	Tense
b.	Pleasant	7	6	5	4	3	2	1	Unpleasant
c.	Informative	7	6	5	4	3	2	1	Not Informative
d.	Stimulating	7	6	5	4	3	2	1	Boring
e.	Self-fulfilling	7	6	5	4	3	2	1	Not Self-fulfilling

20. CONVERSING WITH A JOB SUPERVISOR AT A SOCIAL AFFAIR

a.	Relaxed	7	6	5	4	3	2	1	Tense
b.	Pleasant	7	6	5	4	3	2	1	Unpleasant
c.	Informative	7	6	5	4	3	2	1	Not Informative
d.	Stimulating	7	6	5	4	3	2	1	Boring
e.	Self-fulfilling	7	6	5	4	3	2	1	Not Self-fulfilling

21. TALKING WITH A TEACHER ABOUT YOUR FUTURE PLANS

a.	Relaxed	7	6	5	4	3	2	1	Tense
b.	Pleasant	7	6	5	4	3	2	1	Unpleasant
c.	Informative	7	6	5	4	3	2	1	Not Informative
d.	Stimulating	7	6	5	4	3	2	1	Boring
e.	Self-fulfilling	7	6	5	4	3	2	1	Not Self-fulfilling

22. RECEIVING A CRITICISM FROM A CLOSE FRIEND OF THE SAME SEX

a.	Relaxed	7	6	5	4	3	2	1	Tense
b.	Pleasant	7	6	5	4	3	2	1	Unpleasant
c.	Informative	7	6	5	4	3	2	1	Not Informative
d.	Stimulating	7	6	5	4	3	2	1	Boring
e.	Self-fulfilling	7	6	5	4	3	2	1	Not Self-fulfilling

23. DISCUSSING CURRENT WORLD AFFAIRS WITH A CLOSE FRIEND OF THE OPPOSITE SEX

a.	Relaxed	7	6	5	4	3	2	1	Tense
b.	Pleasant	7	6	5	4	3	2	1	Unpleasant
c.	Informative	7	6	5	4	3	2	1	Not Informative
d.	Stimulating	7	6	5	4	3	2	1	Boring
e.	Self-fulfilling	7	6	5	4	3	2	1	Not Self-fulfilling

24. CONVERSING WITH YOUR FATHER AT A SOCIAL AFFAIR

a.	Relaxed	7	6	5	4	3	2	1	Tense
b.	Pleasant	7	6	5	4	3	2	1	Unpleasant
c.	Informative	7	6	5	4	3	2	1	Not Informative
d.	Stimulating	7	6	5	4	3	2	1	Boring
e.	Self-fulfilling	7	6	5	4	3	2	1	Not Self-fulfilling

Scoring the Assessment Scales

These scales have attempted to provide you with some assessment of yourself as a communicative agent. Involved were four *speech settings* (talking about future plans, receiving criticism, discussing current events, conversing socially); six *other communication agents* (father, mother, friend of the same sex, friend of the opposite sex, job supervisor, teacher); and *five dimensions:* (Relaxed/Tense, Pleasant/Unpleasant, Informative/Not Informative, Stimulating/Boring, Self-fulfilling/Not Self-fulfilling).

For each space in the Profile matrix (page 61), add together the scores on the items listed for the appropriate dimension; then write the total score in the space provided. The numbers printed in the first column identify the scales whose scores apply to the dimensions on the right. For example, scale numbers 1, 5, 9, 13, 17, and 21 deal with the setting entitled Future Plans. So, in the first blank, write in the total of the Relaxed/Tense scores from each of these scales. Proceed in this manner through all of the settings, all of the agents, and all of the dimensions, until the entire matrix is completed. Some interpretations will then be possible.

Interpreting the Assessment Scales

A. For each dimension, you can note the degree to which you can expect it to be present in each of the four settings and with each of the six agents. For each *setting*, possible scores could range from 6 to 42, with an average of 24; for each *agent*, possible scores could range from 4 to 28 with an average of 16. *Compare your scores with these possible ranges and averages.*

B. *Compare your scores for the different settings.* In which communication situation are you most relaxed? Which do you find most informative? *Make similar comparisons for the different agents.* With which person do you feel most relaxed? With which person do you find communication most self-fulfilling? Do you agree with the interpretations which have emerged from this analysis? *Compare your profile with that of a classmate.* In what ways are they most similar? Most different? How do your results compare with the scores of Students X and Y (page 62, Chart B) who participated in this self-assessment exercise in a previous class experiment? What interpretations would you make of their scores?

C. Using a different colored pencil, go over all of the assessment scales again, scoring the items in terms of how *you expect the other person would feel* when talking with you in that situation. Then compare the profile from your point of view with that from the other agent's point of view. Again, your attention is called to the extra, perforated copies of the "Speech Communication Assessment Scales" to be found in Appendix B, pages 354–366.

D. *Correlate your reactions on any two dimensions* by plotting each of the twenty-four pairs of scores as illustrated in the Correlation Chart D, page 62. Are your highest scores on one dimension also highest on the second dimension?

A. Speech Communication Profile

	Scale title numbers to be added together for each dimension on the right	Relaxed/ Tense	Pleasant/ Unpleasant	Informative/ Not informative	Stimulating/ Boring	Self-fulfilling/ Not Self-fulfilling
SETTINGS						
Future plans	1, 5, 9, 13, 17, 21					
Criticism	2, 6, 10, 14, 18, 22					
Current events	3, 7, 11, 15, 19, 23					
Social conversation	4, 8, 12, 16, 20, 24					
AGENTS						
Father	1, 11, 14, 24					
Mother	2, 9, 12, 19					
Friend— same sex	3, 13, 16, 22					
Friend— opposite sex	4, 5, 6, 23					
Job supervisor	7, 17, 18, 20					
Teacher	8, 10, 15, 21					

B. COMPARISON OF   STUDENT X   STUDENT Y

	Relaxed / Tense	Pleasant / Unpleasant	Informative / Not Informative	Stimulating / Boring	Self-fulfilling / Not Self-fulfilling	Relaxed / Tense	Pleasant / Unpleasant	Informative / Not Informative	Stimulating / Boring	Self-fulfilling / Not Self-fulfilling
Future plans	23	21	23	30	22	24	23	31	28	26
Criticism	17	18	30	29	21	18	15	28	28	26
Current events	31	29	29	25	24	18	21	25	25	22
Social conversation	31	30	18	35	28	31	29	17	22	29
Father	9	10	14	18	16	11	10	14	15	13
Mother	15	17	13	22	12	11	10	13	15	13
Friend-same sex	25	23	21	21	19	24	21	21	22	23
Friend-opposite sex	23	19	17	23	19	14	15	16	17	19
Job supervisor	11	13	14	17	12	16	17	20	19	19
Teacher	18	16	21	18	17	15	15	17	15	16

Correlation Chart   Relaxed   Tense

	7	6	5	4	3	2	1
Self-fulfilling 7	1						
6							
5			9				
4							
3							7
2							
Not Self-fulfilling 1							

In this example, which has been only partially filled out, situation 1 was scored 7 on Relaxed/Tense and 7 on Self-fulfilling/Not Self-fulfilling. Situation 7 was scored

1 on Relaxed/Tense and 3 on Self-fulfilling/Not Self-fulfilling. Situation 9 was scored 5 on Relaxed/Tense and 5 on Self-fulfilling/Not Self-fulfilling.

Compare your results with those of the student whose analysis is shown below:

Correlation Chart   Relaxed   Tense

		7	6	5	4	3	2	1
Self-fulfilling	7				1			
	6	16	11	21	15			
	5	3, 5	13, 23	8, 9	7, 17 22	10	14	
	4	24		2, 20		6	18	
	3	4	19					
	2	12						
Not Self-fulfilling	1							

These Speech Communication Assessment Scales are intended to sample your expectations of yourself as an agent of communicative interaction. Prepare a list of other agents, other settings and contexts, and other dimensions which could be considered. These procedures should help you begin a *systematic* self-assessment, and one which you should continue as you study your speech capabilities and abilities.

Appraising Yourself as a Source of Communicable Knowledge

There are, of course, other practical approaches to self-evaluation which intensify and extend the focus upon yourself in the role of speaker, approaches which can help you to expand your self-knowledge and to make you more aware of it. What do you *know?* What are your *interests?* On what topics could you *enlighten others?* What *controversial issues excite you* to the point that you would like to have others agree with your position? These are the kinds of knowledge-appraisal questions that a beginning speaker should put to himself, and take some thought in answering. It is a sad fact that many inexperienced speakers never make this kind of self-assessment. They ask others, for instance, rather than themselves, on what *topics* they should speak. Remember, however, that no one else can ever answer the question of topic selection as well as you can. Your instructor may offer some guidance, but *you* must make the final choice in the light of what you know and feel and think.

Lack of self-appraisal and self-knowledge makes for many student speakers this problem of "getting a topic" the most difficult part of a speech assignment. It therefore deserves special note here.

Often, a beginning speaker will say, "My life has been so *typical,* just like the others, and I have nothing really to say." This is, in large part, a "rationalization." We all feel challenged and somewhat threatened by a speaking assignment, and we all must wish that we had greater resources at hand. But actually no one's life is really "typical" and so like another's. We have not all lived in the same places, participated in the same activities, enjoyed the same interests and hobbies and companions, had the same relatives employed in the same occupations, and so on. What *is* typical is not the life that each of us has led; what is typical is the feeling of inadequacy that each of us experiences in the face of a speaking assignment. This feeling should be recognized for what it is, and it should not be allowed to bring to a frustrated halt our search for a speech topic.

If we take time to assess our accumulation of knowledge about ourselves and our ideas, we will readily recognize those subjects on which we are prepared to speak and those subjects for which additional preparation will be necessary. There is a significant difference between *being* prepared to speak on a topic and *becoming* prepared to speak on it. This is the difference between *general preparation* and *specific preparation* for speaking. This distinction applies equally to giving a public speech or being interviewed for a job. The backlog of the speaker's prior experience, reading, and deliberation about a topic constitutes his general preparation for speaking on that topic. Once the subject is in mind, the additional research, the organization, planning, and practice for the event make up the specific preparation. Admittedly, most student speakers, for reasons of age alone, will probably have had comparatively fewer prior experiences and will need, therefore, a greater amount of specific preparation for any given speech situation.

While your memory may have great retentive capacities, you will nevertheless do well to collect and file away information regarding some of your major interests whenever you come across it. Newspaper columns, magazine articles, lecture notes (all with citations listing the source, author, and date) should be filed systematically for future reference. Such a procedure will provide both general background and a readily available source of materials for topics of special interest to you. Nothing is so inefficient and frustrating as to spend valuable time intended for specific preparation in searching out vaguely remembered materials which would now prove useful. While some of this effort may be unavoidable, the systematic practice of collecting and filing reference materials will reduce it to a minimum. Moreover, once you have given a speech or completed a course, do not discard your research materials, class papers, and class notes. *Hold onto them.* Your research, having been completed for an assignment of the moment, is almost certain to have future value and pertinence for you.

Discovering Your Style as a Speaker

In your self-assessment, you should also try to discover something of your own best personal *style*. By "style" we mean a speaker's distinctive, individualized speaking patterns, the "manner, modes, and means" of his utterance. How would you analyze your style? Formal or informal? Elevated or down-to-earth? Do you like to move from the general to the specific, or from specific to general? Do you like to use vivid, colorful words, or are you characteristically plainspoken? Do you ordinarily employ fairly complex sentences, or do you prefer the short, blunt, unadorned statement?

STUDY PROBE 1

Seeing Yourself as Others See You

Erving Goffman writes about those impressions we "give" while speaking (conscious, planned, deliberate), and those we "give off" (unintended).[1] Try to visualize yourself as you believe you are seen by others in a speaking situation. What impressions do you believe you "give off"? Do you see any consistent patterns in your verbal or nonverbal speech behaviors? Verify your opinions by asking a friend for his honest judgment of the impression you make as a speaker.

[1] Erving Goffman, *The Presentation of Self in Everyday Life* (Garden City, N.Y.: Doubleday & Company, Inc., Anchor Books, 1959), p. 2.

What would you single out as your special strengths and limitations in speaking? In what settings and with what approaches do you feel you are most effective? Some speakers, for instance, fare better in discussing particular cases—facts and figures. Others are better in making more general, grander sweeps over their topic. Some paint the trees, and others the forest. Some are more persuasive with larger groups, while others are more influential with smaller groups. Some excel in more formal parliamentary settings, while yet others are able to function more ably in the informal situations. John Kennedy, Lyndon Johnson, and Richard Nixon—as examples—differed greatly in speech "style." Look both toward your past speaking experiences and also to your present self-image for clues concerning your most effective style and for styles you need to develop. At the

American voters had an unusual opportunity for a close-up comparison of the speaking styles of presidential candidates in the Kennedy-Nixon debates of the 1960 campaign. Although polls showed Kennedy going into the debates with less popular support than his opponent, he won a sufficient number of adherents to gain a narrow margin of victory, and the favorable effect of his speaking style in the debates has generally been credited as the deciding factor. T. H. White, author of *The Making of the President 1960*, said that what the debates "did best was to give the voters of a great democracy a living portrait of two men under stress and let the voters decide, by instinct and emotion, which style and pattern of behavior under stress they preferred in their leader." These pictures of the candidates are from the debate televised from New York on October 21.

same time, keep in mind that speaking styles *evolve;* they must be *flexible;* they can—and should—be *changed* and *modified.* No speaker is totally limited by what he is now. As a student of speech communication, one of your important tasks is to seek that speaking style which utilizes best all of your natural abilities.

Reducing Your Anxiety in a Speaking Situation

Finally, in your self-appraisal, you will want to ask yourself: "How do I feel when I'm faced with the speech communication act? What is my *mental state*—my emotional balance—as I am about to initiate speech with others?" Clearly, a confident, positive mental attitude will carry the speaker a long way toward success. Anxiety is, however, common among beginning speakers; and a certain amount of it is common also to nearly *all* speakers, regardless of age or experience. It therefore deserves some comment here.

Often a speaker, anticipating a communication interaction, visualizes himself with quivering knees, trembling hands, a dry mouth, and a breaking voice. There is much that we do not yet know about speech fear—or stage fright, as it is sometimes called. It has been a common problem, however, for so many centuries that its existence is no mystery. We can be fairly certain, for instance, that speech fear is a part of a larger problem of general anxiety and tension which, to some degree, affects every man and woman. Psychologist Raymond B. Cattell, who has carried out much research on the problem, cites evidence that general anxiety fluctuates in early childhood, rises most consistently in adolescence, declines considerably through early and middle adulthood, and then rises once more as people progress to and through old age—especially after they reach their sixties.[2] So the unfortunate fact is that the level of general anxiety is high when most persons in our society are just beginning their formal speech training.

A compounding difficulty is that in their first classroom efforts in speech communication students imagine their task to be very unlike all of their previous speaking experience. For years, they have talked and conversed with friends without experiencing great anxiety. In Chapter 2, you will recall, we cited a study showing how students, following a speech course, come to see the different speech forms with which they experiment in classrooms as being very much alike, and that even the more formal experiences fit our basic paradigm of "two persons conversing." And, as we have emphasized, in the essentials they *are* alike. Therefore, the sooner you can visualize a public speech as "conversing" with an audience, the more at ease and effective you are likely to become.

Like a self-fulfilling prophecy, undue concern about speech fear may only intensify the existing level of anxiety. If you see anxiety as a problem, realize that it is a very common feeling and that it will never be so apparent to your listeners as you may think.

Further, there are some positive steps which you can take to limit your speech fear. For one thing, *focus primarily upon the ideas you want to communicate* and their *reception by the other agent or agents* for whom you intend them. And, since you will no doubt experience greater anxiety in some speech situations than in others, make a list of those anxiety-provoking circumstances and rank them according to the levels of their severity. Then try to analyze, with your instructor's help if necessary, why the levels vary from situation to situa-

[2] Raymond B. Cattell, "The Nature and Measurement of Anxiety," *Scientific American* (March 1963): 96–104.

tion. Once you have pinpointed the "why," you will have found a fairly sound basis for ameliorating the difficulty. Other important and frequently proffered advice is to prepare thoroughly for every speech occasion, and to gain as many speech experiences as possible. In a sense, the fear of speaking is like the fear of water, which is usually lost in water rather than on land. You can be comforted, too, by the realization that a limited amount of anxiety may be helpful. It helps to keep you alert and concerned about sustaining interaction. An overly confident speaker frequently has problems with effectiveness that are greater than those difficulties generated by ordinary speech fear.

To restate our first principle, then, every speaker should develop a self-awareness—a sensitivity to his own position and possibilities as a communication agent. Unless he has made an accurate self-assessment, he cannot hope to present himself and his ideas with optimum effectiveness.

But in addition to self-awareness, the speaker must also have a *self-concern,* an active desire for *self-actualization.* He must prefer to act for himself—and to be accepted on his own terms for what he is.

Some persons despair at the large degree of "image-creating" that goes on in contemporary society, at the pseudonymous or "surrogate" message-makers that seem to dominate nearly all communication media. We might remember, however, that the ancient Greeks also employed ghost-writers. The "selling" of another and his ideas or point of view is as old as the history of rhetorical practice itself. Occasionally we find the product of the ghost-writer even in the classroom. The practice, even though exploited, is only an extension of a basic truth. In the sense that no man is an island, we can also say that no speech is wholly original. We borrow from others, either consciously or subconsciously.

Yet every speaker in every interaction should desire to add some measure of his own creative power to his speaking efforts. His work should bear his personal stamp. If one merely summarizes and repeats the message of a friend or of a single article from a popular magazine, he does nothing but voice the thoughts, selection of materials, organization of ideas, and wording of another. Little personal growth results from such effort, and little of self becomes part of the interchange.

Understanding How Others Function as Agents

When you are the speaking agent, the other agents in the speech communication context will comprise your listeners—your audience. You should, therefore, learn as much about them as possible if you desire to interact with them effectively. The analysis of audiences begins and is inextricably interwoven with the history of rhetorical theory. In his dialogue *Phaedrus,* Plato asserts that the good speaker must know the nature of his audience—must know their "souls." Aristotle, who also devoted much attention to this topic, discusses in the *Rhetoric* what an audience is likely to consider good. He touches upon several human emotions—anger, fear, love, shame, and pity—and examines the effects produced by the various emotions on listeners and the factors which create those effects. His discussion of the generation gap, hardly a new phenomenon, is a useful model of audience analysis and one pertinent for almost any era. Examine it and decide in what respects (if any) you agree, and to what extent.

Today's generation gap: in what ways comparable to that described by Aristotle?

"YOUNG MEN" . . . . and . . . . "OLD MEN"

¶   Young men have strong passions, and tend to gratify them indiscriminately. Of the bodily desires, it is the sexual by which they are most swayed and in which they show absence of self-control. They are changeable and fickle in their desires, which are violent while they last, but quickly over: their impulses are keen but not deep-rooted, and are like sick people's attacks of hunger and thirst. . . . They look at the good side rather than the bad, not having yet witnessed many instances of wickedness. They trust others readily because they have not yet often been cheated. They are sanguine; nature warms their blood as though with excess of wine; and besides that, they have as yet met with few disappointments. Their lives are mainly spent not in memory but in expectation; for expectation refers to the future, memory to the past, and youth has a long future before it and a short past behind it: on the first day of one's life one has nothing at all to remember, and can only look forward. They are easily cheated, owing to the sanguine disposition mentioned. Their hot tempers and hopeful dispositions make them more courageous
(Continued in column 1, page 69)

The character of Elderly Men —men who are past their prime— may be said to be formed for the most part of elements that are the contrary of all these. They have lived many years; they have often been taken in, and often made mistakes; and life on the whole is a bad business. The result is that they are sure about nothing and *under-do* everything. They "think," but they never "know"; and because of their hesitation they always add a "possibly" or a "perhaps," putting everything this way and nothing positively. They are cynical; that is, they tend to put the worse construction on everything. . . . They are cowardly, and are always anticipating danger; unlike that of the young, who are warm-blooded, their temperament is chilly; old age has paved the way for cowardice; fear is, in fact, a form of chill. They love life; and all the more when their last day has come, because the object of all desire is something we have not got, and also because we desire most strongly that which we need most urgently. They are too fond of themselves; this is one form that small-mindedness takes. Because of this, they guide their lives too much by
(Continued in column 2, page 69)

than older men are; the hot temper prevents fear, and the hopeful disposition creates confidence; we cannot feel fear so long as we are feeling angry, and any expectation of good makes us confident. . . . They have exalted notions, because they have not yet been humbled by life or learnt its necessary limitations; moreover, their hopeful disposition makes them think themselves equal to great things—and that means having exalted notions. They would always rather do noble deeds than useful ones: their lives are regulated more by moral feeling than by reasoning; and whereas reasoning leads us to choose what is useful, moral goodness leads us to choose what is noble. . . . All their mistakes are in the direction of doing things excessively and vehemently. . . . They think they know everything, and are always quite sure about it; this, in fact, is why they overdo everything.

considerations of what is useful and too little by what is noble—for the useful is what is good for oneself, and the noble what is good absolutely. . . . They live by memory rather than by hope; for what is left to them of life is but little as compared with the long past; and hope is of the future, memory of the past. This, again, is the cause of their loquacity; they are continually talking of the past, because they enjoy remembering it. Their fits of anger are sudden but feeble. . . . Old men may feel pity, as well as young men, but not for the same reason. Young men feel it out of kindness; old men out of weakness, imagining that anything that befalls any one else might easily happen to them.[3]

Ascertaining Audience Values and Motives

The analysis of audience behavior is also a central concern in contemporary research in communication. In fact, it has probably received more attention than any other single aspect of the oral interaction process.[4] To know and to study the "subject matter" of an intended message is one task; to know and analyze the nature, inclinations, and biases of other prospective agents to a speech communication act is quite a different task—and a much more elusive one. And, of course, the larger the number of listening agents, the more complex the assessment becomes. Here again, however, you can make certain preparations of both a general and a specific nature.

When preparing to speak with any audience (whether it be one good friend or a thousand strangers), you should try to assess the *dominant values and motives* which will be operative in the audience at the time of the speaking event. Since you will have to make your assessment well before the time you actually meet your audience face to face, your work will not be easy. To an extent, you will have to rely upon generalization and speculation. But regardless of how you formulate your audience appraisal, the procedure can assist you in two important ways. First, it will reveal to you the nature of the audience you will face;

[3] Aristotle, *Rhetoric, The Basic Works of Aristotle,* ed. Richard McKeon (New York: Random House, Inc., 1941), pp. 1403–1406.

[4] See, for example, William J. McGuire, "The Nature of Attitudes and Attitude Change," *The Handbook of Social Psychology,* 2nd ed., ed. Gardner Lindzey and Elliot Aronson (Reading, Mass.: Addison-Wesley Publishing Co., Inc., 1969), v. III, pp. 177–265.

you will become more aware of the types of personalities represented among your listeners. Second, by discovering the present thought-position and nature of your audience, you can more knowledgeably determine the directions and emphases your speaking must take in order to move the thinking of that audience to the desired position on the subject.

One means of accomplishing this goal is to *ascertain the nature of the groups to which the listening agent(s) belong.* Are they, for instance, predominantly members of a single political party, or a church organization, or a certain social group? Do they come from a particular geographical region? Almost always, the individual identifies with one or more groups or collectives. By identifying with a certain group a person places himself in a category: he belongs to X group; he is one of X. When you identify yourself with a group, you associate yourself with and support the attitudes, values, and motivations of that group. If you can ascertain the group memberships of your prospective listeners, you can use their associational attitudes, values, and motivations to bridge the communicational gap, to facilitate closer interaction.

In one research study, for example, a questionnaire containing some items opposing norms of the Roman Catholic faith was administered to two groups of Catholic students. Before filling out the questionnaire, Group I was informed that they were all Catholics; Group II was not so informed. You can anticipate the results. Subjects in Group I answered the questionnaire's critical items in closer accord with the position prescribed for Catholics than did Group II.[5] The awareness of group membership clearly influenced Group I to follow more closely the norms of their religious commonality.

A speaking agent will often wear his Legion cap when addressing the American Legion Convention, thereby calling attention to the customs of the group and letting his audience know that he, too, is a member of their organization—one of them. Even if a speaker is *not* a member of the organization or group to whom he is addressing himself, he often tries to create the appearance of oneness with them by wearing a symbol of their organization or trade. A political campaigner, for example, might wear a hard hat when speaking to a group of construction workers. Almost any group can be expected to respond

[5] See the early studies in Carl I. Hovland, Irving L. Janis, and Harold H. Kelley, *Communication and Persuasion* (New Haven, Conn.: Yale University Press, 1953), Chapter 5.

If safety did not demand it, politics probably did: Senator George McGovern wisely donned a hard hat when appealing to construction workers for their support of his presidential aspirations in 1972.

more favorably to one of its own or to one who shows evidence of a willingness to be "one" with them—especially if the speaker emphasizes visibly their common bond.

Discovering Degrees of Audience Persuasibility

Another means of analyzing an audience—one encountered frequently in behavioral research studies—is to try to relate certain audience characteristics to the factor of *persuasibility*. How susceptible or responsive are listening agents likely to be to persuasive stimuli or messages? While many of the findings are not yet sufficiently clear or definite enough for practical application, a number of the studies indicate that persons with high self-esteem, or with extreme views, or with strong ego-involvement in the topic, or those who are generally hostile or aggressive are more difficult to influence in a speaking situation.[6] Most of these findings you can probably support by drawing upon your own personal experiences and observations as a student. Persons having self-confidence and high self-regard are generally confident of their beliefs and biases. Those holding extreme positions and those who are ego-involved with a topic have made a personal commitment that would be extremely difficult for them to reverse. Hostile and aggressive personalities are usually not receptive to suggestions or new thoughts of any kind. We shall look more closely at this aspect of audience analysis when we discuss Belief-Evaluation clusters in Chapters 5 and 7.

Sex, too, is thought to be a variable of persuasibility. Some studies, including those of this writer, have found women easier to influence than are men. Possibly this is due, in part, to societal norms and role-playing. Women, at least openly, seem less likely to challenge authority figures; but, as almost any television newscast will substantiate, that reluctance is fading fast. Possibly because of their historic acceptance of authority, women students often are easier to teach than are men: they follow instructions and assignments more closely—a trait which has its good and bad features. There is, of course, a possibility that the Women's Liberation Movement will change all this.

Another factor, *intelligence level,* which we might expect to be very significantly related to persuasibility, does not appear to have any readily recognizable correlation with suggestibility through speech.

In the kind of analysis we have been suggesting, the underlying task becomes simply one of trying to "put yourself in the other fellow's shoes," to see things through his eyes, to sense them through his feelings, to respond as he would respond. *Empathize* with him.

---

[6] William J. McGuire, "The Nature of Attitudes and Attitude Change," *The Handbook of Social Psychology,* 2nd ed., ed. Gardner Lindzey and Elliot Aronson (Reading, Mass.: Addison-Wesley Publishing Co., Inc., 1969), v. III, pp. 247–252.

STUDY PROBE 2
Developing Empathy with Listening Agents

As a study of *empathy,* or the ability to place yourself in the position of another and understand *his* feelings, refer again to the *Speech Communication Assessment Scales* on pages 56–59. Using a pencil of a color different from the ones you used the first two times you reacted to the scales, *mark them as you believe one of your friends would "score" them.* Or you may prefer to use one of the duplicate scales which are available in Appendix B, pages 354–366.

Then, as a second phase, *ask this friend to take still a different-colored pencil and mark the scales to indicate how he actually "sees" himself.*

Carefully compare the two sets of responses. In what areas were you most accurate in predicting your friend's feelings? In which situations were you least accurate? You can, of course, further test your empathic abilities by repeating this project with other friends.

In analyzing an audience, then, our advice to you as a speaker is that you should seek out all of the information you can about the other agents who are or will be in the communication setting. Try to discover their views on the topic at hand, their beliefs and evaluations, their values and motives, the groups and viewpoints with which they associate themselves, and such other influenceable characteristics or variables as self-esteem, extremity of view, ego-involvement, hostility, aggression, sex, etc.

This, admittedly, is no small task. It requires patience, perseverance, and a degree of ingenuity; but any speaker who hopes to interact effectively must do it. William Jennings Bryan, one of America's best-known speakers, spoke often and widely on the Chautauqua circuit, that wonderful American institution which brought speakers and performers to countless communities around the turn of the century.[7] His practice was to come to a community well before the speaking occasion, to look around, and to engage as many of the townspeople as possible in conversation. Even with all his experience, Billy Bryan would try to find out as much as he could about the people he would be addressing—their interests, their views. *He* wanted to be influenced by this information, to be able to incorporate it and respond to it in a specific address to a specific audience.

Like Bryan or any other effective communicator, never address an audience you can conceive of only in vague and general terms; *address a specific audience that you are aware of and that you know.* This applies to every communication. Each audience is a *different* audience. And if you fully realize this, you will readily understand why you may on occasion speak to your father very differently from the way you may speak to your mother, or why you would not use the same speech for a political gathering that you would use when addressing fellow graduates at a commencement, although many of the same people might be in both audiences.

Understanding the Context of the Impending Communication

To know yourself and others as source/response agents is highly important, but that is not enough. You must also know the *communication context.* You must make yourself aware of the specific speaking situation or setting, the particular elements which will be multidimensionally, multidirectionally, and simultaneously operant within it and upon the interactants, because

1. The specific context constrains and directs the speaker in his choices of materials and approaches.

[7] A student interested in the history of public speaking in America could begin by reading the first three chapters in Volume I of *A History and Criticism of American Public Address,* ed. William N. Brigance (New York: McGraw-Hill Book Company, 1943).

2. The specific context helps the speaker to determine what is *expected* of him.

3. The specific context helps to define what is *desired* of the speaker.

4. The specific context bears importantly upon what is *required* of the speaker.

5. And, over all, the context strongly influences the *outcomes* of the communication act.

You may recall that in Chapter 2 when we originally analyzed the speech communication process, we noted that context has both physical and psychological dimensions and that those dimensions are significantly influenced by certain social, temporal, and cultural factors. At this point, we want to expand somewhat upon some of the latter, in particular the *contemporaneous, causative,* and *circumstantial influences* which bear upon an impending communication event.

Contemporaneous Influences

Time and timing, as we have previously pointed out, are significant elements of the context. Communicative agents must, therefore, be attuned to the tenor and timbre of the times. What are the common topics and issues of the day? What are the prevailing beliefs and practices? There was a time, for instance, when any self-respecting speaker would wear a beard, if at all possible; those times seem to be returning. The length of speeches, like the length of women's skirts, varies from era to era. Standards for the "ideal" length of a speech change more slowly, however; but some ages do go for maxi speeches while others seem to prefer the mini speech. The typical language (unmistakably a dating factor) of one age will appear ornate and artificial in another. The speaker must have some sensitivity to the contemporaneity of the context.

Causative Influences

A communication agent should also be aware of the impetuses or forces which have conjoined to produce the specific speech situation. What in this context has brought these particular agents together at this particular time? Is the situation one of *negotiation,* where an antagonist and you—as protagonist—will attempt to arrive at a compromise that will bring to an end some impasse between you? Or does the situational milieu require you to enact the role of *arbitrator* in which you will attempt to conduct negotiations among others in order to end an impasse between them? The problems may be similar, but there are different contextual requirements if your role as communicative agent is that of negotiator rather than arbitrator.

Or is the situation, perhaps, one of *debate,* where you are contending against another agent in order to project your view to still other agents? If so, design and marshal your arguments so that they will sway the agents *listening* to the debate. It is pointless to try to influence your opponent in a structured context of this kind.

Circumstantial Influences

As a speaker, you must know within the specific context not only *to whom* you are speaking, but also—and this is equally crucial—you must know what your audience *expects* of you. Are you being called to the specific situation to "present information" in a fairly unbiased manner? In that situation, outright advocacy may be objectionable, out of place, and ineffective. Or the situation might be calling for a polemic before a partisan crowd where you are expected to "pour it on." Is your presence a matter of genuine audience desire, or is it more of a perfunctory appearance? In the latter case you may choose to present "a few fitting and appropriate remarks," however significant, rather than a lengthy discourse. Is it a serious interview or social conversation? Audience expectation should, of course, help to shape every communication context.

Some years ago I was asked to address a group of ladies at a meeting sponsored by the American Legion Auxiliary. The person who contacted me, a lively middle-aged woman, told me the group wanted "something light." Imagining her as a typical member of the audience-to-be, I carefully prepared a very light and (in my view) humorous speech on communication problems in marriage, filling the whole thing with what I considered funny little remarks about middle-aged marital foul-ups, foibles, and fillips—in a Bob Hope style. I was ready. When I arrived to give the speech, I was greeted by the woman who had contacted me, and was ushered into the room set aside for the occasion. As I gazed around at the aged, furrowed faces of my audience, I experienced a sudden, sickly, sinking sensation. I was literally "speechless"—in the awfullest sense of the word! The chairman of the meeting, my contact, was the only woman in the room under seventy! The American Legion Auxiliary, it turned out, was producing a series of programs for the residents of one of the local old people's homes! I was faced with a group of sweet, *very* old ladies—most of them *widows,* with a sprinkling of *spinsters,* I later learned. If you can imagine how I suffered trying to improvise a speech on that occasion, you can be certain I learned my lesson well: never again have I given a speech without first making sure where the speech was to be given, at what time, before how large an audience, composed of what kinds of people, and for what purpose.

Clearly, the circumstantial aspects of the occasion dictate significant differences in the content, thought-direction, and delivery of a given message. A speaker addressing a noontime Rotary Club luncheon on a given topic would not present the identical speech to the same group if they had convened for an evening meeting in a church social hall. As the speaker, you would want to know in each instance what else, if anything, is planned for the program: who and what will precede your speech, and who and what will follow it; whether the general atmosphere of the occasion is to be serious or light; whether you will be seated at the head of a long dining table, or whether you will be speaking to the group from an elevation of some kind. If at all possible, you should make it a practice to inspect the physical facilities and arrangement some time *before* you are to speak. Invariably inquire about the occasion and ascertain the intended order of events—find out what "usually" happens at such a meeting.

To sum up what we have thus far considered, as a basis for speaking and interacting effectively you must know *yourself* as the initiating-source communicator; you must know as much as possible about the *other agents;* you must know the *interactive potentials of the context.* As a speaker you must be aware not only of your own position and role, but you must be sensitive also to the views, values, and comprehension capacities of your listeners; and you must understand how agent-to-agent interplay affects and is affected by the context of the communication situation. This knowledge provides the cornerstones for effectiveness in oral communication. With it, you have a workable foundation upon which to build a further understanding of what happens in communicative interaction and of ways to achieve it—the subject to which we will now proceed.

Facilitating Interaction and Planning Your Adjustments

When we introduced the idea of *interaction* in Chapter 1, we advanced it as the central concept in speech communication. Communicative interaction, as we pointed out in Chapter 2, begins with the agents' recognition of and reaction to *feedback*. And feedback, as we have noted, occurs when both agents to a transaction are sending and receiving stimuli, when both are interpreting and reacting to stimuli from each other, and when *both are aware* of their joint participation. Since feedback undergirds the concluding phase of this chapter, let us look more closely at the way this principle operates.

The Feedback Principle

The thermostat is a common example of a *mechanical* feedback device. It controls the temperature in a room by receiving stimuli indicating temperature levels and reacting with electrical connections with the furnace to produce modifications in the physical environment. When the temperature falls to a certain level, the furnace is activated; when the temperature then rises to a certain level, the furnace is turned off. Mechanisms regulating feedback occur and can be observed throughout nature. The human organism itself, for instance, contains numerous feedback mechanisms which serve homeostatic purposes. They keep body temperature, blood-sugar level, and many other physiological factors within desired ranges.

To pursue our first analogy a bit further, you might ask, "Does the temperature influence the thermostat, or does the thermostat influence the temperature? Which is cause and which is effect?" The correct—and crucial—answer is that *each* is cause and *each* is effect; each is influencing and at the same time being influenced. The key factors in our analogy are *interdependence* and *interaction* of the elements or agents. The agents in the speech communication context operate in an analogous situation: both agents influence and are influenced; both must agree to this joint participation. Erving Goffman appropriately describes this agreement as the "working consensus."[8] The agents must agree on whose claims concerning what issues will be honored at a given moment.

From the vantage point of the speaker (our arbitrary stance for this particular chapter), we need to answer the question: *What can be done to gain and maintain the participation of the listening agent?* In a very large sense, we will find that this willingness to participate derives, first, from the initiating speaker's sensitivity, concern, and respect for the other agent or agents in the communication context. Accordingly, in planning for a speech act you must think in terms of your listeners and must plan with them in mind. In this preplanning, you will find that the principle of *feedback* functions in at least two very useful ways: (1) *it enables you to allow for "feedforward,"* and (2) *it enables you to adjust more readily and effectively to feedback from your listeners during the actual communication of your message.*

The Feedforward Principle

Actually, prior planning is feed*forward,* a counterpart of feed*back.* If you can anticipate what you want to happen—or what is likely to happen—and take

[8] Erving Goffman, *Behavior in Public Places* (New York: The Free Press, 1963), Chapter 6.

careful cognizance of alternative eventualities, true communicative interaction among involved agents is more likely to result.

Audience Rapport

Good *rapport,* the empathy that one human being has for another, and the relationship it seeks to identify should be one of your guiding goals as you plan and incorporate feedforward. You have no doubt heard the expression "having good vibes" to describe a feeling of mutual understanding and sympathy. In the physical world, scientists use the term "sympathetic vibrations." To demonstrate the principle, two tuning forks having equal frequency are placed in fairly close proximity. When one fork is struck and then its vibrations stopped, a similar sound can be heard emanating from the second fork: it has been set into sympathetic vibration by a very small amount of sound-wave energy created by the vibrations of the first fork. If the second tuning fork has a vibration frequency different from the first fork, this phenomenon will not occur. Sympathetic vibration can also be produced with piano strings having the same frequency. The necessary condition for sympathetic vibration is that the two bodies have identical resonant frequencies.

Similarly, if two or more individuals having similar psychological "resonant frequencies" are brought into association in a speech communication context, they seem to have a natural tendency to respond favorably to one another. They apparently have many characteristics in common—backgrounds, beliefs, values, attitudes, experiences, etc.—which seem to cause such agents to respond to an event or events similarly. This is not a matter of mere conjecture. In persuasion, one of the general findings of behavioral scientists is that a person is most significantly influenced by his close friends and associates, and by his family. Voting behavior of the young citizen, for example, appears to be determined to a greater extent by the predispositions of his parents than by the effects of a political candidate's charisma and speeches in a particular election campaign. Of course, this parent-induced "sympathetic" behavior is not an instantaneous or automatic response. One of the reasons is the offspring's constant contact for a long period of time with his parents and their friends—the product of close association, rapport, and previous interaction.

Language Adaptation

As a speaking communicator you should be aware also that two persons having many experiences in common tend to develop similar categories and strategies for reasoning; and you should be alert to the fact—as you plan the phrasing of your ideas, propositions, and arguments—that persons having these similar backgrounds are likely to have similar connotations for *language symbols*. Individuals with a good rapport or who have worked closely together in a school, business, or profession sometimes speak in a jargon which greatly abbreviates their messages—a mutual language which strengthens their communicative bond. Various groups have their own verbal "shorthand"; they can count on the other's ability to fill in a cryptic message with appropriate details. In Tolstoy's novel *Anna Karenina,* for instance, two lovers communicate by using the initial letters of each word, such as I—l—y. If, in planning for feedforward, you take cognizance of the range of language adaptability, you will achieve interaction more easily and effectively.

Not often, unfortunately, do agents in a speech context have the close natural rapport and mutuality that we are describing in this section. Yet your goal as a speaker is to try to discover the extent to which these bonds *do* exist among your listeners, and to strive for the feedforward which can facilitate and broaden their understanding of what you are trying to communicate to them.

To some degree, the functioning of this linguistic commonality is under your direct control as the speaker. Within reasonable bounds, you should adapt and attempt to "speak the language" of your listener. Behavioral research reveals something of the ways in which as a speaker you may effect such adaptation. Professor Helen Franzwa, in exploring the process of adaptation in language selection, considered the evaluative and dynamic dimensions of adjectives selected to describe a speech subject.[9] She found that the communicators tended to select adjectives whose evaluative loading reflected their own personal evaluations of the subject but whose dynamic loadings reflected the audience's evaluations of the subject. In other words, her subjects chose language appropriate for the speech topic and *also* appropriate for the particular audience to be addressed.

[9] Helen H. Franzwa, "Psychological Factors Influencing Use of 'Evaluative-Dynamic' Language," *Speech Monographs,* XXXVI (June 1969): 103–109.

The effect upon human interaction of dissimilarity, as well as similarity, in background and goals is sharply delineated by these two pictures—the one at left showing the hostility which greeted young blacks in a tense racial encounter; and the lower one, the rapport between the late Martin Luther King, Jr., and his followers.

Perhaps a hypothetical case will clarify this concept. Suppose a speaker is advocating the election of a certain political candidate. In his presentation the speaker wishes to make the point, "X is an advocate of tax reform," and he uses a descriptive adjective in the sentence. Since the speaker supports X, he will definitely use an adjective which is positive in evaluation. If the audience members are also very favorable to X, the speaker may use a positive adjective that reveals *also* a high level of dynamism, such as "X is an *aggressive* advocate of tax reform." Franzwa's study indicated, however, that if the audience members are generally opposed to X, then the speaker will still use a positive adjective, *but* will likely use one which is at a much lower level of dynamism, such as "X is a *sensitive* advocate of tax reform." The speaker tends to soften his argument by employing adjectives that are less emphatic when addressing listeners who disagree with him.

The advice implicit in Professor Franzwa's findings should not be interpreted to mean that you ought not to address more than one audience on the same general topic. That, in fact, may be the very thing that you will have to do. Speaking to a Methodist Women's club on water pollution, you may, for instance, relate your proposition to family life and social values. If, later in the day, you speak to the local Junior Chamber of Commerce, you may relate the same proposition to values of economic concern. The important point is that you will obviously be less effective if you attempt to give the identical speech in two different settings. Nor is it enough merely to adjust the introductory material of your speech. The entire message must be fitted to the beliefs and evaluations and values of the audience. This type of adaptation enables you to approach more closely the sympathetic association between communicative agents which facilitates genuine interaction.

In feedforward, what you are doing, then, in your role as a speaker-to-be is to *anticipate* audience reactions and *prepare* for them. And the greater your knowledge of the other agents, the more accurately you will be able to predict their responses. In some special cases, as with a television address, attention to feedforward becomes of utmost importance because your audience is "faceless," and only delayed feedback will be possible. But for most of the other forms of oral communication, including informal conversation, your anticipation of listener judgments and responses can help you achieve the desired interaction.

Stasis

Our study of the facets of feedforward would be incomplete without a consideration of what classical rhetoricians called *stasis* or the "status of the case." Assuming for the moment that you have ascertained with reasonable accuracy the beliefs, attitudes, values, and general backgrounds of your listeners, *in addition* you need to know "where they *now are*" in their thinking about the ideas or propositions you intend to advance. At what point in their thinking and believing will you come upon them as you begin to speak? At what point in the oral process can you most efficiently and effectively *initiate* their consideration and induce their receptivity? At what juncture do you "hook on" to their collective train of thought?

If you assume, for instance, that your listeners have more background knowledge of your topic than they in fact possess, you will "lose" them at the outset; if you assume that they have less than they really have, they may quickly lose interest and become bored.

Cicero and Quintilian taught that the status of a case can be determined by asking certain questions: *whether* a thing is, *what* it is, and of *what kind* it is.

Does the case focus on a question of fact, or of definition, or of quality? For example, take a hypothetical case in which A is accused of murdering B. The first question (of fact) asks: did A kill B? The second question (of definition) asks: did the killing of B fit our legal definition of murder? The third question (of quality) asks: was the act good or bad; was it justified? We can see that, at any given moment, the focus of the argument might fall on one or the other of these states. The issue might be: did A kill B? If it is proved that A did indeed kill B, then the issue could become: was it an act of murder? If murder is proved—or, perhaps, admitted by A—the issue could become: was the murder justifiable (self-defense, for instance), or was it premeditated and in cold blood?

The importance of *stasis* for you as a preplanner of speech communication is that if the communicative agents are to be in close association and interacting, *they must see the status of a given case similarly.* No effective communication will occur if you present an issue and your listener doesn't know enough of what you are talking about to understand your meaning; nor will any real communication take place if you are belaboring an issue already accepted by the listener. I once telephoned a life insurance agent, told him I wanted additional insurance, and described the coverage I wanted. When he arrived at my home, he began immediately to try to convince me that I should have more insurance. I explained that I already thought so, that that was why I had called him, and that he could fill out the necessary papers. He continued, despite my protests, to advance arguments of which I was already *convinced.* Time was wasted; there was no "meeting of the minds"; no purposeful interaction took place; I became restless, lost confidence in the salesman, and decided to take my insurance problems elsewhere.

When you are speaking on social issues, you may sometimes find it necessary to demonstrate the *existence* of a problem and other times necessary to argue the *workability of a specific solution* to the problem. If the listener already accepts the existence of the problem, you should talk about solutions and not waste time trying to persuade the listener of something he already accepts. On the other hand, there is little value in arguing for a specific solution and a new course of action if the listener doesn't feel that a problem even exists. If you hope to have the listener respond maximally to your message, you must sense and concentrate upon the particular concerns, needs, and expectations of that listener at that moment. The degree to which you as a speaker are capable of planning this adaptation will determine in large part the degree of your effectiveness.

STUDY PROBE 3
Adapting Specific Speeches to Specific Audiences

To encourage the study of language usage and audience adaptation in formal, one-to-many speaking situations, Roman students of rhetoric translated Greek orations into Latin. As a student of modern-day communication, examine the texts of a few speeches by great American orators and explore them for some of the ways in which *feedforward* has been used effectively.

1. Find, for example, the text of a speech delivered by a Daniel Webster, an Abraham Lincoln, a Clarence Darrow. Then imagine yourself a speech writer who is revising the manuscript for presentation to a contemporary audience.

2. Find the text of a contemporary speech and ascertain as nearly as you can the kind of audience to whom it was delivered. Then, still in your role of speech writer, rewrite the manuscript as if *you* were to deliver the speech to a *different* audience convened under different circumstances. For possibilities, examine such speeches as "I Have a Dream," or "The Dimensions of a Complete Life," by Martin Luther King, Jr. (the latter speech is included in the Appendix, pp. 345–352); Richard Nixon's Acceptance Speech at the 1968 Republican Convention or his Inaugural Address in 1969; or Malcolm X's "The Ballot or the Bullet," given in Cleveland, April 3, 1964.

3. Prepare drafts of your suggested adaptations in each instance, and hand them to your instructor either as a basis for classroom analysis and/or a written examination of the principles set forth in this chapter.

Adjusting to Feedback from Your Audience

If, in your initial step in planning for a speech situation and event, you have carefully anticipated the nature of your prospective audience, have assessed their preferences and priorities, have taken into close account the variables of feedforward, and feel confident to carry the resultant adaptation into the speech context itself, you are ready to take a second important step toward effective interaction. This step we may describe as adjusting to the feedback from listener-agent(s) *in* and *during* the communication transaction.

This step involves an on-the-spot, face-to-face problem which you can detect and solve only with your actual audience before you: you must correctly interpret other agents' response *as you are speaking,* and you must *adapt* to that response very quickly. The requisite skill is *adaptive readiness.*

One of the key differences between planning for feedforward and adjusting to feedback is that in the former you are, in effect, predicting *probabilities,* but in the latter you are facing *immediate actualities.* In the former you can attempt specific preparation; in the latter you have to rely largely upon general preparation and flexibility. In adjusting to feedback, you must "think on your feet"— and you must think *now.* In planning for feedforward, you are making allowances for what you have reason to believe *might happen* in a possible situation; in adjusting to feedback, you are making allowances for what *is happening* in and to your audience. You must read reactions accurately, devise and assess possible new and unanticipated courses of action—"instantaneous feedforward" —and select the one that seems best to you at that particular instant.

If the facial expressions of your listener(s) reveal puzzlement, you may adjust by reiterating your point and amplifying it with clarifying materials. If your listener(s) appear bored, you may react by interjecting some humorous or novel materials. If your audience is antagonistic or noisily negative, quite probably you will want to react promptly by voicing a pertinent value generally held by most men of good will, or by citing some "common ground" upon which you and your listeners stand.

As an example of successful adaptation to audience feedback, consider an impromptu statement by Henry Ward Beecher. When an audience in Liverpool, suffering from the embargo during the American Civil War, reacted negatively by heckling a point in his speech, Beecher is reported to have said, "All I ask is simply fair play." Fair play apparently was a value embraced by most of the members of his audience, for they allowed the speaker to proceed without further interruptions. In more recent times, the late Black Muslim leader Malcolm X, when speaking in favor of black nationalism to a college audience, sensed a negative audience reaction to his rate and intensity of delivery. He attempted to adjust to this interpreted feedback by saying, "I'm sorry to be talking so fast, but I haven't much time, and I do have a lot to say." If you hope to be effective as a speaker, you must be sensitive to such audience cues, must be able to interpret them accurately, and must be able to react to them in ways which facilitate positive interaction.

STUDY PROBE 4
Experiencing Feedback and Reaction to Feedback

As a study in feedback, familiarize yourself with Figures 1 and 2 below. Then ask a friend to join you in the experiment. Place two chairs back to back; seat your friend in one of them, and provide him with a pencil and a blank sheet of paper. Seat yourself in the other chair, with your back toward the back of your friend, and tell him how to draw Figure 1. Do not look at him or allow him to ask any questions as he tries to draw a duplicate of the diagram.

Now rearrange the chairs so that you and your friend face each other, and repeat the experiment, using Figure 2. This time, however, look at his face and, also, tell him that he may look at yours while he follows your instructions as to the duplication of the diagram. Provide as many verbal and nonverbal cues as you like; permit him to ask questions, and give him the best answers you can— short of actually showing him the drawing in the textbook, of course.

When you have finished, compare his drawings with Figures 1 and 2, and determine under which conditions his diagrams more accurately represent the originals.

Figure 1   Figure 2

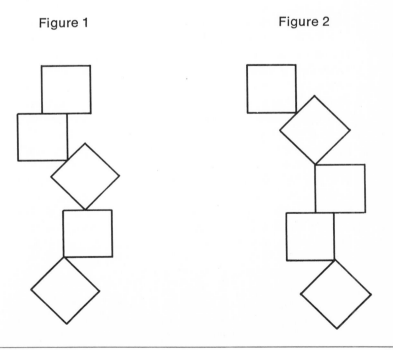

Almost certainly, if you have properly performed the foregoing experiment, you will have found that your friend has been much more accurate in his duplication of Figure 2. By reason of the fact that you have "done things differently" —that you have modified your behavior—you have been able to communicate with him more accurately and meaningfully. At the same time, you have demonstrated another significant facet of the feedback function: *In every act of adapting to audience reaction, the speaker-agent is allowing the listener-agent to modify certain aspects of the speaker's own behavior,* emphasizing again the mutual interdependence and influence which occurs in communicative interaction.

Reacting to Absence of Feedback

Adjustment to feedback has, of course, certain advantages; but it also has its pitfalls; and, as we shall see, the total absence of feedback can produce serious obstacles to human interaction. The able communicator will therefore want to be alert to all of these possibilities.

An early study by Leavitt and Mueller revealed a number of the many positive effects of feedback in communication.[10] In their study (somewhat similar to the one used in the Study Probe above) a speaker described a geometric pattern to a group of listeners who then tried to reproduce it. Feedback conditions ranged from "zero," in which the speaker could not see his audience and no feedback of any kind was allowed, to "free," in which the instructor could see the audience and in which the audience was permitted to ask questions. The study found, in brief, that the more complete the feedback between speaker and listener, the greater the accuracy with which the given information was communicated. Further, free feedback permitted the participants to learn a mutual language (a phenomenon previously mentioned on page 76) which appreciably reduced or even eliminated the need for further feedback. Leavitt and Mueller found also that free feedback was accompanied by a high degree of mutual confidence and mutual good feeling among speaking and listening agents, whereas zero feedback caused low confidence and hostility.

To understand how frustrating and even destructive the *absence* of feedback can be to human endeavor in general and to the process of oral interaction in particular, you have only to recall your feelings while you were performing the Figure 1 phase of the Study Probe 4 experiment above—and to ask your colleague to recount his reactions. At its worst, the inability to respond to others in real life situations is a form of mental illness. And under so-called "normal" day-to-day conditions, failure to provide and receive feedback can do inestimable harm. This detriment can be discerned readily in the many studies of the communicative process conducted in industrial settings.[11] One of the major problems in large organizations is that of "role ambiguity," in which a person feels that he doesn't quite know where he stands, what is expected of him, just how he fits in. He may be uncertain about the "task" elements of his job—his specific duties; or he may feel insecure about the "socio-emotional" elements of the work—his interpersonal relationships. A frequent cause of this role ambiguity, as revealed

---

[10] Harold J. Leavitt and Ronald A. H. Mueller, "Some Effects of Feedback on Communication," *Human Relations,* IV (1951): 401–410.

[11] See "The Social Context of Communication: Introduction" in Dean C. Barnlund, *Interpersonal Communication* (Boston: Houghton Mifflin Company, 1963), especially pp. 164–171. Barnlund's introductions in this book are excellent syntheses of research.

by the studies, is the lack of communication, or feedback, from superiors. No matter how unsatisfactory the role itself may be, ambiguity about it is even worse. The deleterious effects of zero feedback doubtless extend to all speech communication settings. Outright heckling, for instance, is in many ways easier for the speaker to take than no reaction or indifference. As a speaker, you must do all you can to sense reaction in your hearers, and your hearers should do all they can reasonably do to provide "readable" reaction. You must learn to look at your audience, to see people in it, and to see reactions. You must come to read reactions as "interest," "approval," "antagonism," "skepticism," "boredom," "polite blank stares," and so on.

Overreacting to Feedback

At the same time, both as speakers and listeners, you must be firmly on guard against *over*reading or *over*responding to these or any other cues. Inherently, all feedback mechanisms, whether mechanical or human, have in them a tendency to overreact to stimuli. A radar-aimed antiaircraft gun programmed to zero in on a swiftly swerving, expertly maneuvered fighter jet tends to develop a momentum which carries it beyond a correct alignment with the target: it tends to overcorrect itself. The elusive target causes the gun to swing back and forth so rapidly that it has difficulty settling down on a straight line to the plane. Another example of this tendency to overcorrect is the boxer's response to the feinting jab employed by a skilled pugilist to draw his opponent off guard and off balance.

Similarly, in the speech communication situation a speaker may overreact and overadjust for feedback and thereby lose sight of his basic purpose. Stated conversely, an audience—or even a small segment of it—can provide such a strong or vociferous response as to cause the speaker, in turn, to overcorrect, distort, or lose sight of his intended message.

In a classroom circumstance, one of my students was extremely nervous, almost terrified, at the prospect of speaking to a group (although he seemed to have no problem in handling ordinary one-to-one conversation). In some desperation, he suggested that as an alternative to the more formal speaking assignment he be allowed merely to read aloud to the class a funny article he had recently encountered in a magazine. For the sake of at least getting him on his feet, I agreed. The moment came, and he rose with great hesitation and started to read. The first punch line came, and the class laughed. He read on. Came the second punch line, and the class roared. For the first time, the student relaxed and looked at the class. He smiled and read on. They laughed again. It was a metamorphosis. By the end of the reading, the student "reader" was more at ease than I had ever seen him, but he was extremely excited and pleased with his audience's response. In fact, he didn't want to turn it off. He didn't want to stop —he really had lost control. Grinning at his listeners, he exclaimed, "Well, if you liked that, just listen to *this!*" And he proceeded to tell a very crude and not-too-funny dirty story, entirely out of context and unrelated to the immediate circumstance. Almost instantly a chill settled over his listeners; and despite the fact that most of them had probably been desensitized to most of the prevalent four-letter shock words, they didn't laugh at his punch line this time. They didn't even smile. The storyteller had lost them; he had overreacted to their initial response.

Overreaction to audience feedback is by no means exclusively a problem for beginning speakers. Experienced orators and seasoned political campaigners are highly susceptible on occasion. Indeed, there are some speakers, as you no doubt have observed, who are so eager to sense from which directions "the winds of change are blowing"—and to react instantaneously to those currents—that their values and goals seem to come more from their listeners than from themselves. Although they may be public figures and "leaders," they are, in fact, "followers" —the epitome of the other-directed person.

There are significant implications in this reaction principle for you as a speaker-communicator. Don't let a single negative expression or a frown from a listener disturb you disproportionately, and don't, as a result, become unduly defensive in your presentation of a message. Don't allow a lone heckler to bring you to a halt because you react to him only, rather than to the other agents in your much larger audience. While you must indeed look for feedback and react appropriately to it, you should always maintain your self-control in the speaking situation, and try to interpret the feedback in its proper perspective. Rarely, if ever, will all members of an audience react alike and be highly favorable to a speaker. Some will respond negatively, and others not at all; some reactions will be overt and visible; many will not be. What is important above all is that you recognize speech behavior and its potential for influencing and being influenced during human interaction.

In this chapter, working chiefly from the vantage point of the speaker-agent, we have tried to delineate some of the basic "in-action" principles that function to help produce meaningful oral communication with and among listening agents. We have tried to establish the *locus* of these principles within the speech process and to demonstrate—to some extent at least—their *operation*. We have advocated a *preparation* phase and an *application* phase of the process, and we have emphasized two necessities: to be an effective speech communicator you must, first, within a given speech act understand agent-to-agent and agent-to-context relationships; and, second, you must apply that understanding to the making of requisite adaptations for *feedforward* and desirable degrees of adjustment to audience *feedback* as you strive to achieve and maintain a high level of communicative interaction with listener-agents.

STUDY PROBE 5

Testing Feedforward and Feedback

Conduct the following role-playing experiment in a "two-persons-conversing" setting before your class. Before you begin, study the context and the role assigned to you, and then plan feedforward to the best of your ability. During the experiments, attempt to adapt to the feedback from the other agent. Note that the role of professor in each of the experiments is to be played by a student—or a succession of students—not by the instructor.

The Context.

A professor suspects a student of plagiarism on a written assignment. The phrasing of many paragraphs is very similar to works well known to the professor. He calls the student in to discuss the matter.

The Agents.

Experiment 1

Student: The substance of your defense is that you had help from a friend who gave you some materials. You do not feel that you have borrowed unduly from the work of others.

Professor: You are to respond appropriately and spontaneously to the explanation and/or the defense offered by the student.

Experiment 2

Student: The substance of your position is that, while you did in fact paraphrase certain portions of the work, you feel that this is a common practice in research. You claim that most of the work is yours.

Professor: You are to respond appropriately and spontaneously to the argument and defense advanced by the student.

Experiment 3

Student: You plagiarized and you know it. You will, however, deny this and refuse to admit any wrongdoing.

Professor: You are to respond appropriately and spontaneously to the student's denial and his refusal to admit his guilt.

At the completion of each experiment, conduct a class discussion about the proficiency of each participant in the exercise. How skillful were you in predicting the reactions of the other agent in the experiment? How successful were you in adapting your argument to the feedback you received from the other agent?

Speech Communication: Identifying Purposes and Assessing Effects

Earlier we have asserted that if we are to have positive, productive interaction, the speaking communicator must know as much as possible about his listening co-communicators. In Part III we would like first to enlarge and further particularize that knowledge by focusing upon some of the *reasons* why people engage in oral interchange. And, following that, we will examine more minutely some of the *outcomes*—both intentional and unintentional—of such engagement.

There are, of course, many motives which impel man to enter into speech communication as an active agent, forces generated by both internal needs and external impingements. As concerned communicators, we will need to search out and try to understand as many of these motivations as we can. We will try consciously to *affect* our hearers in some meaningful way. But we will want to do more: we will seek to know the extent to which we have succeeded in creating the *effect* we desire. While we are speaking and adapting, we will try—as we have said—to measure our immediate effect by evidence of audience feedback. From the inception of our impulse to speak, however, we will have to be aware that our behaviors and utterances will have numerous *additional consequences,* some of them less discernible, more enduring, and—perhaps—more far-reaching.

As initiators of communication, we will want, further, to assess the effectiveness of our efforts, to apply some kind of yardstick to the achievement of our communicative goals. However, before we can hope to measure the consequences and effects we create by oral interaction, we will need to probe our purposes, our motives, our reasons. This is basic if we are to interrelate, with due honesty and compassion, with our fellow men and women. The resultant knowledge is fundamental if we are to ameliorate to any encouraging extent any of the dilemmas of our society and to enrich thereby our day-to-day experiences.

In sum, we will be attempting in Part III to find answers to two major questions. First, for what *purposes* do human beings speak? Second, what are the *effects* of that speaking upon other human beings? In Chapter 4 we will pursue answers to the first inquiry; in Chapter 5 we will seek substance for the second. In the former we will concentrate chiefly upon the needs and motives which move the *speaker-agent* to action; in the latter we will explore the effects of speech communication as they are experienced by the *listener-agent*.

Throughout, we will want to remember that in actual practice, all purposes—all drives to discourse—and the effects produced by them are interwoven and inseparable; yet, in order to examine them we will have to consider them somewhat arbitrarily as if they were discernible as separate, isolatable entities. Such are the limitations of written communication.

Chapter 4
Why Man Speaks

Our reasons for speaking are ego-centered and intrapersonal, as well as socio-centered and interpersonal—for example, we speak for self-assertion, self-identity, and self-fulfillment, as well as for reducing tensions, establishing social contact, and controlling our environment.

When we ask, "Why does man speak?" we are posing a very broad question. It is an inquiry that asks about *all* of the speech behaviors of humankind—a question on which you will need to be knowledgeable as you engage in practical speaking of your own. If you are to make a meaningful analysis of any aspect of the oral process and apply it intelligently to your own communicative efforts, you must be as fully aware as possible of all the factors which combine to produce speech behavior.

We will try in this chapter to single out and illuminate some of the major ends served by speech. We will raise and—to an extent—try to answer such questions as: What influences constrain a speaker and limit his range of possible speech behaviors in a given situation? What are the influences of self-image, experience, the specific speech context, and other persons upon him? What inner values and tensions move him? To what extent does his speaking contribute to his self-satisfaction and help him to originate and maintain social contact?

In trying to discover what the purposes and ends of communication are, what lies behind and prompts the impulse to speak, there are a number of productive approaches open to us. We might well begin by trying to discover some more or less *basic* communication purpose, a widely inclusive motivation common to all human utterance. If we can do that, we can use that as a vantage point from which to scrutinize some of the equally important but not so generally recognized purposes which impel people to vocalize and interact.

Defining the Basic Communicative Purposes

Grace De Laguna has referred to speech communication as "the great medium through which human cooperation is brought about."[1] This concept clearly implies that a central, major purpose of speech interaction is to enable men and women to make emotional and intellectual contact with one another, consciously and intentionally *to exchange and share information and ideas.* Desmond Morris, in *The Naked Ape,* calls this kind of exchange "information talking," and he maintains that information talking has remained the most important form of vocal communication for our species.[2]

Not everyone agrees, of course, that the getting and giving of information, in its specific sense, is the basic purpose of speech communication, although—as we shall see—it is commonly classified as one highly necessary subcategory of intention. Rhetoricians, both classical and contemporary, see the overriding purpose of communication as *persuasion:* "rhetorical study, in its strict sense, is concerned with modes of persuasion."[3]

Largely, we concur in the latter view. If you will look again at the definition

[1] Grace Andrus De Laguna, *Speech: Its Function and Development* (New Haven, Conn.: Yale University Press, 1927), p. 19. Reissued by Indiana University Press, Bloomington, 1963.

[2] Desmond Morris, *The Naked Ape* (New York: McGraw-Hill Book Company, 1967), p. 166.

[3] Aristotle, *Rhetoric, The Basic Works of Aristotle,* ed. Richard McKeon (New York: Random House, Inc., 1941), p. 1327.

For a contemporary view emphasizing the role of persuasion as one basic, encompassing speech purpose, see *The Prospect of Rhetoric,* ed. Lloyd F. Bitzer and Edwin Black (Englewood Cliffs, N.J.: Prentice-Hall, Inc., 1971).

we advanced in Chapter 1,[4] you will find that it implies that the basic purpose of speech is *to influence others,* which purpose suggests, in turn, at least three sub-goals that spoken interaction always has; namely:

1. To react with appropriate "oralness" when the context calls for it or when a situation would be ameliorated by its use.

2. To formulate messages—both as a sender and as a receiver—and to react appropriately to messages.

3. To influence the thinking, attitudes, and behaviors of others and—if possible—to bring these thoughts, attitudes, and behaviors into a reasonable alignment with our own.

Statements of this kind argue that the basic speech purpose is to *influence* and, for that reason, that the impulse to communicate springs from the plans and purposes of the speaking agent. For the most part, at least, we believe that what we have described in the foregoing paragraphs will be typical of the basic, encompassing communication purpose.

If we can agree that man's overriding reason for speaking is to influence the physical and psychological elements of his environment, then we can profitably survey some of the equally important but not so generally recognized purposes which impel human beings to speak, interrelate, and interact. Among these purposes, we would include primarily those that are (1) *contextually oriented,* (2) *ego-centered or intrapersonal,* and (3) *socializing or interpersonal.*

Contextually Oriented Purposes

As a second approach to understanding communicative motivation, we might rephrase our original question somewhat by asking: What are men's *conscious* purposes when they direct *extended* discourse to others? Here, our answer will be materially affected by *communicators' expectations* and the *contextual climate* which they help to produce.

If you attend a lecture on "Some of the Feminizing Forces Shaping Our Society," you expect to be informed. To be informed is a common audience expectation; and if you are the lecturer, your predominant objective will be to *inform.* If you visit a night club, you anticipate that the comedian will *entertain* you. If a salesman invites you to a formal speech-and-film presentation on the riches to be gained from speculating in Arizona real estate, he obviously hopes to *persuade* you to buy. If, at the end of the presentation, you write him a check as a down payment, he has succeeded in his purpose to *actuate* you. If you witness the dedication ceremonies of a sculpture designed to commemorate man's discovery of atomic energy, you can rightfully expect the orator for the occasion to *stimulate* or, perhaps, even *inspire* you.

This path leads us to approach communicative purposes as the general situational or contextual responses which the speaker seeks to elicit from his listeners: *understanding* of a term, concept, pattern, or a system (to inform); *belief* in a speaker's proposition (to persuade); *enjoyment, amusement,* or *relax-*

---

[4] "Speech communication is the socially learned process occurring when two or more persons are interacting by transmitting and receiving visual and auditory stimuli which are treated as symbolic cues to which meaning is attached." (p. 13.)

ation in the company of the speaker (to entertain); *reaffirmation*—often by ceremony or ritual—of the traditions, virtues, and values held by the state, the church, or a particular segment of society (to stimulate or to inspire).[5]

These general purposes can, in turn, be reduced to more *specific* or *immediate* goal-responses, and their application examined in reference to a number of characteristic speech *forms* or *settings:* public speaking, debate, group discussion, oral reading, and other communication situations of a more or less formal nature.

We must not, however, make the mistake of assuming that audience expectations, however categorized, are neatly isolatable. We "individualize" them only to facilitate discussing them. All kinds of communicative goals may, in fact, be evident in the agents' messages and the contextual atmosphere. Within a given context, a speech which informs, for instance, can also entertain us, stimulate us, or even persuade us to believe or to act. Usually, however, by reason of contextual circumstances and speaker/audience expectations, one of these purposes will predominate. Nor should we think of such purposes only in terms of formal, extended, or public communication; they can pervade all levels of communicative interaction.

However, if we employ these kinds of differentiations to analyze communicative intention, we must recognize that, while they may be useful and widely practiced, they tend to produce a somewhat *static* view of speech rather than the ongoing, dynamic, verbal/nonverbal *process* which we have been emphasizing.

Today, when scholars of communication theory and the behavioral sciences are searching as never before for human motivational principles—principles often found in disciplines other than speech—in order to understand communicative interaction more fully and precisely, we need to minimize the category of settings in which speaking occurs and the generalizing classes of purposes which appear to prompt it. In searching for what is characteristic and relatively predictable in all speech behavior, we need to look more at the *commonalities* rather than the differences among speech acts—a view reflected in our paradigm of two persons conversing.

Ego-Centered/Intrapersonal Purposes

Very often, instead of using speech to influence others, we use it to influence the thinking we do about *ourselves.* We employ it to serve *intra*personal needs or drives. Among these "self" serving and self-actualizing purposes we find:

Asserting self-existence
Establishing and projecting a self-concept or self-image
Finding and enlarging self-satisfaction—self-actualization
Diminishing or dissolving tensions within ourselves and others

[5] For a more thoroughgoing consideration of these purposes, see:

Alan H. Monroe and Douglas Ehninger, *Principles and Types of Speech,* 6th ed. (Glenview, Ill.: Scott, Foresman and Company, 1967), Chapters 20–24.

Donald C. Bryant and Karl R. Wallace, *Fundamentals of Public Speaking,* 4th ed. (New York: Appleton-Century-Crofts, 1969), Parts III and VI and Chapter 22.

W. Norwood Brigance, *Speech: Its Techniques and Disciplines in a Free Society,* 2nd ed. (New York: Appleton-Century-Crofts, 1961), Chapters 7 and 23.

Again, we remind you that these egocentric purposes are never in fact separable or independent. We have attempted a categorical isolation only for the purpose of talking about them. Nor does the order of their listing reflect any predominance of any one of them over any other.

Asserting Self-Existence

Of the many ways that speech can be used to serve the self, one of the most pertinent is to proclaim our existence. We could use a modification of Descartes' famous phrase and say: *I speak, and therefore I am.*[6] If we are *silent,* others may treat us as if we do not exist. But when we speak, we assert—along with everything else—that we *are.*

In a study conducted for an undergraduate speech course, a student made detailed observations of the speech behavior of preschool children as they played together. The student's research was prompted by the writings of Piaget and Vygotsky concerning social-versus-egocentric speech behaviors.[7] She observed in particular a small child who was playing alone and talking aloud to himself. He was addressing no one in particular; nor, apparently, was anyone listening. Eventually, for one reason or another, the other children drifted out of the room, one by one. When all the others were gone, the observer noted that the lone child stopped talking. Later, as the other children came back into the room, the "loner" started talking aloud to himself again.

The research worker who was conducting the study manipulated the situation so that the above conditions were replicated, and the same result was noted. When alone, the child played silently; when others were present but playing independently in the room, the youngster talked aloud to himself. In the presence of the others, he seemingly employed overt speech not at all for the basic communicative purpose of influencing anyone, but rather to assert for anyone who cared to listen, and especially for himself, that he was there—that he *existed.*

In a comment which tends to reinforce this interpretation, Meerloo writes:

> *The built-in intention and goal of communication is always to arrive—at least for oneself—at a greater feeling of certainty and security, in short, to a better adaptation, but also to the experience of meaning in the mutual transaction. Besides the information imparted, communication should contain an actualization of the self, a creative rhetorical assertion.*[8]

Another manifestation of the need to assert self-identity can be seen in small group discussion. If one of the supposed discussants does not speak and elects to remain silent for an extended time, the other participants begin to act as if the nontalker were not there at all. They do not look to him for comment,

---

[6] René Descartes (1596–1650) was a French philosopher, mathematician, and author. The basis of his philosophy is summed up in the words: *Cogito, ergo sum.* ("I think, therefore I am.")

[7] Jean Piaget, *The Language and Thought of the Child,* trans. Marjorie Gabain (New York: The World Publishing Company, 1955).

Lev S. Vygotsky, *Thought and Language,* ed. and trans. Eugenia Hanfmann and Gertrude Vakar (New York: John Wiley & Sons, Inc., and The M.I.T. Press, 1962).

[8] Joost A. M. Meerloo, "Contributions of Psychiatry to the Study of Human Communication," *Human Communication Theory,* ed. Frank E. X. Dance (New York: Holt, Rinehart & Winston, Inc., 1967), p. 132.

nor do they address him; and if he begins a remark, they often react as if he were intruding and pay little attention to what he says. They have come to expect him *not* to speak. This kind of response by the group is less likely to happen if the "nontalker" has made some comment early in the discussion and then merely waits for a long time before venturing another remark. But if he says nothing at all in the beginning and maintains silence for an extended interval, his existence seems almost to be denied by the active, participating discussants. He has failed to use speech to assert and actualize his being. Having waited too long to speak, he tends—like wallpaper—to merge into the background and disappear.

STUDY PROBE 1
Nonparticipating Agents and Their Relationships in a Group

As you participate in classroom, community, or family groups, observe the "silent" or rarely participating members of these groups. Make notations as to the frequency or infrequency with which they attempt to interact orally with others. Also, on those occasions, note in particular the ways in which other, more active agents react to the "silent" ones.

The significance of this for you as a speaker is that you will—often must—assert your identity in varying ways and with varying emphases from time to time as you attempt interaction. Sometimes you may feel impelled to do it openly; often you will do it subtly. If you overdo it, of course, quite likely you will be marked as a bore; if you fail to do it sufficiently, you place yourself in danger of being completely ignored. And neither of these conditions is conducive to productive oral interchange.

The public speaker, for example, will usually approach his audience in such a way that they will, in effect, say to themselves, "Here is a calmly, reasonably disposed human being, poised in his bearing, confident in his manner, and obviously in control of himself and his thoughts." Ordinarily, too, a public communicator will pause, survey his listeners, and wait until they have focused their attention upon him before he begins to speak. By this nonverbal means, he is saying to them: I *am*. I *exist*.

Establishing and Projecting a Self-Concept or Self-Image

No man, it has been argued, can hate until he can love, and no man can respect another unless he can respect himself. Similarly, it may be argued that no man can establish contact and interact with another "self" unless he has some conception of his *own* self. In Chapter 1, we cited George Mead's suggestion that each of us establishes a concept of self as a result of interaction with others in our environment.[9] Projecting a clear image of the self you desire to present serves a highly positive purpose in initiating and maintaining effective communi-

[9] George Herbert Mead, *Mind, Self, and Society: From the Standpoint of a Social Behaviorist,* ed. Charles W. Morris (Chicago: University of Chicago Press, 1934).

cation. Failure to project your self-image—or to project it wrongly—can seriously impair your credibility as a speaker and your acceptance by other agents.

Affirming and Confirming Self-Images

No doubt we fantasize a great deal about the self that we would like to be, the "picture" that we would like others to have of us. Doubtless, too, our self-images tend to slip in and out of focus with great frequency, and often may be lost or changed entirely—especially during our more formative years. But regardless of the concept that we hold or would like to hold of self, we can only test the usefulness and validity of that concept through oral communication. In every speech act, one of our insistent purposes will be to try to discover or to affirm whether listeners' judgments and expectations concerning us are congruent with our own continually developing self-concepts.

This necessity to *be*—or to appear to be—what we like to believe that we are cannot be denied or minimized; it is insistently evident. In nearly every society, and especially in the structured ones, men try to live up to the expectations of their fellows, "to fit in," even to be what others think they are. While we can never be (and ought not hope to be) totally what others expect of us, we will discover when we try to interact with them that their expectations, their "impression," their image of *us* exert a powerful force in helping to shape what we are or hope to become.

Throughout life, of course, others communicate with us; and in that communicative collaboration, these others will characterize us and "type" us. So, at least, *we* believe. On the basis of such beliefs, we learn to take on certain roles and to *internalize* those roles. In this way, our original intent to create a self-concept may be validated, altered, or even destroyed. In this way, others' interpretations of what we should be contribute to determining what we will be. And in this sense, we may become—to a greater or lesser degree—what others *say* we are. Probably most of us cling tenaciously to our most cherished self-images, aided and abetted by a kind of self-pride. But even so, despite our best efforts to the contrary, we will be categorized, stereotyped, and pigeonholed.

In elementary school the skinny kid with glasses may become a "brain" because he is given that role by his classmates. If he accepts it, he is likely to spend more time on his homework, and thereby verify the impression which his peers have of him. Or, as another example, one theory—debatable, but probably not wholly wrong—maintains that a child may become a stutterer if his parents call him one, and treat him as one.

We could cite examples of "other-imposed" self-concepts that are less unique than the two we have mentioned above. If you have brothers or sisters, quite early you very probably discovered your "pecking order" in the family. Studies of families having several children show clearly that significant role differences between first-born children and those born later evolve and are learned through family interaction.[10] Your effectiveness as a speaking and listening communicator will depend in no small degree upon your discernment of your own self-image, the extent to which that image is accepted and affirmed by other agents, and the interplay of *your* image and *their images of you.*

[10] Edward Zigler and Irving L. Child, "Socialization," *The Handbook of Social Psychology,* 2nd ed., ed. Gardner Lindzey and Elliot Aronson (Reading, Mass.: Addison-Wesley Publishing Co., Inc., 1969), v. III, pp. 547–548.

Implicit in the self-affirming purpose of speech is the fact that, whether we will it or not, others are constantly observing our communicative behavior and trying to sift out information and clues by which they can shape and confirm their image of us. While we are speaking, others are "discovering" who we are. Such is the multidirectional nature of human interaction.

What kinds of clues and identity indices do we advertently or inadvertently reveal to others in order that they may form and confirm their conceptions of us as speakers and as persons?

Our *patterns of word* choice and our *vocal dynamics* work together to provide some of these clues. In societies where "class" differences are drawn fairly sharply, speech patterns tend to reveal a speaker's socio-economic orientation almost immediately. He speaks as he "should." His choice of words and the manner of his enunciating them may show that he is from the "working" class. If he "sweats," for instance, he is likely to be a "member" of the lower class or the upper class; only middle-class people "perspire." When I attempted to speak Dutch in the Netherlands, my accent was so clear (clearly American) that by the time I had managed to utter only a very few sentences, an Amsterdammer would smile tolerantly and begin to speak English to me.

As students and practitioners of oral communication we have to be aware that there are, so to speak, "two sides to the coin" of the self-assertive speech purpose. As we use speech to develop and present our own self-image, so do we use it to investigate and understand the images of others. Within a given situation, *all* communication agents share in the inputs and the "out-takes" of communicative exchange. Through interaction with others we find out what they are and what they would like to be or to feel, and thus we are better able to predict and to judge the nature and possible dimensions of our relationships with them. In sum, the self-assertive purpose of speaking serves the very useful function of revealing to interactants the *mutuality* of their intelligence, background, experience, and values.

STUDY PROBE 2
Inferring Political Attitudes from Language or Voice Variables

Language and voice variables can of course re-reveal more than a speaker's "class" and background. Olga A. Carlisle, granddaughter of the Russian poet Leonid Andreyev, wrote:

> *I have found that for an outsider like myself, Russian voices reveal not so much a person's education, as his political attitude. Young militant Communists seem to have overly articulated intonations; they often sound like didactic teachers.*[11]

Orally or in writing, particularize several language or voice variables from which you feel you could infer political attitudes of speakers. As an alternate assignment, you might prepare a list of linguistic and vocal variables which might help a listener identify the occupations or professions of others involved in an oral exchange.

[11] *Voices in the Snow* (New York: Random House, Inc., 1962), p. 174.

Concealing a Self-Image

Not often, unfortunately, do we want to reveal ourselves as we truly and totally are. Indeed, most of us have large fears about revealing *too much* about our inner selves; we are reluctant to be "too open."

Psychiatrist Irvin Yalom has conducted investigations yielding some understanding of the dimensions of our inner fears and secrets.[12] Working with groups as diverse as persons undergoing group psychotherapy and Peace Corps workers and clinical psychologists, Yalom has asked individuals to write down, anonymously, their "top secret," the fact about themselves that they would least like the other members of their group to know. The "secrets" were collected, shuffled, and categorized. The categories of secrets were remarkably similar for the various groups of individuals involved, and they centered around three themes: (1) *feelings of personal inadequacy* (a feeling of incompetence or intellectual bluff); (2) *feelings of interpersonal alienation* (feeling that one does not or cannot really care for or love another person); and (3) *some kind of sexual secret* (fears based on homosexuality, premarital or extramarital sex, and the like).

STUDY PROBE 3
Self-Concealment versus Self-Revealment

With the clear understanding that participation in the experiment is entirely optional and voluntary, your class may wish to try the Yalom project. If so, let those students who choose to participate take home a blank 3 x 5 card and typewrite on it the secret which they would least like their peers to know about them. Of course, this experiment must be approached in a genuinely thoughtful, serious, and highly introspective frame of mind.

At the next class meeting the cards can be collected, carefully shuffled by the instructor, and then read aloud. The class can attempt to categorize the cards on the blackboard under Yalom's classifications:

PERSONAL INADEQUACY   *ALIENATION*   *SEX*

A number of observations can then be made:

(1) The class can use their results to check the validity of Yalom's findings. Do most of your secrets fit under his headings?

(2) Do any of the individual secrets surprise you? Probably not—and this realization of the universality of many of our fears may be the most significant observation of this study.

(3) The class can discuss the effect of such fears upon communication. How might each of these secrets constrain a speaker-agent?

Should anyone attempt to pry such a secret from its possessor, he would quite likely encounter stubborn or sullen silence, instant rebuff, or even violent anger. Any attempt of this kind, once recognized, would generate a fear which could quickly evolve into distrust and closely guarded behavior on the part of the

[12] Irvin D. Yalom, *The Theory and Practice of Group Psychotherapy* (New York: Basic Books, Inc., Publishers, 1970), pp. 10–11.

secret's "owner." Such conditions, of course, would hardly be conducive to productive and positive human interaction.

This fear that we will overexpose the dark underside of our mind to another sometimes prompts us to overcompensate by speaking for the purpose of *concealing* ourselves. We may—and sometimes do—speak for the purpose of portraying ourselves as something that we are not, usually in an attempt to mislead or deceive our listeners as to our actual identity, role, motivations, and values. And, conversely, we have observed speakers who were attempting to deceive us, or themselves, about reality. You may, for instance, have known of politicians who were notorious for their communicative duplicity and who seem to have made a career out of maintaining multiple public identities.

A certain glibness or "oiliness" may serve to effect the desired self-concealment for some. Others try to exclude from their speech behavior all clues about the self. The speaker who tries this tends always to be defensive and tense—constantly on the alert *not* to reveal himself, not to "give himself away." He is not likely to succeed, however, for as psychiatrist Joost Meerloo points out:

> We can recognize the psychic level of such well-guarded expressions by its different sound. The musical tone is gone, and the voice sounds mechanical, monotonous, and stripped of emotion.[13]

Finding and Enlarging Self-Satisfactions Through Speech

As we have illustrated, the fulfillment that we experience from identifying ourselves through speech and asserting our self-images contributes much to our self-satisfaction. Related to—but extending beyond—those purposes is the *creative* motivation for speaking. Essentially, speech in nearly all of its manifestations involves some degree of creativity. But sometimes, as its "creators," we derive a special, *added* kind of satisfaction—a kind of "above and beyond" satisfaction that results from an *act of creation*.

Using Creative Speech for Inner Satisfactions

Most of us take pleasure in producing and creating. We experience a glow of pride when we feel we have said something "just right," something uniquely suited to the circumstances. The remark doesn't have to be poetic, certainly; it doesn't even have to be clever. If our attempts to create interaction succeed, if the desired audience response is greater, or more enthusiastic, or more intense than we had anticipated, we know at that moment that we "have done something": we have *created orally*. The speech process thus allows us an opportunity for almost unlimited self-fulfillment. If successful, every communicative collaboration—every speaker/audience confrontation—can be an intensely satisfying, self-actualizing experience in creativity. Earlier in these pages, Meerloo stressed the psychological importance of this creativity potential in making a rhetorical assertion. The personal experiences and intimate glimpses of famous orators and great public speakers also attest repeatedly the special gratification and creational exhilaration they have derived from facing and moving an audience. Clarence Darrow (1857–1938), celebrated defense attorney, champion of the underprivileged, and the antagonist of William Jennings Bryan in the Scopes

---

[13] Joost A. M. Meerloo, "Contributions of Psychiatry to the Study of Human Communication," *Human Communication Theory,* ed. Frank E. X. Dance (New York: Holt, Rinehart & Winston, Inc., 1967), p. 142.

"monkey" trial, revealed a measure of his satisfaction in the following account of one of his early speeches:

> *I had discovered enough about public speaking to sense that unless a speaker can interest his audience at once, his effort will be a failure.*
>
> *The audience hesitated and began to sit down. They seemed willing to give me a chance. I had at least one advantage; nothing was expected of me; if I could get their attention, it would be easier than if too much was expected. Not one in twenty of the audience knew much about me. As a matter of fact, I had taken great pains to prepare my speech. The subject was one that had deeply interested me for many years, one that I really understood. In a short time I had the attention of the entire audience, to my surprise. Then came the full self-confidence which only a speaker can understand; that confidence that is felt as one visits by the fireside, when he can say what he pleases; when the speaker can, in fact, visit with the audience as with an old-time friend. I have no desire to elaborate on my talk, but I know that I had the people with me, and that I could sway those listeners as I wished.*
>
> *I have talked from platforms countless times since then, but never again have I felt that exquisite thrill of triumph after a speech. That was forty years ago, and even now I occasionally meet some one who tells me that he heard my speech at Central Music Hall the night I was there with Henry George.*[14]

[14] From *The Story of My Life* by Clarence Darrow. Reprinted by permission of Charles Scribner's Sons.

One of Darrow's most celebrated defense efforts was on behalf of Nathan Leopold, Jr., and Richard Loeb in their trial for the murder of Bobby Franks. This picture, taken at the arraignment, shows (left to right, foreground) Leopold, Darrow, and Loeb. Thanks to Darrow's plea, the defendants escaped the death penalty, but both were sentenced to life imprisonment. In part, Darrow had pled: "You may hang these boys . . . but in doing it you will turn your face to the past . . . . All life is worth saving, and . . . mercy is the highest attribute of man."

Darrow's statement, in addition to making clear the memorable, creational pleasure he experienced in interacting with his audience, supports our view that a speaker addressing a large audience is much more likely to be effective if he can see the communication situation as similar to a visit with "an old-time friend"—as closely related to our paradigm of two persons conversing.

Another highly persuasive speaker in this century, Malcolm X (1925–1965), a leading spokesman for the black nationalist movement, described a similar inner awakening and exciting self-discovery in being able to move and influence others:

> . . . *debating was a weekly event there at the Norfolk Prison Colony. My reading had my mind like steam under pressure. Some way, I had to start telling the white man about himself to his face. I decided I could do this by putting my name down to debate.*
>
> *Standing up and speaking before an audience was a thing that throughout my previous life never would have crossed my mind. Out there in the streets, hustling, pushing dope, and robbing, I could have had the dreams from a pound of hashish, and I'd never have dreamed anything so wild as that one day I would speak in coliseums and arenas, and the greatest American universities, and on radio and television programs, not to mention speaking all over Egypt and Africa and in England.*
>
> *But I will tell you that right there, in the prison, debating, speaking to a crowd, was as exhilarating to me as the discovery of knowledge through reading had been. Standing up there, the faces looking up at me, the things in my head coming out of my mouth, while my brain searched for the next best thing to follow what I was saying, and if I could sway them to my side by handling it right, then I had won the debate—once my feet got wet, I was gone on debating. Whichever side of the selected subject was assigned to me, I'd track down and study everything I could find on it. I'd put myself in my opponent's place and decide how I'd try to win if I had the other*

The strength and control that made Malcolm X a spokesman for the black nationalists are evident in this picture which was taken at a militant labor forum, two months before his death at a gunman's hands.

side; and then I'd figure a way to knock down those points. And if there was any way in the world, I'd work into my speech the devilishness of the white man.[15]

Clearly evident from this testimony is the fact that both of these effective speakers found speech making a uniquely creative experience and gained a great measure of self-satisfaction from their interaction with others in the speech communication process. We can also note in passing that (1) they had something they wanted to say, and (2) they prepared carefully for the speech event.

STUDY PROBE 4
Recalling Self-Satisfaction from Communicative Interaction

Recall some of your speaking experiences from the past: classroom speeches, interviews, family "councils of war," a role in a dramatic play, or some other communication situation in which you experienced a personal satisfaction and/ or a feeling of creativity similar to that described by Malcolm X or Clarence Darrow. Can you cite any specific evidence—audience response, feedback—to verify your feeling of triumph, or was it entirely an inner satisfaction?

If, by any chance, you cannot recall such a circumstance, try to remember a communication circumstance in which you *wanted* or *hoped to* experience that kind of satisfaction but were unable to.

Then, whether or not you were successful or merely wanted to be, try to describe the event and your own reactions to it at the time.

Using Consumatory Speech for Inner Satisfactions[16]

Some speakers mouth words as if they were good food. Through verbosity and redundancy they savor what they consider a good thought. Often, the speaking they do is done for its own sake, as if the words were made to be tasted —delicious morsels to be turned temptingly on the tongue. The unfortunate caricature of the "windbag" Senator Phogbound illustrates one form which the consumatory speech purpose may take.

From the foregoing, you may have inferred our definition of consumatory speech (coming from the verb *to consume*). Largely, and certainly initially, consumatory communication is "internal" in that its primary purpose is *to generate satisfaction within the speaker,* to enable the speaking communicator *to derive some inner gratification, to express his inmost emotions or feelings* because—first of all—to do so somehow allows him to "feel better."

Clevenger and Matthews make a useful distinction between what they term "consummatory" (based on the verb *to consummate*) and "instrumental" speech, saying:

[15] From *The Autobiography of Malcolm X* by Malcolm X with the assistance of Alex Haley. Reprinted by permission of Grove Press, Inc. and Hutchinson Publishing Group Ltd. Copyright © 1964 by Alex Haley and Malcolm X. Copyright © 1965 by Alex Haley and Betty Shabazz. P. 184.

[16] Some of these thoughts have come from the author's interaction with his former colleague Edmund C. Nuttall.

A relish for phraseology and delivery that was unabashedly archaic and sentimental put the late Senator Everett McKinley Dirksen in a class by himself as a master of consummatory speaking. *Time*, in its obituary for the Senator, referred to his "floriated prose," and specifically to his periodic appeal to have the marigold named our national flower: "It is as sprightly as the daffodil, as delicate as the carnation, as aggressive as the petunia, as ubiquitous as the violet and as stately as the snapdragon." But it was the nuance and the delivery, as much as the content, that gave Dirksen's speech its characteristic flavor and caused him to be called "the Wizard of Ooze." Observed *Time*, "When he spoke, there issued forth . . . diapasonal sounds like a Hammond organ in a dense fog."

> *Even when the primary purpose of the communication is instrumental—for instance, to secure concessions or to quell a riot—such consummatory elements as profanity, irrelevant attacks on "the establishment," moralistic generalizations, etc., are very likely to manifest themselves. Thus, we may say that whenever content appears in a communication without regard to its intended effect on some group of receivers, it represents consummatory communication.*[17]

This definition is similar to ours in many respects, and both suggest that a consumatory speech purpose, by and large, produces negative effects. While this is not entirely the case, it is true that at its worst it can seriously impair or even destroy desirable human interrelationships. At best, it can serve only to provide a limited measure of self-stabilization or self-reassurance for the user.

To the degree that consummatory speech helps us to "let off steam," it may serve beneficially to reduce tensions—a subject we will examine in some detail in subsequent pages. There have been those times when, using speech as a pressure-escape valve, we have "told someone off," and we have experienced great self-satisfaction for *the effective way in which we did it*. So proud are we, indeed, that we repeat the incident over and over silently to ourselves, or aloud to friends, co-workers, or anyone who will listen. Relating the tale of our verbal prowess—like the pleasure of chewing a good piece of steak—enables us to derive the greatest possible satisfaction from the event. At other times, if the "telling off" did not turn out so well, we repeat over and over what we "should have said."

[17] Theodore Clevenger, Jr., and Jack Matthews, *The Speech Communication Process* (Glenview, Ill.: Scott, Foresman and Company, 1971), p. 162.

STUDY PROBE 5
Discovering Additional Uses of Consumatory Speech

In addition to the functions it serves in enabling us to "savor" words for words' sake and to recall real or imagined verbal triumphs, consumatory speech serves other purposes for human beings. Enumerate some of these other purposes, especially those which are less obvious and, if possible, more positive in their fulfillment of self-satisfaction.

In certain situations such as those involving salesmanship, auctioneering, and carnival operation, the consumatory speech purpose may take on a different, almost *combative* turn. We have mentioned the case of the "high-pressure" life insurance salesman who insisted on giving us the "hard-sell" even though we had already made up our own minds to buy what he had to offer. He is typical of some speakers, especially those whose work or occupation is by nature *aggressive* or *combative,* who are unable to accept victory without a contest. For them, a large part of the reward of victory exists in the verbal battle. The means have thus become an end in themselves.

Staking out Verbal Territory

Another ego-centered purpose for which we sometimes speak is to lay claim to certain social or psychological "domains" which we want to dominate or control verbally. We tend to feel that if we verbalize loudly and insistently enough we can establish the boundary lines and keep out all would-be "trespassers." In this respect, we are not unlike other earthly creatures. Male birds sing to attract female birds, but they sing also to make territorial claims, to establish audibly the boundaries they wish to control. Speech serves a similar purpose for us human beings. You may have known persons, for instance, who used nonstop speech and increased voice volume to dominate a conversation (and, often, the surrounding ones as well). Like birds, they chatter and chirp to make their presence known and noisily strive to lord it over what they characteristically view as their private verbal domain. It is possible to employ this purpose skillfully, subtly, and creatively—particularly if you are clever at "games" and one-upmanship. Since most of us probably are not, we have to be cautious, lest what we *are,* or are trying to be, speaks so loudly that others cannot hear what we *say.*

Diminishing Tensions Within Ourselves and Others

In an over-populated and tension-ridden society such as ours, people must have the means to dissolve or reduce their tensions so as to maintain mental equilibrium and a sense of well-being. Scholars of psychology and behavioral science have shown us that much of human behavior is motivated by the need to minimize or balance internal tensions, to eliminate "cognitive dissonance."[18] Speech provides us with one means of accomplishing this.

[18] Leon Festinger, *A Theory of Cognitive Dissonance* (New York: Harper & Row, Publishers, 1957). An interested reader might want to follow up with Leon Festinger, *Conflict, Decision, and Dissonance* (Stanford: Stanford University Press, 1964).

A concise description of cognitive dissonance theory and some of the related research is given in Leonard Berkowitz, *Social Psychology* (Glenview, Ill.: Scott, Foresman and Company, 1972), pp. 15–17.

Often the sharp pain from an accidentally bumped shin can create an internal sensation that erupts in an emotional exclamation which, in itself, seems somehow to relieve the hurting. Similarly, guilt or frustration or the anxious desire to see social change can produce inner tensions which can be reduced appreciably by the act of speaking about them. We have all experienced that satisfying relief derived from discussing a distressing personal problem with a friend. *Saying* it—"getting it off our chest"—dissipates some of the physical and emotional tautness associated with the problem. If we feel strongly that one candidate for an important position or a political office is much better qualified than another, that inner conviction can create tensions which may very well drive us to speak out for the man of our choice.

In contrast, if you have nothing that you *need* to say, if you try to present a speech devoid of your convictions and inner feelings, you will almost surely provide a time-wasting and, perhaps, nerve-tightening experience for your hearers. At the same time, your own tensions will multiply. If you are essentially an honest person, a lack of inner enthusiasm will make you feel and behave insecurely. If you fail to speak from a burning *desire* to speak, listeners will be quick to detect your lack of conviction; and your uncertain feeling—rather than your message—will communicate itself to them. In either case, there will be tensions; in either event, you cannot hope to interact successfully with other agents. This is why we have said so often: In any speech communication situation, and especially in the classroom, your chances of being maximally effective will be far greater if you choose a topic that is so *vital to you* that you experience an emotional release when you are speaking about it.

Occasionally, it is true, we *cannot* speak out with genuine conviction. We may be frustrated, perhaps, because we feel that we lack the ability to act in a given situation. The job may require more than we know we can accomplish by acting alone. Or we may not feel qualified for the task; we can see no solution for the problem, or we may have some other good reason to be fearful of the outcome. If you face such a dilemma, do not try to rely on bluff or "big talk" to accomplish verbally what you cannot accomplish in actuality. If you have observed speakers who have attempted to bluster their way through taut situations, you know that such an approach can create more tensions than it can eradicate.

Prolonging Speech to Moderate Tensions

By the advice offered in the foregoing paragraph we do not mean to imply that you ought not to speak unless you can be decisive and conclusive—unless you know "all the answers." Sometimes one of your tension-relieving purposes will be *to prolong consideration of an important question or issue.* Here, to a large extent, you will be trying to diminish tensions in others. You may find yourself in a situation in which you realize that the ideal timing for a desired action is not quite yet. So, because the problem and/or proposed action are so important to all concerned, you prolong the oral interchange to prevent the matter from being dropped from attention or lost sight of. Legislators, for instance, know well that with "much talk and little action" a final decision may be postponed while more planning and (we may hope) constructive evaluation can be given to the problem.

Many times, this tactic may be condemned—and rightly so—as a stalling of progress or filibustering. However, if reasonably and fairly employed, speaking for the purpose of prolonging a decision can be a viable, even valuable, tool for a group desiring social or economic changes which, though justifiable, do not as yet have broad support. For such a group, this speech purpose helps to maintain tensions at a "live-withable" level, hold the membership together, and extend the hope that *eventually* a perplexing problem can be solved or an unfair or oppressive condition ameliorated through successful interaction. In our country, for example, a number of third-party and minority movements have led ultimately to significant social, political, and jurisprudential adjustments. Frequently these efforts began with a high talk-to-action ratio. By prolonging talk, these groups have been able to keep the issue in the public eye until the propitious moment when the proposed action became more generally acceptable and achievable.

STUDY PROBE 6

Analyzing "Talk-to-Action" Ratios of Organizational Communications

Identify some current movements or organized groups which appear to have wide public support and some which seem not to have it. Select one "have" and one "have-not," and compare a number of their typical communications (press releases, advertisements, public speeches, etc.) to determine whether you can find in them attempts to fulfill an intention other than the basic communication purpose. Compare their "talk-to-action" ratios, and describe the results to the class, orally or in writing.

Avoiding Silence to Reduce Tensions

Silence can communicate, both constructively and destructively. It can either create or diminish tensions. Certain societies cultivate the practice of "communing" in silence. Some religious groups encourage periods of silence and group meditation: each individual may reflect quietly, and there is no need for speech.

Quite properly, we need not speak until we have something to say. In our society, however, silence is not necessarily golden. In fact, it often creates great inner tension. Not uncommonly we penalize or punish one another by according the "silent treatment." Frequently parents use silence to punish children by seeming to withhold attention and, therefore (in the child's eyes), affection; and children, in turn, employ silence to register their rebellion.

This negating, tension-producing purpose of silence is evident in a vast number of human relationships and at almost every level of our society. What, for instance, is more stressful than to be host or hostess at a very quiet party where the guests refuse to converse—if not wittily, at least perfunctorily? What is less enjoyable than finding yourself at a cocktail party where most of the guests —strangers all—arrive in cultural or professional or conversational strait jackets and most of the "good spirits" are contained in bottles? Indeed, in very many social contexts we place such a high premium on *not* being silent that we are willing to engage in any kind of talk—however empty, fatuous, caustic, malicious, or ego-destructive—in order to fill the void and thereby relieve our tensions and soothe our fears. Most of us would probably agree how pointless and even harmful such void-filling chatter can be. But what we are willing to put up with for the sake of *preventing* an "awkward" silence should be proof enough of how even the prospect of it can trigger tensions.

In our consideration of the ego-centered/intrapersonal purposes of speech communication we have examined such commonly shared human needs as *asserting self-existence, establishing and projecting a self-image, generating and enlarging self-satisfactions through self-expression,* and *reducing and eliminating tensions within ourselves and others.* Singly, in combination, or in their totality, these drives and motivations enable us as human entities to adjust—at least in part—to our physical, psychological, and social environment, to "adapt" that environment to *us* to the extent needed for survival, and with some satisfaction to interact with one another in day-to-day and moment-to-moment speech communication. It seems appropriate, therefore, as a concluding consideration, to note briefly a few of the ways in which that oral interaction may be utilized to extend and broaden our person-to-person capabilities and how we are able, through language—the audible "tool" of speech—to exercise a greater measure of control over our surroundings.

Socio-Centered/Interpersonal Purposes

Through vocal utterance and the multiplicity of motivations which impel us to use it, we human beings have vastly enhanced our ability to *initiate, establish,* and *extend* the range of our interhuman contacts and to exert a degree of control over our surroundings. Our concern here, then, will be twofold: (1) *the social-contacting purpose of speech,* and (2) *the control-of-environment purpose.*

The Social-Contacting Purpose of Speech

Man has been called a social animal, mainly—we may suppose—because without the sensual warmth and supportive nurture of his fellows, he could not survive as a species or, probably, bear to endure his loneliness. The comparative brevity of his jaunts to the distant moon and back lends credence to this notion. On those journeys, very frequently pre-eminent in his behaviors was the obvious need for the solace, reassurance, and human contact afforded by his use of "speaking through space"—back and forth, again and again. And even when on this orb, his own habitat, he is physically crowded elbow to elbow and bumper to bumper, his psychological singularity and aloneness persist.

To see how apart—how really isolated and lonely—man can be in our society requires no great discernment. As we look about, we can see many groups, big and small, having distressing differences and whose interrelatedness is either nonexistent or severely strained and disrupted by feelings of distrust, hate, or indifference. We have, of course, cautioned against viewing communication as a cure-all for the many human ailments and conflicts. But, even so, through no means other than vocal collaboration are we likely ever to be able to reduce our social, economic, intellectual, religious, and generational gaps and "bring ourselves together." Mutual silence and separation, whether physical or of the spirit, can maintain human harmony only if absolute isolation were possible. It isn't. The natures and numbers of men and the conditions under which they dwell together make such a prospect baseless and utterly barren. Given man's will to socialize, to fulfill himself and his needs through close contact with and dependence upon others, we must recognize as imperative to our survival a willingness to search out common ground, a willingness to constructively modify—and mollify—by speech. Only in speaking together can men and women

Partisans must have a willingness to initiate and sustain communication with the opposing side if any solutions are to grow out of the interchange. In the disturbed Ulster community these residents, at least, showed some willingness to "talk through" the problems dividing them.

hope to allay their fears and fulfill their longings and expectations. To this end, the social-contacting purpose of speech must play an increasingly productive role, a role that is, in itself, worthy, compelling, and lifelong.

In their wild state, animals can be observed in the act of grooming one another. This social grooming establishes cooperative, nonaggressive, social contact among them. Writing in *The Naked Ape,* Desmond Morris finds the human equivalent of such grooming in what he terms "grooming talking":

> *This is the meaningless, polite chatter of social occasions, the "nice weather we are having" or the "have you read any good books lately" form of talking. It is not concerned with the exchange of important ideas or information, nor does it reveal the true mood of the speaker, nor is it aesthetically pleasing. Its function is to reinforce the greeting smile and to maintain social togetherness. It is our substitute for social grooming. By providing us with a non-aggressive social preoccupation, it enables us to expose ourselves communally to one another over comparatively long periods, in this way enabling valuable group bonds and friendships to grow and become strengthened.*[19]

By means of such "grooming talking," and verbal stroking, man establishes contact—a touching-together which describes itself in such terms as openness, friendliness, personal warmth, congeniality and conviviality, and even simple courtesy.

We are not taking the position, certainly, that all social-contact speech has

[19] Desmond Morris, *The Naked Ape* (New York: McGraw-Hill Book Company, 1967), p. 167.

to be pointless politeness. What we are emphasizing is that man must affirm his social nature, and the speech communication process provides him with the most direct and personal means for establishing contact with his fellows.

In research conducted in the small group discussion setting, this author and a colleague have found that in problem-solving situations nearly one half of the comments made by discussants were statements confirming, or further clarifying, or further substantiating ideas already before the group.[20] In other words, much of the talking that went on was not logically necessary for the development of a decision by the group. What did appear to be psychologically necessary, however, were the *oral play on an idea* and the *verbalization of concurrence.* We can view such psychological needs as related to "grooming talk." Clearly, comments made for mutual clarification and confirmation of agreement are important in establishing social interchange. This sense of contacting and social bonding, basic to small group discussants' loyalty to the group's decision, is also influential in other forms of speech communication.

Some people, it is true, seemingly view the socializing purposes of speech with a degree of disdain. Usually these are the "no-nonsense—just give me the facts" people. Perhaps they fear that unless they appear to be decisive and firm in their reactions and judgments, they will be marked as trivial by others. Such disdainers may be somewhat akin to those defensive persons we mentioned earlier who try to eliminate all vocal clues which might reveal more than is absolutely necessary for what they deem the basic communication purposes. Most of us, probably, would agree that providing some means for making and maintaining social contact may well be one of the most significant purposes for which human beings employ speech communication.

[20] Thomas M. Scheidel and Laura Crowell, "Idea Development in Small Discussion Groups," *Quarterly Journal of Speech,* L (1964): 140–145.

The ecology movement has necessarily generated a great deal of communication of both a verbal and a nonverbal kind. Young people in particular have brought a sense of dedication and commitment to the solution of this environmental problem.

The Control-of-Environment Purpose of Speech

In a sense, all of the speech impulses and motivations we have thus far discussed enlarge our capability to exert influence and exercise control over ourselves and others in the communication context. In this respect, it is closely related to and involved in what we have described as the basic, encompassing speech purpose: *to influence*. For this reason, having come full circle, it merits a concluding and climactic position in the hierarchy of oral intention.

There are a number of ways in which we may achieve this purposive control over our environment, but here we will consider only one—a major one. As you may have suspected, much of our ability to shape and dominate our psychological and physical environment is bound up in the unique nature of *language*. Later, in Chapter 6 (pages 171–179), we will examine in greater detail the relationships of language to speaking and thinking. Here, for the purpose we have under consideration, we will note very briefly only one of the numerous implications.

At one time or another, quite probably, you have been told that if you cannot express an idea clearly, you do not have the idea clearly in mind. This correctly implies that when we attach a word-label to an object, we gain a measure of control over that object. Once we provide the label, with all that *that* implies, we are able to manipulate the object *symbolically*. We can think about it in the abstract and in its absence. We are able to freeze it in time and place. We are able to communicate with others about it; that is, we can "put it into words." Until we have symbolized the object, we cannot do these things—things which are the essence of making speech.

To cite an example, if we did not have a word "dog," we could still collect sensory impressions of the animal and create an "internal" image which would enable us to *think* about "dog." However, if we wanted to *talk with others* about this particular kind of animal, we would have to invent a "dog" word or devise a label of some kind. The same is true for all objects and concepts that we name, label, and symbolize. In this way, the use of language and speech gives us a certain control over a portion of our environment.

In response, then, to our question, "Why does man speak?" we find that there is not one answer, but many. The conscious desire of one person intentionally to influence another is by no means the only purpose served by speech communication. If, as students of speech behavior, we are to make a meaningful *analysis* of any aspect of this oral process, we must be as fully aware as possible of all of the factors and forces which combine to produce it. If, as practitioners of oral communication, we are to produce a meaningful message or series of messages—to make oral utterance in such a way that others will notice, accept, and deem it worthy of response—we must intelligently and discriminantly *utilize* certain of these factors and forces, combining them so as to ensure to the greatest extent possible the interaction we desire and the purposes we hope to accomplish.

As we have progressed through these pages, we have tried to single out and illuminate some speech purposes that are largely contextually oriented, others that appear to be primarily ego-centered, and still others that have as their intent the extension of our social, person-to-person relationships and the control of our environment.

In trying to answer the questions which we originally raised on page 90, we have examined the influences which constrain a speaker and limit his range of possible speech behaviors in a given situation. We have analyzed the influential effects which self-image, experience, the specific speech context, and other persons can have upon a speaker. We have considered the inner drives and tensions which move him. And we have attempted to determine the extent to which his speaking contributes to his self-satisfaction and helps him to originate and maintain social contact.

Such questions gain added significance if and as we accept the view that speech communication serves multiple purposes, and as we attempt to search out and investigate those many purposes. Answers to such questions should be sought seriously by the student who desires to improve his own speaking, or who studies and evaluates the *effects* produced upon him by the speech of another.

The identification and assessment of some of these effects—particularly as they have impact upon us as listeners—provide the thrust and substance of the chapter which follows.

Suggested Readings

Charles T. Brown and Charles Van Riper, *Speech and Man* (Englewood Cliffs, N.J.: Prentice-Hall, Inc., 1966). This paperback book pursues in some detail the many and varied purposes served by man's speaking. It is interesting reading.

The following two sources present some contrasting theories about why man speaks and how speech communication develops in man:

Lev S. Vygotsky, *Thought and Language,* ed. and trans. Eugenia Hanfmann and Gertrude Vakar (New York: John Wiley & Sons, Inc., 1962).

Jean Piaget, *The Language and Thought of the Child,* trans. Marjorie Gabain (New York: World Publishing Company, 1955).

Chapter 5
Effects of Speech Communication

The influence which a speaking agent exerts upon
the *thought patterns* and *behavior patterns* of listening agents
has vast significance for and impact upon
successful, productive speech interaction.

"Why," you might ask, "do we use 'effects' in the plural sense? Why not simply 'effect'?" After all, you could argue, a speech either has an effect or it has not. If a speaker seeks contributions to a United Fund, the listeners either contribute or they do not. If he presents information about modern art, his auditors either learn or they do not. Purpose and response either "match" or they don't. But this view, looking as it does to the speaker's specific purpose and to the listener's more or less immediate response, is far from complete.

The Cumulative, Accretive, and Retroactive Nature of Speech Effects

Aside from producing actions which bear on the speaker's immediate and specific objective, speech interaction generates many other significant and long-range effects. Just as the speaker has numerous intentions in addition to his basic, encompassing communicative purpose, so the listener may experience numerous effects *in addition to* what might appear to be the immediate and overriding one. The multi-purposive and multidirectional nature of oral communication makes inevitable the fact that as listeners we will be affected in a wide variety of ways and with varying degrees of directness, intensity, and duration. Consequences never come singly; they are *plural;* they are *accretive* and *cumulative;* and—not infrequently—they are *retroactive.*

As we suggested at the outset, the most readily apparent effects of speech communication can be seen by comparing the evidence (admittedly often fragmentary and incomplete) of the listener's "major" accretive, cumulative response with the explicit, specific purpose of the speaker. Thus if the speaker's intention is to cause his listener *to act* or *to behave* or *to think* in a certain way, and if the listener appears to act or behave or think in that way, the speaker has achieved his purpose because the listener has acted in response to an accumulation, an accretion, of certain of his own attitudes, beliefs, and values.

We use the terms "cumulative" and "accretive" because the *why's* of the acting or behaving or thinking can be found somewhere on the usually long and often circuitous road between speaker-selected stimuli and listener-accumulated responses—between vague desires and their fulfillment. And there are many hidden obstacles and only a few known or suspected facilitators en route. We may say, somewhat arbitrarily, that the listener arrives at the desired "destination" by one or both of two means: (1) *learning new information and beliefs* and (2) *modifying his existing Belief-Evaluation clusters.* This is why we emphasize the pluralism of effects and the accretive, cumulative nature of the process by which we arrive at those effects.

If, therefore, we are to have a comprehensive view of what speech can do, we will need to try to consider as "separately" as we can several kinds of results and possible outcomes *beyond* the effects usually noted. If, as speaking and listening agents we hope to achieve fruitful human interaction, all of us must be acutely aware of the possible—as well as probable—consequences of our speech behaviors. A major intent of this chapter is to make more evident some of these contingent outcomes and effects. And as we proceed, we must remember that, as was the case with speech purposes, the effects of speech communication acts can be "isolated" only for purposes of observation and analysis.

Learning New Information and New Beliefs

Speech communication will result, quite likely, in the acquisition of some new information by those who listen. This new information may be unrelated to anything the listener now knows, and may open up a whole new category of meaning for him. More frequently, however, such information may be taken in by a listener and integrated into his *present* categories of meaning, into his *existing* patterns of beliefs and evaluations. That is to say, most of the new information presented by a speaker *adds to what his listeners already know*. It adds to and fills in their presently held categories of comprehension.

Consider an example. In one of his famed television presentations, composer-conductor Leonard Bernstein discussed the term "syncopation." His listeners probably had heard of the term before, and had at least some vague notion of its meaning. But Bernstein's explanation, complete with musical examples, developed the meaning of the term by making it more complete and, at the same time, clearer and more specific and definite. Thus he added new specific information to the listeners' understanding. Most of them probably knew more about syncopation after the presentation than they did before. They had experienced enlarged insight by reason of accumulation and accretion. In sum, we may say that a major effect of speech communication is the addition of new information which we as listeners can integrate into our understanding and with which we can increase and enrich our categories of meaning.

Modifying Existing Belief-Evaluation Clusters

A second and related major effect of speech communication is that the listener is influenced to modify and restructure his existing attitudes and views. As he listens to what the speaker is saying he may experience changes of beliefs in directions advocated by that speaker. A speaker may, for instance, argue for a charitable cause, and our belief level in the value of that cause may increase. Such an increase may, in turn, prompt us to make a financial contribution or sign a pledge card. A speech against birth-control pills may lower our belief level in the safety of that form of birth control and may, therefore, alter our willingness to accept or advocate its use.

Because our beliefs and evaluations play such significant roles in the effects which, as speakers, we create in our listeners, we need to examine more closely these concepts and a few of the ways in which they operate in influencing communicating agents.

Beliefs and Evaluations

As human individuals, each of us will have a number of beliefs and evaluations about any entity, activity, or concept of which we are aware. The object of "judgment" can be a person (one of your instructors, for instance), or a place (San Francisco), or an activity (skiing), or an action proposed by your community (fluoridation of the water supply), and so on. In fact, the subject of our beliefs and the values we attach to it can be any conceivable thought: past, present, or future—real or imagined.

Let us take "San Francisco" as an attitude-object. Any one of us can hold many beliefs about San Francisco. For example:

San Francisco is a city in California.

San Francisco is a large urban complex.

San Francisco has scenic hills and water areas.

San Francisco has available numerous cultural activities.

San Francisco has a moderate climate.

San Francisco has traffic-congestion problems.

San Francisco has air-pollution problems.

Obviously, we could have varying degrees of belief in these "attitude statements." Some statements we might hold to be absolutely certain, while others we would hold with qualification. Statisticians describe probability as varying between 0 and 1, with 0 meaning no probability of occurrence, and 1 indicating certainty. We could use this scale and say that one belief statement is held with a probability level of 1, another with a level of .90, still another with .40, and so on.

In each of the statements listed, the concept *San Francisco* is located within a larger category. For example:

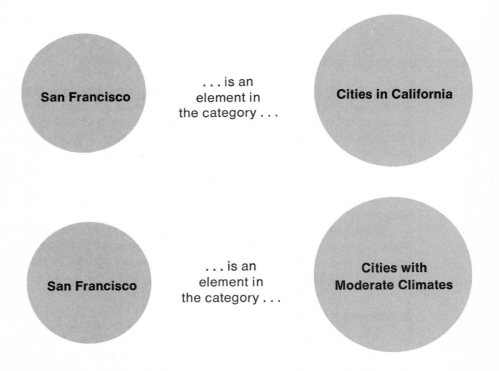

San Francisco   ... is an element in the category ...   Cities in California

San Francisco   ... is an element in the category ...   Cities with Moderate Climates

When we locate an attitude-object within a larger category of objects, all of the evaluations and feelings we attach to that larger category usually become associated with the specific attitude-object. Again, these evaluations could be held to vary between 0 and 1, with 0 indicating the lowest possible evaluation and 1 indicating the highest possible evaluation. We may feel very positive about "cities with moderate climates" (.90), but evaluate "cities with air pollution" very low (.00).

Belief-Evaluation Clusters

The combination, then, of all of our beliefs and evaluations about a concept make up our attitude toward that concept. Beliefs and evaluations are clearly related in a Belief-Evaluation *cluster* (B-E). If you dislike "air pollution," your attitude toward San Francisco will be determined in part by the level of your belief that San Francisco has polluted air, and this element will then be a negative factor in your B-E cluster. If you do not believe that San Francisco has polluted air, your negative feelings about polluted air will not matter. Similarly, your level of belief that San Francisco is a large urban complex and your evaluation of large urban complexes will contribute to your total attitude or B-E cluster, and so on with all of the other associations.

Every individual will, of course, have his own unique B-E cluster for any given attitude-object; these elements will differ from person to person. Some concepts will have many beliefs associated with them; others will have few. Quite likely, as we learn more about a subject or have more experience with it we will have more beliefs concerning it and more evaluative reactions toward it. As we hear more about an idea, an entity, a process, or an object—or think about it, or talk about it—we will be adding belief and evaluation elements to that cluster. This means that our B-E cluster regarding any given attitude-object will change from time to time; and even in a short span of time, we will have different reactions and formulate different judgments as certain beliefs and/or evaluations become more salient or evolve as the point of focus at any given instant. In sum, at any given moment, the beliefs and evaluations which, consciously or unconsciously, come to mind at the mention of an object or concept will comprise our *attitude* toward that object or concept *at that moment*.

Now consider how this bears upon speech communication. One of the major effects of all oral interaction is to induce agents to focus upon certain attitudinal elements and thereby to influence the content and structure of their B-E clusters—even if only temporarily. If a speaker, for instance, in presenting and developing his subject dwells on negative belief-evaluations to which you are sensitive, those negative elements may outweigh the positive elements you hold in your cluster but are not focusing upon at that particular moment. Similarly, in every act of speech communication, *the speaker's basic communicative function involves to a very significant extent the influencing (developing, modifying, restructuring) of listeners' beliefs and belief-evaluations*.

As a speaking agent, you have a number of alternative means of effecting this influence: you may attempt to *add new belief-propositions* not yet a part of the belief system of your listeners; you may try to *associate your subject with "meaning" categories* which you know your listeners value highly, or with categories they dislike; you may attempt to *change listeners' existing belief levels* or to *change listeners' existing evaluation levels*. In Chapter 7, "Decision Making," we will explore these options in some depth as we extend there our analysis of Belief-Evaluation clusters and examine more minutely further implications and practical applications. For our purposes here we will only emphasize that any oral communication having as its objective the influencing of other agents to accept your viewpoint or position must strive in some degree to effectuate that acceptance by means of developing and/or modifying the B-E clusters of the receivers of your message.

STUDY PROBE 1

Analyzing Your Beliefs

Select an issue or "article of faith" concerning which you hold a quite firm attitude. Samples:

> "Women should in all respects—sexually, socially, educationally, economically, and occupationally—be the equal of men."

> "If a man and a woman marry, have children, and decide to separate—obtain a divorce—the man should be required by law to pay all necessary and reasonable expenses involved in the upbringing of the children, but he should not be required to pay alimony to his divorced wife."

Now make a list of the *specific beliefs* which have influenced you to adopt, hold, and defend the attitude which you selected as the initial phase of this Probe.

Rate those beliefs, giving to each a number ranging from .00 (weakest) to 1.00 (strongest) in order to reflect the strength with which you hold them.

Try to formulate a line of persuasion or argument which you feel that a speaker might present to move you to reorder the values you've attached to these particular beliefs.

Retroversive Effects and Countermeasures

Our considerations up to this point suggest that there are certain effects over which the speaker exercises a fairly large measure of control. New input of information is one. And to the extent that this new input disposes listeners favorably toward the speaker's position, we may say that modification of beliefs and evaluation levels is another.

Obviously, however, in pursuing his purposes, the speaker will find it impossible to anticipate or to exercise control over all of the effects he will be creating in his auditors. He must realize—and so must we as his hearers—that in moving us, he may have moved us *too far* or in a totally *opposite direction* from what he had intended. In trying to influence us, he may have overinfluenced us. His communicative efforts may have created in us certain consequences which he probably had not anticipated and which he may not have purposed. This is, in part, what we meant when we remarked earlier that the path to persuasion is beset with many unforeseen and often unforeseeable obstacles.

For illustration and analysis we will single out four of what might loosely be described as retroversive or retroactive outcomes in speech communication:

1. Boomerang Effect
2. Regression Effect

3. Sleeper Effect
4. Focusing Effect

Then we will propose two measures which can help to counteract or counterbalance such effects:

Immunizing
Campaigning

In employing this arbitrary set of distinctions we do not wish to create a judgmental impression that retroversive or retroactive effects are necessarily all "bad" or invariably negative in the end results they produce. Quite probably, after a little thought and some observation you will be able to cite situations in which the overall outcomes contain elements of both "goodness" and "badness" —in which they appear to have operated either positively or negatively in the broad span of human interaction.

Boomerang Effect

For some listeners a speech effort may backfire. Its impact may be such as to move the hearer in a direction almost exactly the *reverse* of what the speaker intends. This is a phenomenon we may encounter with some frequency. In almost every speech-research study, scholars have found a few audience members whose beliefs and evaluations change in a direction opposite from that advocated by the speaker. Seemingly, these auditors are somehow offended or perhaps somewhat alienated by the speech, and so they react negatively. Not only does the speaker fail to influence them toward the position he is advocating, but—worse—he causes them to retrovert, to move in a counter direction, away from the very position they are being urged to adopt. This kind of "boomerang" reaction has been largely neglected as a topic for research, but it is of sufficient significance to us as students and practitioners of communication that we should at least speculate on some of the possible reasons for this effect.

Suppose that a speaker argues against a position that you, a listener, support. His speaking may have little effect upon you at all; you may be unmoved. Your beliefs and evaluations relative to the subject remain essentially what they were before he started to speak. But suppose that a college administrator, in arguing against the ability of college students to make their own academic decisions, speaks against your position in a manner that you consider unfair or untruthful. You may then react negatively to him and be prompted to favor your own "side" of the issue or topic even more strongly than you did originally. This retroversive response-effect is a very human and understandable one: our reaction, generally, to people who treat us unfairly or who lie to us is markedly negative and personal.

STUDY PROBE 2
Analyzing Boomerang Effects

Listen critically to some televised commercial messages, and examine advertisements in newspapers and magazines and on billboards.

Select at least five of the messages which you find in some way offensive, and analyze what seems to you to be the "persuasive appeal" underlying each of them. Examples:

Message: USE BRANDEX HAIR CREAM!

> *Persuasive Appeal:* "Tiger Thompson, the snaky, scrambling quarterback of the great Tulsa Toolers football team, wouldn't be caught in the crunch or anywhere else without his Brandex Hair Cream dressing!"

Message: BUY NOPAIN ASPIRIN!

> *Persuasive Appeal:* "Our expert 'Answer Man' recommends Nopain highly. It's great for highbrows, lowbrows, and middlebrows!"

Be prepared to identify, either in class discussion or in writing, the elements of the actual appeals you single out as being personally objectionable to you, and explain why they would probably produce a boomerang effect in you. (*Note:* In the interests of enlarging the concept of "persuasive appeals," examine the discussion and analysis of it in various other textual sources.[1])

[1] See, for example:

Alan H. Monroe and Douglas Ehninger, *Principles of Speech Communication,* 6th ed. (Glenview, Ill.: Scott, Foresman and Company, 1969), especially pp. 342–354.

Donald C. Bryant and Karl R. Wallace, *Fundamentals of Public Speaking,* 4th ed. (New York: Appleton-Century-Crofts, 1969), Chapters 16–21.

Thomas M. Scheidel, *Persuasive Speaking* (Glenview, Ill.: Scott, Foresman and Company, 1967), Chapter 4.

When a con man approaches you with his get-rich-quick scheme, you are likely to be repelled by the evident fact that he seems not to have followed his own advice. If he had, you may reason, he could now be relaxing at home rather than peddling his dreamed-up deceit. Any such evidence of insincerity or dubious motive which you attribute to a speaker, or in which you perceive an incongruity between a speaker's *ethos* and what he advocates, may produce a boomerang effect.

Listeners, in their turn, need to be on guard against what may be *for them* a possible adverse consequence from this type of negative reaction. In one sense, you may say that if a speaker causes himself to be perceived as a person of ill will, then he deserves the reaction he produces. But, as a listener, you will do well to attempt some *independent* judgment of the subject matter of the speech and of the *ethos* of the speaker. If you do not, sometimes your *over*reactions to an obnoxious advocate can drive you to positions that are too extreme. You may then find yourself trapped into supporting a policy or position beyond that in which you really believe. Or, conversely, your retroversive responses may cause you to "clam up," to restrict your position unduly. And, worse yet, if you are called upon to present *your* views, your presentation may itself show an incongruity between the position you now feel compelled to advance and the Belief-Evaluation structure with which you support it.

STUDY PROBE 3
Overreacting to a Speaker's Message or a Speech Communication Situation

Recall an oral communication situation in which you "overreacted" and were driven to argue for a position *beyond* that which you could honestly support.

Describe that situation, singling out the factors which caused you to over-respond.

Assess the outcome of the oral interchange on that occasion, and offer suggestions—or encourage other class members to offer suggestions—as to what you might have been able to do in order to "rebalance" your reaction in such a way as to generate a more satisfactory and productive outcome.

Regression Effect

With the passage of time following a speaker's presentation of a message, audience attitudes tend to move back toward their original positions—the positions held by the hearers prior to experiencing the communication. Perhaps because—in time—the memory of the speaker's position, point, or persuasiveness blurs, some of the immediate effects of that speech communication act will necessarily erode or will eventually fade. A belief originally held at a moderate level may be moved to a higher level during or immediately following a speech, only to regress slowly back to the earlier moderate level within a few days or a few weeks.

Notice, for instance, the vast acceleration with which the public's belief level and enthusiasm for "the ecological urgency" was caused to soar and blossom into nationwide prominence. Scores of speakers spoke on the subject; some scientists made dark and dire predictions concerning the ultimate destruction of our environment; radio stations issued urgent messages; television producers presented documentaries as proof that something must be done. And we all agreed. Now, however, some observers note a drop in the belief level of the public; they see it as dropping—perhaps not too slowly—to a lower level, one approaching apathy.

Or, as an illustration drawn from a somewhat different domain, consider the recurring complaint of a number of the men who coach some of the country's leading college football teams. "It's almost impossible," they say, "to 'get the team up' (its enthusiasm, that is) week after week, for one big game after another!" It is as though the coaches' rhetorical and oratorical "batteries," repeatedly overcharged and overworked, "run down." They find it harder and harder to elevate and sustain the belief levels of the players. In the "ecological urgency" the public is experiencing a regression effect; in the locker-room crisis, the football teams are experiencing it.

STUDY PROBE 4
Recalling and Analyzing a Regression Effect

Try to remember situations in which you, as a listener, have experienced a regression effect. In preparing your analysis of what happened and why, select a situation in which you were moved to accept the view or position advanced by the speaker at the time of the speech. Then describe:

1. Your position on this issue or point *before* you heard the speech.

2. The extent and direction in which you were moved from your position *at the time you heard the speech* or *immediately following it.*

3. *The time elapsed between hearing the speech and reverting toward your original position or view*—that is, the "regression interval."

Try to discover (a) *why* you did not continue to hold the view or position you held immediately after the speaker had presented his views and had tried to persuade you to his position or viewpoint, and (b) what the speaker might have done in order to *sustain* your acceptance of his argument and to prevent you from regressing.

Sleeper Effect

Another finding from research studies which bears significantly upon the speaker's efforts to modify existing Belief-Evaluation clusters has been labeled the "sleeper effect."[2] The phrase names the phenomenon wherein *a source and a message become disassociated as time passes, and the influence of the source tends to be separated from the influence of the message.* As we have previously pointed out, experimentation supports the view that a speaker's prestige or lack of it will add to or diminish his persuasive influence accordingly. A high-prestige source will be more influential than a low-prestige source if both present identical messages.

However, an examination of the *long-term* effects of persuasive messages has led to some surprises. Research has revealed that the positive or negative effects of the source upon the listeners' reception and acceptance of the message tend to disappear as time passes. For example, when a high-prestige source spoke for a position, the audience was initially more favorably disposed toward that position. As time passed, however, audience attitudes regressed to their earlier positions. In contrasting cases, when a low-prestige source presented a message, the persuasive effect (change in belief-evaluations) immediately following the speech was *less* than the persuasive effect when it was measured several weeks after presentation. A plausible explanation is that the negative effect of the low-prestige speaker was lost as time passed and the audience no longer associated that speaker so strongly with the point of view he had advocated.

Typically, in experiments of this kind, the experimenters prepare a carefully worded and carefully structured speech on a given topic and record it on tape. "Free Speech and the Law" could be an example. Next, they attempt to measure the attitudes and belief-levels held for this topic by two groups of listeners, A and B, both tested by means of a "semantic differential" scale of some kind.[3] Then, to Listener-Group A the speech is introduced as having been given originally by a high-prestige source, possibly by former Supreme Court Chief Justice Warren. To Listener-Group B the speech is introduced as having originated with a low-prestige source, for example, a high school sophomore reporting on the subject of his term paper. Then, following the speech, the experimenters again measure the belief-evaluation levels of the separate groups. Some time later, possibly in six or eight weeks, the experimenters again apply their

[2] William J. McGuire, "The Nature of Attitudes and Attitude Change," *The Handbook of Social Psychology,* 2nd ed., ed. Gardner Lindzey and Elliot Aronson (Reading, Mass.: Addison-Wesley Publishing Co., Inc., 1969), v. III, pp. 254–256.

[3] One way to measure a person's attitudinal reactions is to use a measuring device called a "semantic differential." For further information, see Charles E. Osgood, George J. Suci, and Percy H. Tannenbaum, *The Measurement of Meaning* (Urbana, Ill.: University of Illinois Press, 1957). Chapter 5, "Attitude Measurement and the Principle of Congruity," is particularly helpful.

measurements in order to try to determine the extent to which the two groups have disassociated the message from the presumed source.

In certain respects, the "sleeper" effect is similar to the "regression" effect, in that both are erosive, and in each a passage of time is at work. The major difference between the two is that in the latter the listeners' retention of the message and its immediate effect become blurred and indistinct with the passing of time, allowing the "pre-speech" view to return to dominance; in the "sleeper" effect, the speaker-as-message-source becomes disassociated from the message-impact. The integrity-influence of the speaker as such—whether high or low, "good" or "bad"—tends to become decreasingly important to the hearer from the moment the message is communicated to him. What the speaker *says,* rather than what he *is,* persists in the listener's memory and—all other factors being comparatively constant—therefore tends to become increasingly significant in shaping the attitudes of the latter.

Here again the durability, if not the power, of the speaker's *ethos* is involved; and, here again, all of the "evidence" is by no means in. There is enough, however, to suggest that as you approach the speech-making task you cannot afford to overlook the potentially erosive consequences of the "sleeper" effect.

Focusing Effect

We have all seen photographs in which some subjects are in focus while others blur into the background. The subjects in focus are the ones which gain our attention. When looking out a window, we can focus on either the window glass itself or on some object beyond it. In the first case we may notice scratches and bits of dirt on the window glass, whereas the distant tree is a blur. Or we can focus on the distant tree and see it clearly, in which case we no longer see the scratches on the windowpane. We cannot focus on both objects simultaneously, and here is an important analog to speech communication. In a speech setting, some elements will be emphasized and focused upon. For the moment, these elements will become the focus of our attention while others blur into the background. Let us examine in some detail how this works.

As we pointed out earlier in this chapter, as a listener you will come to the speech setting with a more or less fully developed set of beliefs and evaluations. You may hold these beliefs and evaluations at varying levels and with different degrees of salience or prominence. Some, obviously, will be more prominent in your awareness than others. This set will represent your usual position on or predisposition toward the topic.

As you listen to the message, however, your attention will be channeled in *new* directions. The speaker will emphasize certain points and ignore others: he will be *selective.* He will develop some aspects of the topic in detail, and others only briefly. Perhaps the speaker will focus upon positive elements in the subject and let negative elements fade into the background. Or he may, for instance, focus on economic elements and largely ignore aesthetic considerations.

As long as the speaker maintains this new focus for you the listener, his speech quite probably will appear to have a positive effect upon you. *Later,* however, when you return to your usual environment, the effects of this new focus will be reduced because you will very likely see the topic with the relative saliences you held earlier. Your "thinking" will tend to slip back into its previous, comfortable configuration.

Because the focusing process operates in this manner, it is partially responsible not only for the immediate effects observable following a communication event, but it also partially explains the regressive reaction. *What we are focusing upon at a given moment will be most influential in determining our behavioral response to the speaker's purpose at that moment.*

STUDY PROBE 5

Focusing the Attention and Interest of Listeners

Draw from your own experiences and observations as a speaker and a listener four or five elements, devices, or factors which you, as a communication agent, might employ to "focus" the attention and interest of other agents.

> *Examples:*
> 1. Amount of time devoted to the topic.
> 2. Vocal emphasis.
> 3. Repetition.

Then, using as a reference source such books as those cited in Footnote 1, (page 120), examine relevant chapters bearing upon the topics of Interest and Attention. Itemize the elements, devices, or factors discussed there, and then compare your original list with the results of your survey.

As you plan your speech communication, then, you will want to consider carefully the possibilities of retroversive/retroactive effects, among them: *boomerang, regression, sleeper,* and *focusing.* Any one of these or all of them—since they tend to create a reversion of audiences' attitudes toward their original positions—can seriously vitiate fulfillment of your purpose as a speaker, or may even obliterate it entirely. A boomerang effect can, of course, obstruct and frustrate your intent from the outset. If your specific purpose calls only for an immediate consequence, then the regression, sleeper, and focusing effects may pose no special problems. But if your goal is to produce a long-range and more enduring objective, your speech planning and presentation must be infused with some efficient countermeasures for combating all of these purpose-eroding effects.

Earlier in this chapter we mentioned two such counteractants, *immunizing* and *campaigning,* which can prove of possible assistance to you as a speaker. We will, therefore, take a brief look at each.

Immunizing

Some research studies have suggested "immunization" as a useful means of combatting the possible loss or deterioration of immediately achieved speech effects. Immunization calls for the "open consideration of the other side of the argument." Some investigators have found that speakers may be more effective in the long run if—in addition to presenting the positive and constructive supports for their sides of the arguments—they take up and refute the counterarguments that are likely to be advanced by their opponents. If you reflect on this for a moment and try to marshal a few arguments and counterarguments on a given proposition, you will be better able to see why this happens.

If a speaker presents only his side of the issue, he may achieve the immediate effect he desires to create in his hearers. But suppose that you are one of those hearers and that as time passes you are confronted by a *different* speaker, one who brings up some *opposing viewpoints* or who questions you about the other side of the issue or proposition. Thus confronted, you may be swayed in the direction advocated by the second speaker. If, however, the *original* speaker—in first addressing you and the others—brings up and sensibly refutes the major opposing arguments, you will tend to be immunized against these counterarguments which are likely to be advanced at a later time by another speaker. You will have been prepared for them. You will already know the refutation to opposition arguments and will have been made less susceptible to their counter-influence; you will have given "open consideration" to both sides of the issue.

Admittedly, this kind of immunization cannot eliminate all later reverses in audience attitude, but it can help to reduce erosion. And we must admit also that there is a precaution signal to be observed here, too. If a listener is not very knowledgeable and discriminative, to confront him with more than one side of an issue may confuse him. If this happens, of course, you will be lessening the influence-impact which your message might otherwise have had. In the final analysis of your audience, especially when you are readying yourself to engage in controversial or issue-centered speaking, you will need to consider very carefully whether you can afford to take the time to answer the possible objections and obviate the alternate choices to which your listeners may be exposed in the future. You must, at the same time, decide whether you can afford *not* to anticipate those objections and dispose of those alternatives. This involves *decision making,* a subject which we will examine in quite some detail in Chapter 7.

Campaigning

As speech communicators, very early in life we became aware of the power of *repetition* in accomplishing our immediate purpose. As children, we didn't ask for a piece of candy *once;* we asked and *kept on asking* until we got it or concluded that our plea had been utterly rejected. And, of course, the skilled speaker knows the value of reiterating skillfully the central point of his message several times while he is presenting it. In public, one-to-many communication settings, most of us do not have an opportunity to present our message more than once.

But when we do, we need to recognize that one of the best means for achieving lasting effects for purposive speaking may well be the use of a *campaign.*[4] A series or succession of message presentations, all strategically developed to accomplish the speaker's intent, and distributed over time, are almost certain to have a much greater effect than the simple sum of the effects of a single message which is presented only once.

Nearly all of us, as teachers or students or parents, recognize the importance of such repetition in the learning process. Leaders in business and industry are well aware of it, and often exploit it. Probably no business management these days would consider presenting a single, for-one-time-use-only advertisement for the purpose of selling its product or service. In advertising, corporate and promotional thinking runs invariably to mounting a campaign: several or numerous presentations of an identical (or nearly identical) message repeated day after day, week after week, in carefully selected media. We daily witness countless advertising campaigns and the seemingly endless repetition—on radio, television, billboards, in newspapers and magazines—of a single, insistent message for each "client." Like it or not, we are compelled to admit its obvious effectiveness.

The speaker—in his way—should do no less if his purpose is to "sell" his idea, position, or proposition to others. If you are a speaker-advocate who desires long-lasting effects for your cause, you should be fully cognizant of the possible advantages and purposive impact to be gained from a campaign. As you plan speech communication messages, try to view your objectives in a larger context; and, if at all possible, look to a *series* of speech encounters as perhaps the most effective means for advancing and establishing your position. While this approach to counteracting erosive effects may have its greatest strength in public communication, it also has implications and value in one-to-one settings. Few therapists, for instance, would hope to accomplish their corrective or therapeutic ends in a single session.

In sum, the acquisition and integration of new information and the modification of existing Belief-Evaluation structures in listeners are the most immediate and probably the most frequently noted results of speech communication. The persistence of these major and usually very desirable effects may be seriously weakened or negated, however, by (1) boomerang effects, (2) regression effects, (3) sleeper effects, and (4) focusing effects. Therefore, in the planning stages of your speech communication you will be wise to include provisions for *immunizing* your listeners against possible counterarguments and for combating deteriorative reactions by using a series of messages—a *campaign*—to ensure to the greatest extent possible the permanence of your persuasive purpose.

In addition to the effects we have thus far examined in this chapter, the speech communication act almost always produces a good many other outcomes and consequences. As a speaker, no doubt, you will sometimes see these other effects as problems; always, however, they will be fraught with challenging possibilities for facilitating and improving speech interaction. Two which appear to fit the latter description primarily and which you will want to take into account are (1) *developing second-level communicators* and (2) *transferring effects to related topics.*

[4] William J. McGuire, "The Nature of Attitudes and Attitude Change," *The Handbook of Social Psychology,* 2nd ed., ed. Gardner Lindzey and Elliot Aronson (Reading, Mass.: Addison-Wesley Publishing Co., Inc., 1969), v. III, pp. 211–212.

Developing Second-Level Communicators

Potentially, any speech-communication setting offers opportunities for the speaker to create second-level communicators. An illustration will help to define our use of the term. Research on the spread of information originating in the mass media has singled out a group of people who have been labeled the "opinion leaders." This small but concerned group is comprised of the most frequent and regular users of mass-media sources: television, radio, magazines, and newspapers. These "leaders" take from *their* sources information about government, current events, fashions, and advertised products, and proceed to pass this information along in interpersonal contacts to a larger group of acquaintances. The majority of these "second-level recipients" who have been surveyed on this matter seemed to get more of their views from the "opinion leaders" than from the mass media directly.

In writing about this phenomenon, Elihu Katz describes the process as the "Two-Step Flow of Communication" and makes the point that in many groups these opinion-shapers serve as *intermediaries* between the communicated messages and the other members of the group.[5]

The concept of second-level communicators might be depicted thus:

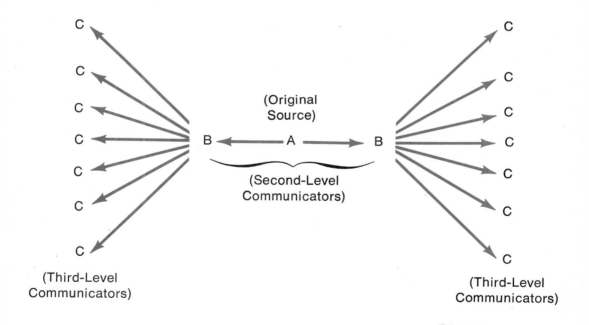

The possibility that in every speech context some of the listeners may very well become second-level communicators has much practical significance for the student and practitioner of speech communication. We may note that this concept of second-level communication may take at least two forms: a *disciple* effect and an *intermediary* effect.

[5] Walter Weiss, "Effects of the Mass Media of Communication," *The Handbook of Social Psychology,* 2nd ed., ed. Gardner Lindzey and Elliot Aronson (Reading, Mass.: Addison-Wesley Publishing Co., Inc., 1969), v. V, especially pp. 142–143 and 169–172.

Disciple Effect

Second-level communicators ordinarily can be expected to "spread the word" of the speaker's pronouncements, position, or views to a still *larger* audience. This serves to extend and reinforce the initial impact of the speaker's message. One of the aims, therefore, of every speaking agent should be to develop—as an added effect of his presentation—some second-level communicators. This potential "disciple" effect underscores again the desirability of your presenting, within the available time, the fullest possible case during the initial speech act. As we pointed out on pages 124–125, if you can develop all of the essential lines of an argument in the beginning, you will tend to immunize your hearers against the countereffects of opposing arguments. Here, we further emphasize that by providing this kind of thoroughgoing development you will also be providing your listeners with resources which they, in turn, will need in order to achieve maximum effectiveness as second-level communicators.

STUDY PROBE 7

Using a Second-Level Communicator to Attain Desired Outcomes

Try to recollect at least three important decisions that you have been faced with in your lifetime—significant decisions which hinged to a major extent upon the approval or concurrence of someone else, possibly a parent, a wealthy acquaintance, an influential dean, or some similar authority figure. Ideally, these decisions should have involved situations and other agents—contexts in which you asked (or should have asked) an intermediary to intercede or negotiate for you.

Report the outcomes in each instance, indicating whether—in the main— you succeeded or failed to obtain the approval, concurrence, or permission you desired in order to make the decision you *wanted* to make.

If you did not involve a second-level communicator, speculate as to whether and in what possible ways the decision might have "gone your way" if you had done so.

The benefit to be derived from second-level communicators need not by any means always be an indirect, secondary, or incidental one. As a speaker, you may want to plan—as a direct, immediate, and primary part of your specific purpose—to *create* such agents. For example, this approach to communication is sometimes employed in work with urban juvenile gangs. A social worker may not be able to make contact with the gang as a whole because its members distrust him and believe that he would be unlikely to hold the views and values they do. So he works to establish direct contact with the gang *leader*. Partially because of the natural cohesiveness of groups and also because leaders tend to recognize the probable effectiveness of "two persons conversing," an outsider (social worker in this case) can manage to establish a meaningful relationship with a single insider (gang leader) more readily than he can with the group. The social worker, therefore, communicates first with the leader and tries to prevail upon him to serve as the worker's spokesman within the gang.

The use of second-level communicators is not simply a strategy for cheap manipulation. If significant progress is to be made, it is sometimes the only course possible. Elijah Muhammad needed a Malcolm X as a recruiter for his Black Muslim movement. Most organizations, in fact, need at least a few especially able adherents or converts to serve as second-level communicators. As a speaker you will be well advised always to ask yourself: Whom do I wish my message to reach finally? Who else in the group has the ear of this or that particular listener? Shall my plan be to make a direct, frontal, verbal effort myself? Or will my purpose be better served if I can develop a second-level communicator to carry my message?

We are thinking here, really, about communicating across gaps. And we are saying that the development of second-level speaking agents is one way to bridge them. Obviously, there are many causes for communication gaps. Age is one. But even this one is not simple; a generation gap implies many differences beyond longevity. Earlier, a quotation cited from Aristotle (pages 68–69) pointed to a number of key characteristics which are concomitant with age differences. Each of the differences he singled out could conceivably cause breakdowns in communication. Thomas Hardy, in describing one of his characters, pointed to another dissimilarity inherent in the generational dilemma:

> He had just reached the time of life at which "young" is ceasing to be the prefix of "man" in speaking of one. He was at the brightest period of masculine growth, for his intellect and his emotions were clearly separated: he had passed the time during which the influence of youth indiscriminately mingles them in the character of impulse, and he had not yet arrived at the stage wherein they become united again, in the character of prejudice, by influence of a wife and family. In short, he was twenty-eight, and a bachelor.[6]

Of course, not all communicative agents are twenty-eight, and bachelors. But Hardy's point prompts us to ask: Is youth indeed impulsive and age prejudiced? If so, how then can the two be brought together? We hope that the comments made throughout this volume concerning ways to achieve communicative interaction will help create desirable understanding and a unifying effect. Recognizing the potentiality of second-level communicators may further contribute to that empathy and unity. Frequently, the development of this type of communicator is an incidental—even accidental—effect of speech communication. More frequently, perhaps, it should be a carefully planned component of a speaker's specific purpose.

[6] Thomas Hardy, *Far from the Madding Crowd* (New York: The New American Library, Inc., 1960), p. 15.

STUDY PROBE 8
Identifying and Locating a Breakdown in Speech Communication

Using our concept of speech communication as agent-context-interaction and our paradigm of two persons conversing, formulate your view of the so-called generation gap. (Review, if you wish, pages 68–69 in Chapter 3 wherein Aristotle stated his view.)

If you see this gap as a communication problem—a breakdown of some kind—try to determine at what juncture in the process or the relationship the breakdown seems to occur. What obstacles, if any, seem to you to impede or prevent productive oral exchange between your generation and, for example, that of your parents or your grandparents?

Prepare, briefly, a statement of four or five specific speech behaviors which, if you were to employ them, might enable you or at least help you to narrow or close the generation gap if one does indeed exist.

In addition to—or, perhaps, in lieu of—possible breakdowns in speech communication, what other factors do you discern as contributing to the generational barrier?

Intermediary Effect

There are, of course, numerous conditions under which productive human interaction can be achieved more readily and successfully through the *intermediation* of second-level communicators than through direct, face-to-face confrontation of agents themselves. We can observe this in situations ranging from arbitration of labor-management disputes to matrimonial matchmaking. Possibly, points of difference between the principal agents will be so salient and divisive that when these agents are in face-to-face contact, even the mutual desire for a solution to the common problem will be overridden. Characteristi-

Henry Kissinger became one of the best-known second-level communicators in recent history through his successful efforts to set up a meeting between President Nixon (with whom he is conferring at right), and the Chinese leaders Mao Tse-tung and Chou En-lai. The lower photo shows Kissinger with Chou En-lai.

cally in such circumstances agents tend to resort to verbal attacks upon one another, and physical assaults are not beyond the realm of possibility. Some observers see this kind of communication breakdown as resulting in riots and violence on the one hand and in a rigidly arbitrary, overly strict meting out of punishment to the dissidents on the other. In both, the verbal and physical acts serve the *actors* as a form of emotional release. Agents thus involved—as well as neutral bystanders—would, if pressed, have difficulty in pointing to any enduring and positive accomplishments of confrontation at this level.

Here, as elsewhere, in situations where sharp differences and disagreements are likely to develop, the second-level communicators representing and speaking for the leaders of differing factions should come together under the conditions of "two persons conversing." Such conditions can increase the probability of productive, solution-finding interaction. A word of caution, however, is in order. If tension is high, the *number* of agents—of whatever level—should be kept to a minimum. Too many agents may spoil the context. It may, in fact, be highly desirable that the principal agents meet alone, or that their second-level counterparts meet alone. If the contending leaders meet with their followers in attendance, each of the main antagonists may be inclined to shout or to try to put down his opponent for the benefit of his followers rather than to speak reasonably and intelligently with each other. Thus, when the likelihood of communication conflict is great, the serious speaker of good will should explore conscientiously the possibilities of *indirect* interaction or intermediation through the use of second-level communicators.

Transferring Effects to Related Topics

Effect-transferral by listeners is another common consequence of speech communication, an outcome often not anticipated and planned for by the speaker. The fact that you may categorize a topic or a concept or a belief in a given way does not mean that your listener will categorize it similarly. He may see it differently or he may not; he may see possibilities and make associations that you may not. Furthermore, we need to remind ourselves constantly that *a concept that fits into one category may also fit very well into others*. Suppose that, as a result of your communicating a speech message, you change your listeners' belief in or evaluation of a certain concept. The influence exerted by your message will not necessarily limit itself to that one concept. Some influence of the same message may transfer to *other* concepts in the same category, even though the secondary influences are not directly related to the specific purpose of your speech. When a listener's beliefs and values for one concept or topic "rub off on" some other related or seemingly unrelated concept or topic, the result is described as the *transfer effect*. Although you may seldom use the term, you are no doubt familiar with the experience.

Suppose we view a film presentation which moves us to feel very favorable toward a certain candidate for a political office. That positive effect may, in turn, cause us to feel more positively disposed toward other candidates who represent the same political party. This can happen even though the other candidates have not been considered overtly or directly in the message we have seen and heard.

You are perhaps even more familiar with these transfer effects as they occur in the stereotyping of individuals and groups. If we hear one bearded student advocate violence, we may generalize and become suspicious of other bearded students we see. As another example, some research done by this author showed that a speech arguing against federal aid to health and education had significant transfer effects to such related but unmentioned topics as federal aid to farms and federal public-works programs.[7]

In speech communication, transfer effects often are unforeseen and unforeseeable. At the time of the communicative exchange, such effects may be submerged and extremely difficult to detect, only to surface later in the form of a noticeably different consequence. In this sense, transfer effects may have reverberations and *extensions*. An illustration may help to clarify this. Suppose that you are arguing a special case on your campus and you feel that the particular circumstances are such as to call for *special* and *unusual* action. In your view, these circumstances demand that temporary, special curricular considerations be made for black students, or perhaps for veterans. If the actions you are calling for are indeed unique and special, or if you intend them to be only temporary, you had better spell out very clearly for your listeners the singular nature of your proposal. Otherwise, transfer effects may occur, and your listeners—inadvertently misled as to your true position—may generalize your proposition as applicable to *all* students on campus and for an unlimited time.

Further Effects of Speech Communication: Influencing Behavior and Thought Patterns

As we have seen, one of the most significant effects of speech communication is the influence which the speaker, in one way or another, exerts upon the listener. Indeed, as we explained in Chapter 4, since the basic, encompassing *purpose* of the speaking agent is to influence the listening agent, we must conclude that —overall—in order to succeed, he will have to cause his hearer to "behave" and "think" as he wants him to.

We would go further. As a speaker, clearly, you will not succeed in your purpose—any purpose—unless you are able to alter and adjust in some way and to some extent the *behavioral patterns* and the *patterns of thinking* of those to whom you are directing your message.

[7] Thomas M. Scheidel, "An Exploratory Study of the Relationships Between Certain Organismic Variables and Response to a Persuasive Speech," unpublished Ph.D. dissertation (University of Washington, 1958).

STUDY PROBE 9
Recognizing Thought Patterns That You Use

Outline, briefly, four or five of the "thought patterns" that you customarily employ in organizing and expressing your ideas and attitudes to others.

To what extent, if any, have you observed the use of such patterning in others: your mother, father, brother or sister, an uncle, a minister, a teacher you've admired, or someone else with whom you have been in comparatively close and frequent contact?

Observe the speech behaviors of other speakers in one-to-several or one-to-many situations, and describe any idiosyncratic thought patterns which call unfavorable attention to themselves and which could, conceivably, interfere with effective interaction between or among the respective agents.

Affecting patterns of thought and behavior has far-reaching import both upon the speaker and upon those he is attempting to influence. Like many of the other effects we have discussed, the ways in which and the degree to which listeners' "thinking" and "behaving" patterns are modified ordinarily are not immediately discernible. Nevertheless, the interaction, whether fertile or futile, will have affected in some way and over some period of time the manner of our physical and mental functioning in contemplated or occurring speech communication events. The influence which a speaking agent exerts upon the *thought patterns* and *behavior patterns* of listening agents has vast significance for and impact upon successful, productive speech interaction. In the ensuing pages we will endeavor to explore that significance in some detail and to identify some of the more evident and ascertainable patterns. Because, for the most part, the ways in which speakers modify listeners' *physical behaviors* are usually more readily discernible, let us look first at those.

Modifying Physical Communicative Behaviors

Imitative, Associative Factors

In a physical behavioral sense, our vocalities and gestures are largely imitative, at least at first. In no small part we acquire our "ways" of speaking from our forebears, respected relatives, peers, teachers, and churchmen. As listeners and consumers of communication we tend to identify with those we respect or admire. And we do this from a very early age. We try, especially when we are very young, to emulate our elders and to model our behaviors—including our speech behaviors—after them. Recognizing this, when we are older we try to be "model" parents, to "set a good example." Citizens in a dynamic society, no less aware of this tendency to identify and emulate, see in it both a responsibility and an opportunity when they endeavor to set good examples in interpersonal interaction.

When you observe the presentation of a speech, either in class or in your community, you are likely to see with some frequency speakers who copy some of the gestures, vocal emphases, intonations, and even some of the transitional physical movements typically used by current politicians and television heroes. In your classrooms this term you doubtless have some fine teachers who—very probably—are still posturing and clearing their throats in the manner of some of *their* fine old teachers. The effects of their speaking patterns have been transmitted "from generation unto generation."

Frequently, all of us identify with, emulate, and imitate others—sometimes intentionally, but more often unwittingly. Many of these vocal-gestural behaviors we test out in terms of our self-images and also for their appropriateness and effectiveness with other listener/watchers. Some of these behavior patterns we discard rather quickly; others we may try to retain, possibly in modified form, as an integral part of our personality and speaking style. We can further refine and enrich our presentational style by listening to good vocal models on the radio and in recordings and by observing skillful communicative behavior evidenced on the rostrum, the stage, the motion picture screen, and the television tube. Needless to say, particularly in these days when we are being electronically cannonaded with all kinds of messages, we need as never before to sharpen our sense of discrimination between good and not so good examples.

Speech Skills as Patterned Behavior

When we practice to learn or perfect a speech skill, we are of course trying to assimilate desirable vocal, gestural, or "physical control" patterns. Typically, we are motivated—from within or without—to identify the vocal pattern of a certain phonetic sound or the meaningful intonation of a word in a line of poetry or the physical configuration of a useful gesture of reinforcement or illumination. Then we *repeat* it. We practice or rehearse the pattern over and over, assimilating it, perfecting it, making it a habit.

In Chapter 10 we will be commenting more fully on the necessity for and the importance of oral practice for public communication. Here, we submit that the *components* of such practice are:

1. *Identifying* potentially effective vocal/gestural behavior patterns as we observe them in various speech contexts.
2. *Experimenting* with these patterns in order to determine their probable usefulness and appropriateness for the particular impending speech communication event.
3. *Selecting* those patterns which are most suitable.
4. *Integrating* such patterns with the message content.
5. *Repeating* them until the desired degree of pattern-assimilation has been achieved.

The importance and permanence of such assimilation and the extent to which we will allow it to shape our vocal/gestural behaviors will be influenced, certainly in part, by the *ethos,* charisma, and status-roles of the model speakers with whom we have identified and whose communicative skills we are attempting to emulate.

In one way or another, then, subsconsciously or by intent, we are continuously being influenced by the vocal and physical behavioral patterns of other agents. And unless they have adopted communicative patterns that are visually or audibly so idiosyncratic as to call unfavorable attention to themselves or otherwise interfere with desired and desirable oral interaction, the total cumulative *effect* can be positive and beneficial.

Modifying Thought-Process Patterns in the Listener

Much more important, perhaps, but certainly less immediately discernible, are the effects which the speaker creates in the *thought-patterning* of his listeners—

upon their "habits of thinking." We are not referring here to the propositional substance of the speaker's message, although that may be of much greater immediate importance to him and his hearers. What we wish to emphasize is that just as listeners "take on" some of the vocal/gestural behavior patterns of the speaker, they also assimilate—less consciously, but just as surely—some of the *mental-process patterns* of speakers whom they admire or respect.

The attentive listener may learn not only the substantive content contained in a communication act, but he may also learn the *form* and *modality* of that act: the way in which the information is organized and structured for presentation. As hearers, if we sense that the speaker's thought-process patterns are useful modes for organizing and giving utterance to our own ideas and thoughts, we will tend to take on these patterns and make them an integral part of our own. If we repeatedly hear from a respected authority-source or much admired person a particular ideational/formational pattern or thought-structure, or what appears to us to be a viable "approach" pattern for developing and arranging verbal positions and propositions, this design will begin to impinge upon our minds. This *schema* will begin to impress itself upon our ways of thinking and relating our ideas as we prepare, in turn, to communicate them to others. We will employ the pattern in our own idea making; we will tend to speak with that pattern. Furthermore, this pattern-extensionality will play a crucial role once a speech act has been initiated and when agents perceive one another in an interactive context.

Thought-Structuring and Thought-Utterance: Desirabilities and Dangers

The consequences of thought-modification patterns can be far reaching and long lasting. The transferral and assimilation of concept-structuring and thought-patterning are both necessary and, usually, highly desirable in a society which is trying to advance, to make progress, through means of more reasoned and reasonable interaction.

Familial, educational, religious, political, and economic systems (to name only a few) are deeply rooted in and committed to the extension of thought-creational and thought-presentational patterns. Indeed, almost any system may be said to be a complex of patterned "approaches to thinking." The very effectiveness of societal systems depends to an impressive extent on the communicative ability of speaking agents: parents, teachers, ministers, politicians, industrialists, labor leaders, economists, public relations people, news commentators, and the like. These and similar agents effect an efficient, enduring, and thorough-going transferral and embedment of particular sets of thought-patterns in the young and the not-so-young. *Teaching* is a usefully descriptive word in this connection. *Indoctrination,* because of its authoritarian connotation, is perhaps less so. *Brainwashing* is, of course, much farther away on the continuum; but a continuum it is, nevertheless.

When we discussed the ways in which a speaker may modify the physical communicative behaviors of others, we pointed out that the factors of *imitation, emulation, assimilation,* and *sensitive discrimination* play an important role. These same factors are also operant in the modification of listeners' thought-process patterns. When we emulate thought patterns that are clear, fair, and reasonably objective (no easy task), the encompassing and enduring results tend to be positive and desirable. But when and if we carelessly or indiscriminately take on faulty, incomplete, or self-deluding ways of producing our thinking and communicating its essence, the possibilities of constructive, genuinely rewarding interaction with other agents can be seriously jeopardized or even destroyed.

Few would deny the obvious dangers to us and to those things we value if, as listeners and speakers, we limit the range of our perceptual, thought, and linguistic orientations. And we stand in danger if we structure the outputs of our thinking in such a way as to distort our personal value systems, if we resort to rhetorical devices to conceal our real motives or to create self-serving ends exclusively. To be imitative—up to a point—is both desirable and necessary, but we must bring more to our proposition or our reception of a speech-idea. To fail to do so fails to take into account the importance of *self* as a thinking, discriminating "process" selector. As we noted when we examined the concept of Belief-Evaluation clusters (pages 117–118), how we *feel* about something—our attitude toward it—is heavily influenced by the beliefs we hold and the relative importances and urgencies we accord to those beliefs.

Within broad limits, at least, we may say that the value we attach to an idea, concept, person, or object is largely the product of "how we think about" it. The implications of this and our responsibilities in regard to the recognition and use of clear and rational patterns of thinking cannot be overstated. The manner of people we emulate and our sensitivity to *their* patterns of thinking and their motivations become overriding concerns. It is to sharpen our sense of discrimination in these matters that we pursue the discussion that follows.

Propositions, Premises, and Patterns: Definitions and Examples

From time to time, in the context of this and preceding chapters we have used the terms *proposition, premise,* and *thought pattern.* As a result, probably you have at least inferred meanings for them. As we move ahead in our considerations, however, in this and ensuing chapters we will be using these terms with increasing frequency. We should, therefore, establish some specific, workable definitions for them.

Some Definitions

By *proposition* we mean, mainly, a statement of a communicator's viewpoint or position. It is what he wants other persons to understand and/or agree with. Verbally, it is the act of presenting or proposing an idea or notion to be considered by listeners—something which the proposer hopes they will accept, agree to, or do. In a strict rhetorical sense, a proposition is a statement or a problem offered as a basis for discussion or argument—a contention presented for affirmation or rejection by others.

A *premise* is a declarative statement or sentence, usually, of something assumed or taken for granted—at least at the start of an oral interchange. It is a presupposition or generally accepted stipulation which, we may assume, will lead to a *conclusion* of some kind. In the sense that a proposition may have been "antecedently" or presupposedly proved, it may also be a premise. The assertion that "All men are created equal" may be both premise and proposition. We shall take a more searching look at this matter of premises when we examine Aristotle's syllogism in the ensuing chapter, pages 180–184. For our immediate purposes, however, the foregoing definition should suffice.

The subject of our immediate focus, *thought pattern,* we may describe as a repetitively established, identifiable, and sequentially structured verbal output which is observable by and comprehensible to other agents in a communicative interaction. Obviously, insofar as the speaking agent himself is concerned, as listeners or observers we do not know whether a thought exists or is in the making until and unless a verbal, audible configuration of some kind comes to our attention, or is made observable by the speaker for us. The speaker *may* be thinking, either in language symbols or in nonlanguage elements of some kind. But unless and until he makes an "intelligible" utterance which we can detect and interpret through sensory channels, we cannot know what his thinking is or how he may be patterning it.

Our definition of thought pattern, then—loosely formulated and not necessarily accurate in all scientific respects—is *an established design or verbal configuration used for communicating orally certain portions of the thought-substance of the speaker to the comprehension of the listener.* The pattern is the rhetorical *form* in which the speaking agent states his premises; it is the "practical" *plan* by which he advances his propositions.

Again, as we shall emphasize in Chapters 6 and 7, much is yet to be discovered and understood about human thinking and the thought-creation process. A thoroughgoing examination of what is known cannot be contained in a book of this size; nor is it necessary in a volume of this nature. We can be certain that human thought and the processes which originate and generate it are extremely complex and that even the simplest act, verbal or otherwise, requires a uniquely intricate and as yet little-understood physiological/neurological/psychological involvement.

Thought-Process Pattern: An Example

As a detailed example of this involvement, consider the simple act of putting on your shoes and tying the laces. As an adult, you would probably say that the task of putting on one's shoes is so easy that you scarcely need to think about it at all: it's automatic.

But it was not always so. Try to recall when, as a two- or three-year-old child, you tried for the first time to put on your shoes and tie them. Or, better still, imagine yourself an older brother or sister or a parent trying to communicate the nature of the task to a youngster and to guide his "thinking" in such a pattern as to enable him to accomplish the task. Assume that he has never, for some reason, *seen* anyone else put on shoes. Also, you cannot *show* him; you must *tell* him how to "think through" and perform this very elementary act.

Ultimately, after much trial and error, you would succeed in guiding the child to develop a physiological/neurological/psychological pathway which, if he retravels it carefully and often enough, will become a pattern for "Putting on Shoes with Laces." And if you were to "program" the process, it would look something like the diagram shown on the following page.

This "thinking through" process, if successful and if repeated often enough so that the child can perform the task without pausing to ponder its constituent steps, will serve to exemplify what we mean by *thought pattern.*

Putting on Shoes with Laces[8]

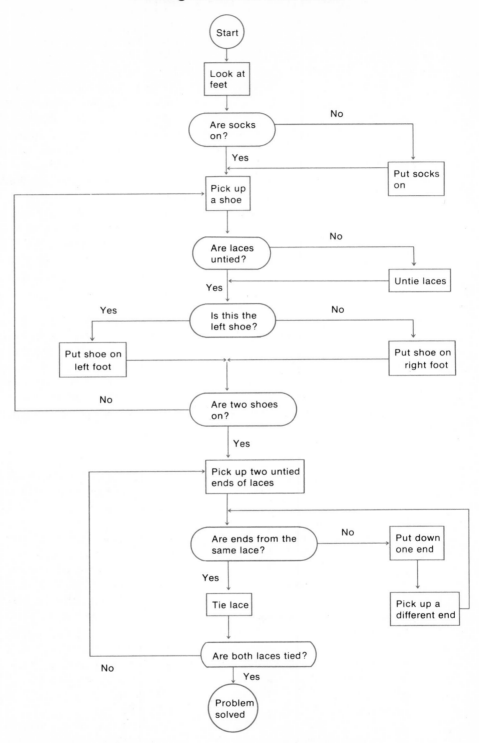

[8] Figure 9–1 "Putting on shoes with laces" by S. M. Dowdy, *Mathematics: Art and Science*. Copyright © 1971 by John Wiley & Sons, Inc. Reprinted by their permission.

Some Patterned Approaches to Thought-Structuring and Thought-Utterance

To attempt to catalog anything like a complete list of thought patterns, even for one individual, would of course be impossible. Hence we will try only to touch very briefly upon a few *categories* which in our society have come to be recognized and recognizable, namely:

1. Linguistic/Syntactic Patterns.
2. Intonational/Emotional Patterns.
3. Limited Focusing Patterns.
4. Associative/Transferential Patterns.
5. Causative/Inferential/Assumptive Patterns.

As we move into our specific consideration of these patterns, the difficulties of trying to classify them with any degree of exclusivity must become readily apparent. Admittedly, our ways of thinking and of giving voice and language to that thinking are not neatly classifiable and separable. They overlap, one upon the other; elements of one pattern may combine with the elements of another or of several others; at times, one pattern may even "work against" some other pattern. In fact, it is conceivable that the effects of one pattern may negate or cancel the effects of another. Obviously, much experimentation and study of human thought patterns, their presentation, and functioning remain to be done. However, because of the significant effects they create in communicative agents prior to, during, and following interaction, they merit our scrutiny and should prove of interest and value as we endeavor to enlarge our view of how human beings think and behave when they try to communicate.

Linguistic/Syntactic Patterns

As we have emphasized heretofore, thinking and speaking are not identical; and they are not necessarily sequential: one does not have to precede the other. Each is a significant *part* of the other, but the two processes are far from being synonymous. Nor, within the reasoning processes are *language* and *thought* identical—a subject which we will explore at much greater depth in the next chapter. But, even so, the fact remains that we do use such linguistic elements as syllables, words, phrases, clauses, etc., and that we do arrange them in various syntactical patterns and formations in order to create the human expression which informs and influences us as we speak or listen. The way we structure, phrase, and utter a sentence is certainly a clear reflection of "the way we are thinking"; it reveals a particular thought pattern.

If, as in some languages, for example, the language of our society called for placing verbs at the ends of sentences, we would nearly always *hear* that syntactical sequence, and we would become habituated to *using* it. And, characteristically, in our modes of reasoning and in the expression of our thinking we would tend to employ that pattern when interacting with others. Some of our thought-formational patterns and the ways in which we voice them are necessarily imitative of our society as a whole. Moreover, as we shall see, this patterning principle extends itself to other aspects of our thinking, vocalizing, and decision making.

The few linguistic/syntactic patterns which we survey fleetingly here are essentially *compositional.* And when we compose our thoughts and convert them into communication, *clarity* becomes paramount. To communicate clearly we ought to say what we suppose or hope or believe that we are saying. This necessitates the use of language and syntactic forms which, in turn, requires that intelligible utterance must deal—as we indicated above—with meaningful units of speech: syllables, suffixes, prefixes, words, phrases, sentences, and paragraphs. It is by this means that the people within a society *understand:* they attach to these linguistic units and their arrangement a certain commonality of meaning. We try, therefore, to organize these units syntactically to compose the thoughts we wish to utter.

Linguistic limitations being what they are, an utterance can never be complete in the full sense of the word. But we can hope that it will be sufficiently composed to be recognizable as a "whole" statement, proposition, or premise. As the whole becomes enlarged by the addition of new ideas, concepts, etc., the speaker will necessarily have to drop out certain other elements of meaning. The premise or claim or whatever may grow more and more complex and become increasingly generalized and abstract. Usually, because of the way these processes function in a communicative context, we recognize the inevitability of losing something. And so we do not expect a speaker to be able to "say it all." We "know" what is meant; we fill in the gaps. When we consider categories and language in Chapter 6, we shall see more fully how and why this happens.

In composing a generalized and abstracted thought-utterance, however, we must not mistake the whole for the part or the part for the whole. We cannot, for instance, affirm of the whole that which holds true of one or more of the parts taken separately. We can categorize and pigeonhole only up to a certain point if we wish our statements to have much validity. After that, we face the danger of having to abstract *too much,* of stereotyping people, places, objects, ideas, etc. As we transform our thought patterns into orality, we must remember that a few specific cases or instances cannot "type" all members of a race, a religion, a nationality, an occupation, or a political party.

If we cannot affirm of an entire entity that which holds true of one or more of the parts when taken separately, conversely, we are in error if we say that what is true of the whole is necessarily true of each of the parts if considered independently or separately. Suppose Congress has voted a tax increase, and Mr. X is a congressman. Obviously, we cannot correctly conclude that Congressman X voted for the tax increase. The measure might, in fact, have passed despite his zealous opposition. In developing and using a compositional pattern of this kind, we will need to be sure that we are not "tarring all with the same brush."

Not far removed from this thought pattern is that of the *sweeping, unsupported assertion.* While the abstractive nature of language often compels us to speak in generalities, we must exercise caution that our statements do not become so broad and so general as to become meaningless. Examine critically the statement, "The true patriot will hold high those democratic ideals that bring pride to the hearts of every American mother." Note in particular the very high level of abstraction in the terms "true," "patriot," "democratic," "ideals," "pride," and "every American mother." If you try to arrive at essential, criterial subcategories for each, you will quickly realize that the assertion has become so overloaded with broadly inclusive generalities as to crowd out almost any specificity. Any real *specific meaning* has been supplanted by verbal "grandeur." For this kind of statement to create a meaningful effect, the speaker would have to explain, support, and enrich it with examples, specific illustrations, special connotations, and the like. He would have to take into account the linguistic and experiential commonalities of his hearers by injecting *specificity*. But string together a succession of such sweeping and unsupported assertions, and meaning tends to become lost in the empty thunder and roll of verbosity.

Another pattern for creating and presenting thought-substance involves selecting and drawing listener attention to a *single, special case* and then generalizing from this isolated and often atypical instance. In this manner, the speaker may try to create his effect by linking a number of discrete, actually separate, and often unrelated instances together, allowing listeners to infer or suppose a connection among them. By looking only at special cases and implying a general conclusion therefrom, a speaker may impose a kind of mental "gaposis" pattern in the thinking of the listener; and this listener—when he becomes speaker—may try to impose the same pattern upon the thinking of others. This kind of rhetorical card-stacking can of course produce inaccurate or even biased conclusions. This is a pattern which most of us, no doubt, employ from time to time. We generalize from insufficient evidence, saying in effect: This particular circumstance is true; therefore all of the other possible circumstances must also be true. In legal parlance, we are thus "convicting on insufficient circumstantial evidence."

Among the numerous linguistic/syntactic patterns we may also observe those of a *transpositional* nature. A speaker, in creating his effects, will of course want to use variety, to state a point differently, to "change things around" a bit. While this is greatly to be desired, there are pitfalls to be avoided in such patterning. For example, in changing the statement of a proposition from an affirmative to a negative form, we must be careful not to change or distort our meaning. "All university students are eligible for reduced bus fares," can be changed to "No university students are ineligible for reduced bus fares" and our intended meaning will remain more or less intact. But if we change the proposition to "No non-university students are eligible for reduced bus fares," we have obverted the meaning.

Similarly, if we wish to transpose the subject and the predicate of a proposition-statement, we should be aware that such conversion may alter the meaning we intend. "All naked apes are animals" obviously does not mean the same thing as "All animals are naked apes."

Relying, as we are compelled to do, upon the often complex symbolism inherent in language labels, we can expect numerous misunderstandings and errors to occur as we try to communicate meanings to others. The *obversion* and *conversion* patterns cited above are instances of this problem; and to them we might add a third: *ambiguity*. If our modes of thinking and speaking are vague or carelessly formed, ambiguous grammatical patterns are likely to result. To demonstrate this point, devise a sentence or two in which you deliberately attempt to confuse a listener by causing him to derive *two* possible meanings from your words. As a sample statement consider the oft quoted "The Duke yet lives that Henry shall depose." Or the simpler "Twice two plus three." This could yield either *seven* or *ten*. In both samples, the confusion arises from the grammatical patterning rather than from the choice of words.

To sum up this brief and admittedly far from complete survey of what we have termed linguistic/syntactic patterns, we have noted those involving *composition, division, abstraction* or *generalization, transposition,* and *ambiguity*.

Intonational/Emotional Patterns

Whereas most of the linguistic/syntactic patterns bear centrally upon the *clarity* of a communication, many of the intonational/emotional patterns seem to emerge from what Martin Scheerer calls the "cognitive-emotional-motivational matrix" characteristic of human beings.[9] With considerable frequency we are prompted from within to "express our true feelings" about something. Sometimes we feel called upon to do this; more often, probably, we cannot avoid doing it. In either type of circumstance, we rely heavily upon *emotional coloring* and *vocalized accent* to pattern and project our meanings. In terms of speaker output, these patterns are most apparent in stressful moments, in situations characterized by aroused feelings. And very often these patterns reveal our true reactions and responses to other agents and certain contexts. By whatever name—accent, intonation, or emphasis—these are the types of patterns which most frequently impair or impede communicative interaction. These are the patterns that creep into the voice despite our best efforts to conceal them.

By stressing or accenting a particular syllable, word, or phrase, the speaker can strongly influence the listener's interpretation of a given remark. Consider the Commandment, "Thou shalt not bear false witness against thy neighbor." If emphasis is given the final word, the hearer may interpret the statement to justify bearing false witness against everybody *except* one's neighbor. A speaker need not misquote the words of a source to create an erroneous impression; he need only change the vocal stress to lead a listener to a flawed conclusion. Reread Marc Antony's oration at the bier of the assassinated Caesar and see again the powerful rhetorical effect created by the repetition of the simple statement ". . . Brutus is an honorable man," uttered each time with a slightly changed stress or inflection.

Earlier we spoke of generalizing from a specific, single case. When we accent our communications emotionally, we may carry the generalization to an even higher level and reduce the essence of the instance to a single word. This is sometimes called a *labeling* or *name-calling* pattern. The word may, of course, work along a continuum and be applied to a whole class of ideas, objects, concepts, or entities; and the inflectional toning may also move along an emotional-motivational continuum. The label "doting mother" may range in meaning from a kind and loving and generous parent to a thoroughly domineering and tyrannically despicable dowager. The intonational coloring and the context in which the label is used creates the effect, and the pattern works its influence upon both speaker and listener from early childhood through adulthood and old age. Very early, human beings discover that a lone word may be used to invoke warmth and affection, to engender scorn or disdain, to put down, and even destroy. We know that a word may damn or endear, depending upon the intonation with which we utter it. The pattern is easily used; it is economical; it is facilely imposed and quickly learned. It has its advantages—but it has inherent dangers; and we cannot escape its effect, either as listening agents or as speakers. One word of derogation usually calls forth another from your opponent; and when the substance of a communicative endeavor is reduced to a "you're-another" status, productive interaction goes out the window.

[9] Martin Scheerer, "Cognitive Theory," *The Handbook of Social Psychology,* 1st ed., ed. Gardner Lindzey (Reading, Mass.: Addison-Wesley Publishing Co., Inc., 1954), v. I, p. 123. This "matrix" will be considered at greater length in Chapter 6, pp. 192–193.

Limited Focusing Patterns

From the opening pages of this book we have underscored the multidimensionality and interrelatedness of the agent and the message he communicates. In the behavioral, process view, certainly we ought not to separate the message from the source. But, despite our best intentions, we sometimes try to do just this. Sometimes, because of status differences, Belief-Evaluation clusters, and the limitations of just "plain human nature," we employ patterns of thinking and speaking which restrict the focus we bring to the communicative context. As we have seen, a certain amount of this selecting and focusing is both necessary and desirable. However, on occasion, most of us have probably used a limited focus pattern to assail a message maker and have chosen to ignore the content of his message. If we are opposed to a proposition advanced by another, but feel that we are unable to develop a sufficiently strong counterproposition, we may be tempted to center our verbal fire on the personality of the proposer rather than on his ideas. The Romans had a phrase for this, *argumentum ad hominem;* and they used it to describe a verbal appeal against or an attack upon the character, principles, or beliefs of another person rather than on the subject matter of the controversy. In our own era you have probably observed a speaker or commentator who, by attacking a man's past actions, tried to diminish that man's credibility on a current issue while never mentioning the issue as such.

We may see a variation of this pattern in a situation in which a speaker strives to create his effect by selecting *out of context* an act or statement made by an opponent in some other circumstance and at some earlier date. In this pattern we can detect an element of division, too, in that the speaker endeavors to advance a single part of an earlier communication as if it were the whole of the matter.

Although you may share Scheerer's view that all human behavior, including communicative behavior, is inextricably interwoven in a cognitive-emotional-motivational matrix, you have surely observed that speakers sometimes pattern their messages in such a way as to focus primarily upon the passions and prejudices of listeners. In so doing, they are able to avoid the central issue as such. A politician may, for instance, focus on our love of country and appeal to our "patriotism" to accept his proposed action because he is fairly certain that we would not accept it on the basis of its fiscal soundness or social potentialities. When a speaker asks us to pay higher taxes in our community, he will probably be more persuasive if he tells us that we "owe it to our children" to build bigger and more costly school buildings. If an ecologist warns us that within twenty years we will have buried ourselves under our own garbage unless we act on his proposal to prevent such an occurrence, our fears may move us to take favorable action now.

Another prevalent pattern involving limited focusing we might describe as an *either/or dichotomy* or a *single/multiple orientation.* In speaking, as in life, we are frequently faced with a clear-cut choice between two alternatives—and *only* two. We must say either "yes" or "no"; "I will" or "I will not"; "I can" or "I cannot." Even if we can discern a continuum in a given case, we have to assign an arbitrary term to each end of that continuum. We may conjecture that the tendency arises from our need to balance our cognitions. But whatever the reasons, we do tend to think in dualities, in opposites: rich *or* poor, fair *or* unfair, clean *or* dirty, black *or* white, tall *or* short, man *or* woman. In many circumstances, obviously, such a pattern is both desirable and necessary.

There are also many other circumstances, however, in which it is to our great advantage to discover, consider, and weigh the multiple choices available to us before making a final decision or taking a conclusive action. In general, it seems fair to assert that the more knowledge and the more experience we have, the more likely we are to discern viable options. This is a subject to which we shall devote full attention in Chapter 7 when we talk about communicatively induced decision making. At this juncture, it will benefit our considerations to take special note of the requirements of *understanding, patience,* and *tolerance* upon which the decision-making process must be predicated. Much of the comment and discussion we hear on social issues is necessarily presented in a problem-solution pattern. The speaking agent identifies, describes, and amplifies the problem as he sees it, and then presents his solution. This pattern is, of course, employed often in public speaking and small group discussion settings. Quite generally, it is a useful one, but one which usually must be structured sequentially and given broad focus if it is to achieve maximally productive re-sults. A number of steps are involved, and we must take time to make the careful analysis needed to identify the problem, locate its symptoms, discern its prob-able causes, and develop some possible alternative solutions.

However, if we feel hurried, impatient, angry, frustrated, or fatigued, we may be strongly tempted to bypass some or all of the required steps. If we yield to this inclination, we limit our focus: We employ an *ellipsis* of the pattern —one which moves too quickly and too directly from the "problem" stage to the "solution" stage of the decision-making process, leaving out some of the highly useful and essential intermediate steps; thus:

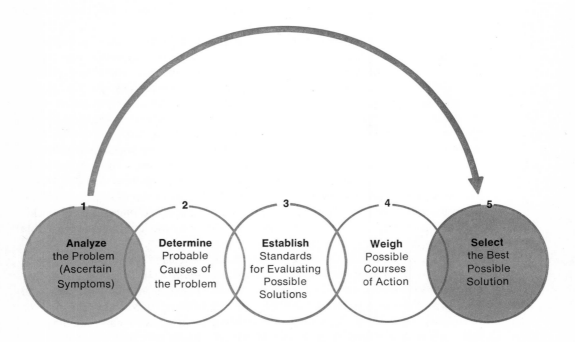

As the diagram suggests, if we hear "problem," our immediate response-reaction should not be "solution," but rather "analysis," "probable causes," "alternative courses of action," and—*finally*—"best solution." We are urging against an elliptical pattern of thinking which may, over time, create an intolerance of and an impatience with sound decision making.

The single/multiple orientation patterns present problems for us as speakers and as listeners when we confuse or ignore the set of circumstances for which a given pattern might prove the most appropriate and productive. If we choose the either/or pattern when we are analyzing a proposition fraught with multiple choices, we are obviously short-circuiting the thought-creational and thought-expression processes. If, on the other hand, we elect to impose a multiple-choice orientation when such options do not exist, indecisiveness and unwarranted delay may frustrate communicative interaction.

As students and practitioners of speech communication, we must recognize that some beliefs, propositions, etc., can be seen as "yes" or "no," "true" or "false," "worthy" or "worthless"; and, at the same time, we must realize that other beliefs, propositions, etc., *cannot* be so viewed. Moreover, we need to be aware that quite probably we will not facilitate communication if we pattern our thought-expression on a take-it-or-leave-it or an all-or-nothing basis. To do so rules out *compromise*—often an indispensable ingredient of successful and conclusive interaction. In sum, if we hear the disjunctive "either . . . or" with great frequency, our own patterns of thinking may tend to become largely two-valued. We may then fail to detect the subtle and significant shades of difference or degree along a continuum. The main point that we need to hold in our minds about all of this is that if a problem has in fact only two possible solutions, we ought to recognize that fact and act accordingly; if the multiple-choice or continuum pattern is likely to be more useful and accurate for propositions we want to analyze and/or advance in speech communication settings, we ought to recognize that fact and—again—behave accordingly.

Associative/Transferential Patterns

Although we may assert our independence often and insistently, we are in fact quite *dependent* upon our fellow beings for support, reinforcement, and concurrence. Additionally, the more powerful, influential, and prestigious those beings are, the more likely we are to want to *associate* ourselves, our ideas, and our positions with them. By such association, we hope, some of their power, influence, and prestige will automatically *transfer* itself to us. As a result, many of our patterns of thinking and speaking are associative and transferential, especially as they may involve an *authority* figure or an authoritative concept of some kind. Generally, we are inclined to respect or at least defer to someone who has more wisdom, experience, or special knowledge than we have.

Authority and our deference to it play a major role in our society. Indeed, authority is a key structural force; without it, we would not have the society we have. At the same time, we may chafe at the constraints it places upon us. A paradox of human nature is that we tend to resent authority—except when it is "on our side." When a personage or an institution or a law or a custom or a tradition—in a word, an authority—reflects or concurs with our view of the world, we tend to *invoke* that authority. When, in an interaction with another person, we find ourselves faced with the possible acceptance of a decision which we see as going against our preferences or presumed best interests, we look around for help; we try to appeal to a "higher authority." This particular pattern of behavior is, for example, basic to our entire legal system. But all of us have experienced and employed numerous variations of the pattern, from childhood onward. How many times, for instance, have you heard such actual or implied appeals to authority as "I'll tell Papa on you!" "Just wait till Mama sees what you've done!" "My big brother is bigger than your big brother!" "Just wait until your father comes home!" "Call the police!" "I'll take you to court!" Obviously, patterns of associating our beliefs and evaluations and positions with an authority pervades much of human activity, including communication.

Many speakers quote Jefferson and Lincoln and heroes from all fields, attempting thereby to transfer a degree of status to their case or cause. By those in the advertising field, to name but one, we are incessantly being reminded that some of the prestige and public admiration attributed to a motion picture star, a television personality, or a successful athlete may extend itself to the product or the claim of a particular manufacturer.

Associative/transferential patterns have numerous variations and may work in many directions. Not only is it possible to improve the status of a proposition or elevate a cause by authority-association or transfer; it is also possible to reverse the effect by using the pattern to assail an opponent's position or to detract from his cause. We have heard the comment that a man is known by the company he keeps; and, to a certain extent, he is also known by the company that keeps *him*. In almost any political campaign, for instance, there will be situations in which one candidate will denounce the opposing candidate as being "the Mayor's man" or "the Governor's handpicked choice." The speaker thus makes the strong implication that if the policies of the mayor or the governor are in any way flawed or suspect (and in politics they are often claimed to be both), then the selfsame flaws and suspicions have necessarily "rubbed off" on the candidate of their choice.

This kind of guilt-by-reason-of-association pattern is often combined with devastating intonational coloring, and we may detect in it also some elements of the labeling and over-generalizing patterns mentioned earlier. In certain circumstances, to damn by association may be justifiable and necessary. Much oftener, we would hope, the associative/transferential patterns will be employed in a more positive and discriminative manner.

There is another problem of which we must be aware when invoking authority or employing a pattern of testimonial transfer. *Who* is, in fact, the authority in the following expressions:

"They say . . ."

"A highly reliable source, who refused to be identified, intimated today that . . ."

"According to informed government sources . . ."

"The silent majority feels . . ."

"In the interests of the common man . . ." (Has any man ever allowed himself to be so identified?)

When we hear such expressions, or such phrases as "The Pepsi Generation" or "peer group" cited as an authority-source, we should be aware of the *identity gap* inherent in those patterns. We should not unwittingly play the game of Follow the Faceless Leader. If we hear many claims documented by the equivalent of "They say," we may well come to a point where we eventually see "they" as an authoritative mystique, and stop questioning sources.

Obviously, when we associate our communications with an authority-source or when we try to transfer to our own position or view the power, prestige, and/or testimony of another, we take on certain rhetorical and ethical obligations. Among other concerns, we are obliged to *identify the authority accurately.* If we restate or paraphrase his words, at the very least we must present them *correctly, fairly,* and *representatively:* we are not entitled to lift the quotation or the implied concurrence of the authority out of context. Nor, in arguing a case, should we substitute an appeal to an authority for a weighing of the facts at hand.

In sum, associative/transferential patterns, if used with discernment and the best judgment of which we are capable, can be very useful to communication. Later, in the culminating chapter of this text, where we consider achieving interaction with many others in a public communication context, we will urge that you employ authoritative testimony as one of the most influential and persuasive means by which to enlarge and support the main points of your message. The advice is, of course, applicable in speech communication settings of all kinds. The *ethos,* experience, expertise, and reputability of a well-chosen authority can lend considerable credence and attractiveness to a speaker's case or argument.

Causative/Inferential/Assumptive Patterns

Surrounded and enveloped as he is by the endless succession of stimuli crowding in upon him from every direction, it is amazing that any one, single human being is able to differentiate and objectify any one particular event from all of the many possible occurrences in his environment. The fact that he can do so is, of course, an essential element in his humanness. From first to last, in an effort to identify the world, man has been fascinated with his origin and his ultimate destination; and he tries over the span of his lifetime to bridge the expanse by continuously asking: *Why?* To *what* can I attribute this occurrence? What is the *cause?* Often, the asking takes the form of trying to distinguish—through observation and much trial-and-error experiencing—between those happenings which threaten his survival and those that seemingly sustain, nourish, and bring to him a sense of security and gratification.

And even if we cannot find very many answers to our "why's," we must go on forever seeking the "because's." It should not be surprising, therefore, that large numbers of our thinking and speaking patterns reflect the search for a *connection* between event and event, between what we presume to be a *cause* and what we suppose to be its *effect.* This chapter itself has, of course, been such a search—a seeking to discover some possible effects generated by asking "Why does man speak?" Indeed, as we shall see in the chapter to come, causal reasoning is one of the most important and at the same time one of the most complex means by which man seeks to relate himself to his universe and, in particular, to the formation, analysis, and listener-reception of those propositions, premises, and ideas shaping his communications.

Our causative/inferential/assumptive patterning reflects the fact that we like to believe that many events occur in a so-called "logical" sequence: one happening follows another in a certain natural and inevitable order of some kind. Of this sequence and order we tend to say—as did the Romans—"*After* it, therefore *because* of it." Actually, of course, the ancients recognized—as we do —that events are rarely, if ever, so simply and neatly arranged. But in the more primitive and supposedly less informed stages of civilization, men and women assumed that because one event *followed* another in time, the former must be the cause of the latter. When they could not discern or discover a cause, they invented a deity and attributed to him those events that seemed to occur mysteriously and without detectable cause. In our own time, thanks to a degree of increased knowledge of self and physical environment, we consider ourselves generally more sophisticated as to matters of causation.

Nevertheless, vestiges of primitive patterns remain today in our thinking and speaking processes. A very evident vestige can be seen in our superstitions:

> "If I walk under a ladder, I'll have 'bad luck.' "
> "I'd better be careful—today is Friday the thirteenth."
> "Don't allow a black cat to cross your path."
> "I always carry this charm with me—it brings me 'good luck.' "
> "Every time I've worn this old T-shirt, we've won the game."

In these and scores of similar statements, we are inferring a *sequential* relationship between a cause and an effect. The "ladder," "Friday the thirteenth," "black cat," "charm," and "old T-shirt" are all presumed causes of a possible or presumed *effect* that will supposedly occur at a later date.

Ordinarily, however, we are aware that merely because an event took place at an earlier point in time it did not necessarily "cause" one which took place subsequently. Usually, when we are trying to relate one or more events to some other event or events, we recognize that some of those events *may* be causes, that some of them *may* be effects, and that some of the events which—at first glance—might appear to bear a relationship to some other event or events may, in fact, be totally *unrelated*.

The task of drawing accurate and valid distinctions among the "eventful" stimuli impinging upon our consciousness is a major one confronting humankind. To help ensure accuracy and validity, human beings have devised certain patterns for thinking and speaking. These, in turn, facilitate the interhuman understanding which we have to have if we are to function intelligently. We are entitled to expect some kind of discernible connection or relationship (not necessarily a causative one) between the statements or assertions which a speaker makes. If one statement does not lead understandably to another or does not appear to relate to what has gone before, we say that we cannot "follow" his reasoning. If he asserts a conclusion that doesn't follow from his premises, we are puzzled by the *non sequitur.* Mr. X may in fact be a good husband, father, churchman, war hero, astronaut, and movie actor. But from these accomplishments alone—admirable though they may be—a speaker cannot claim that Mr. X will therefore make a good congressman. Nor should we as listeners be led to make that inference or assumption. The speaker is asking us to believe that because Mr. X has been successful in certain *past* activities or ventures he will, for this reason, be successful in his *next.* But, as we have said, there can be no reasonable guarantee that former events will in any way cause a certain future event: there is no causative relationship in the case of Mr. X.

In our insistent probing for causes of events, or of events as they may be interpreted for us by fellow communicators, the *question* is no doubt the most appropriate and valuable tool. As a pattern of thought-creation and thought-utterance, we encounter it and employ it with considerable frequency. Much of the progress made by man is attributable to the questions he asks and the ways in which he asks them. Intelligent inquiry is, as we know, fundamental to scientific experimentation and discovery of causes. It is basic also to much of the communicative interaction between persons and groups of persons.

If one of the aims of communication is to discover causes, listeners should direct frequent questions both to themselves and to speakers. Speakers should be prepared to encounter and answer these questions. They should be willing and able to respond with *directness, honesty, fairness,* and *good will.* To the extent that speakers are willing to meet questions "head on" they strengthen and extend their *ethos,* they firm up their rhetorical positions, and they enhance their reliability and reputability in the minds of their hearers.

The effective communicator cannot afford to ignore the questions inherent in his position; he dare not ignore or evade the central issue of his proposition if he wishes to gain acceptance of it. If his listeners sense that he is intentionally mistaking the point of a question or misrepresenting an opponent's point in order to make refutation easier, they are generally quick to lose confidence in the speaker and what he has to say. Sometimes, especially when we feel we are being backed into a verbal cul-de-sac and have no other way out, we may be tempted to dodge the question. But ordinarily it is a temptation we should work to avoid. The pattern of ignoring the question appears to be one employed with unfortunate frequency in many speech settings—especially those involving public communication. However, as you may have observed, the public is fairly quick to perceive evasiveness; and we may hope that there is truth in the claim: "You cannot fool all of the people all of the time."

The listening agent, too, has some obligations when he elects to formulate and ask questions. He should state them fairly, clearly, and without any attempt to mislead the speaker or other listeners as to the true intent of his inquiry. If you seek an honest answer, ask an honest question; do not assume that you know the answer before you ask the question. You may seek *confirmation* for an assumption, certainly; but do not try to entrap a fellow communicator by asking him a "loaded" question—a question which *assumes* the very thing you appear to be trying to prove. Such an assumption is obvious in the classic example, "Have you stopped beating your wife?" The questioner, by the pattern of his query, assumes the guilt of the alleged wife-beater while attempting to prove it. While our illustration is an old and humorously exaggerated one, it serves to demonstrate the manipulative effect of this assumptive pattern. As communicators, we will encounter such patterns from time to time; and when they are employed by a skilled phrase-maker, they can create a strong effect in listeners.

In these few preceding pages we have surveyed some of the further effects of speech communication, especially as those effects work to originate, modify, and otherwise influence the communicative behaviors and thought patterns of participants in an oral interaction. We have defined *thought pattern,* quite broadly and somewhat loosely, as a discernible and repetitively established verbal design or configuration used for communicating orally certain portions of the thought-substance of the speaker to the comprehension of the listener. We have then proceeded to examine briefly five generally recognized categories in which thought patterning seems to be discernible and identifiable, namely: (1) *linguistic/ syntactic patterns,* (2) *intonational/emotional patterns,* (3) *limited focusing patterns,* (4) *associative/transferential patterns,* and (5) *causative/inferential/ assumptive patterns.*

What we have set forth in these pages should at least help suggest the wide-ranging and lasting effects created in the minds of listeners by the speaking agent. We have emphasized that the *patterns* of our thoughts, as well as the contents, are learned and reinforced in our speech interaction with others. Generally, as communicators we have a tendency to focus primarily upon content. We are somewhat accustomed to questioning and evaluating message content: we want to understand it; we test it; we do not want to be deceived by it. What we have tried to stress here is that as listeners we should try with equal discernment and diligence to evaluate the form and configuration—and the *effects*—at work in the thinking and presentational modes of the speaking agent. One of our continuing concerns has been the effects of *pattern imposition* and *extension* in oral interchange, the necessity and desirability of such imposition and extension, and their potential dangers. At the very least, we hope we have opened up new possibilities while, at the same time, providing some useful means and standards for identifying thought formation and expression as we encounter and/or employ it in speech communication settings.

This section should serve also as a useful introduction and referential base from which to launch our exploration of some of the more advanced and complex forms of thinking and reasoning as those processes grow out of human sensing, perceiving, categorizing, and linguistic labeling—the substance of the chapter which ensues.

STUDY PROBE 10
*Recognizing Speakers' Influence upon Physical Behavior and
Thought Patterns of Listeners*

In this section we have singled out for brief analysis a number of the possible effects which a speaker, in trying to achieve his purpose, may create in the thought patterns and physical behavior patterns of listeners in speech communication contexts. Read several speeches in current issues of *Vital Speeches of the Day,* especially those touching upon contemporary social problems, and try to detect *additional* kinds of influences which a speaking agent may possibly exert upon the listening agents. Formulate a list and include influences and patterns of both a positive and negative nature.

Modifying Patterns of Thought and Behavior in the Speaker

Thus far, our concentration has centered primarily upon the effects of speech communication as they bear upon listeners. Now, what about the effects of speech communication upon the *speaker?* How might the speech act influence *him?* In our discussion of the ego-centered/intrapersonal speech purposes (Chapter 4, pages 92–106), we pointed out a number of these influences. The speech context was shown to be a setting in which development of a self-image is facilitated. That context also allows for a measure of self-satisfaction by providing a social setting where inner tensions may be reduced and personal creativity made evident. We saw, too, that speech can serve the speaker as a substitute for immediate, definite action when the latter is untimely, inappropriate, or impossible.

We should note now that the speech process can produce certain other effects in the speaker—effects which are unplanned for and which may have an indirect impact upon him. For one thing, the concept of feedback, as we have explained it, allows the listener to exert a measure of influence over the speaker. If, in adapting to his listeners, a speaker modifies his original position, and if that modification is rewarded by listeners' responses, the *speaker's* Belief-Evaluation cluster may thus be altered. The position he subsequently supports may be basically the same, but the components of his viewpoint may have been changed. Following the speech, he may even see certain aspects of his subject or proposition differently, as being more salient or less salient than at the start of his talk. He may be conditioned to consider more positively the material to which his listeners have responded most positively, or he may be prompted to rethink points that his listeners appeared to doubt, or to which they did not respond as he had anticipated. In a somewhat different speech setting, we may observe how a nightclub entertainer continues to "test out" his act before successive audiences, building up those portions of his materials which appear to evoke the strongest listener response and dropping out other portions.

Similarly, a campaign speaker—uncertain as to the constituency of his possible audiences—may advance a number of points in his initial appearances, and will then dwell longer upon those that receive the most immediate and favorable listener response. Later, as he continues to speak on the same topic, he may be inclined to restructure his speech in order to place even more emphasis upon those points received most favorably in the initial setting. This demonstrates again a significant aspect of the oral communication process: the speaker is not solely the influencer in a speech event; he is also the influenced.

We have made much of the fact that a speaker's influence upon listeners may appear in the *form* as well as in the *content* of a communication. The reverse is also true: listeners may create appreciable effects upon the thought-making and thought-utterance patterns of speaking agents. Research studies on "verbal conditioning" have found that a number of speech behaviors (such as the use of plural nouns, "hostile" verbs, or speech rate), if positively reinforced by listener responses, will occur with increasing frequency in the speakers' verbal behaviors.[10] Once again, listener influences speaker.

As we have stressed repeatedly, in the reciprocity of the speech context both speaker and listener are to be viewed as speech agents, each interacting with the other, each exerting influence upon the other. We should not find it surprising, therefore, that just as a listener may be changed by the speech act, so may a speaker be changed. Each creates effects within the other, and each is impelled to adapt to those effects. The essence of speech interaction is this *mutual adaptation and change* toward the position and understanding of the other.

In this interacting, a further potential effect produced by the listener upon the speaker is a *changed commitment*. A speaker may persuade himself. A number of experimental studies have pointed to occurrences of this "self-persuasion."[11] In an early Army study, for example, soldiers in a public-speaking training course were required to prepare and give speeches favorable to Army life. The results revealed, among other things, that some "chronic kickers" showed marked improvement in morale. This reflects John Dewey's thinking that we learn by doing—a principle of "self-conditioning." And in that self-conditioning we are

---

[10] Leonard Krasner, "Studies of the Conditioning of Verbal Behavior," *Psychological Bulletin,* LV (1958): 148–170.

[11] William J. McGuire, "The Nature of Attitudes and Attitude Change," *The Handbook of Social Psychology,* 2nd ed., ed. Gardner Lindzey and Elliot Aronson (Reading, Mass.: Addison-Wesley Publishing Co., Inc., 1969), v. III, pp. 238–240.

learning to find or restructure a concept which will, in turn, lead to a new view or a changed commitment. Whereas communicating a restructured concept may lead to behavior change, the reverse is also true: following a new course of action may lead to restructured concepts.

As a further illustration of this point, a research study found that subjects could learn the phonetic alphabet more easily if they were required to rehearse or repeat the phonetic sounds aloud rather than simply watch a filmstrip showing the various sound formations. In another study, group discussion involving active participation by all members in the group was found to be more influential than a lecture in which the group listened to only one speaker. The active participation required of any speaker can influence him to restructure a concept or view; and this may, in turn, result in his own self-persuasion. Operating here is the fact that the principle of reconstructing an idea or concept can work in two directions:

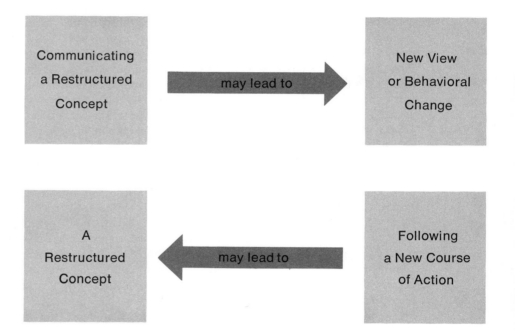

In these ways, a speech communication act may, through the actions of the listener or of the speaker himself, produce significant effects upon the thinking and behavior of the speaker. A speaking agent, entering the communicative interchange, should try insofar as he is able to anticipate the potentialities of these indirect effects and to plan his messages to allow for such influences.

The Extent and Limitations of Speech Communication Effects

Clearly, speech communication acts create multiple and multifaceted effects. Some of them are the result of consciously intended and planned efforts; many of them are subconscious, unintended, and unplanned. These effects may be subliminal or subtle; they may be dramatic. They may be short-lived or enduring. Sometimes the effect of a particular act of orality may occur at a later and, perhaps, quite unexpected time, as if the purpose which generated it had for an interval lain dormant and unsparked, finally to appear as a "sleeper" effect. And, as must be all too readily apparent, some speech communication seems to have little or no detectable effect at all.

The potential for speech communication effects admittedly has some limits. Research in mass-media communications indicates that messages from these media seem more likely to channel or reinforce *existing* dispositions among readers and listeners than they are to reverse dispositions or create new ones. Klapper has written:

> *Regardless of the condition in question—be it the vote intentions of the audience members, their tendency toward or away from delinquent behavior, or their general orientation toward life and its problems—and regardless of whether the effect in question be social or individual, the media are more likely to reinforce than to change.*[12]

Similar limitations have been found in research with brainwashing, subliminal persuasion, and even with psychotherapy.

At times speech communication messages appear to *follow* rather than to lead public opinion. Studies of social reform movements indicate that some *general, latent support* must exist for an idea if the voicing of that idea is to create any immediate effect. Without such support and commonality of feeling, the bases for interaction may not be available. About one hundred years ago an interesting phenomenon occurred in Russia. Many young student members of the intelligentsia, largely from middle and upper classes, went out to live and work with the peasants in order to help them improve their living conditions. These, in brief, were the results:

> *All in vain. The peasants refused to listen to the gospel of the crusaders, preached in what Kropotkin called that "mad summer" of 1874. No point of contact developed. Neither side understood or talked the same language as the other. Never was dichotomy between the outlook of the intelligentsia and educated classes and that of the "dark masses" more dramatically revealed.*[13]

[12] Joseph T. Klapper, *The Effects of Mass Communication* (Glencoe, Ill.: The Free Press, 1960), p. 8.

[13] Lionel Kochan, *The Making of Modern Russia* (Harmondsworth, England: Penguin Books, Inc., 1963), p. 191.

STUDY PROBE 11

Familiarizing Yourself with Factors Limiting the Range and Force of Speech Communication Effects

Using as a basis the outcome of what Kropotkin describes as the events of that "mad summer" of 1874 in Russia, cite a number of possible *contemporary* parallels in our own country. In terms of comparative consequences, do these "parallels" appear to have been successful or unsuccessful?

If, in your view, these parallel events and outcomes are (or were) successful, suggest some communication behaviors which might have contributed to that success.

To the extent that the outcomes may have been unsuccessful, suggest a number of speech communication behaviors which might have helped to bridge the chasm between intention and fulfillment.

In general, we maintain, in the vast majority of instances speech communication can and does generate significant effects in producing social and political change. As we review the history of our country, we can see effective speaking and resultant influential consequences at every turn in the road toward progress. We see it, typically, in the lives and works of such men as Alexander Hamilton, Daniel Webster, Wendell Phillips, Franklin D. Roosevelt, and Martin Luther King, Jr.—to cite only a few of the many.

In isolation, the effects of spoken discourse may seem limited and transitory; but it unquestionably has been—and almost surely will continue to be—a powerful and uniquely sharp cutting edge for forces already tending toward some social action or change. Speech communication can, quite clearly, serve either as a first and necessary step in a series of citizen actions leading to significant social and political change or as an added impetus to forces already in motion.

The overall effects that do result from oral communication acts extend far beyond the immediate horizons of any particular observer or analyst. Because every effect creates others, every *single change* imposed on or within a system will produce *other changes* in that system. As one illustration of this, consider the case of DDT. With considerable talk, many claims, and much discussion, this pesticide was introduced some years ago to kill mosquitoes which spread malaria and yellow fever, to eliminate potato beetles which destroy crops, and so on. DDT's advantages and benefits were proclaimed far and wide by speakers and writers, and DDT did indeed prove very effective. It seemed to warrant all of the communication made for and about it.

Only later was the discovery made that the chemical elements of DDT do not break down and assimilate easily. For instance, when scientists checked one field that had been sprayed with the pesticide seventeen years earlier, they discovered that forty percent of it remained in the soil. Soon came another discovery: the action of wind, rain, and flowing water has spread DDT over the entire world. It has been found even in the fatty tissue of polar bears in the Arctic. So now we are faced with another problem on an international scale: what to do about DDT? Already its effects have created considerable *new* communication and some *new* actions, and inevitably there will be more.

The introduction and widespread adoption of the use of birth-control pills provide still another interesting illustration. Initially, the pills created a considerable quantity of communication—much of it favorable at first, but less favorable and more controversial once certain possibly harmful side effects were observed and commented upon by the media and circulated by word of mouth. Human population control and human speech have thus created some obvious effects and countereffects, each upon the other.

These illustrations help to substantiate the conclusion that by reason of speech communication any social, political, or economic change sincerely, skillfully, and persistently recommended and advocated by a speaker is almost sure to lead to effects of some kind.

STUDY PROBE 12

Tracing Speech Communication Effects Beyond Those Originally Intended by the Speaker

Using our DDT illustration as a basis, draw from your own observations, newspaper reading, and television listening an *actual, detailed instance* in support of the assertion:

> "The overall effects that do result from speech communication acts *may extend far beyond the immediate intention of any particular speaker or of any particular political or social observer.* Every communication effect creates other effects; every single change imposed upon or within a system will produce other changes in that system."

Remember that you will be dealing here with an actual *example* of a social, political, economic, religious, or cultural situation which has in very large part come about by reason of *oral interaction* among the people of our society.

Concentrate upon effects that appear *not* to have been anticipated by the original speaker or speakers *at the time the utterance was made,* and trace the development of your example in some detail.

In summing up the limits and limitations of the effects of speech communication, we should emphasize the potential for numerous *types* of effects, side effects, and countereffects. And we should bear in mind, too, that possibilities for the *spread* of effects always exist. Certainly, anyone who engages knowledgeably and purposively in communicative interaction should, to the extent of his ability, weigh and consider all of the potential and likely consequences of his speech behavior, and also the ways in which he may respond to those consequences sensitively and sensibly.

Suggested Readings

William J. McGuire, "The Nature of Attitudes and Attitude Change," *Handbook of Social Psychology,* 2nd ed., ed. Gardner Lindzey and Elliot Aronson (Reading, Mass.: Addison-Wesley Publishing Co., Inc., 1969), vol. III, pp. 136–314.

This general source has been cited often in this textbook; and McGuire's chapter, in particular, has much that is important to report about speech communication effects.

George A. Borden, Richard B. Gregg, and Theodore G. Grove, *Speech Behavior and Human Interaction* (Englewood Cliffs, N.J.: Prentice-Hall, Inc., 1969).

This work affords significant materials dealing with speech communication effects as they are found in the intrapersonal, interpersonal, and public communication contexts.

Part IV

Deriving Speech Substance, Advancing Propositions, and Making Decisions

Whence the *substance* of human speech? What *propellants* prompt it into being? Which factors and forces shape that substance into *communicable, propositional form* and generate its potentially persuasive thrust? What determines the *degree of decisiveness* with which spoken messages are advanced, accepted, or rejected? In short, what leads a human being to formulate and promulgate orally a rhetorical proposition and urge fellow human beings to make a positive decision regarding it?

We have already commented upon many of the deep-set and far-reaching reasons why man speaks; we have noted in some detail the effects which he thereby creates in and upon his listeners; we have observed some general ways in which speaking and listening agents modify the physical behaviors and thought patterns of one another in communicative contexts. But what brings us to assume and urge the particular ideational positions that we do and to support them as we do? By what means and in what manner are we enabled to draw in sensory stimuli from our environment and transform them into perceived and ordered experiences? By what communicative "alchemy" is it possible for us to endow our perceptions and experiences with categorical labels, give voice to them in linguistic symbols, and organize the whole into rhetorical formulations requiring sometimes simple, but more often complex problem-solving decisions? What accounts for the specific advocacies of Abraham Lincoln, Martin Luther King, Jr., Indira Gandhi, Golda Meir, Ralph Nader? How have these men and women arrived at their views? How do you come to the views that *you* support and argue for? What are the important steps leading from basic, environmentally originated sensation to a decision to extend and defend a definite view in a speech communication situation?

In Part IV we shall seek possible answers to such inquiries. We shall also familiarize ourselves with certain established guidelines and methodologies which can help us to a fuller understanding of how we "think" and "reason" as we try to solve our human dilemmas communicatively. In order to accomplish this, we shall employ a number of terminological and conceptual frameworks, all of which should prove pertinent and important to you as you function as an agent in speech communication—whether as a speaker, a listener, or as a critical observer of the communicative behaviors of others.

Chapter 6 examines ways in which the basic processes of sensing and perceiving help us to become oriented and adaptive to our stimulus-laden environment; it explores materials bearing upon the perception and manipulation of sensory data and experience; it notes some of the ways in which perceptions are filtered in certain instances and filled in or completed in others. Attention is then directed to the processes by which the data of our perceptions are categorized and given man-made labels, and how such labeling permits us, in turn, to communicate with other agents by means of symbolic cues. The chapter culminates with a consideration of thinking and reasoning—deductive, inductive, and causative—and draws a distinction between the demands of language for one's own thinking and for communicating with others. Overall, the emphasis falls upon the smaller, simpler, and more singular elements involved in developing speech propositions.

Chapter 7 treats somewhat broader concerns: the processing of data leading to complex viewpoints and propositions of advocacy. Primarily, the focus here is communicatively induced decision making, and is problem-solution centered. Initially, we survey some of the general approaches and typical patterns for problem solving, and then proceed to develop a contemporary paradigm of practical, day-to-day decision making, building it upon a conceptual foundation of Belief-Evaluation clusters, prevailing value systems, and motivational needs. This paradigm should assist us in making an analysis and evaluation of our own decision making as well as the decision making of others as it is revealed in the communicative context. Cumulatively, the emphasis of Chapter 7 is upon that decision making which involves significant and complex social problems.

Taken together, these chapters are intended to serve two basic functions. First, they outline the essential antecedents to rhetorical propositions, explaining what lies behind and leads to those propositions which we advance as agents in speech communication contexts. Second, they provide useful tools and systems by which we may analyze and evaluate speech communication effects.

Certain fundamental ideas
about sensation, perception,
language, and reasoning
bear most centrally upon
how we form our ideas and feelings,
how we arrive at our convictions
and values, and—ultimately—upon
how we use the speech process
to communicate them to others.

Chapter 6
Speech Communication: Sensation, Perception, Language, and Reasoning

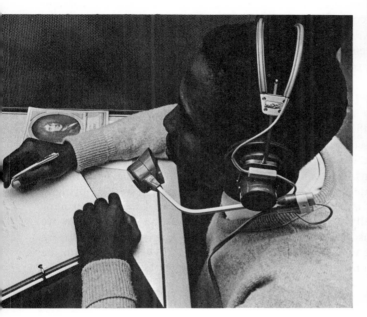

The contemporary model of speech communication in Chapter 2 (page 35) shows the oral interaction process occurring within a context which exercises an influence upon the outcome of that process. Not only do we speak within a context; we also *live* within one. Our thoughts and potential actions are limited by the ranges of our vision and hearing, by the breadth of our reading and experience, by the extent of our travel, and by the nature and frequency of our contact with others. As we have previously noted, our particular human ways of interpreting, adjusting to, and ordering our environment influence the development of the ideas, positions, and propositions which we bring to any specific communication situation. The context within which we live will determine, in part, the stands which we will take and, therefore, what and how we will communicate.

Why did Demosthenes cry out against Philip? Why did Hamlet choose to stage a play as a means of discovering who murdered his father? Why did Wendell Phillips sacrifice so much to speak out against slavery? Why did Lenin preach revolution in 1917? Why did President Kennedy journey to speak in Dallas? Why does John speak words of endearment to Mary, but quarrel with his father and argue with his history teacher? Why do all of us frame the kinds of messages we do and cast them into one form rather than another? The wellsprings of human motivation and action fascinate us all.

For obvious reasons, we cannot attempt to survey all knowledge of human behavior in a single chapter or even an entire book. We can, however, highlight certain fundamental ideas about sensation, perception, language, and reasoning which bear most centrally upon how we form our ideas and feelings, how we arrive at our convictions and values, and—ultimately—how we use the speech process to communicate them to others. Let us begin at the beginning: with the processes by which man receives and organizes stimuli from his environment.

Sensation and Perception

Sensation is the "intake" process by which we draw information and experience from our contact with our environment. It is the much-studied process of the ways in which our sense organs respond to stimulation by light, sound, touch, pressure, taste, and olfaction, thereby producing the individuality and totality of our so-called sensory experience. By reason of these stimulations we become aware of such sensations as color brightness, the vibrational energies of vocal pitch and loudness, tactility, tangibility, weight, warmth, piquancy, pungency, and so on. *Perception* is the complex process by which we select and organize our sensations into patterns that are more or less complete. It is at this basic level of sensation and perception that speech propositions are born.

Sensation and Environmental Change

Basically, sensation is a response to *energy change*. A change or differentiation in stimulation rather than the sheer amount of stimulation is what attracts our attention. Antithetically, to experience warmth we must have known cold; to be aware of sound we must distinguish it from silence. A perfectly homogeneous or absolutely unchanging environment would be like none at all. This is why many animals—for safety's sake—"freeze" when frightened, rather than run from danger. By remaining motionless, they not only help to camouflage their presence, but they also produce minimal change in the sensation of their enemies and are, therefore, more likely to remain unseen by those who would threaten them. As we pointed out in Chapter 4, the participant in a group discussion meeting who says little and does little tends not to attract attention and to remain unnoticed. In various communication settings, some persons do, in fact, "freeze" like any other fearful animal. They are frightened by the occasion, and they hope not to be noticed. An animated speaker, on the other hand, because he provides many energy changes in his listeners' environment and produces multiple, varying, and successive sensations in the receptors of those listeners, has numerous natural advantages in gaining and holding their attention.

STUDY PROBE 1
Analyzing Movement and Attention in Speaking

Observe persons who are conversing. Catalog the postures and gestures which they appear to use frequently. Do the speakers "mirror" one another's nonverbal behavior, employing similar stances, postures, and gestural activities? Identify and contrast animated and lifeless conversationalists. Describe the types and specific examples of movement which seem to attract and hold the attention of others in the conversational interchange.

Aptly illustrating the idea that speakers often tend to mirror one another's nonverbal behavior are these photos of encounters between: (top right) a father and his little girl; (lower right) a demonstrator and a policeman; and (lower left)—perhaps the most classic example of all—a baseball manager and an umpire.

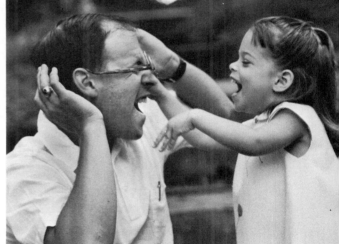

Suggest several guidelines for effective speaking which might be derived from the fact that it is a *change* in stimulation rather than the amount of stimulation that tends to attract our attention.

Energy change—movement and differentiation—is a unique and significant factor, then, in activating and sustaining the speech process. Such change accounts for much of the initial stimulation which we receive from our environment; and it also accounts, in no small measure, for our capacities to stimulate other agents in a speech communication context.

Orientation Through Sensation

Another important aspect of sensation is that we must make some differentiations and distinctions among sensory intakes in order to orient ourselves appropriately to our environment and maintain the necessary cognitive balance. We must have sensation to know where we are and what is happening. If we are deprived of sensory intakes, we lose our sense of *identity* and *reality*. Experiments have been conducted to test the effects of sensory deprivation. Typically, each of the subjects in these studies was isolated in a separate room and placed in bed. The temperature of the environment was maintained at a comfortable and stable level. The subjects were blindfolded, and their hands were padded and enclosed in cardboard tubes. Aside from being properly fed and allowed to take care of bodily functions, the subjects were kept as free as possible from changes in external stimulation. The results of this deprivation were striking. The great majority of those participating in the study experienced hallucinations and other unusual sensations. They reported seeing weird geometric designs and strange figures. Their minds, without differentiated inputs, supplied an "unreal" set of sensations.[1] In the literal sense of the phrase, they truly lost contact with the real. Human beings simply require sensory intake as a condition of "normality." In the speech communication process this means that an agent must receive and be aware of continuing feedback-response (sensory inputs) from his listener if he is to be fully aware of where he is and how effectively he is interacting with other agents in the physical/psychological context.

Adaptation to Sensation

Our human senses are capable of adaptation to the stimuli they receive. The central nervous system can regulate the quantity and nature of the sensory inputs directed to it, becoming more sensitive or less sensitive to suit the conditions of the moment. If there is very little energy change in the environment—if our senses receive very little stimulation—we may become maximally sensitive, able to detect low intensities and small stimulus differences. Human hearing is not as acute as that of many other animals, but in a very quiet auditorium people with normal acuity can hear a pin drop at a considerable distance. When bombarded with stimuli of great intensity, on the other hand, we have internal protective devices which will effectively reduce our sensitivities. Our middle-ear

[1] Floyd L. Ruch and Philip G. Zimbardo, *Psychology and Life,* 8th ed. (Glenview, Ill.: Scott, Foresman and Company, 1971), pp. 299–300.

mechanism, for instance, has features which hinder the transmission of harmfully intense stimuli—a most useful and necessary protection in a society subject to many varieties of "noise pollution."

Not only do our senses adapt to changes in stimulus thresholds; they also adapt to the *duration* of the stimulus. We may be shocked, for example, by the cold when we first dive into a pool, but we soon adjust and no longer feel the cold. Or if one takes drugs, he may find the adaptation process working against his desires as it becomes necessary over a period of time to take increasingly larger doses to reproduce the original effect.

Furthermore, our senses establish adaptation-levels on the basis of the *comparative magnitude* of the stimuli. That is, we judge the magnitude of one stimulus in comparison with other stimuli considered to be in its same class. For instance, a certain foreign car may seem small when compared with an American automobile, but large when viewed alongside any one of several other European makes. As another illustration of the way in which the human senses adjust to stimuli-input and effect adaptation-levels, consider the popular taste as to the length of public speeches. Today, in our society, a one-hour speech may seem too long. But in many other contemporary societies, and in our country only a few decades ago, a one-hour speech would be considered too brief. Three- or four-hour speeches are not uncommon in Latin nations, for instance.

One barrier to the effective functioning of speech communication today is our impatience when listening to speeches: our adaptation levels appear to be highly variable and inconsistent. We are able—most of us—to sit for a full evening steadily watching the sporadic television presentation of pieces of "dramatic" programs and old movies, liberally interspersed with varied, jarring, and irrelevant commercials. And ordinarily in these circumstances our senses don't "protest" enough to produce any behavioral change. Our adaptation levels in this case seem flexible and capacious. We tend, however, to judge by a different standard the stimuli produced by speeches. If the President plans to address the nation on a major foreign-policy matter, we will allow him thirty minutes. He can't have thirty-five minutes because his speech would then overlap our favorite television serial, "Beverly Bonanza in Burbank," and we would miss the scenes which are key to the plot. (Have no fear about missing the commercials!)

STUDY PROBE 2
Lengthening the Attention Span in Speech Communication

Suggest at least three means by which we might help to lengthen listeners' attention spans in order to give more thoroughgoing, communicative consideration to social issues confronting society. Compare your list of suggestions with those made by your classmates, and develop an outline which could serve as the basis for a general class discussion.

Observe current programing by television networks, especially on education channels, and prepare a list of programs which probably contribute to increasing the attention span and adaptational levels of listeners. Prepare a second list which, you suppose, would tend to decrease the attention span and stimulus-tolerance.

As long as we insist on being spoken to in brief "speechettes," we will receive about what we deserve. While thirty minutes is not enough time to allow a speaker to develop an adequate explanation on a major question at issue and to present supporting facts and evidence, it does allow him enough time to present an "image"—a public exposure of the self he wishes to assert or to aggrandize in that particular circumstance. Many speeches now seem to be narrowed in focus for the express purpose of such image-presentation.

The image and its substantiality—or lack of it—and the *effect* created thereby are frequently the only subjects of discussion in journalistic commentary following some of our contemporary political speeches. Perhaps our sensory mechanisms could *adapt* once again to longer speeches featuring substance and content, rather than merely speaker-image. However, this would call for a change in our present patterns of sensing and perceiving public speeches—a greater range of adaptation-levels, especially for those public speech communications directed our way through electronic channels.

Journalistic attention to images of 1972 presidential contenders is evidenced by the Fischetti cartoon about Edmund Muskie (right) and by comment concerning the "new" George Wallace (below, left). Newsman Stephan Lesher, discussing Wallace's new image, cited his more stylish appearance and less extreme political stance—some distance removed from that of the "old" Wallace who (below, right) barred the door of the University of Alabama to blacks.

Fischetti

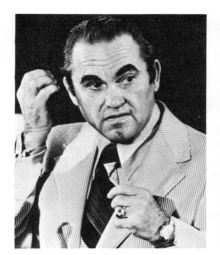

So conscious of image projection have we become that apparent indifference to one's image will provoke comment. For example, consumer advocate Ralph Nader's non-mod look was described by *Time* (May 10, 1971) as making "no concession to the generally young, liberal audience he addresses." Here, Nader speaks at St. Cloud State College in Minnesota.

STUDY PROBE 3
Analyzing Image Development

Study the materials of a political campaign: texts of speeches and press releases, contents of television and radio broadcasts, "news" coverage, in-action photographs, etc. Determine which materials relate solely to the supposed issue and which ones seem intended primarily to create an "image" of the speaker and his party. Using as a basis those materials which seem to you mainly devoted to "image-building," cite several specific instances in which you feel that such items have been used to "manipulate" sensory inputs of listeners.

Filtration of Sensations and Perceptions

Within the general ranges we have suggested, the human central nervous system can regulate the kind and number of the sensory inputs it will "accept," and hence the perceptions we can make. Seemingly, it ordinarily *selects* and *facilitates reception* of certain sensations; and—at other times—it appears to block out certain sensations entirely. Thus our sensations and perceptions are *filtered*. We see a fairly obvious manifestation of this in a listener who is slightly hard-of-hearing. He may miss some of what is said, perhaps a great portion of it. Or, again, we may see this sensory filtration at work in a listener who is foreign born and is only now acquiring the use of English as a second language. The vocabulary or syntax in some parts of what he hears will be confusing for him, and he may not receive useful sensory impressions of them at all. In a speech communication situation, the speaker may have among his listeners the man who is slightly deaf, the man of foreign birth, another listener who may be intellectually dull, another who is sleepy, and still another whose thoughts are primarily focused on a problem he must face tomorrow. For any of these reasons, large portions of the speaker's message simply may not be received by anyone in his audience.

Further, the human nervous system can filter out sensory "materials" and perceptions that are *potentially threatening* to the organism. These materials could be the actual sensations themselves, or they might be *images* that are centrally excited sensations. Materials of this kind would be found, for instance, in profanity or pornography. Studies in "perceptual defense" have investigated this phenomenon.[2] Words and pictures are flashed on a screen for very brief periods with a tachistoscope. Some of these words and photographs are "neutral" in emotional stimulation while others are "loaded." "Dirty words," for instance, appear to be loaded—sometimes overloaded—with stimulus ranges which greatly excite the central nervous system, and for this reason profanity and obscenity often are consciously or unconsciously threatening to many people. In these cases, the "neutral" materials—those having less exciting stimulus ranges—appear to be more easily and quickly accepted by the human nervous system. Thus our sensory receptors help us to filter out excessive excitation, and our perceptions thus defend us against material which, we fear, might be threatening to our values or status, or which might insult our self-esteem.

STUDY PROBE 4

Overcoming Listeners' Tendencies to Filter Messages

Enumerate several steps that a communicator might take to combat listeners' tendencies to filter out sensory stimuli and perceptions necessary to ensure reasonably full comprehension of his messages. Compare your suggestions with those of your classmates.

With another member of the class, present a role-playing situation resembling as closely as possible an everyday conversation, and employ several of the anti-filtering steps or procedures you have formulated in the first phase of the Probe. Try to implement the more useful of these techniques in your speech communication behaviors.

Just as our perceptions may be blocked, so may they be facilitated. We may see and hear what we *want* to see and hear. Suppose we were to perform an experiment in which we presented to a general audience a speech that advanced some arguments favoring the Democratic party and some arguments

[2] Floyd L. Ruch and Philip G. Zimbardo, *Psychology and Life,* 8th ed. (Glenview, Ill.: Scott, Foresman and Company, 1971), pp. 296–297. The Ruch-Zimbardo chapters on "Awareness of the World We Live In," pp. 258–307, and on "To Think, To Reason, To Create," pp. 308–335, can serve very usefully as supplementary reading in connection with this chapter.

favoring the Republican party. If we then administered a retention test to all members of the audience, what would you expect to happen? Actually, this experiment has been performed a number of times, and the findings generally coincide. The Democrats in the audience will tend to remember more of the material favoring their position, and the Republicans will tend to remember more of the material favoring their views. This result will occur even when the audience is cautioned prior to the speech to remember *all* of the content for a test to be given immediately following the speech. If you will look again at the experiment described in Chapter 3, where we were stressing the importance of the speaker's ascertaining audiences' values and motives (p. 70), you will see in it another instance of this kind of perceptual facilitation.

In another study of this type, a ten-minute speech was presented which contained, as nearly as possible, equal amounts of material favorable and unfavorable to the New Deal, a name for the socioeconomic policies of President Franklin Roosevelt during the Great Depression of the 1930's. Three groups of subjects listened to the speech: a group favorable to the New Deal, a group with neutral feelings toward the New Deal, and a group unfavorable to the New Deal. Following the speech, a recognition test was administered to all of the listeners involved in the experiment—a test which contained equal numbers of items (twenty-three each) based on material which could be construed as favorable and as unfavorable to Roosevelt's policies. The table below shows the mean number of pro-New Deal and anti-New Deal items recognized by each of the three groups:

	Pro-New Deal Items Recognized	Anti-New Deal Items Recognized
Listeners favorable to New Deal	16.1	9.9
Listeners neutral to New Deal	12.8	11.8
Listeners unfavorable to New Deal	10.9	13.0

The effects of filtering during the receiving phase of the communication process are evident. Subjects favorable to the New Deal remembered more pro-New Deal material, and subjects with the opposite bias remembered more of the anti-New Deal substance. The study concluded:

> . . . *it is almost impossible to expect objectivity and accuracy in perception, learning, remembering, thinking, etc., when ego-involved frames of reference are stimulated. Our behavior is too much determined by our desires, wishes, beliefs, attitudes, and values for us to expect anything other than what we find, namely, highly subjective responses.*[3]

[3] Allen L. Edwards, "Rationalization in Recognition as a Result of a Political Frame of Reference," *Journal of Abnormal and Social Psychology*, XXXVI (1941): 224–235.

STUDY PROBE 5

Overcoming Predispositions of Listeners

"The fact that a listener receives more readily ideas which he favors means that an agent should never advance ideas and arguments with which his listener disagrees." React negatively or affirmatively to this statement. If your reaction is affirmative, provide a detailed explanation and defend your position at some length. If your reaction is negative, indicate the circumstances under which material "disagreeable" to the listener should be communicated to him, and provide a number of useful guidelines which may well facilitate such presentation.

Studies on "selective perception" phenomena, such as the pro/con New Deal experiment, indicate that a listener tends to filter speech communication messages according to his needs, his expectations, and his prior knowledge. If a man is hungry, he may focus on that part of a speaker's message which promises food and may fail to hear with equal acuity that part of the message which prescribes or implies the violence needed to get it. And it is not surprising that a partisan will receive from a speech more easily and retain longer those items to which he is favorably inclined and/or with which he is familiar, while forgetting or "filtering out" the material less favorable to his cause. In these and similar ways listeners devise their *own* messages by selecting from the messages they receive from other sources and by reconstructing those received messages in accordance with their personal predispositions and preferences.

STUDY PROBE 6

Analyzing Some Factors in Selective Perception

Review the Aristotle and Thomas Hardy materials bearing upon the generational gap (pages 68–69 and 129), and try to relate those materials to *selective perception*. Prepare a careful analysis of the ways in which the groups of different ages seem to selectively perceive contemporary phenomena differently. Specify the various needs, expectations, values, and prior experiences which seem to underlie the selection process as reflected in the dichotomies described by Aristotle and in those implied by Hardy.

Completion of Perceptions

Given the natural limitations of human sensing mechanisms, our sensory impressions and our resultant perceptions can never really be complete. They are destined, it seems, always to be partial and therefore subject to all of the dangers and problems inherent in that partitiveness. It is to both our advantage and our disadvantage that when our perceptions are incomplete, we tend to try to complete them. Despite any "missing parts," in the process of perception the incoming stimuli are organized into what we like to believe are "whole" and "complete" patterns. If, for example, we see the figures below, we tend to complete them and see not an arc or a series of dots but a circle and a triangle.

If adjacent dots of light flicker alternately, we may "see" movement. In this "phi phenomenon" we complete our perceptual experience by adding non-existent, intermediate dots of light and experience the sensation of motion. Many of the advertising signs and displays that are frequently evident on our streets and highways utilize this principle of "incomplete-perception-made-complete." When still pictures are flashed before us in rapid succession, we see motion in the pictures *as such.* The "in-motion" images seen on movie screens are made visible and believable by this means. These are not processes of filtering something *out* of a message, but rather are processes of *adding something to* messages as they are received. This kind of completion seems to be what McLuhan is getting at when he writes about viewer-involvement and the manner in which the viewer "completes" what he sees on a television screen.[4]

There are, of course, variations and extensions of this way of completing our perceptions. If, for instance, our perceptions are ambiguous, we may interpret them and add meaning, as suggested by the illustration below:

In Escher's woodcut "Heaven and Hell," when you are looking at the devils, the angels become background; but when you are looking at the angels, the reverse happens. Despite attempts to keep from shifting, you are likely to see one and then the other alternatively.[5]

[4] Marshall McLuhan, *Understanding Media: The Extensions of Man* (New York: McGraw-Hill Book Company, 1964), pp. 268–294.

[5] See Floyd L. Ruch, *Psychology and Life,* 7th ed. (Glenview, Ill.: Scott, Foresman and Company, 1967), p. 304, for an amplification of this.

Studies of learning by conditioning have shown a somewhat similar effect which has been termed *stimulus generalization*. Once a conditioned response has been established for a given stimulus, that response may be elicited not only by the controlled stimulus but also by a variety of similar stimuli. If, for instance, a subject is conditioned to react in a certain manner following the stimulus-input of a 1000-cycles-per-second tone, he will later respond similarly to tones having close to 1000 cycles per second.

This type of perception-completing behavior can also be observed in speech communication settings. The generalizing or transferring effect discussed in Chapter 5 (pages 131–132) is one example of the human tendency to seek internal consistency and completeness. If an individual is persuaded as to the validity of two or three specific cases bearing upon a particular issue, he tends to complete the persuasiveness of the whole by adding other related cases. The fact that man needs to provide order and completeness to his perceptions of his environment confronts him with certain challenges and unique opportunities in deriving his speech communication, some of which should become apparent to you as you work with Study Probe 7.

STUDY PROBE 7

Analyzing Personal Experiences with Perception-Completing Behaviors in Communication

Recall an occasion in which you and another agent were engaged in an argument and in which you—in order to convince yourself in your own mind—completed that agent's argument by supplying additional supporting examples drawn from your own perceptual experience.

Recall a second occasion, one in which you drew from your own perceptual experience for supportive materials, but which—instead of completing and reinforcing the other agent's argument—tended to work against your acceptance of it.

Prepare fairly detailed notes describing those portions of the experiences which seem to you to involve *stimulus generalization*. Next, compare these notes with those made by two or three other students in the class.

Then, as a final step, formulate some conclusions concerning the principle of *stimulus generalization* as it relates to various kinds of speaking situations.

Obviously, our human need to infuse perceptions of our environment with order and completion places a number of special demands on us as speech communicators. Our individual needs, expectations, and previous experiences will all influence the ways in which we will employ the principle of stimulus generalization to "round out" what we have seen and heard. In a speaking situation, if we expect "illogical ranting" from "that buffoon on the platform," we will probably hear it. If we expect cogency, we are likely to hear that. If we approve of the viewpoint of a speaker who is speaking to us from a considerable physical distance, we may see him as taller or handsomer than he really is. If he says something which—coming from another speaker—would be objectionable, we excuse the comment with the paraphrase, "When he said . . . , he meant . . . ." In this interpretative manner we often add to a transmitted message. In these and similar ways we often help to fulfill our own expectations.

In this section we have considered how we sense and receive stimuli from the world about us. A knowledge of these matters is important to the student of speech communication because it is through the processes of sensation and perception that an individual forms his initial reactions to and assessment of his environment. Through these processes he begins to develop the ideas and feelings which eventually will constitute the substance of the messages he sends to others. Before these messages can more closely approximate a final form, however, the sensations and perceptions in which they are grounded must be organized into *classes* or *categories*. As we have suggested from time to time in the preceding chapters, one of the important ways in which this classifying and categorizing is accomplished is through the instrumentality of *language*.

Language: Categories, Language Labels, and Symbols

Let us now consider how language affects our adaptation to our environment.[6] With language we can impose order on those aspects of nature which we can perceive. We can create order by developing categories or constructs and treating them *symbolically* with the use of language. The implications of this capability are of course multitudinous and multifaceted.

Our human senses are capable of discriminating seven million different colors; that is, if we could be shown all possible degrees of color brightness, hue, and saturation, we would be capable of distinguishing seven million different combinations. If a name were to be provided for each of these combinations, seven million names would be needed to describe distinguishable colors. Imagine trying to learn the names of seven million colors! If we were to find it necessary to treat each color possibility as a separate and equal entity—with a name for each—obviously, our understanding of color would break down. We could never learn the necessary vocabulary or remember it, much less communicate with it.

Categories Are Needed for Understanding

Because of the vastness of the problems, human beings have evolved another way to cope with this pervasive and prevailing need: *they organize their sensations into categories and give them word-labels*. Having this capability, we do not always have to consider the unique and separate entities of this world as such. We are able to deal with them more efficiently by combining them into sets or categories. With this process we are able to provide order to the ways in which we perceive our environment, organize our perceptions into cognitions, and try—when necessary—to communicate them to others. We have attempted to show how this is done with color. With the terms (categories) *red, orange, yellow, green, blue, indigo,* and *violet*—seven names rather than seven million—

[6] The reader may profit by reading Hubert G. Alexander's *Meaning in Language* (Glenview, Ill.: Scott, Foresman and Company, 1969) in connection with this section.

we find it possible to do much of our thinking and our communicating about color. By subdividing these sets and using the concepts of *brown, black, white,* etc., we can—with only sixty or seventy terms—carry on a very specific conversation about the color of sweaters or paint for a dining room. Or, in this same manner, consider the variety of perceptions we can include in our categories of "dog," "school," and "politician."

When we concern ourselves with the categorizing capability and activity of human beings, there are a number of important ramifications which deserve special emphasis. The first is that categorizing is a necessary process for allowing us to better understand and manipulate our environment. If we could not *abstract* and *generalize,* we would be overwhelmed by the sheer number of sensations which constantly bombard us, and we could not reason efficiently or communicate at all. This categorizing process permits us to reduce the complexity of our environment; it permits us to relate *classes* of events rather than individual events.

The capability to reduce—and thereby, to a degree, to simplify—rational and linguistic complexities is uniquely human and is inseparable from the roots of rhetoric. Aristotle, for instance, emphasized that rhetoric is concerned with *classes* and not with individuals when he said, "Rhetoric is concerned not with what seems probable to a given individual like Socrates or Hippias, but with what seems probable to men of a given type."[7] Aristotle's discussion of classes of men (pages 68–69) can be used again here to illustrate the abstracting and generalizing process. He characterizes *young men,* you will remember, by contrasting them with men of other ages: they have strong, but unsteady, desires; they are easily deceived; all their mistakes are on the side of intensity and excess, etc. In this description Aristotle abstracts: he does not describe everything about every youth but rather focuses on those *key criterial aspects* of all youth as he sees them. In making the description, he generalizes: he extends his ideal description to cover *all* entities in the class *(all young men).* Exactness, the dimension of precise specificity, is lost in the process of abstraction and generalization, but this loss is necessary. In categorizing, for the sake of general applicability of our terms we must sacrifice precision and completeness in describing the individual case.[8]

[7] Aristotle, *Rhetoric, The Basic Works of Aristotle,* ed. Richard McKeon (New York: Random House, Inc., 1941), p. 1331.

[8] A good source of information about language and reasoning from the view of general semantics is Harry L. Weinberg, *Levels of Knowing and Existence* (New York: Harper & Row, Publishers, 1959).

STUDY PROBE 8
Understanding Categories and Connotations

1. Using concepts, processes, human entities, or physical objects as a basis, select five categorical classes and apply "descriptive word-labels" to each. Specify connotations for feelings that accompany the descriptions.

2. Indicate a number of the connotations that you have for the following word-label categories:

Blacks	Teachers
Catholics	"Hard Hats"
Republicans	Jews
Bankers	Democrats
Hippies	Unitarians

3. Put your connotations in note form, exchange the notes with other students who are taking the course, confer, and compare your respective responses.

Think about the ways that you abstract and generalize. Earlier we asked you to consider the variety of perceptions you could include in your categories of "dog," "school," and "politician." What are the *significant* and *criterial aspects* of your concepts in each of these instances? What features must any specific entity have for you to classify it in one of these categories? What features are usually related to the entity but not essential? Must a "dog" have four legs, hair, and be man's best friend? Must a "school" have a building, a teacher, a desk, and a football team? Must a "politician" be a speaker, an opportunist, a wheeler-and-dealer, and have powerful friends in City Hall? You can see that the essential traits for classification are really few, and are abstracted from the many possible, specific characteristics which can be perceived in any particular entity, object, or idea. When we abstract, we *select* from among the many characteristics or qualities which we can perceive; and then we say, in effect: "These are all of the characteristics needed to understand what I mean when I use the word 'dog'; these qualities are 'common' to *all* 'dogs.'" Thus, when we speak of "dog" in the abstract, we are not talking about Fido, or Spot, or Rover; we are generalizing on the basis of a few canine qualities in order to distinguish a *class* of creatures which we arbitrarily name "dog."

Categories Are Man-Made

From the foregoing comments, you can no doubt readily infer that our categories or sets are *man-made inventions,* not discoveries; they exist in man rather than in nature. Again consider the color spectrum. The boundaries for *green* certainly do not exist on that continuum. These boundaries are established *arbitrarily* by man, and the single label *green* is applied to all shades falling within those boundaries. We suppose these boundaries, these dividing lines, to exist; but actually they may not. Even the most carefully defined categories can overlap. The greater the perceptual range of our knowledge and the broader the scope of our sensory experiences, the less distinct the categorical boundary lines are likely to become. As laymen, we speak freely and easily about the "living" and the "dead," and about "animals" and "plants." But scientists are hard pressed in some cases to label a single instance as "living" or "dead," "plant" or "animal." Conveniently for us, most of the instances we observe appear clear-cut and easy to categorize. Because of the commonality of human experiencing and the conditioning that we are subject to in our homes, schools, churches, etc., our personal categories often coincide quite closely with those of others. However, even when we examine what we suppose to be exceptional cases, we can see how the dividing line between categories is not fixed in nature, but is determined and imposed by human beings. For this reason, thought and communication—to the extent that they are dependent upon the use of language—can never be exact. Room for error is inherent in the very nature of language.

Although the boundaries of our categories are established arbitrarily, we must emphasize that they are not set capriciously or without viable purpose. Our categories often are set up to satisfy criteria of some kind. We usually choose and maintain categories that are able to stand up to pragmatic tests, that are usable and useful. For instance, the boundaries on the color spectrum for the seven labels mentioned above are approximately equally spaced along the color continuum (as measured in Angstrom units). Other standards, inherent in our makeup, may also be imposed. As we shall develop in Chapter 7, when we discuss "consistency" and "balance" theories, human beings seemingly have a strong need and desire for equivalence, parallelism, and completeness in their cognitions; and this factor also seems to influence the invention of many categories. Moreover, we are constantly working to test their validity, accuracy, and appropriateness in reasoning and communicating situations.

STUDY PROBE 9

Familiarizing Yourself with Language Development

To demonstrate our assertion that language, like categories, is man-made and, therefore, always changing and developing, we offer the graphic examples shown below.[9] Taken from Biblical sources, these are parallel passages from Matthew 8:1; and they show the modifications that have taken place in the English language over a thousand-year span.

A = *Old English* (Ca. 1000 A.D.)
B = *Wycliffe Version* (Ca. 1400)
C = *King James Version* (17th Century)
D = *Revised Standard* (20th Century)

A: Soþlice þa se Haelend of þaem munte nyþer astah, þa fyligdon him micele menigu.
B: Forsothe when Jhesus hadde comen doun fro the hil, many cumpanyes folewiden hym.
C: When he was come down from the mountain, great multitudes followed him.
D: When he came down from the mountain, great crowds followed him . . .

To extend further your understanding of some of the ways in which language can change and be changed, select a passage of several lines from *The*

---

[9] These examples are taken from Bernard F. Huppé and Jack Kaminsky, *Logic and Language* (New York: Alfred A. Knopf, Inc., 1957), p. 107.

Canterbury Tales or *Beowulf;* write it, first, in its original form; then rewrite it as it might appear in the English language today; and, finally, present both versions aloud.

List five words or phrases which seem to have more or less "disappeared" from our language in the past fifteen years. Then list ten additional words or terms which have come into use during the past five years.

Categories Include Both Physical and Psychological Properties

Although we can form categories or sets which reflect our reactions to physical objects or sensations resulting from external influence, not all categories refer to discernible objects or events. We create categories also for nonobservable or even hypothetical concepts and imaginary objects. Just as we form categories for the physical properties of color, we also form categories for psychological properties, categories which encompass sets of feelings or values or internal fractional responses. To certain circumstances or events or feelings we attach the labels "just" or "fair." To an even larger set of circumstances, happenings, and reactions we attach the labels "good" or "bad." These categories represent psychological attributes—feelings and values—just as "green" and "hard" reflect physical properties. Again, we do all of this—in part—in order that we may be able to talk about data and impressions that we are aware of.

Language Labels Are Applied to Categories

In the sense that categories provide boundaries for grouping our experiences, they fence off sets of experience. This "fencing" is facilitated by means of labels. One of the primary functions of language is to assign labels or names to these categorical groupings or sets of human experience. The processes of categorizing and labeling are *interdependent:* categorizing establishes the boundaries; labeling establishes the names. Labeling, like categorizing, involves the processes of generalization and abstraction. A language label must reflect the condition that the category it names applies not so much to the total of the individual entities in the set as it applies to certain real or imagined properties of those entities. Since the important common elements in or "properties" of the set are combined and narrowed in the making of the category, it is this narrowed "meaning" of the category to which the label applies. Consider how the word *bottle* stimulates not a recollection of every bottle we have ever seen but rather an abstractively narrowed set of generalized criterial "meanings" which we have come to attach to that word.

Man tends to give labels to all the different categories he discriminates; and, conversely, he discriminates among the different categories for which he has labels. Anthropologist Franz Boas has pointed out, for example, that the Eskimo discriminates among many different categories for snow and ice and has dozens of labels for their various conditions. Fine shades of difference in the condition of ice and snow are extremely important to the Eskimo's daily functioning and survival, and the ability to discriminate among them is more necessary to him than it is, for example, to those of us who live in less frigid surroundings. All of this again emphasizes how we use categories and language to impose order upon our environment so that we can better understand and control our own existence, and communicate with others concerning the many essential commonalities bearing upon that existence.

Language Labels Are Used as Symbols

As we use a word-label to name the perceptions we have organized, abstracted, and generalized into a category, the label becomes a linguistic *symbol* for the category. It "stands for" the category. The labels applied to our categories thus provide a code with which we can manipulate *symbolically* the perceptual and experiential groupings into which we have analyzed our universe. This code of symbols enables us to deal with the physical world by means of language labels. We use the "word" in place of the "entity" it symbolizes.

Language mediates between man and his environment. Imagine the enormity of the difficulties we would experience if we could communicate about only those objects, entities, and processes which we would have immediately at hand or before us at the moment we wanted to converse with someone. Jonathan Swift reveals something of what our dilemma would be when he describes in a humorous, satirical vein the linguistic theories of the wise men of his mythical Laputa. Some of these sages proposed that human beings carry along with them, in large sacks, all of the various objects to which they might wish to refer in their speaking. And he relates the plight of a couple of these wise men "almost sinking under the weight of their packs . . . and who, when they met in the streets, would lay down their loads, open up their sacks, and hold conversation for an hour together; then put up their implements, help each other to resume their burthens, and take their leave."[10]

Obviously, language is the great facilitator of human action and communicative interaction. Suppose, for example, that two of us are trapped in a burning building. One of us is familiar with the place; the other is a stranger to it. We need not, under these circumstances, race randomly about and try all potential or imagined escape routes solely by trial and error. Language—used first, perhaps, as "inner speech" and later as meaningful utterance—makes it possible for us to travel each route *symbolically*. We can stand for a moment, "think through" and, if necessary, talk about each particular escape route, and take the trip symbolically to its possible consequences. Then, ultimately but quickly, we can choose the route that seems to offer the highest probability for safe escape from the holocaust. In this manner, among many others, language can mediate between man and his physical world.

Language also mediates between man and man. By means of a labeling code, you can communicate with your fellow human beings. You can vocally transmit to a listener the symbol *fire* and hope that, because of the common cultural environment in which both of you learned that label, *fire* will call up in that listener a set of reactions essentially similar to those that *you* experience in response to that symbol. The internal reactions we feel when confronted with a symbol are probably the best definition of the "meaning" that symbol has for us; and to the extent that our utterance of that symbol causes our listeners to experience similar internal reactions, they will apprehend the "meaning" we are trying to communicate to them.

[10] Jonathan Swift, *Gulliver's Travels* (Garden City, N.Y.: Doubleday & Company, Inc., 1945), pp. 186–187.

COMMUNICATING VIA NONLINGUISTIC SYMBOLS

Nonlinguistic symbols used in communicating encompass innumerable kinds, of which only a few are shown here. The cross and the flag (top photos) have traditionally been used by their followers for purposes of identification and unification. The zodiac and its symbols (center) have become invested with astrological meanings, yet the diagram itself is simply a convenient way of showing the positioning of the twelve constellations whose appearance dictated the choice of symbols to represent them. In the two lower photos, symbols are used to get across a specific message—the one having developed out of recent needs and conditions, and the other having seen service through the centuries in warning the unwary.

Clearly, the experiential congruence which human beings have for their linguistic symbols underlies and greatly facilitates the speech communication process. Some commonalities are readily arrived at; others are much more difficult to achieve. Some categories—and the word-labels for them—are seemingly more "appropriate," "fixed," and "verifiable" than others. The likelihood that a speaker and a listener will have essentially similar reactions is greater for the symbol *fire* than it is for the symbol *freedom*. The sensations which produce a response of *fire* are easily and quickly identifiable: we smell the smoke; we see the flames; we feel the waves of heat emanating from them. If necessary, as in the instance of a stove, furnace, or an electric iron, we can measure the intensity of these emanations with scientific instruments such as thermometers, thermostats, etc. We could stabilize our judgments on that label with relatively high reliability; and if we wished to invest the required effort, we could obtain fairly general agreement in setting the boundaries of *fire* in terms of thermal units. But the symbol *freedom* is a broader and higher level of abstraction. As contrasted with the boundaries for the "hotness" and "coldness" of *fire,* the boundaries for the category or set delineating responses we label *freedom* are not nearly so clear. In fact, we are not at all sure that *freedom* is a single-dimensional concept. It might be viewed along many dimensions and would then require many sets of boundaries; to understand its "meaning" might require familiarity with *clusters* of categories, all interrelated and all interacting. The continua, if analyzable, would certainly not be as clear as are the wave length of reflected light or the distinctions we can draw for *fire.*

These, then, are some of the important and useful considerations that we need to hold before us as we conclude our explorations of how we use language and before we move on to our study of the relationship of language to thinking and reasoning. Specifically, we have observed that:

1. With language we can improve our adaptability to our environment.

2. With language we can impose a semblance of order and selectivity on our perceptions, constructs, and cognitions.

3. We can use language to help us create, define, refine, and distinguish categories.

4. We can use language to devise and arbitrarily attach word-labels to the categories we invent and to communicate these categories to other agents with whom we wish to interact.

5. We can use language to evolve a code of "meanings" with which we can *symbolically* manipulate the categorical sets and concepts which seem to us to comprise our environment.

6. Language is facilitative and "economical" in that it precludes the necessity of manipulating real entities and actual objects; it enables us to use the *word* in place of the *entity*.

7. Language can help us to develop and communicate connotative "meanings."

8. Language enables us to think about events, even in their absence, and to communicate about those events with others.

9. Language changes with increased inputs of data, with the shifting of perspectives, and with the passage of time.

10. As between one human being and another, the greater the linguistic commonalities—the more congruent the residual symbolisms—the greater the likelihood of effective communicative interaction.

11. We can use language to discover and interrelate *commonalities* of concepts and "meanings" which can, in turn, enlarge understanding of ourselves, others, and the communicative context.

While recognizing the many advantages of language, we must at the same time admit certain serious limitations. The use of language prohibits exactness in ways which make "perfect" communication between human beings impossible. The fact that general language labels are derived originally from fallible perceptions, that they progress through a process involving a fairly high level of abstraction and generalization, and that they ultimately emerge as symbolic representations means that such labels can never be as precise and—at the same time —as complete as a single entity which has been categorized and symbolized. Thus we find inherent in the very nature of language some significant barriers to effective communication.

STUDY PROBE 10
Discovering and Using Word "Meanings"

For this probing, do not look to the dictionary. Look to yourself.

Define the "meaning" of:

> democracy
> freedom
> age
> wood

With pencil and paper beside you, think about these words and write out the reactions, feelings, impressions, and specific events or instances which each of these terms brings to your mind. Make an appropriately detailed listing for each of the four terms. The sum of the listings in each case should represent the "meaning" of the particular term for you.

Ask a friend, someone in your family (your father, perhaps), or a roommate to make a similar list. Then compare your list with his. Using both lists, designate a number of the reactions, feelings, impressions, and specific instances which, in your opinion, might serve to *facilitate* communicative interaction between you and the maker of the other list. And, again using both lists, point out some elements which would very probably *impede* productive communication between you.

As a second phase of this Probe, consider such broad and abstract terms as "justice," "freedom," "truth," etc., and describe a number of the ways in which their use would make a speaker's task more difficult. Also, describe a number of ways in which their use could make his task easier.

Thinking and Reasoning

Psychologist Norman Munn has defined reasoning as *the sequential arousal and manipulation of language symbols.*[11] One way man reasons is by associating—in some kind of pattern or order—the language labels he has applied to categories of experience. This association, or the relating one to another of these symbols, allows for *inference,* the process by which a person derives new propositions or conclusions from previously established or assumed propositions and facts. Scholars representing many different disciplines and ages have assiduously studied the subject of reasoning and have written about it at length.

Some Basic Approaches to Reasoning in Speech Communication

In this section, we will review some of the long-used and well-recognized approaches to reasoning and inference-making. In particular, we will direct attention to (1) *deductive reasoning,* (2) *inductive reasoning,* and (3) *causal analysis.*

Deductive Reasoning

Deductive reasoning aims at *valid* or *necessary* conclusions. Given the acceptance of certain premises, and following certain rules for relating these premises, we arrive at necessary conclusions. Consider the following dialogue:

John: I think water-skiing is a dumb sport, and anyone who likes it is stupid.

Bill: Why, I was just talking with your fiancée, and she said she loves to water-ski!

John: Oh.

The conclusion is obvious—and necessary—and John knows it. He is trapped by a necessary deductive inference.

The deductive form: the categorical syllogism. Aristotle gave much attention to the deductive form of reasoning, and his efforts resulted in the *categorical syllogism* with rules for its application. With this rhetorical invention he was attempting to develop standards or tests to be applied to thinking in order to insure its validity whenever possible.

The categorical syllogism contains three statements: *a major premise, a minor premise,* and *a conclusion;* and all three are usually stated in the form of a simple, declarative sentence. Given major and minor premises, stated in proper form and meeting certain standards, then the proper conclusion must follow; and it will be valid. Surely the most frequently cited categorical syllogism is:

All men are mortal.   *(major premise)*

Socrates is a man.   *(minor premise)*

Therefore, Socrates is mortal.   *(conclusion)*

In diagramming this mode of reasoning in terms of categories or sets as we have described them, we begin with the three terms constituting the elements of the syllogism: the set (or category) of *all things that are mortal,* the set (or category) of *all men,* and *Socrates;* thus:

[11] Norman L. Munn, *Psychology,* 2nd ed. (Boston: Houghton Mifflin Company, 1951), p. 228.

Then we show the relationship specified in the major premise. It states that all entities in the category MEN are included within the category of THINGS MORTAL, and we depict this relationship thus:

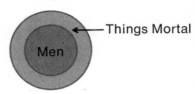

We then add the relationship specified by the minor premise, that SOCRATES is included in the category of MEN, thus:

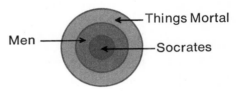

From the completed diagram we can draw the inevitable and obvious *conclusion:* Socrates is mortal.

The syllogism can appear in many different forms.[12] All possible moods and figures of the syllogism would, in fact, produce a total of 256 combinations, of which 24 would be valid when tested against the seven rules for categorical syllogisms. The valid form we have presented above is:

> All A's are B's; C is an A; therefore, C is a B.

Other examples would be:

All A's are B's.
Some C's are A's.
———————
∴ Some C's are B's.

All A's are B's.
All A's are C's.
———————
∴ Some C's are B's.

All A's are B's.
No C's are B's.
———————
∴ No C's are A's.

All A's are B's.
No B's are C's.
———————
∴ No A's are C's.

Testing premises for validity. Earlier in this discussion we alluded to the "rules" for testing the validity and the relationships of premises. Books on logic usually discuss such rules in detail. For our purposes, however, to examine a typical one and to consider a violation of it will suffice. The rule which we will consider here bears upon the *distribution* of a major or minor term within a

12 Harold A. Larrabee, *Reliable Knowledge: Scientific Methods in the Social Studies,* rev. ed. (Boston: Houghton Mifflin Company, 1964), pp. 67–80.

premise. A term may be considered "distributed" when it is used in a statement that refers to all members of a class. If it does not refer to all such members, it is "undistributed." As Blyth and Jacobson point out in their *Class Logic: A Programed Text:*

> . . . *the term "cat" in "All cats are feline" is clearly distributed because a claim is made about every member of the class of cats. However, the term "feline" is undistributed in that same statement because cats constitute only part of the class of felines.*
>
> . . . .
>
> *In the . . . statement "Some cats are long-haired," however, the term "cat" is undistributed. Similarly, the subject term is undistributed in "Some cats are not long-haired."* [13]

The formal rule governing this aspect of distribution prescribes that *the middle term must be distributed in at least one premise.* Further, *a term which is distributed in the conclusion of a syllogism must also be distributed in the premise.* If the middle term is undistributed in both premises, the syllogism is said to commit "the fallacy of the undistributed middle term." This fallacy, probably one of the most frequent violations of the rules governing syllogisms, can be seen in the following form:

Criminal elements oppose wiretapping.	*(major premise)*
My opponent opposes wiretapping.	*(minor premise)*
Therefore, my opponent is one of the criminal elements.	*(conclusion)*

If diagrammed, the major premise contains categorical relationships which could be shown thus:

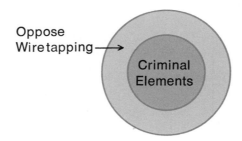

But the relationships expressed in the minor premise, "My opponent opposes wiretapping," would be properly illustrated in two *different* ways:

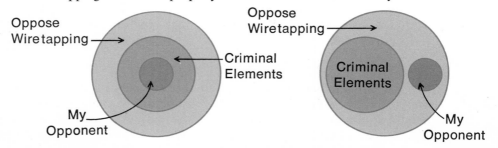

[13] John W. Blyth and John H. Jacobson, Jr., *Class Logic: A Programed Text* (New York: Harcourt Brace Jovanovich, Inc., 1963), p. 323.

The conclusion, "My opponent is one of the criminal elements," may or may not be true and cannot be necessarily and validly drawn from the premises as stated. The "fallacy" is inherent in the major premise: It does not state that criminal elements are the *only* persons who oppose wiretapping.

STUDY PROBE 11

Diagramming Syllogisms

Diagram the following syllogisms in order to check the validity of the conclusions indicated. Ascertain, specifically, (a) whether the conclusions follow necessarily from the premises, and (b) whether the conclusions are true.

Syllogism A

Some men who have not been to college are failures.
Some businessmen have not been to college.
Therefore, some businessmen are failures.

Syllogism B

All children like candy.
Bill does not like candy.
Therefore, Bill is not a child.

If you are diagramming a premise that states "Some A's are B's," how could you relate the circles representing the two concepts? *Hint:* You might overlap them thus:

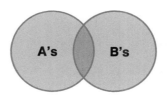

Applying syllogistic tests to speech analysis. Over the years, the structure of the syllogism and its appropriate tests have been applied to the analysis of speeches. Such application, however, cannot always be directly and easily accomplished. Because we rarely find a fully stated syllogism *as such* occurring in a speech, we must analyze the material and search out *unstated premises.* One concept which may be of help to us in making this kind of analysis is the *enthymeme.*

Aristotle pointed to the *enthymeme* as the rhetorical syllogism—essentially the deductive form of reasoning as it is usually found in propositions advanced by speakers. Since the enthymeme is a syllogism in which one premise often is *unexpressed,* it deals in probabilities, potential uses, and premises which are familiar to listeners and which can, therefore, appear in abbreviated forms because they may draw unstated premises from these listeners. For example, a speaker may state as his argument, "Socrates is mortal because he is a man," thereby requiring his hearers to fill in the unstated major premise, "All men are mortal." The application of syllogistic tests to the *enthymeme* has some value when and as we try to analyze such rhetorical statements as "My opponent opposes wiretapping, and so do criminal elements."

STUDY PROBE 12
Understanding Deductive Reasoning

Examine a number of examples of speech communication materials, and locate portions in which arguments are presented in a deductive or syllogistic form. In each instance write out the stated or unstated premise upon which the speaker's argument rests.

As a second phase of your analysis, cite those instances in which you conclude that the *middle term* may not be distributed.

As a third and final phase of the Probe, draw diagrams of the arguments in order to verify or validate your evaluations of them.

In the Middle Ages the deductive pattern of reasoning was predominant to the point of being extreme, and it is still condemned today for some of the excesses of that period. At that time the absolute truth of too many premises was assumed, and dogmatic acceptance of the resulting conclusions was demanded. We now recognize, of course, that the deductive mode is only a *part* of the total reasoning process. So long as our methods of making inferences and drawing conclusions are balanced within the rational perspective, attention to the deductive mode can be helpful to us as we endeavor to formulate sound judgments and decisions and communicate them to others.

Inductive Reasoning

Whereas deductive reasoning is concerned with the necessity and validity of conclusions, inductive inference is concerned with the *probability* and the *reliability* of conclusions. The inductive mode of reasoning allows *relative* "truth" and probable conclusions.

STUDY PROBE 13
Comparing Deductive and Inductive Inference

Examine the following brief exchange between John and Bill, noting particularly what is taking place—rhetorically—in John's concluding line.

    John: I have known a number of water-skiers who were really stupid.
    Bill: Why, I was just talking with your fiancée, and she said she loves to water-ski!
    John: Isn't she an exceptional girl!

Recall that earlier in this chapter you encountered a somewhat similar bit of dialogue (page 180). There, in slightly different form, it was cited as an example of deductive inference. Compare the Bill/John dialogue shown here with the earlier exchange, and then stipulate the differences you can detect between the deductive and the inductive modes of reasoning, as you understand them.

The inductive form. Induction we may define as the process of using evidence concerning some members of a categorical class as a basis for asserting probability about other members of that class. Suppose we designate entities *a, b, c, d, e,* and *f* as members of one set or category, thus:

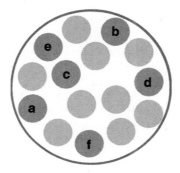

Having noted certain common properties among these entities (*a, b, c, d, e,* and *f*), we make the inference that those particular properties are common to *all* members of that set and will be found in other, as yet untested entities in that set. Having observed *a, b, c, d, e,* and *f* in the set and finding that they all have X trait (fewer dental cavities, for instance), we infer that the other, yet untested members of the set will also have X trait. Stated another way, we are assuming that entities *a, b, c, d, e,* and *f* are *typical* "examples" of all entities in the set or class.

Rhetorical uses of inductive reasoning. Aristotle described this kind of argument from "example" as the rhetorical use of inductive reasoning. Using this form of argument-by-example, a politician once argued:

> *When this present communist party did come into power in Russia, they promptly wiped out all other parties and took the whole people under a firm and dictatorial grip. In each of the other countries—Poland, Hungary, Yugoslavia, Romania, Bulgaria, Albania, and finally Czechoslovakia—the Communists used the blessing of legality as an aid to organizing an underground movement, and finally betrayed the liberties of the people and brought them under the domination of the Kremlin in Moscow.*[14]

This was an inductive inference made from a number of examples or specific instances pointing to the conclusion that a legalized Communist party can work overground and underground to gain control of a nation.

[14] From *Vital Speeches of the Day,* v. XIV, No. 16 (June 1, 1948), p. 484. The statement, by Harold E. Stassen, was made in the Stassen-Dewey debate, "Should the Communist Party in the United States Be Outlawed?" which occurred on May 17, 1948.

STUDY PROBE 14
*Locating Examples of Inductive Inference
in Contemporary Social Issues*

Examine communication materials developed in contemporary discussions of social issues, and single out examples of inductive inference which you find in
them. Make a list of specific cases cited in each by the speaker seemingly for the
purpose of drawing inductive conclusions. Then ask yourself the following questions:

1. Are the specific cases (in each example) *typical* cases?
2. Are the cited cases *adequate in number?*
3. Are the cited cases *broad enough in scope* to cover the class or set as a
   whole?
4. How did you determine the *standards* for "typical," "adequate," and
   "broad enough"?

Compare your answers with those of your classmates, and arrange to explain
your findings with others in a small group discussion.

Inductive/deductive reasoning: strengths and weaknesses. When compared,
the deductive and the inductive modes of reasoning will be found to contain some
complementary strengths and weaknesses. The deductive form assures validity,
or internal consistency, to the development of a proposition or the line of argument. Deduction helps to assure us that we do not entertain as a result or conclusion of our reasoning some statement that is inconsistent with the premises
from which we began. If we follow the rules for syllogisms, the conclusion must
follow validly from the premises. However, as we have pointed out, the deductive form is *analytical* in the sense that the conclusion is implied by the premises,
and does not add anything to them. It merely analyzes or makes specific what
is implied in the premises. Or, to state it another way, the conclusion is already
contained within the premises and makes only *a part* of their content explicit.
In this respect, the deductive pattern of reasoning is limitative and insufficiently
"exploratory."

The conclusion of an inductive inference, on the other hand, is not contained solely in the instances upon which it is based. The inductive conclusion
goes beyond the data and is *nonanalytical* in the sense that we have used the
term above. It thus lends itself well to scientific studies, experimentation, and
the probing of social issues. At the same time, there is danger that the "examples" supporting the inference may be inadequate in number and too narrow
in scope to cover the entire class or set, and might not, therefore, ensure
typicality.

The Scottish philosopher David Hume pointed out this nonanalytic character of induction thus: "Even if every crow we have seen was black, and we
believe all crows are black, yet it is possible that the next crow we shall see
will be white." An early textbook in argumentation presented this as an example
of a complete or perfect induction:

Mercury revolves on its axis; so do Venus, the Earth, Mars, Jupiter, Saturn, and Neptune. But these are all the planets, and therefore all the planets revolve on their axes.[15]

But these are not *all* of the planets, and it is conceivable that there may be others of which we are still not yet aware. As this should serve to demonstrate, induction can never be complete or perfect. We may always find the exceptional case. In sum, the strength of induction is that its conclusion goes beyond the data in making an inference, but the weakness is that induction cannot assure necessary validity to that conclusion.

The inductive and deductive modes, being complementary, can be combined in the formulation of most positions, propositions, and arguments advanced in speech communication situations. For this reason, as students of oral discourse and co-agents in communicative interaction, we can expect to encounter both of these patterns of reasoning very frequently. It will be to our great advantage, therefore, to understand how induction and deduction can help us as we attempt to analyze and test the propositions and arguments that we hear and/or may wish to advance.

Causal Analysis

The third basic mode or pattern of reasoning which we employ to organize and extend the data derived from sensation is *causative* in character. What are the "reasons" for what takes place in our environment? What lies behind, or is the cause of, a certain event? What factors caused the inflationary spiral that flawed the country's economy in the late sixties and early seventies? What led to the riots in our large cities? What will be the effects of continuing use of drugs by the youth of our society? The cause—the *why*—of any phenomenon or event, rhetorical or otherwise, endlessly intrigues human intelligence and intellect.

Patterns of causality. Reasoning about causation falls into three basic patterns:

1. Reasoning *from cause to effect.*
2. Reasoning *from effect to cause.*
3. Reasoning *from effect to effect.*

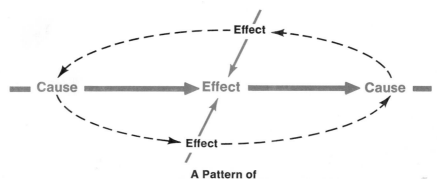

A Pattern of
Argument from Antecedent Probability
and Some Other Cause-Effect-Cause Interrelationships

[15] James M. O'Neill, Craven Laycock, and Robert L. Scales, *Argumentation and Debate* (New York: The Macmillan Company, 1917), p. 121.

The pattern that moves from cause to effect is also known as *argument from antecedent probability*. In a murder trial, for example, the prosecuting attorney can argue from an established motive *(cause)* to an inferred crime *(effect)*. Or, an ecologist can argue from the fact that industrial wastes are being dumped into a city's water supply *(cause)* to the inference that harmful consequences will ensue *(effects)*.

A second pattern of reasoning moves in just the opposite direction: *from effect to cause*. Observing that dead fish suddenly litter a river bank *(effect)*, we infer that some toxic agent is present in the water *(cause)*. Or, if we know that a crime has been committed *(effect)*, we immediately seek the motive *(cause)*; for we assume that there is a reason for every criminal act.

A third pattern of causal reasoning is that *from effect to effect*. We infer from the presence of the dead fish *(effect)* that unless some action is taken to remove or neutralize the cause of their death, more fish in that stream also will die *(effect)*. Or if we know that a student receives high grades *(effect)* because he is by nature a conscientious and industrious person, we infer that because of these same qualities he will be a success in his chosen profession *(effect)*.

Methods for discovering causes. For as long as man has sought causes, he has also searched for systematic ways in which to discover them. In *A System of Logic,* John Stuart Mill (1806–1873) provided five methods that are useful in this search.[16] In addition to the guidance which Mill's methods provide as we attempt to analyze and use causal reasoning in speech communications, these methods have played an important role in developing the experimental studies which are so extensively employed in the physical and behavioral sciences today. Quite possibly you are familiar with the *practice* underlying Mill's approaches to causal analysis, but you may not be conversant with the statement of the *principle* involved in each instance. Because of the compressed and somewhat technical terminology required by such statement, our procedure here will be, first, to present a definitive description of each method as concisely as possible and, second, to extend the definition *by example*.

Method of Agreement

If two or more instances of a phenomenon under investigation have only one circumstance in common, the circumstance in which alone all the instances agree is the cause (or effect) of the given phenomenon.

Example:

A group of persons varying widely in age, pattern of life, and general state of health, suddenly become violently ill and are rushed to the hospital. Upon investigation, the attending team of physicians find that although in all other discoverable ways the activities of the stricken ones on the preceding day differ, all of them attended the same church picnic and ate the homemade ice cream that was served there. It is, therefore, assumed that bacteria or some other foreign substance in this ice cream is the cause of the illness.

[16] John Stuart Mill, *A System of Logic* (New York: E. P. Dutton and Company, 1905), Chapter 8.

Method of Difference

If an instance in which the phenomenon under investigation occurs, and an instance in which it does not occur, have every circumstance in common save one—that one occurring in the former—the circumstance in which alone the two instances differ is the effect, or the cause, or an indispensable part of the cause, of the phenomenon.

Example:

Two groups of elementary school children, matched for intelligence and stage of educational development and taught by the same teacher, are chosen to participate in an experiment in the teaching of mathematics. One group is taught by traditional methods, the other by the methods of "the new math." Tests administered at the end of the school year reveal that the second group is well advanced beyond the first in its grasp of number concepts and in its ability to solve various sorts of problems. The "new math" is, therefore, pointed to as the cause, or an indispensable part of the cause, of this superior performance.

Joint Method of Agreement and Difference

If two or more instances in which the phenomenon occurs have only one circumstance in common, while two or more instances in which it does not occur have nothing in common except the absence of that circumstance, the circumstances in which alone the two sets of instances differ is the effect, or the cause, or an indispensable part of the cause, of the phenomenon.

Example:

Cities A and B differ in all relevant respects except one: each has recently established a scientific crime detection laboratory as part of its police department. A second pair of cities, C and D, also differ in all relevant respects except one: neither has a scientific crime detection laboratory. In Cities A and B there has been a significant increase in the number of law violators apprehended; in Cities C and D there has been no such increase. The work of the crime detection laboratory is, therefore, assumed to be the cause, or an indispensable part of the cause, of the increased apprehension rate.

Method of Concomitant Variations

Whatever phenomenon varies in any manner whenever another phenomenon varies in some particular manner, is either a cause or an effect of that phenomenon, or is connected with it through some fact of causation.

Example:

A radio station finds that whenever it includes more items of local interest in its hourly news summaries, the number of listeners increases, and whenever it omits such items in favor of items of national or international develop-ments, the number of listeners decreases. The station manager, therefore, concludes that it is interest in local news items that draws hearers to these broadcasts.

Method of Residues

Subduct from any phenomenon such part as is known by previous induc-tions to be the effect of certain antecedents, and the residue of the phe-nomenon is the effect of the remaining antecedents.

Example:

A college alters its degree requirements so that students seeking a B.A. de-gree no longer need to take two years of study and training in which to learn a foreign language. At the same time the college introduces a new and highly attractive program of studies in Far Eastern thought and affairs. After these subtractive and additive changes have been in effect for two years, the registrar discovers an interesting phenomenon: While student enrollment in courses in French, German, Spanish, and Italian languages has decreased considerably, enrollment in courses in Chinese and Japanese languages has increased. Generalizing from the experience of other colleges, the registrar concludes that the reason for the decrease in the study of French, German, Spanish, and Italian is the fact that the language require-ment for the degree has been removed. The increase in the study of Chi-nese and Japanese languages he then attributes to the fact that interest in these languages is increasing because of the new program of Far Eastern studies made available to the students by the college.

Mill's canons for systematic approach to discovering causal relationships are somewhat difficult to apply, especially where a matter of human behavior is in question. It is not easy to isolate and measure most phenomena which appear in social issues. We may narrow the differences between two events to a single factor, but that factor may be caused by still *another* factor which we have not yet detected. Earlier, when we were discussing the communication process, we commented that it is not always easy to distinguish between sender and receiver; similarly, in the process of causation there sometimes appears to be no clear line between cause and effect. As a candle burns, the burning wick melts the wax—but the melted wax enables the wick to burn. So which is cause and which effect? This is like asking which comes first, the chicken or the egg.

Catalytic agents as a causative factor. The factor of *catalytic agents* poses still another difficulty when we try to determine causation. In human affairs, as in chemistry, catalytic agents may be necessary for the production of an effect, and yet take no part in that effect. In social situations the presence of a third person may, without intention or action on his part, strengthen or weaken the bonds between two other individuals and thereby facilitate or impede communi-cative interaction. When we are assessing social problems and their possible solu-tions, we may well ask whether a catalytic agent should be considered a cause.

STUDY PROBE 15
Causal Analysis

Look for current speech materials in which various communicators attribute a certain event to another event by causation: "A has caused B." Find examples demonstrating that the speakers are arguing (1) from *cause to effect,* (2) from *effect to cause,* and (3) from *effect to effect.*

Apply Mill's canons of causation to these examples in order to determine which, if any, of the five methods your communicator-sources have employed in their reasoning. Select specific instances of what you judge to be "sound" reasoning and "unsound" reasoning, and describe your reasons for so concluding in each case.

From among the pressing social problems of our time—inadequate housing, air pollution, over-population, poverty, escalating costs of living, etc.—select one which particularly interests you. Treat it *causatively* and construct a "case" for it in which you view it first as a cause and lay out a number of possible effects from it. Then view it as an effect and lay out a number of similar effects which can seemingly be "traced" to the specific cause.

As your experience with Study Probe 15 must have shown clearly, the discovery of causes is far from a simple task. Yet it must also be clear that if we are to understand a given phenomenon, one of the first inquiries we must make is into those factors which lie behind it. We must then work with whatever means we have available to provide sound and supportable standards for causal inferences.

All of the approaches we have discussed thus far—deductive, inductive, and causal analysis—provide us with some ways for viewing the human reasoning process and with some tools for the analysis and testing of that process. While individually each of these methods has limitations and weaknesses, when taken together they provide some indispensable aids for judging inference.

Some Common Misunderstandings About Reasoning

In concluding this chapter, we should take note of two common misunderstandings about human reasoning. The first is the view, held by many, that "logical" reasoning will automatically and inevitably lead to truth. The second is the supposition that there exists an inherent and essential conflict between our logical and our emotional natures.

Logical Reasoning Does Not Necessarily Lead to Truth

Regarding the first of these common beliefs, we should emphasize that logical thinking serves primarily to make our reasoning *consistent,* but it cannot guarantee the infallibility or "truth" of our conclusions. Given certain premises, we may find what kinds of conclusions can and cannot follow; but we are told little about the validity of the premises or the basic beliefs from which we start.

A man's reasoning may be rigorously logical; but if his initial grounds for so thinking are false, his inferences and conclusions will likewise be false. The delusions of a mentally ill person may be entirely consistent with one another and fit the tests of sound, logical reasoning. Such individuals are well-reasoning persons, even if not rational. Their problem is a lack of contact with reality—not a faulty manipulation of reality. The categories for their reasoning do not accurately represent the ranges of experience they are supposed to generalize.

Reason and Emotion Are Not Dichotomous

The second supposition, involving a conflict between reason and emotion, has long been a source of difficulty to students and scholars of oral communication, especially those who write about its persuasive aspects. Some have written of reason and emotion as distinct, separate, even opposed elements; as a speech contains more of one, it contains less of the other. Occasionally, too, a distinction has been drawn between appeals to reason and appeals to emotion. Such dichotomies find little confirmation in contemporary studies and experiments, and can prove to be extremely misleading.

A more defensible position is that reason and emotion are always conjoined in any communicative act. Writing on cognitive theory, Martin Scheerer maintains:

> *In principle, then, behavior may be conceptualized as being embedded in a cognitive-emotional-motivational matrix in which no true separation is possible. No matter how we slice behavior, the ingredients of motivation-emotion-cognition are present in one order or another. As Adams succinctly expressed it, "For there is a conative or dynamic component in our most disinterested, scientific, and objective cognition, or we would not make the observation. There is likewise a cognitive component in our blindest lust or rage, or their expressions would not have even the minimum of direction that they seem invariably to have.*[17]

From this point of view, we see that no communicative interaction can fail to appeal to emotion, to touch upon our affective systems. At the same time, no communication in which we participate can fail to involve the arousal and manipulation of symbols; and this is the process of reasoning as we understand it and have tried to present it in these pages.

Here, again, the problem—in part—is man's long-standing need to have his actions be explainable, reasonable, rational. This need causes us to rationalize frequently, to invent plausible reasons if we cannot find probable ones. Have you, for example, never reasoned thus: "I do have a test tomorrow, but the movie would be relaxing. And besides, if I don't know the stuff now, I never will." If you haven't justified a conclusion in some such fashion, you are indeed the exception to us all.

Not only are emotional responses and reasoning processes conjoint; we have some evidence that they are positively correlated. Psychologists Hebb and Thompson report:

> *Evidence from species comparison suggests that emotional susceptibility*

[17] Martin Scheerer, "Cognitive Theory," *The Handbook of Social Psychology,* 1st ed., ed. Gardner Lindzey (Reading, Mass.: Addison-Wesley Publishing Co., Inc., 1954), v. I, p. 123.

increases with intellectual capacity. Man is the most emotional as well as the most rational animal.

. . . .

> *Such phylogenetic and. ontogenetic correlations between increasing intellect and increasing emotionality would suggest that thought and emotion are intimately, essentially related. There must be doubt concerning any treatment of emotion as a state or process independent of intellectual processes, and having a separate seat in the nervous system.*[18]

The point being established by Hebb and Thompson is that, between species and within species, emotion and reasoning are positively interrelated. From rat to dog to chimpanzee to man (moron) to man (genius), intellectual capacity and emotional capacity increase steadily, and they increase together.

At first glance, this finding seems to conflict not only with the human need to appear rational but also with our observations of everyday life. Not often do we observe an intelligent man showing extreme, overtly emotional reaction to a stimulus or set of stimuli. How is this seeming calm and dispassion to be explained if we do not assume a dichotomy between reason and emotion? One explanation, certainly—and one which we must take into serious account—is that man can use and does use his intelligence to avoid those situations in which his responses would be, or would appear to be, extremely emotional. Moreover, so-called "civilized" man is *conditioned* from infancy onward to "control" (conceal) his emotions. We know very early in life that in situations invoking fear, anger, despair, great pleasure, excessive excitement, etc., we can reveal *too much* of the self to others. And so we are conditioned by parents, by peers, and by ourselves to be calm and poised and not to "wear our hearts on our sleeves." Hence, the more intelligent and conditioned the human being, the more capable he is of avoiding or at least controlling emotionally explosive behavior. However, when involved in an emotionally reactive circumstance or when thrust unexpectedly and against his will into an explosive situation, the emotional response of even the most intelligent man or woman is almost sure to be more variable, more visible, and more intense.

We may summarize these observations on the reason/emotion involvement in speech communication by saying that the reasoning process involves the sequential arousal and manipulation of mediating language symbols, that this capacity for reasoning is positively correlated with emotional sensitivity, and that while reason and emotion (like any other language categories) may be considered separately in the abstract, they are necessarily conjoined in any concrete, communicative context.

In this chapter as a whole, we have attempted to outline those significant and indispensable processes in which man receives stimuli from his environment, perceives them as sensations, categorizes and organizes those perceptions, attaches language symbols to them, and then manipulates those symbols in reasoning about and in drawing inferences concerning his existence. The flow from

[18] D. O. Hebb and W. R. Thompson, "The Social Significance of Animal Studies," *The Handbook of Social Psychology,* 1st ed., ed. Gardner Lindzey (Reading, Mass.: Addison-Wesley Publishing Co., Inc., 1954), v. II, pp. 553–555.

human sensation to human reasoning and the overlapping of necessary and successive phases with intermediate phases should now be readily apparent. The resultant concepts and possible patterns of sensing, perceiving, categorizing, word-labeling, and rational thinking should provide us with increased understanding and continuing flexibility as we attempt to analyze and prepare to function in speech communication contexts.

Suggested Readings

A number of books, interestingly written and combining and extending the concerns for language and reasoning, develop additional perspectives on the basic concepts which we have focused upon in this chapter. They also provide a wealth of illustrative substance. Among those which we would particularly recommend are:

Harold A. Larrabee, *Reliable Knowledge: Scientific Methods in the Social Studies,* rev. ed. (Boston: Houghton Mifflin Company, 1964).

Bernard F. Huppé and Jack Kaminsky, *Logic and Language* (New York: Alfred A. Knopf, Inc., 1957).

John W. Blyth and John H. Jacobson, Jr., *Class Logic: A Programed Text* (New York: Harcourt Brace Jovanovich, Inc., 1963), esp. p. 323.

Chapter 7
Decision Making

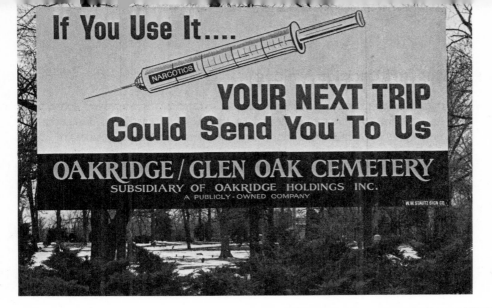

Beliefs and evaluations are central to the speech communication process and are therefore central to any decision making that we may do.

Problem Solving and Decision Making

The preceding chapter introduced important concepts and surveyed some pertinent approaches to perception, language usage, and reasoning. The emphasis there was upon the smaller and more singular elements in these processes. There, too, we discussed the development and logical manipulation of single propositions. In the present chapter our concerns will be broader: we will examine complex decision making, especially as it is *communicatively induced*. Few social decisions are made in this world without the use of speech communication. Wherever we go—to the classroom, the lecture hall, the PTA meeting, the political rally, the student center, the dining hall, or the TV set—we are constantly exposed to speech communication calculated to formulate, alter, or firm up our decisions. One of our major concerns in this chapter will be to learn something new and useful about problem solving and decision making where *communication* is a determining variable governing what does or does not happen.

We know that decisions on significant social issues usually involve more than single and simple propositions. Typically involved are *numerous* propositions and numerous *conflictive, intersective,* and *interactive* propositions. We also know that carrying our decision making to the point where we are willing to advocate it orally is not always a simple matter. All of us, from moment to moment, arrive at decisions of relatively minor import to anyone else—decisions that we don't need to shout from the housetops. We may believe strongly—and even "decide"—that it will rain tomorrow, but we are not likely to give a speech in support of that decision. We may decide to buy a hamburger without being moved to the point of public advocacy or public justification of that decision.

But as we move to the broader aspects and implications of decision making, our decisions *are* likely to be communicatively induced and oriented. Only a little observation and thought will make clear the fact that every phase of the speech communication process, and every setting in which it occurs, involves choices and requires decisions. Whether we will speak or remain silent, whether we will speak to reveal or to conceal our true beliefs and motives, whether or not we will make optimum use of feedback and feedforward—these typify the kinds of to-speak-or-not-to-speak decisions which we must make every day.

Now, some of the ways of talking about these matters will tell us more about what *ought* to happen than about what *does* happen. We shall first review some of the standard "oughts" because they contain some good and useful advice, and then we shall examine some of what is known today about the actual psychological events that *do* take place whether we work as we "ought" or not.

Finally, when we have explored these elements and facets, these generative factors and forces of decision making, we shall inspect in some detail what actually *did* happen when two politicians clashed with one another a century ago about a specific problem, some unsolved aspects of which are still with us today.

By traveling this route and observing as many of the road signs and twists and turns as possible, we may hope to arrive at an understanding of some of the *ideals* of problem solving—at a workable familiarity, perhaps, with some of the actual decision-making processes which can lead us "right" or "wrong." We will have found a way of describing to ourselves what goes on before, during, and after a clash or controversy in which speech communication is the crucial impetus for decision making. And always, to the greatest extent possible, our chief concern will be upon those aspects of human "deciding" in which speech communication is the prominent generative force.

Let's begin with an historical example. In the 1858 Lincoln-Douglas Debate at Freeport, Illinois, Lincoln put the following question to his opponent:

> *Can the people of a United States Territory, in any lawful way, against the wish of any citizen of the United States, exclude slavery from its limits prior to the formation of a State constitution?*

Douglas answered:

> *. . . in my opinion the people of a Territory can, by lawful means, exclude slavery from their limits prior to the formation of a State constitution.*[1]

A simple question and a straightforward answer. But they are the observables. With this conflict, as with an iceberg, nine-tenths of the substance rests below the surface. The many interrelated propositions drawn together in the decision making here are too involved for any simple "logical" analysis of the question and the answer by themselves. We will return to this case later in the chapter and point out some of what lay below the surface.

For a somewhat different but more contemporary event, consider the 1967 Report of the National Advisory Commission on Civil Disorders. This Commission asked three straightforward questions about the racial disturbances which occurred in many American cities in 1967:

> *What happened?*

> *Why did it happen?*

> *What can be done to prevent it from happening again?*[2]

The answers to these questions were not so simple or straightforward. Again, the mass of interrelated propositions involved in the attempt to answer questions of this kind is nearly overwhelming. If we were to approach them with the intention of diagramming Aristotelian syllogisms, we would almost surely become frustrated.

What is needed, therefore, is a system for the analysis of multiple and complex propositions. In the present chapter, we will present such a system. Our approach, drawn especially from contemporary behavioral science research and decision theory, can be used for the analysis of speech materials as well as of speech effects. As we shall see, much of speech communication behavior is decision-making behavior: Will I speak? What will I say? How should I say it? In short, we will attempt to examine here those elements of decision making which ultimately generate and influence communicative interaction.

Problem Solving: General Approaches and Typical Patterns

Let us begin with a view of three somewhat older and more or less general systems which have been advanced to describe and explain problem-solving behavior. In Chapters 5 and 6, you may recall, we discussed certain patterns of

[1] All quotations bearing upon the Lincoln-Douglas controversy are drawn from *Abraham Lincoln Speeches and Debates,* Centenary Ed. (New York: The Current Literature Publishing Co., 1907), vols. 3 and 4.

[2] *Report of the U.S. National Advisory Commission on Civil Disorders* (Washington, D.C.: U.S. Government Printing Office, March 1, 1968).

thinking. Here the patterns become more complex, and the concentration is upon patterns which will help to identify, locate, and sort out possible solutions to a problem.

A "Reflective Thinking" Approach: John Dewey

One of the best-known and widely cited systems for the analysis of problems is to be found in the "Steps to Reflective Thinking" developed in 1910 by the noted philosopher and educator, John Dewey (1859–1952).[3] Dewey distinguished five steps or stages in the process:

1. *A felt difficulty*. Something perplexing and puzzling occurs in our experience. Things are unsettled and not right. A new situation occurs for which we have no answer, or perhaps an older "tried and true" solution breaks down and no longer fits the needs. We have a problem.

2. *Location and definition of the difficulty*. Observations are made and data are gathered to make clear just where the difficulty lies and what it is. Different approaches are made so that we may discover fully the nature of our problem.

3. *Suggestions of possible solutions*. Alternative hypotheses and potential answers explaining the problem are advanced at this stage. These suggestions grow out of the careful analysis made as a result of the second step.

4. *Mental exploration and elaboration of alternative hypothesized solutions*. The meaning and the implications of the various possible solutions are probed. The consequences are investigated. One reasons, "If this hypothesis is true, then it follows that . . ."

5. *Further observation or experimentation*. Here one tests by specific and planned observation the proposed hypotheses and their implications in order to accept or reject them on empirical grounds.

[3] John Dewey, *How We Think* (Lexington, Mass.: D. C. Heath & Company, 1910).

Pictured in a characteristically reflective pose is John Dewey, who guided generations of people through the intricacies of problem solving by means of his five-step delineation of what the process involves.

Previously, you may recall, in Chapter 5 we mentioned an ellipsis of the problem-solution pattern. Later, in Chapter 9, when we consider small group interaction, we will examine the five steps in Dewey's problem-solving sequence in still another perspective.

Dewey's system seems highly reasonable and descriptive of the progression of steps you may have followed in solving some of your own problems. Note how closely it is related to the three essential steps frequently associated with scientific inquiry:

1. *Observation* and *description* of phenomena.
2. *Explanation* by means of hypothesis and theory.
3. *Testing* of hypotheses and theories.

A "Creative Thinking" Approach: Graham Wallas

Another early pattern was developed by Wallas in 1926, and it analyzed problem solving as proceeding in accordance with the following steps:[4]

Step One: *Preparation.*

Step Two: *Incubation.*

Step Three: *Illumination.*

Step Four: *Verification.*

This scheme has been employed to explain the process by which some scientific discoveries have been made, and also as a means of describing the processes of "creative thinking." When faced with a problem, according to this pattern, we should first *prepare*—marshal all the available material on the problem and go over it in our mind. Then we let the problem "rest" while we turn to some other activity: the *incubation* period. Hopefully, this is followed by the *illumination*—the sudden insight; from the unconscious level comes the answer we have sought: "Aha!" (hence the designation "Aha phenomenon"). Finally, one tests the insight in the *verification* step.

Numerous case studies have been presented in which the processes of creative thought do seem to approximate these steps. One scientist is said to have experienced his insight while sitting in a bathtub; another while stepping aboard a bus. Perhaps you, too, have experienced this sort of insight. In attempting to solve a mathematical problem you may have puzzled over it at some length and without success, then gone on to another activity, only later to have the answer flash before your mind. A somewhat related phenomenon occurs with *recall.* A person's name, previously known, may not come readily to mind when we meet him again, and we can't think of it. Then later, when we are engaged in an entirely unrelated activity, the name flashes before us.

This is an appealing pattern, and most of us probably try to use it from time to time. Unfortunately, since many of us are especially adept at "incubation," we eagerly turn to other activities while waiting for the "lightning to strike." But incubating an infertile egg will not accomplish much. Note that the step is labeled *incubation*—not procrastination. For speech preparation, the incubation phase can be of great value if one has *first* filled himself with the many nuances of his topic in the preparation stage.

[4] Graham Wallas, *The Art of Thought* (New York: Harcourt Brace Jovanovich, Inc., 1926).

An "Observational-Deducing" Approach: Sherlock Holmes

With an interest in traditional approaches to problem solving, we may learn something from personal testimony. Who was the greatest problem solver of all? Sherlock Holmes, of course, and we may profit from his advice:

The ideal reasoner . . . would, when he had once been shown a single fact in all its bearing, deduce from it not only all the chain of events which led up to it, but also all the results which would follow from it. As Cuvier could correctly describe a whole animal by the contemplation of a single bone, so the observer who has thoroughly understood one link in a series of incidents, should be able to accurately state all the other ones, both before and after. We have not yet grasped the results which the reason alone can attain to. Problems may be solved in the study which have baffled all those who have sought a solution by the aid of their senses. To carry the art, however, to its highest pitch, it is necessary that the reasoner should be able to utilize all the facts which have come to his knowledge; and this in itself implies, as you will readily see, a possession of all knowledge, which, even in these days of free education and encyclopaedias, is a somewhat rare accomplishment. It is not so impossible, however, that a man should possess all knowledge which is likely to be useful to him in his work, and this I have endeavored in my case to do.[5]

Holmes, you see, stressed the importance of background knowledge of *facts, careful observation,* and *incisive reasoning.* His shrewd inferences always followed a specific observation to its implications, and a combining of circumstances into a total integrated view of the matter.

[5] From *The Adventures of Sherlock Holmes* by Sir Arthur Conan Doyle. Reprinted by permission of the Estate of Sir Arthur Conan Doyle and John Murray (Publishers) Ltd.

Familiar to old-movie buffs are the characterizations of Holmes and Watson by Basil Rathbone and Nigel Bruce. In *The Hound of the Baskervilles,* a bit of evidence leads to a "deduction" by Holmes who, as usual, explains his findings to Watson.

After listening to the problem of a stranger, he turned to his friend Dr. Watson and pointed out:

Beyond the obvious facts that he has at some time done manual labor, that he takes snuff, that he is a freemason, that he has been in China, and that he has done a considerable amount of writing lately, I can deduce nothing else.

Mr. Jabez Wilson started up in his chair, with his forefinger upon the paper, but his eyes upon my companion.

How, in the name of good-fortune, did you know all that, Mr. Holmes? he asked. How did you know, for example, that I did manual labor? It's as true as gospel, for I began as a ship's carpenter.

Your hands, my dear sir. Your right hand is quite a size larger than your left. You have worked with it, and the muscles are more developed.

But the writing?

What else can be indicated by that right cuff so very shiny for five inches, and the left one with the smooth patch near the elbow where you rest it upon the desk?

Well, but China?

The fish that you have tattooed immediately above your right wrist could only have been done in China. I have made a small study of tattoo marks, and have even contributed to the literature of the subject. That trick of staining the fishes' scales of a delicate pink is quite peculiar to China. When, in addition, I see a Chinese coin hanging from your watch-chain, the matter becomes even more simple.[6]

It would be interesting to know something of the thought patterns used by Sir Arthur Conan Doyle, author of the Sherlock Holmes adventures. What steps might *he* have followed in developing one of his stories?

But not everyone can make of himself a Sherlock Holmes, and the traditional patterns of problem solving outlined here cannot ensure "truth" any more than could the syllogism. Rather, these general systems should be seen as ideal patterns, as models of how people may and perhaps "should" solve their problems; we must not confuse these systems with the way people "do" solve their problems. For these patterns to be accurate descriptions of how people do reason we would have to assume that the world is "reasonable," that we have conscious control over our thinking, and that men think more or less alike. But nature may not be so clearly ordered; not all of reason is a conscious activity, and not all men can or do reason alike.

Some Contemporary Views and Implications

Rationality and Language

An important philosophy of our age is existentialism. In his *Irrational Man*, William Barrett considers aspects of our contemporary culture, ranging from

---

[6] From *The Adventures of Sherlock Holmes* by Sir Arthur Conan Doyle. Reprinted by permission of the Estate of Sir Arthur Conan Doyle and John Murray (Publishers) Ltd.

science to music and art; and he emphasizes the many frames of reference from which we can get glimpses of a nature that may, at bottom, be irrational and chaotic.[7] In our time, according to Barrett, we see definite limits to reason. He argues that science in this century, with the work of Heisenberg in physics, and Godel in mathematics, has at last caught up with Kant who nearly two centuries ago attempted to show that there were insurmountable limits to the power of reason. In our earlier discussion of language, we saw how the boundary lines between categories are determined and set by man rather than discovered by him. We saw also that language labels for categories are arbitrary and determined by mankind. The fact that we, as human beings, *impose* an order upon nature in these ways should be a clue to the realization that there is not a complete, obvious, and consistent-to-all ordering of our environment.

Toulmin's Inferential Pattern

While the modern view does acknowledge some limits to reasoning, attempts are still being made, nevertheless, to develop some satisfactory means of analyzing the inferential process. One such attempt is that of Stephen Toulmin.[8] In his pattern, Toulmin incorporates some of the essentials of the syllogistic approach which we discussed in Chapter 6. According to his description in *The Uses of Argument,* we infer from *data,* to a *claim,* by means of the connector of a *warrant* or general proposition. His plan may be clearer if we substitute the word "evidence" for data, and "conclusion" for claim. Thus:

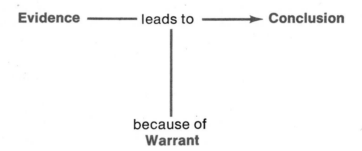

Toulmin suggests that the warrant itself may be given support, called *backing,* and that the conclusion might yet not follow if countered by objections, called *rebuttal.* He also recognizes the danger in absolute categorized claims and includes a *qualifier* for the conclusion. His full model for an argument (or line of reasoning), with our changes in terminology, is represented by the following diagram:

---

[7] William Barrett, *Irrational Man: A Study in Existential Philosophy* (Garden City, N.Y.: Doubleday & Company, Inc., Anchor Books, 1962).

[8] Stephen E. Toulmin, *The Uses of Argument* (London: Cambridge University Press, 1958), especially "The Layout of Arguments," pp. 94–195. *Note:* The first two diagrams on this and the facing page are based on Toulmin's scheme; the third is redrawn from Toulmin, ibid., p. 105. © 1958 by Cambridge University Press.

Also see Douglas Ehninger and Wayne Brockriede, *Decision by Debate* (New York: Dodd, Mead & Co., 1963), Chs. 8–9, pp. 98–167.

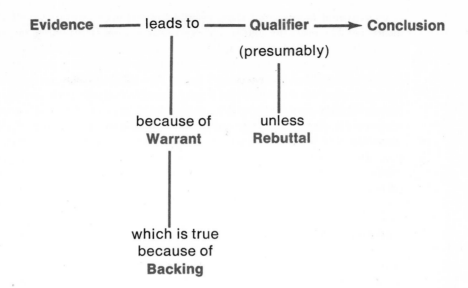

Toulmin's warrant represents a generalization which has already been arrived at or accepted, and evidence represents a fairly specific item of information. The inferential process attempts to subsume the specific evidence under the generalization of the warrant. Once this is done, an association is drawn between the evidence and other specific statements (including the conclusion) also subsumed under the warrant. This association of particulars through the process of categorizing and generalizing is the essence of inference. It represents the overlapping of language and thought.

An example used by Toulmin illustrates the procedure by which a person might draw the inference that Harry was born in Bermuda. The inference is laid out as follows:

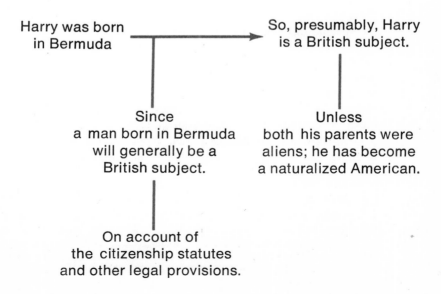

It would appear that the Toulmin approach to the process of inference is more flexible than the categorical syllogism and will probably be more useful for the analysis of decision making in speech communication. It does present a reasonable means for analysis, for breaking a proposition or argument into its constituent parts so that we can inspect the adequacy of each part in isolation, as well as for viewing the relationship between the parts. Toulmin's system will be useful to us also because it contains as elements the *backing* for the *warrant,* the specific recognition of *possible lines of refutation,* and the *qualifier to the conclusion*—all elements that occur in the process of oral discourse.

If we attempt to fit the earlier Aristotelian syllogistic model (pages 180–184) to real propositions and decision making which we encounter and employ in our everyday experience, we may find it to be rather inflexible and somewhat difficult to apply. If we think for a moment of the origins of such systems, we may better understand why this is so. In the early days of man, his decisions and their consequences occurred close together in time. A decision was often tested immediately. When stalking wild game, a man may be allowed only one mistake. A wrong inference could well be the last inference. As humankind developed the use of language and—with it—abstract thought, decisions and consequences no longer occurred so close together. Greek logic was an attempt, as we have tried to suggest, to provide immediate tests and principles for abstract thinking, the consequences of which could not be seen immediately. Rather than abandon such an approach, it is probably better that—as Toulmin has—we continue to modify and adapt it for use with our special analytical and communicative purposes.

At the same time, although Toulmin's system is flexible and adaptable, it is by no means the final answer in our search for ways to understand human thinking and problem solving. We know, for example, that not all thinking is done on a conscious level and that man has, therefore, only a limited ability to govern his own reasoning. The "Aha! phenomenon" is a label for the occurrence of a sudden insight, but the label surely does not explain it. A number of experiments have made abundantly evident the fact that we can form, retain, and manipulate categories or concepts "unconsciously."[9] These studies show that neither the formulation of a concept nor the application of a principle requires the conscious recognition of the common elements or relationships involved in the specific instances. From studies of language usage, for example, we know that children who learn to speak a language can use and distinguish proper from improper grammatical patterns without ever being aware of the applicable or governing linguistic "rules." Children, seemingly, are able to fit a specific sentence into a system they have assimilated over time. In short, they unconsciously "know" and apply rules in the manipulation of language symbols that they do not consciously know and cannot spell out.

Michael Polanyi makes a similar point in his work *The Tacit Dimension* when he argues that "we can know more than we can tell."

> *We know a person's face, and can recognize it among a thousand, indeed among a million. Yet we usually cannot tell how we recognize a face we know . . . most of this knowledge cannot be put into words.*[10]

[9] See, for example, Bernard Berelson and Gary A. Steiner, *Human Behavior: An Inventory of Scientific Findings* (New York: Harcourt Brace Jovanovich, Inc., 1964), Chapter 5, "Learning and Thinking," pp. 133–237.

[10] Michael Polanyi, *The Tacit Dimension* (Garden City, N.Y.: Doubleday & Company, Inc., Anchor Books, 1967), p. 4.

The fact that we can "know" more than we can "put into words" has obvious implications for our views about decision making, language usage, and especially about speech communication.

Studies of decision making and also of research work in the theory of games reveal that there are varying patterns of reasoning in the actual practice of problem solving; not every man approaches a given problem in the same way. In terms of Toulmin's description of argument, for example, it is likely that some persons focus more on the evidence than they do on the warrants; their most careful checks are applied to evidence. They especially want "just the facts." Other people are more concerned with general principles, focusing more upon warrants and what lies behind them. Some are keen to sense possible rebuttal; others appear oblivious to these possibilities.

Scanning and Focusing

And there are still other ways of describing patterns for manipulating symbols so as to arrive at new understandings. In *A Study of Thinking* Bruner, Goodnow, and Austin identify and describe such patterns as simultaneous scanning, successive scanning, conservative focusing, and focus gambling.[11] These terms identify such operations as the following. In solving a problem, one person may attempt to see the overall picture: He is engaging in *simultaneous scanning*. Another may try to view the overall picture but look especially for the elements that test the particular hypotheses he advances, one at a time: He is attempting *successive scanning*. Another may focus upon and vary one element of his perception at a time: He is engaging in *conservative focusing* behavior. Still another may narrow his alternatives (as is typical of focusing behavior), but allow more than one element to vary at a time: He is *focus gambling*. Some persons will favor one of these differing approaches much more than others, and some will take yet other paths. Obviously, much research work yet needs to be done on patterns of reasoning in speech communication settings.

STUDY PROBE 1
Scanning Versus Focusing

Which of these two patterns, *scanning* or *focusing*, is more typical of your problem-solving behavior? When making decisions do you try to envision several alternatives at once and weigh them against one another collectively, or do you take one alternative at a time, weigh it, and decide upon it before moving on to the next possibility? Or is there some *other* pattern that seems to you to be characteristic of your problem-solving attempts?

The problem-solving systems which we have thus far described and briefly scrutinized are limited in that they represent *abstractions* of the process. They provide only a *model,* and they possess both the benefits and the disadvantages of a word label. Yet, like road maps, they are helpful for pointing the way. No description or model, however, can *lead* a man to the solution of a problem.

[11] Jerome S. Bruner, Jacqueline J. Goodnow, and George A. Austin, *A Study of Thinking* (New York: John Wiley & Sons, Inc., 1956), especially Chapters 4–8.

If a person is perceptive, aware of what he is doing, and follows a particular pattern, he may facilitate his search for a solution. These patterns and models, like others we have discussed, can be extremely helpful as guides and servants— but only in that capacity.

Decision Making in Practice: Generative Factors and Forces

Let us turn from the idealized descriptions or models of problem solving to inspect some decision-reaching *processes* and the human factors which strongly influence decision making. We are defining decision making as the process of "choosing among alternatives." What are the factors which influence our formulation of decisions, and which of these factors are significant in our speech communication? What happens when we analyze multiple and complex propositions? In this section we hope to provide some analytical tools for finding answers to such questions.

Attitudinal Components and Measurements

Attitude and *attitude change* are central concepts in any serious consideration of decision making and/or decision changing. There are many differing views about the components of attitudes and attitude structures, and of how attitudes affect human behavior. Let us begin with a brief survey of some of the particular notions we shall later draw upon in setting out a general view of decision making.

Cognition-Feeling-Response Tendency

Krech, Crutchfield, and Ballachey maintain that attitudes are developed over a period of time and can be changed or modified.[12] They propose that the attitude of a person toward any object is composed of three interrelated elements:

1. Cognitions.
2. Feelings.
3. Response tendencies.

Cognitions are the beliefs of the person about the object. We may believe that George is tall, has blond hair, has a good sense of humor, is loyal to his friends, and is fun to be around. These are the beliefs we hold about George. *Feelings* are the emotions connected with an object. We may feel pleased to be in George's company; we may like George. These are our emotions toward him. *Response tendencies* are the action predispositions or behavioral readinesses associated with the object. We may seek out George's company; we may support positions he takes in a meeting. These are our response tendencies toward him. These three elements, then, combine to form, constitute, and sustain our total attitude toward George.

Beliefs-Affects

A somewhat related conception of attitudes has been proposed by psychologist Martin Fishbein. Fishbein suggests that attitudes have two interrelated components: (1) *belief,* which is the probability dimension of attitude, and (2)

---

[12] David Krech, Richard S. Crutchfield, and Egerton L. Ballachey, *Individual in Society* (New York: McGraw-Hill Book Company, 1962), Chapters 5, 6, and 7.

affect, which is the evaluative dimension of attitude. These two components are conceptually much like the "cognitive" and "feeling" dimensions of the Krech, Crutchfield, and Ballachey conception. Fishbein's special contribution has been his attempt to provide a means of measuring those dimensions.[13] He has used the semantic-differential type of scaling, such as the following:

Belief Scale

Fluoride treatments prevent tooth decay.

Likely ____ ____ ____ ____ ____ ____ ____ Unlikely

+3 +2 +1 0 −1 −2 −3

Affect Scale

Prevention of tooth decay.

Good ____ ____ ____ ____ ____ ____ ____ Bad

+3 +2 +1 0 −1 −2 −3

The first item, a belief scale, measures the level of probability the respondent would assign to the association stated by the sentence attached to it. The second item, an affect scale, measures the evaluation level the respondent associates with the concept by the word or phrase attached to it. Both items are scored from +3 to −3, according to the level where the respondent places his mark.

Fishbein maintains that an individual has many *beliefs* (probabilistic views) toward any given psychological object. An individual believes, at some level of probability, in the existence of the object; and he believes, also at varying levels of probability, that certain elements are associated with that object. Related to his belief structure, an individual has *affects* (evaluative feelings) toward those associated elements. Also, according to Fishbein, *the sum of all the scores on the belief elements multiplied by the scores on their associated affective quantities expresses the individual's total attitude toward the concept under consideration.*

Consider the total attitude of one individual toward the concept, "fluoride treatments." This person would hold a number of beliefs about fluoride treatments, and hold them at different levels of *conviction.* For example:

Fluoride treatments prevent tooth decay.	(belief level = +3)
Fluoride treatments are costly.	(belief level = +1)
Fluoride treatments are inconvenient.	(belief level = 0)
Fluoride treatments are not helpful for adults.	(belief level = +2)
. . . And so on.	

Each of the associated terms would also have an *affect* level for the individual:

Prevent tooth decay.	(affective level = +3)
Costly.	(affective level = −2)
Inconvenient.	(affective level = −1)
Not helpful for adults.	(affective level = −2)
. . . And so on.	

[13] See Martin Fishbein, "A Consideration of Beliefs, Attitudes and Their Relationship," in *Current Studies in Social Psychology,* ed. Ivan D. Steiner and Martin Fishbein (New York: Holt, Rinehart & Winston, Inc., 1965), pp. 107–120.

The total attitude of the individual toward "fluoride treatments" is the sum of the belief-affect products for all beliefs-affects held; thus:

Attitude Toward Fluoride Treatments

Belief-Affect Term	Belief Level		Affect Level		Product
Prevent tooth decay.	+3	×	+3	=	+9
Costly.	+1	×	−2	=	−2
Inconvenient.	0	×	−1	=	0
Not helpful for adults.	+2	×	−2	=	−4
. . . And so on.	. . .	×	. . .	=	. . .

Total Attitude = (+9) + (−2) + (0) + (−4) . . . (all other products)

The number representing the total attitude in this calculation has no absolute meaning in itself. But the total can range from a high positive number to a high negative number, depending on whether the person strongly or weakly believes good or bad qualities are associated with the *attitude-object*. The more highly positive the number, the more favorable the attitude. This procedure is useful because it considers attitudes to be composed of *multiple* propositions, and it provides a means for the analysis of those propositions. According to this view, attitudes could be shown to be influenced by adding new beliefs or affects to a person's system, or by changing his belief levels, and/or by modifying his affect levels.

Utility-Probability

A somewhat different approach to how we explain choosing from among alternative solutions, but one yielding a similar and certainly compatible view, is a pattern that is derived from decision theory and the theory of games.[14] Decision theory attempts to describe the variables in an immediate situation which influence behavioral choices in that situation. The principles derived from the theory can be applied to real human problems in real settings. This is why decision theory has attracted attention in such varied fields as economics, business, applied statistics, and psychology. The two major variables considered in decision theory are (1) *utility,* the judgment of the relative attractiveness of a choice; and (2) *probability,* the judgment of the relative probability of a choice. If we were to choose between choices X or Y, for example, our decision would be determined by the *utility* of X and Y (the relative attractiveness, usefulness, and desirability of these two choices), and the *probability* of X and Y (the relative likelihood or chances of obtaining X or Y).

[14] Ward Edwards and Amos Tversky, eds., *Decision Making* (Baltimore: Penguin Books, Inc., 1967).

STUDY PROBE 2
Identifying Some Components of Attitude Structures

In this section of the text we have outlined three category-systems for mental processes, the components of which are shown in the three columns below. In column 1 we have listed the components of the Krech, Crutchfield, and Ballachey system; in column 2 we have listed the components of the Fishbein system; in column 3 we have listed the components described by Edwards and Tversky.

1 *Krech / Crutchfield /* *Ballachey System*	2 *Fishbein* *System*	3 *Edwards / Tversky* *System*
Cognition Feeling Response Tendency	Belief Affect	Utility Probability

In the text we suggested a relationship between the Krech-Crutchfield-Ballachey system and the Fishbein system. Review the three classification-systems as a whole, and distinguish as many relationships (similarities and differences) among them as you can.

We have suggested that the Belief and Affect components of the second column parallel the Cognition and Feeling components of the first column. How would these systems relate to the components of the third column? Would the Cognition-Belief-Probability components have many common subelements? Would the Feeling-Affect-Utility components have many common subelements? In short, discern the common elements underlying the three analytical systems.

In making your analysis, do you *scan* or *focus?*

The overlapping elements in the three different approaches to the study of attitude and behavior, as we have reviewed them here, must be readily discernible. As students of speech communication and also as people who are frequently faced with the necessity of making decisions, we will find it generally useful to be familiar with the meanings of the terms presented. We can employ those terms to describe the elements of many problems that we may choose to analyze.

Beliefs and Evaluations as Factors in Decision Making

Now, drawing upon the views we have just examined, and also upon our discussion of beliefs and evaluations in Chapter 5 and upon our consideration of categorizing and language usage in Chapter 6, let us attempt to develop an understanding of how decisions are formulated, particularly as that formulation relates to the process of speech communication. Our basic premise will be a continuation and an extension of one which we have previously advanced; namely: *Beliefs* (B's) *and Evaluations* (E's) *are central to the speech communication process and are therefore central to any decision making that we may do.*

As we emphasized then (pages 115–118), as individuals each of us holds a number of beliefs about and attaches a number of valuations to any idea, entity, or activity of which we are aware. The object of our belief and evaluation may be a person (our doctor), a place (Timbuctu), an activity (snowmobiling), or a proposed action (birth control). The belief-evaluation "object" may be drawn from any time—past, present, or future; it may be real, supposed, or suspected.

In our earlier example we used *a place,* San Francisco, as our attitude-object. For our illustration here let's select *a proposed action* and make some characteristic "belief" statements about it. Most of us probably hold a number of convictions—some positive, some negative—about the taking of birth-control pills. Some typical ones might be:

> The Pill is the best scientific approach to keeping national population in check.
>
> The Pill is less costly than having children.
>
> The Pill can eventually solve the problem of urban overcrowding.
>
> The Pill can indirectly reduce the pollution of our physical environment.
>
> The Pill can help to reduce "dependency" taxation.
>
> The Pill can jeopardize the health of those who take it.
>
> The Pill violates the Christian Ethic.
>
> The Pill violates human rights.
>
> The Pill can endanger the capitalistic, producer-consumer system.

Each of us could, of course, attach varying degrees of belief-value to each of these assertions. And, faced with making a decision about a policy of birth control, we could place each one in a hierarchical framework: Some statements we might hold with complete conviction; others we would probably be less certain about, and still others we would exclude from our hierarchy almost entirely. To those beliefs we hold with certainty, we might assign a probability level of 1.0; to those about which we have some doubts we could assign, say, a level of .9; to another, .4; and so on down.

In each of these belief assertions the category of the proposed action, *taking birth control pills,* is located within a larger category. For example:

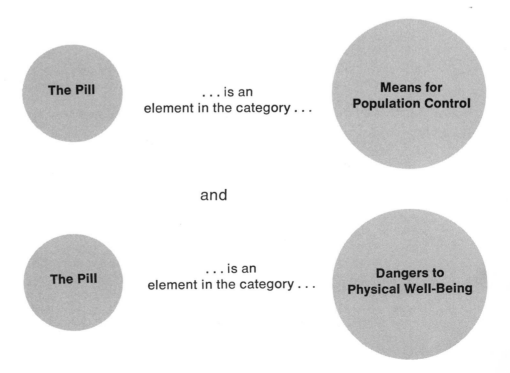

. . . and so on. When we locate the Pill (attitude-object) within a larger category of concepts (Population Control, Physical Well-Being, etc.), all of the feelings we have for and the evaluations we make of the larger category become associated with the smaller category—in this case, the Pill as the attitude-object.

And, of course, the evaluations (degree of personal feeling) we hold for the concept in the larger category could be rated somewhere within a range between 0 and 1, with 0 representing the lowest possible evaluation and 1 representing the highest possible evaluation. We may, for instance, feel very positive about "Population Control" (1), but believe that "Urban Overcrowding" is very undesirable (0).

Belief-Evaluation Clusters in Decision Making

Clearly, any decision we make—or any problem that we need to solve in order to make that decision—is going to involve an *aggregate* of all of the beliefs and evaluations we happen to hold in a cluster with reference to the central concept, entity, or activity upon which a potential or impending communicative interaction is to be focused. In any given case, while we may feel that we are "basing" our decision on a single belief-evaluation, actually we are *ordering our priorities* among *all* of the operant B-E's within the total cluster. And in this ordering, our B-E's are conflicting, intersecting, and interacting to produce the decision.

If your listener dislikes "violation of human rights," his attitude toward the Pill will be determined in part by the level of his belief that the Pill violates such rights, and then this belief-level will be a negative factor in his B-E cluster. If he does not believe that the Pill violates human rights, his negative feelings about such violation will not matter. Going further, the individual's level of belief that the Pill is a sound, scientific approach to keeping population in check and his evaluation of the need to hold down the number of the country's inhabitants will contribute to his total attitude or B-E cluster. Similar assessments could be made for all of the other associative elements.

In some research on this subject, Martin Fishbein proposed that the relationship between belief and evaluation is multiplicative and that the products of that interrelatedness are additive.[15] Additional studies are needed on this and other relationships involving beliefs, evaluations, and attitudes. There is ample evidence, however, to support the conclusion that the total cluster of beliefs and evaluations we associate with an entity, object, or concept—combined with the ways in which these associations intersect and interact with one another—are of great importance in speech communication.

[15] Martin Fishbein, "A Consideration of Beliefs, Attitudes and Their Relationship," *Current Studies in Social Psychology,* ed. Ivan D. Steiner and Martin Fishbein (New York: Holt, Rinehart & Winston, Inc., 1965).

STUDY PROBE 3
Beliefs and Evaluations: Self-Assessment

In Study Probe 1 of Chapter 5 (page 118) you were asked to assess your attitudes and beliefs regarding a particular issue. Here, you are asked to select a number of subjects—two or three at least—and formulate a fairly detailed *Belief-Evaluation cluster* for each of them.

More specifically, as a first step, list for each of your chosen topics all of the *beliefs* you hold about it or associate with it. Second, attempt to determine the *level of probability* at which you hold each belief. Use a scale of .00 to 1.00. (Let .00 represent impossible and 1.00 represent certain. Most of your judgments will, of course, be relative and will fall somewhere between these two extremes.) As a third step, for each relevant evaluation, use a similar scale to depict the level of that evaluation. (Let .00 represent absolute dislike, and let 1.00 represent the highest possible favorable evaluation, with your judgments falling somewhere in between.)

The interrelationships among the various elements of your B-E clusters, if carefully worked out as suggested, should provide you with an enlarged understanding of how you "feel" about certain things and why you "believe" as you do.

Using Belief-Evaluation Clusters to Induce Decision Making in Others

In the beginning, this associating, clustering, and interaction of beliefs and values goes on inside our minds and assists us toward making our personal decisions. But when and if we reach the point where we feel impelled to *communicate* these decisions to others and to influence others to "decide" as we have, we must give very serious consideration to what is likely to be going on inside the minds of those others.

Assessing B-E Clusters of Others

Fortunately, there are some reasonably sound assumptions we can make— assumptions that will help us communicate our decisions and the desirability of those decisions to others. We can begin by recognizing that *every other person*— like us—has his own unique Belief-Evaluation cluster for any given attitude-object. This being the case, we can of course expect the elements comprising the cluster in any given instance to vary from individual listener to individual listener.

Typically, there will be some concepts for which a listener will hold many beliefs. For other concepts he will hold only a few, if any. Many of the constituent elements in the B-E cluster of Listener A, for instance, may more or less coincide with those of the speaker. This listener may associate many beliefs and levels of belief with the concept or proposed course of action advocated by the speaking agent; he may "believe" largely as the speaker does.

Listener B, in contrast, may have only a few beliefs about the central idea or proposal. As he approaches the communicative event, he is neither "convinced" nor "unconvinced" of the appropriateness of the advocated position or proposed action. He may be moderately "concerned," but no more than that.

Listener C may have scarcely any beliefs at all about the central concept or the proposed action or the problems therein. Conceivably, the cluster of Listener C's belief-evaluations may in no way resemble those of Listener A, Listener B, or the speaker. Seemingly, he is indifferent to the whole business, and soon may decide only that he doesn't "belong" in this context.

Listener D, on the other hand, is anything but neutral or indifferent. The individual elements to be found in his B-E cluster may be substantively similar to those contained in the speaker's cluster, but the *evaluations* he places upon them may be completely the reverse of those given priority by the speaker. Indeed, some—perhaps many—of Listener D's cluster elements may be such as to interact in a highly conflictive manner with the idea or action advocated by the speaking agent.

We could proceed in this fashion to describe many different types of listeners, but these four should be enough to suggest the nature and dimensions of the communicator's task as he attempts to "analyze" his audience and formulate his procedures for communicatively inducing co-agents to interact positively and productively in the decision-making process. Obviously, in the circumstances we have described, we see again the significance of a point we have stressed with some frequency in these pages: The agent must know the other agents; he must know the context; and he must know—to the greatest extent possible—what is likely to happen when the B-E clusters of all agents are involved in a communicative interaction.

Interacting with Others on the Basis of B-E Clusters

Let us look at a few specifics of what *is* likely to happen.

In the decision-*inducing* stage of the communication process particularly, the speaker needs to know as much as possible about how his listeners are likely to "feel," react, and behave. In earlier pages of this book we have proffered a number of means by which the speaking agent may try to predict such behavior. Belief-Evaluation clusters provide some additional means.

In a broad sense, we may assert that:

a. The more a listener knows about a particular, potential attitude-object—the greater his familiarity with it—the more *beliefs* he is likely to have about it.

b. The larger the listener's experience with the focal attitude-object, the greater the range of his *evaluations* is likely to be.

For instance, if Listener A holds a great many of the beliefs held by the speaker and if his evaluations of those beliefs are quite similar to those of the speaker, the two will tend to "agree," and Listener A will very probably and readily decide as the speaking agent wants him to.

Since Listener B holds only a few beliefs about the speaker's proposal and apparently attaches no really strong evaluation to any of them, his B-E cluster will be limited in scope and probably comparatively simple. The fact that he is present in the situation may indicate that he is sufficiently concerned to want to learn more about the problem and may, in fact, be seeking additional beliefs which will enable him to concur in the speaker's position and/or the means of implementing the proposed action.

Listener C, knowing little or nothing about the whole matter and apparently indifferent to the problem or the need for a decision, will probably tend to be quite open to new information and quite susceptible to the speaker's influence, if he decides to remain in the context.

Listener D will present the speaker with his greatest challenge. Since he is particularly prejudiced against the idea or action being advocated, his B-E cluster very probably will be rigidly and persistently held. He "knows what he knows"; and that "knowledge," such as it is, cannot easily be changed. If the speaker is to induce coincidence-of-belief and congruent evaluation in this listener, his most effective approach will probably be through Gradual Reciprocal Increments, a procedure which we will explore at some length in Chapter 8 (pages 252–253).

The implications of this kind of analysis must be clear. When a speaker is communicating for the purpose of inducing others to make a decision which coincides with or is at least compatible with his own, he must direct his efforts toward influencing in some positive way and to a significant degree the Belief-Evaluation clusters of his listeners. He must communicate and interact with them in such a way as to *add to, subtract from,* or *reorder* the belief-evaluation structures of the other agents involved in the context. For problem-solving decision making to be achieved successfully, the speaker must devise ways to develop, modify, and/or otherwise reconstruct the attitudes of listeners toward his proposal.

How, specifically, may the speaker hope to accomplish this? Certain options (procedural decisions) are available to him. For one thing, he may attempt to *add new belief propositions or knowledge* not heretofore a part of the belief system of the listener. Essentially, this is an *additive* process. The speaking agent supplies new information, and—quite possibly—by focusing upon it he provides the listener with some possible paths leading toward favorable interpretation of that information.

As another option, the speaker may try to lead his listeners to *make new evaluations of beliefs presently held.* One usually effective means of accomplishing this is for the speaker to try to associate his subject or proposed action with other and, perhaps, larger categories that he knows his listeners value highly. He could, for example, "tie in" his own particular B-E cluster with such larger and ordinarily-believed-in categories as fairness, productivity, efficiency, individuality, etc.

Still another option which the speaker may elect is to reverse the foregoing procedure by trying to associate possible objections or counterpositions with categories that he knows his listeners dislike, fear, or abhor. In circumstances of this kind the speaker could, for instance, tie his opponents' counterpropositions or counterarguments to high taxes, corruption of public morality (with all that may mean), pollution of the environment, highway death tolls, etc. We would urge most strongly, however, that the speaker make every effort to be truthful and objective as he tries to link the positions or propositions of his antagonist to objectionable or negative categories of the kind mentioned.

Turning to a *subtractive* means by which to affect the Belief-Evaluation clusters of his hearers, the speaking agent can attempt to *change listeners' existing belief levels.* In this procedure, the speaker may attempt to "subtract" old or previously established propositions to which the listener has presumably committed himself. "Usually it is an honor and a privilege," he might say, "to fight and die to protect and preserve the nation's honor. But," he might declare, "it is neither an honor nor a privilege to die *on foreign soil* thousands of miles from the homeland. Nor is it an *obligation* to be shot and killed in Vietnam, for *there* unwilling soldiers are being commanded by ambivalent officers to die for persons who do not know or care what the issues are."

Or, as still another option, the speaker may attempt to *modify the affect-level* of his listeners. He might, for example, cause his listeners to adjust their level of belief in the desirability of using oral contraceptives by arguing that decreased population by means of birth-control pills will, in the long run, seriously endanger our long-established producer/consumer economic system (producing an affect-level of, say, .55 rather than .90).

As a speaker, then, you may attempt to affect the beliefs and belief-evaluations of your listeners by:

    a. Supplying new information and new "interpretations" of new information.

    b. Inducing new evaluations of listeners' existing beliefs by:

        (1) Associating your proposition with larger categories admired by listeners.

        (2) Associating counterpropositions with categories objectionable to listeners.

    c. Changing listeners' belief-levels by subtracting ideas or propositions to which the listeners have previously committed themselves.

    d. Modifying the affect-levels of listeners—increasing or decreasing the intensity of convictions heretofore held by them.

To return to our earlier example, by exercising these options you could attempt to provide new information about birth-control pills, alter the belief-structure of your listeners concerning them, and instill or obliterate certain category-associations—of a positive or negative character—with regard to the desirability of controlling population by such means. To the extent that you are able to utilize these procedures effectively you may induce others to concur in your decisions.

Taking Cognizance of B-E Temporality

In weighing the efficacy of the B-E cluster approach to decision making, we must not lose sight of the oft-mentioned fact that speech communication is a *process,* and as such it cannot be "frozen" in time. Belief-evaluation structures not only vary from person to person but *they also change from moment to moment.* And at any given time, the beliefs and evaluations which come to mind, consciously or subconsciously, at the mention of an idea, entity, or object comprise our attitude toward that idea, entity, or object *at that particular instant.* And, even in a very short span of time, differences in B-E clusters may develop as certain elements become more salient or move to the center of our attitudinal focus at a given moment. As we learn more about a subject, or think about it, or talk about it, very likely we will be adding elements to that cluster and/or modifying some of the elements that exist within it.

As a speaker presenting and developing a subject, position, or proposition, if you dwell on the negative B-E elements to which your listeners are sensitive, these negative elements may be made to outweigh the positive elements which the listeners hold but are not focusing upon at that particular moment. Hence both *timing* and *focal emphasis* assume extreme importance.

Weighing "Informative/Persuasive" Considerations

Note that under this system of communicatively induced decision making you are providing new data, new value systems, new viewpoints, etc. That is to say, you are both "informing" and "persuading" your hearers to think, believe, or act as *you* think, believe, or act. Not infrequently, speech textbooks attempt to draw a distinction, more or less sharply, between speaking *to inform* and speaking *to persuade.* From the view we have presented here, however, this distinction cannot be sharply set. Any speech communication, whether "informative" or "persuasive," must inevitably effect changes in the B-E clusters of those listening and reacting to speaker messages. We may say, perhaps, that the so-called informative speech presents relatively more new items having "neutral" connotations, whereas the so-named persuasive speech tends to seek a greater modification of existent beliefs and scales of values. However, both "types" of speaking present new elements and modify prevailing beliefs and evaluation structures.

Regardless of its "type," any oral communication having as its objective the creation or inducement of decision making in others must strive in some significant degree to originate and shape that decision by enlarging, decreasing, or restructuring the B-E clusters of listening agents. Taken from this perspective, *the whole end of speech communication is to influence B-E clusters.*

Relationship of Attitude to Behavior

Before moving on to the other generative factors bearing upon decision making, there is still another aspect of beliefs and evaluations which we must consider. The current literature of behavioral science raises some questions concerning the relationship of attitudes to behavior.[16] In the past, it has often been assumed that there must be a direct relation between the two and that attitude must be almost synonymous with behavior. In fact, attitudes have been defined by some as "predispositions to behave." More recently, however, there has been some recognition of the general fact that attitudes may not predict behavior accurately and adequately.

A frequently cited study on this point was done by Richard La Piere.[17] He traveled through the United States with a Chinese couple. During the trip, they stayed at more than sixty hotels and ate at nearly 200 restaurants, and they were rarely refused accommodation or service. Following the trip, La Piere mailed questionnaires to the hotels and restaurants they had visited, asking whether they would accept Chinese guests. Nine of every ten responses were negative. This finding seemed to argue that what people *say* and what they *do* may differ appreciably. Because of La Piere's conclusions and a number of other studies which have produced similar findings, some investigators argue that attitudes cannot be used successfully as predictors of social behavior.

Such conclusions, however, present certain difficulties. B-E clusters change from time to time, as we have said, so they cannot be perfect predictors even of themselves. Moreover, as we have also observed, B-E clusters involving social issues are comparatively large and complex. Only an overly simplified study could pretend to measure any one of these clusters completely. Too, since in many of these studies attitudes were measured at a very different time from the occurrence of the behavior, some of the incongruities could be attributed to the passage of time. Additionally, the attitudes measured were often quite general, whereas the behaviors observed were specific.

The problems can be illustrated easily. Suppose one day you asked a person whether he preferred hamburger or steak, and he replied "Steak." Later you observe his behavior in a grocery store. He looks over all the meats and buys hamburger. Would you be shocked? Would you think perhaps he had lied to you?

[16] Leon Festinger, "Behavioral Support for Opinion Change," *Public Opinion Quarterly,* XXVIII (1964): 404–417.

[17] Richard T. La Piere, "Attitude versus Actions," *Social Forces,* XIII (1934): 230–237.

Would you say that his attitudes have little to do with his behavior? Probably not, for you would realize that his earlier and generally favorable response to steak was not the sole determiner of his present specific action. He may not have money enough to buy steak at the moment, or the available steak may not look very good to him, or he may even have had steak at his last meal. We might better consider his attitude toward the "buying of steak" at the moment he is making his decision. We must realize that factors other than attitude may also influence our decision making.

Value Systems Operant in Decision Making

Other systems of values play an unmistakable role in any decisions we make. *Values* are higher-level abstractions and more general than the B-E clusters we have discussed thus far. In fact, values may be seen as *clusters of B-E clusters*. Value systems are learned, developed throughout our lifetime, and determine our life style. We need, therefore, to understand something of the impact these systems have upon our thinking and how they affect decision making.

"Value-Types of Men": Spranger

Eduard Spranger, a German scholar, developed a theory of human behavior in which he maintained that there are certain primary types of human beings, identifiable according to the dominant values held by each.[18] Although Spranger agrees that an individual certainly has more than one set of values influencing his behavior, he argues that one value system will predominate. He describes six primary value-types, as follows:

> *Theoretical Type* — Values the pursuit of and discovery of truth, the "intellectual" life.
>
> *Economic Type* — Values that which is useful, practical.
>
> *Aesthetic Type* — Values form, harmony, and beauty.
>
> *Social Type* — Values love, sympathy, warmth, and sensitivity in relationships with people.
>
> *Political Type* — Values competition, influence, and personal power.
>
> *Religious Type* — Values unity, wholeness, and a sense of purpose above man.

According to Spranger, our lives are dominated by systems of value. An "economic" man will want to speak and hear about economic topics and propositions. He will be more sensitive and responsive to economic issues. His interpretation of almost any topic will bear the economic stamp.

[18] Eduard Spranger, *Types of Men,* trans. P. Prigors from the Fifth German Edition (Haale [Saale]: M. Niemeyer, 1928).

STUDY PROBE 4
Adapting to Value Systems of Others in a Job Interview

Suppose you are applying for a summer sales job in a downtown department store. To obtain the position you must engage in a personal interview with the store manager. Somehow, prior to your talking with him, you learn that he is what Spranger would describe as a "theoretical" man. Plan your interview accordingly and describe the approach and procedure you would follow in the interview.

Supposing, in turn, the store manager to be each of the other "types"— *economic, aesthetic, social, political, religious*—prepare what you believe to be a workable approach and plan in each of these hypothetical instances.

The American Value System: Ruesch

Psychiatrist Jurgen Ruesch, in *Communication: The Social Matrix of Psychiatry*, advances a different classification of values. He asserts that American values show five emphases:

1. Puritan and pioneer morality.
2. Equality.
3. Sociality.
4. Success.
5. Change.

Ruesch writes:

> *The American psychology has been described as being governed by the premises of equality, sociality, success, and change, which are thought to be interconnected by the multiple premises of puritan and pioneer morality. These four values, together with the core of moral principles, can be conceived, on the one hand, as pivotal points around which American life revolves, and on the other, as cornerstones upon which communication is based.*[19]

While it is impossible to draw up a specific list of value systems held by all men, these attempts by Spranger and Ruesch serve to clarify what we mean by a "value system" and to indicate the potential influence of these systems in speech communication, as well as in other kinds of human behavior. Value systems cannot be turned on or off at will; a strong value system will pervade and tend to persist in an individual's behavior.

Value systems affect the decisions of speakers and listeners alike. Because a man's values are so central to his thinking, he cannot speak for long without revealing what those values are. As listeners, we expect a speaker in a certain role to conform to the values typical of that role. Occasionally, we see politicians whose essential values do not all seem to be "political." Eugene McCarthy may be an example. Such a man presents an enigmatic figure. Our analysis of any speaker must include some consideration of the values he embraces and reveals. His values, along with more specific B-E clusters, will influence the decisions he makes and attempts to communicate.

Motivation and Decision Making

We may arrive at decisions on the basis of the interplay of our Belief-Evaluation clusters and systems of values; but for significant behavior to occur,

---

[19] Jurgen Ruesch and Gregory Bateson, *Communication: The Social Matrix of Psychiatry* (New York: W. W. Norton & Company, Inc., 1951), p. 95.

we need *motivation* to energize and provide further direction for our behavior. As we view man in his environment, we can note that he often seems impelled to action. The living human, in fact, is never completely at rest. It is not easy, however, to detect just what it is that thus impels him. Human motivation is, unfortunately, one of those complex subjects about which we do not have as many answers as we should like. Yet, progress is being made.

A number of psychologists have seen motivation as the product of primary and secondary motives—a rather useful and usable classification of human striving. *Primary* motives are taken to cover those basic physiological needs which must be satisfied if the life of the individual and his species is to continue. *Secondary* motives are the learned, social needs—the needs he has for functioning effectively and well within his society.

Hierarchy of Prepotent Needs: Maslow

Somewhat more detailed and helpful is the general theory of motivation developed by A. H. Maslow.[20] He lists five basic needs, rank-ordered according to their prepotency or priority:

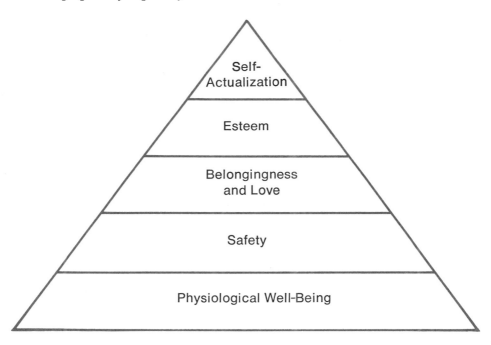

The *physiological needs* are the demands of the individual for:

Food.

Water.

Procreation.

Homeostasis or balance.

These needs are basic to life and must be satisfied *first*. They form the base of his "priority pyramid." *Safety needs* are on a higher level. Man desires an

[20] A. H. Maslow, *Motivation and Personality* (New York: Harper & Row, Publishers, 1954), especially Chapter 5, "A Theory of Human Motivation."

orderly, smoothly functioning world in which sudden, unexpected, and potentially dangerous events do not occur often. He wants to feel settled and at ease, rather than threatened.

The *need to belong* and *to be loved* reflects man's social nature. Man desires to be loved by family and friends. He wants to belong, to be "in."

On the next level are the *esteem* needs. Man likes to have self-esteem, self-respect, a reasonably high evaluation of himself; and he desires the esteem and respect of others. He seeks status; he likes to be recognized and appreciated.

The need at the highest level is *self-actualization* or self-fulfillment. Most of us know or at least know of persons—artists, writers, political leaders—who seem to have satisfied all the other needs, but who are still motivated to further action. Maslow would call this behavior the product of self-actualization; a man must be what he *can* be.

Maslow's theory holds that these needs form a hierarchy of prepotency—in other words, the physiological needs take precedence over all others. If the physiological needs are reasonably well satisfied, then the higher-level needs will serve as motivators. Maslow realizes, of course, that this hierarchy is not rigid and that our lower-level needs do not require complete satisfaction before the higher-level needs begin to influence activity, to generate motivation for us. But we should not look for much evidence of self-actualizing behavior unless the lower-level needs appear to have been fairly well met.

Functional Autonomy of Motives: Allport

Another helpful concept for an understanding of motivation is that of the "functional autonomy of motives." This principle, developed by psychologist Gordon Allport, maintains that behaviors and desires which are learned in order to satisfy basic needs may eventually become motivators themselves, even in the absence of the basic and originally associated need.[21] For example, many of us probably had a grandfather who worked hard to provide food and shelter for his family in difficult times. Even after he had provided the necessities of life and all the members of his family were comfortable, however, he continued to work hard. Strenuous effort had become a part of him, and he was driven to it for itself alone long after the original need for such work had been satisfied. From this example we can see how the value systems mentioned earlier could become functionally autonomous and serve as motivators of behavior.

For the most part, motivations are necessary and helpful; they provide the drive and help shape the direction of our behavior. They are, however, a mixed blessing. The blocking of a goal, coupled with the continuance of a drive, can lead to frustration. Frustration, in turn, can lead to aggression or to even less adaptive behavior, such as flight, negativism, defeatism, and even withdrawal from reality. And, of course, none of these behaviors is conducive to positive, productive speech interaction.

Consistency and Cognition Balancing

Another view of motivation which has been applied frequently in studies of communication derives from psychological "consistency" theories.[22] The general

---

[21] Gordon W. Allport, "The Functional Autonomy of Motives," *American Journal of Psychology,* L (1937): 141–156.

[22] See the review in Roger Brown, *Social Psychology* (New York: The Free Press, 1965), Chapter 11.

explanation of these theories is that we are all motivated to achieve *a balance or harmony among our cognitions.* Cognition, as defined by the theorists, covers all of our knowledge, beliefs, and judgments about ourselves or our environment. If anything should happen to create an imbalance or state of dissonance in our cognitions, then we are motivated to adjust those cognitions to achieve a *new* balance.

As an instance of the theories which have been developed on these premises, consider the "congruity" approach of Osgood, Suci, and Tannenbaum.[23] To test their hypotheses, a number of sources (speakers, writers) who had been evaluated by a group of subjects as either positive or negative were afterward positively and negatively associated with concepts which the subjects themselves had evaluated as positive or negative. The predictions of Osgood, Suci, and Tannenbaum were largely supported by the results of this study.

If you wanted to test a "consistency" theory yourself, you could produce an experimental message in which former President Kennedy (*positive source here*) supposedly spoke out against (*negative association*) a proposal to improve higher education (*positive concept*). According to Osgood, Suci, and Tannenbaum, if a speaker we respect (+) speaks against (−) a proposal we favor (+), our cognitive balance will be upset, and we will be motivated to adjust our evaluations of source and concept in order to strike a new balance. As a result of the experiment, presumably we would see Kennedy somewhat less positively, but also see the proposal for higher education somewhat less positively. If Kennedy were to speak against crime, our cognitive balance would *not* be upset, and we would have no need or motivation for making cognitive realignment. If he (+) spoke in favor (+) of a policy we opposed (−), then the balance again *would* be upset, and cognitive change should occur. We should then achieve a rebalance by respecting Kennedy a little less and favoring the proposal somewhat more.

STUDY PROBE 5
Discovering Examples of Cognitive Balancing and Congruity

Familiarize yourself with a number of current speech communication events and find in them examples that, for you, represent each of the eight possible contexts listed below:

    a. Positive source for a policy you like.
    b. Positive source for a policy you dislike.
    c. Negative source for a policy you like.
    d. Negative source for a policy you dislike.
    e. Positive source against a policy you like.
    f. Positive source against a policy you dislike.
    g. Negative source against a policy you like.
    h. Negative source against a policy you dislike.

---

[23] See Charles E. Osgood, George J. Suci, and Percy H. Tannenbaum, *The Measurement of Meaning* (Urbana, Ill.: University of Illinois Press, 1957), Chapter 5.

Earlier we commented about a politician who does not reveal a value system that is primarily "political." We cite him here again as another instance of the creation of cognitive imbalance. We must strive for a mental consistency either by changing our mind's image of what a politician must be or by removing the candidate from our category of "proper politicians." Seemingly, it will always be easier to shift our judgment of a specific case than to change our view of a general category. The "final verdict" on these matters, of course, is not yet in. Nevertheless, theories of cognitive balance and consistency hold promise and deserve further research, as does—in fact—the entire subject of motivation in speech communication.

Summary Examples

To help summarize our considerations thus far, let us look at a few examples. Suppose that an individual in a politically powerful position declared, "I have decided that busing school children is not a workable or desirable means for bringing about integration." Or, in a very different context, suppose that a father tells his son: "I have decided that you may not use the car this weekend."

These statements of decision, in themselves, are relatively simple and straightforward. Their meaning is clear. They do not, however, reveal anything about the context from which they were derived or about the issues that prompted their utterance. If we want to know about the decision-making process which has produced the statements (necessary, certainly, if we hoped to *change* those decisions), we would have to look beyond the declarations themselves.

It is this "looking beyond" that we have been concerned with in this chapter, and to that end we have tried to suggest some of the means for the simultaneous analysis of a complex series of beliefs and evaluations and have emphasized the necessity for considering critically underlying human values and motives. And, in so doing, we have endeavored to provide some useful procedures pointing to a more discerning analysis and thoroughgoing understanding of the processes of decision making, especially as those processes may bear upon social issues.

Limitations on Decision Making

As we try to understand and practice perceptive decision making, we will almost certainly encounter certain *limiting factors*. Given Belief-Evaluation clusters, value systems, and motives which "ought" to lead in a certain direction, we may see man take yet another—and entirely unexpected—turn. Much as we might like to have them, there are no infallible "predictors" of human decision-making behavior. As with our friend who told us he preferred steak and then bought hamburger, there is sometimes more involved in a decision than we have counted on. It will be useful to our purpose here to examine, at least briefly, some of the factors which tend to place limitations on the formulation of decisions which we make and try to communicate.

Internal Limitations

Initially, we need to examine the constraints which are placed on our decision making by factors within ourselves. Specifically, we should note: (1)

capacities and abilities of agents, (2) *habit-fixed behaviors,* and (3) *constraints on sensation and perception.*

Individual Capacities and Abilities

As most of us are painfully aware, the ends men strive for cannot always be achieved. Natural endowments and learned abilities set definite limitations on human behavior. We cannot see, hear, or smell those stimuli which fall outside our sensory thresholds. We cannot think beyond our intellectual powers or act beyond our physical strength and endurance. If the resources are not available, they cannot be used. A deafened Beethoven composed great music, but a congenitally deaf Beethoven could not have. One of the most awkward questions for a teacher comes when a conscientious student who is working well and at about his best level asks what he can do to raise his grade. More than a grade-making decision is involved here: the teacher must decide whether to tell the student merely "to keep trying," or to speak realistically of limited abilities and capacities. All of us have these limitations; and although they may not become evident, they will work to alter the decisions we make and communicate to others.

Habit-Fixed Behaviors

Habit and "custom," once they are firmly established, tend to shape and often constrain our decision-making capabilities. Habit, we may say, is a "fixed" behavior; decision making—until an actual and final choice is made—is a *potential* behavior. The fixed behavior tends, generally, to be the more potent, the more decisive, when both are operant in a context.

Our habits are somewhat like our categories: they are ways of generalizing and abstracting experience. When we are learning to perform a complex task, such as driving a car or doing a new dance step, in the beginning we must concentrate all of our attention on the activity *as such*. We focus as much as possible on the specific task and are acutely aware of each individual substep of the process. As our learning progresses, the complex series of interrelated steps blend together; and, gradually, we are able then to perform the entire task without consciously focusing upon each of the successive phases or elements of it. If we are driving, we can pay more attention to the road and to passing and oncoming cars, without having to think about such individual component acts as shifting gears or applying brakes. If we are dancing, we can converse with a partner (in dance forms where proximity is possible) or focus on other dancers without having to concentrate on what our left foot is doing at the moment. In short, we have developed habits.

Habituated behavior thus allows us to perform complex tasks while we are engaged in additional or peripheral activities. It allows us a broader scope of behavior and, often, to apply our consciousness to higher levels of abstract thought. At the same time we must recognize that, as they become strong, habits do much to regulate—even limit—our potential behavior.

For example, accuracy of speech articulation is largely habitual. As children, while we were learning to speak, we were "monitoring" or listening closely to our own articulation. Quite quickly, however, we developed language habits that allowed us to drop that conscious and active monitoring. If the articulation habits we had then formed were socially and communicatively desirable, all was well. But if those learned habits of speech do not fit the modes and expectations of the society in which we *now* live, then our choices are too limited and relearning is necessary. Trying to change articulatory or grammatical patterns in adulthood dramatically demonstrates the fact that when the new behaviors we are trying to learn run counter to our fixed habits, the new learning can be especially difficult.

Sensory and Perceptual Constraints

In Chapter 6 we took cognizance of the factors which limit sensation and accurate perception, and these same limitations can constrain our decision making. Adaptation, selective perception, and perceptual defense may affect our decisions. When we are ego-involved in a topic, we will make and judge statements about it, and we will do this differently from the ways in which people who are *not* ego-involved will do it. As we have emphasized with some frequency, when we focus on certain elements or aspects of a subject, other elements or aspects fade or become blurred and distorted. Similarly, when we try to make and communicate our decisions, we will tend to selectively perceive our "reasons" and perceptually defend our "choices."

Externally Imposed Limitations

Just as one's decision-making behaviors are checked by limitations within his person, so are they further directed and checked from without. Among those we must allow for are the impingements of environmental and societal factors and the unexpected and exploratory behaviors of people themselves.

Environmental-Societal Impingements

Man's actions are often determined by his adjustment to his physical environment, to his culture and society, to his immediate family, and to his peer group. Signs of these adjustments and influences are everywhere: the Eskimo wears warm clothing and eats foods which are most accessible to him; the Dobuan adopts the rituals, mores, and taboos of his culture; the Frenchman speaks the language of his society; the upstate New Yorker tends to vote for the same political party as did his father; the college senior usually accepts a larger number of the values of his peer group than does the college freshman. These behaviors are not the products of free choices. They are guided and determined from without. One may be driven from within to seek the esteem of others, but may be directed by them in the behaviors by which he seeks it.

Change-Impelled, Exploratory Behaviors

A final limiting factor we should mention is that wonderful, perverse tendency of man occasionally to take the unexpected turn. Laboratory studies of rats in learning situations show that those animals occasionally make shifts in the strategies used to reach their goals. They do this without any special reason and even when there can be no chance to improve their payoff or rewards. The only motive seems to be a desire for some *change* and for "exploratory" behavior. If laboratory rats can show this curiosity, then we should not be too surprised to find it in human problem-solving behavior. This does imply, however, that our predictions of human behavior can never be made with certainty, and that there can be no end to the investigations of human decision making.

A Specific Case for Study and Analysis

In order to integrate the materials we have been developing and to illustrate their application in a speech communication context, let us return to the specific case referred to early in this chapter. Over a period of two months during the fall of 1858, Stephen A. Douglas, the incumbent Senator from Illinois, and Abraham Lincoln, his political opponent, met in seven joint debates over the pressing issues of that day. The immediate prize was the Senate seat then held by Douglas. We will consider these debates briefly in the light of some of the decision-generating concepts developed in this chapter. What choice was being presented to the voters in that election? Which side would you have supported if you had been voting in that year? Is it enough to say that Lincoln opposed slavery and Douglas did not? Which man won the debates?

We use this case to illustrate the point that instances of genuine communicative interaction can best be described and evaluated with the kind of multidimensional approach we have outlined in the foregoing pages of this chapter. Single and simple propositions can rarely represent more than the surface concerns of any issue. Hence we will be dealing here with a more complex and far-ranging *set* of propositions, many of the effects of which are still with us today.

In 1858, Lincoln and Douglas were *agents interacting in a context*. Our considerations may be facilitated if we refresh our memories as to the factors which helped to formulate that context. Although those debates occurred only a little over one hundred years ago, we must remember how greatly life in those

Aside from the availability of public-address systems or the lack of them, an obvious contrast between the present context and that of the 1858 debates is in the length to which speeches may run. In that day people came willing to listen to a three-hour discussion of issues, as in this scene at Charleston, Illinois, September 18.

times differed from what we have experienced. Today our fifty United States have a combined population of over 200 million. We are concerned about threatening overpopulation, the unsteady state of the economy, pollution of our environment, whether to make more trips to the moon and explore the planets, our relations with many foreign powers, and with questions of human rights. When Lincoln and Douglas met, there were only thirty-two states in the Union with a total population of 30 million (fewer than in New York and California today). Illinois itself had become a state during the lifetime of the speakers. Many conveniences of modern life which we accept so casually today —the automobile, electric lighting, the telephone, the typewriter, and television —were then all accomplishments for the future. Yet the concerns of the day were not totally different. Questions were raised then, too, about foreign relations and about human rights. At that time, human slavery existed as a fact and was a critical issue.

In the beginning of this chapter we presented one exchange between Lincoln and Douglas. In their second debate, which took place on August 27 at Freeport, Illinois, Lincoln asked the following as the second in a series of four questions:

Can the people of a United States Territory, in any lawful way, against the wish of any citizen of the United States, exclude slavery from its limits prior to the formation of a State constitution?

Douglas answered:

I answer emphatically, as Mr. Lincoln has heard me answer a hundred times from every stump in Illinois, that in my opinion the people of a Territory can, by lawful means, exclude slavery from their limits prior to the formation of a State constitution. Mr. Lincoln knew that I had answered that question over and over again. He heard me argue the Nebraska bill on that principle all over the State in 1854, in 1855, and in 1856, and he has no excuse for pretending to be in doubt as to my position on that question. It matters not what way the Supreme Court may hereafter decide as to the abstract question whether slavery may or may not go into a Territory under the Constitution, the people have the lawful means to introduce it or exclude it as they please, for the reason that slavery cannot exist a day or an hour anywhere unless it is supported by local regulations. Those police regulations can only be established by the local legislature; and if the people are opposed to slavery, they will elect representatives to that body who will by unfriendly legislation effectually prevent the introduction of it into their midst. If, on the contrary, they are for it, their legislation will favor its extension. Hence, no matter what the decision of the Supreme Court may be on that abstract question, still the right of the people to make a slave Territory or a free Territory is perfect and complete under the Nebraska bill. I hope Mr. Lincoln deems my answer satisfactory on that point.

Lincoln's question and Douglas's answer appear simple enough on the surface. Yet this exchange probably attracted more attention and had greater influence on subsequent events than any other in the debates. Some highly significant decision making lay behind the raising of the question and the eliciting of the fateful response to it.

It has been reported that Lincoln decided, against the counsel of some of his advisers, to put this question to Douglas in the hope of forcing him to take a position which would further split the national Democratic party. Douglas was at odds with President Buchanan and his Administration because of Douglas's opposition to the President's Lecompton policy. The South was also wary of Douglas. When Douglas broke with the Administration on the Lecompton matter, a charge had been made that he was planning to switch to the Republican party whenever circumstances made such a move possible. Lincoln referred to this charge in one of the debates.

In earlier years Douglas had said the question posed by Lincoln was one for the Supreme Court to decide. The Supreme Court, in the Dred Scott decision, had ruled essentially in the negative. Lincoln believed Douglas would now shift his view and answer in the affirmative, a position popular with Illinois voters. Lincoln's advisers argued that an affirmative answer would help Douglas retain his Senate seat. But Lincoln knew the South would not accept as *President* a man who held this view, and reportedly replied, "I am after larger game; the battle of 1860 is worth a hundred of this."

Lincoln, clearly, had his eye on a bigger prize than a Senatorship; and he was beginning to set in motion a daring decision-making process. He determined to make the most of Douglas' shift of position and pressed the point as the debate continued:

> In the Senate of the United States, in 1856, Judge Trumbull, in a speech, substantially, if not directly, put the same interrogatory to Judge Douglas, as to whether the people of a Territory had the lawful power to exclude slavery prior to the formation of a constitution. Judge Douglas then answered at considerable length, and his answer will be found in the *Congressional Globe,* under the date of June 9, 1856. The judge said that whether the people could exclude slavery prior to the formation of a constitution or not was a question to be decided by the Supreme Court. He put that proposition, as will be seen by the *Congressional Globe,* in a variety of forms, all running to the same thing in substance—that it was a question for the Supreme Court. I maintain that when he says, after the Supreme Court has decided the question, that the people may yet exclude slavery by any means whatever, he does virtually say that it is not a question for the Supreme Court. He shifts his ground.

And as Lincoln had anticipated, the South later accused Douglas of the "Freeport heresy." Senator Benjamin of Louisiana declared in the Senate:

> We accuse him [Douglas] for this: to wit, that having bargained with us upon a point upon which we were at issue that it should be considered a judicial point; that he would abide by the decision; that he would act under the decision, and consider it a doctrine of the party; that having said that to us here in the Senate, he went home, and under the stress of a local election, his knees gave way; his whole person trembled. His adversary stood upon principle and was beaten; and lo! he is the candidate of a mighty party for the Presidency of the United States. The Senator from

Illinois faltered. He got the prize for which he faltered; but lo! the grand prize of his ambition to-day slips from his grasp because of his faltering in his former contest, and his success in the canvass for the Senate, purchased for an ignoble prize, has cost him the loss of the Presidency of the United States.

Thus Lincoln's decision making proved to be sound. Douglas was indeed reelected Senator from Illinois in 1858. But Lincoln won the Presidential election in 1860—an outcome materially influenced by the splitting of the Democratic votes between Douglas and the Southern candidate, Breckinridge.

There was much involved in Lincoln's decision to put that simple question to Douglas. Lincoln must have held the *belief* (at some level between 0 and 1.0) that Douglas would answer the question affirmatively. Lincoln must have had many *beliefs* about the consequences of such an answer. Would it make Douglas' reelection to the Senate more probable (.80 rather than .60, perhaps)? Would it make Douglas' possible Presidential election less likely (maybe .20 rather than .50)? What were the probabilities that Lincoln's political future would be improved?

Lincoln's *evaluations* were also involved. How much did he value the Senate seat for himself in 1858? How much did he value a potential Presidential nomination for himself in 1860? How strongly did he feel about widening the split in the Democratic party? Also bearing on Lincoln's decision were his more pervasive *values:* his general opposition to slavery, and his respect for lawful means of effecting change. There is little doubt that Lincoln was a "political" type, and was *motivated* to self-actualization in that realm.

Of course, Douglas also made a decision, and it must have involved many of these same propositions, although with different levels of belief and with different levels of evaluation. We cannot know all of a man's private thoughts in decision making, but at least we have here some tools for speculating about them.

The background to this entire series of debates was complex. Perhaps the views of each of these men were clear and internally consistent. Yet they involved many elements, some of which were made explicit, while others were not. "Good" reasons were always given, but sometimes we may wonder about the "real" reasons.

Douglas was opposed to any view of equality between blacks and whites. He strongly advocated a policy of "popular sovereignty"—each state or territory has its own peculiar problems and needs and should be free to do as it chooses on all matters, including slavery, without Congressional interference. The following excerpts reveal something of Douglas' views.

 I am opposed to negro citizenship in any and every form. I believe this government was made on the white basis. I believe it was made by white men, for the benefit of white men and their posterity forever, and I am in favor of confining citizenship to white men, men of European birth and descent, instead of conferring it upon negroes, Indians, and other inferior races. . . . I do not believe the Almighty ever intended the negro to be the equal of the white man. If he did, he has been a long time demonstrating the fact. For thousands of years the negro has been a race upon the earth, and during all that time, in all latitudes and climates, wherever he has wandered or been taken, he has been inferior to the race which he has there met. He belongs to an inferior race, and must always occupy an inferior position. I do not hold that because the negro is our inferior, therefore he ought to be a slave. By no means can such a conclusion be drawn from what I have said. On the contrary, I hold that humanity and Christianity both require that the negro shall have and enjoy every right, every privilege, and every immunity consistent with the safety of the society in which he lives.

. . . .

Now, I hold that Illinois had a right to abolish and prohibit slavery as she did, and I hold that Kentucky has the same right to continue and protect slavery that Illinois had to abolish it. I hold that New York has as much right to abolish slavery as Virginia has to continue it, and that each and every State of this Union is a sovereign power, with a right to do as it pleases upon this question of slavery, and upon all its domestic institutions.

. . . .

Now, my friends, if we will only act conscientiously and rigidly upon this great principle of popular sovereignty, which guarantees to each State and Territory the right to do as it pleases on all things, local and domestic, instead of Congress interfering, we will continue at peace one with another.

. . . .

I believe that this new doctrine preached by Mr. Lincoln and his party will dissolve the Union if it succeeds. They are trying to array all the Northern States in one body against the South, to excite a sectional war between the free States and the slave States, in order that the one or the other may be driven to the wall.

Lincoln's position, too, was multifaceted. He opposed slavery and thought that it should be lawfully (and therefore gradually) exterminated. For the slave he sought freedom rather than equality. The following statements, some of which are drawn from the debates and some of which come from earlier pronouncements, reveal something of his beliefs and prevailing values.

 The real issue in this controversy—the one pressing upon every mind —is the sentiment on the part of one class that looks upon the institution of slavery as a wrong, and of another class that does not look upon it as a wrong. The sentiment that contemplates the institution of slavery in this country as a wrong is the sentiment of the Republican party. It is the sentiment around which all their actions, all their arguments, circle; from which all their propositions radiate. They look upon it as being a moral, social, and political wrong; and while they contemplate it as such, they nevertheless have due regard for its actual existence among us, and the difficulties of getting rid of it in any satisfactory way, and to all the constitutional obligations thrown about it. Yet having a due regard for these, they desire a policy in regard to it that looks to its not creating any more danger. They insist that it, as far as may be, be treated as a wrong, and one of the methods of treating it as a wrong is to make provision that it shall grow no larger. They also desire a policy that looks to a peaceful end of slavery some time, as being a wrong. These are the views they entertain in regard to it, as I understand them; and all their sentiments, all their arguments and propositions, are brought within this range.

. . . .

While I was at the hotel today, an elderly gentleman called upon me to know whether I was really in favor of producing a perfect equality between the negroes and white people. While I had not proposed to myself on this occasion to say much on that subject, yet as the question was asked me I thought I would occupy perhaps five minutes in saying something in regard to it. I will say then that I am not, or ever have been, in favor of bringing about in any way the social and political equality of the white and black races—that I am not, nor ever have been, in favor of making voters or jurors of negroes, nor of qualifying them to hold office, nor to intermarry with white people, and I will say in addition to this that there is a physical difference between the white and black races which I believe will forever forbid the two races living together on terms of social and political equality. And inasmuch as they cannot so live, while they do remain together there must be the position of superior and inferior, and I as much as any other man am in favor of having the superior position assigned to the white race. I say upon this occasion that I do not perceive that because the white man is to have the superior position the negro should be denied everything. I do not understand that because I do not want a negro woman for a slave I must necessarily want her for a wife. My understanding is that I can just let her alone.

. . . .

I will say here, while upon this subject, that I have no purpose, either directly or indirectly, to interfere with the institution of slavery in the States where it exists. I believe I have no lawful right to do so, and I have no inclination to do so.

We believe as much as Judge Douglas (perhaps more) in obedience to, and respect for, the judicial department of government. We think its decisions on constitutional questions, when fully settled, should control not only the particular cases decided, but the general policy of the country, subject to be disturbed only by amendments to the Constitution as provided in that instrument itself. More than this would be revolution. But we think the Dred Scott decision is erroneous. We know the court that made it has often overruled its own decisions, and we shall do what we can to have it to overrule this. We offer no resistance to it.

When I so pressingly urge a strict observance of all the laws, let me not be understood as saying there are no bad laws, or that grievances may not arise for the redress of which no legal provisions have been made. I mean to say no such thing. But I do mean to say that although bad laws, if they exist, should be repealed as soon as possible, still, while they continue in force, for the sake of example they should be religiously observed. So also in unprovided cases. If such arise, let proper legal provisions be made for them with the least possible delay, but till then let them, if not too intolerable, be borne with. There is no grievance that is a fit object of redress by mob law.

These statements from the Lincoln-Douglas debates reveal a portion of the beliefs, evaluations, values, and motives of the antagonists. They provide bases also for inferences about additional factors bearing upon their views. Taken together, these statements serve to indicate the complexity of the positions joined in these social-political issues.

The case study included here illustrates another significant fact about decision making. This case occurred a century ago and yet, while the specific issues may have changed, the basic problems of dealing with minority and repressed groups in society are still with us. The underlying questions of these debates concerning individual beliefs, social values, and lawful social change are most contemporary. A problem solver today must know that he will not be solving problems for all time. We make decisions and take actions in our time and for our time. Decision making, as speech communication, is a *process* that is ongoing and never ending. This fact should create in us more interest in what has happened in the past, more concern for how our actions may constrain decision makers in the future, and more humility regarding our own powers to deal with significant social problems.

STUDY PROBE 6
Analyzing Contemporary Decision Making in a
Social, Political, Economic, or Religious Setting

Search the contemporary scene for what appears to you to be a significant conflict; and when you have found it, make an analysis of it which is similar in treatment and scope to the Lincoln-Douglas example which we have just examined.

Specifically, list the many propositions (especially the conflicting ones) held by each party to the disputation or controversy.

Try to assess the levels of belief and evaluation in the B-E clusters of the respective opponents. Determine what values and motives appear to be most salient in the context.

At what points does the clash between the differing viewpoints occur?

If you were a negotiator, how might you use this analysis to work out a compromise between the principals? If you were arguing for one "side" or the other, suggest some of the ways in which you could use this analysis to construct your arguments.

As a second phase of this Probe, attempt to apply the foregoing type of analysis to some interpersonal conflict which you may presently have with some other person, or one that you have had with this person at some time in the past. Try to discover by making this analysis what lies behind the conflict and also some possible means for resolving it.

Positions such as those suggested by Study Probe 6—positions involving social problem solving which occurs in real speech communication settings— may be seen as resulting from the piling up of interrelated propositions representing varying levels of beliefs and evaluations, and influenced by broad and pervasive values and motives. Clearly evident now should be the conclusion that not all of a man's beliefs lie parallel to one another on the same plane. They conflict, intersect, and interact. For example, Lincoln's opposition to slavery would have been simpler if coupled with a desire for complete racial equality. His opposition to slavery must have been somewhat frustrated by the value he attached to lawful change. *Absolute* positions are nearly always straightforward and uncomplicated. For the sake of simplicity we often try to interpret the positions of another as absolute and, therefore, as definite and clear. However, the real positions that speakers take and the decisions they make must be *relative* and must contain overlapping, interacting, and partially conflicting elements. They can never be absolute and unqualified; they must be *multidirectional* and *multidimensional.* For these reasons we have tried in this chapter to provide some useful approaches and procedures for the multidirectional and multidimensional analysis of decision making as it occurs in the speech communication process.

Suggested Readings

Since in this chapter we have proposed some approaches to decision making and have tried to develop some useful procedures, the readings most to be recommended would be those works which present detailed analyses of problems characterizing our contemporary society. The following source may be considered as a typical and useful one:

Confrontation: Psychology and the Problems of Today, gen. ed., Michael Wertheimer (Glenview, Ill.: Scott, Foresman and Company, 1970). This work presents materials under the following headings, all of which could be useful for analyses bearing upon communicatively induced decision making:

1. Identity and Identity Crisis.
2. Conformity, Compliance, and Integrity.
3. Racism and Race Relations.
4. Violence and Aggression.
5. Conflict and Conflict Resolution.
6. Human Control Over Human Behavior.
7. Man and Technology.
8. Education, Creativity, and the Student.

Also recommended for suggested readings for purposes of this chapter are various government documents such as the *Report of the U.S. National Advisory Commission on Civil Disorders* (Washington, D.C.: U.S. Government Printing Office, March 1, 1968).

Part V

Speech Communication in Action: Advanced Concerns

In the preceding chapters we have examined some of the basic ideas, formulations, and interrelated processes underlying the use of speech communication as a means for achieving productive human interaction. With certain exceptions—encountered most often in the Study Probes—our focus has been largely theoretical, analytical, and conceptual. Now, in this final section, we shall consider in some detail the practical concerns and procedures that are especially relevant when we, as *speech practitioners,* prepare to engage in communicative acts involving interpersonal, small group, and one-to-many relationships.

Part II of this book introduced some of the preliminary phases of oral practice and performance, and we return to those matters now. In the ensuing chapters, we shall be enlarging and broadening an "in-action" view of speech. We shall be directing particular attention to some of the ways in which previously considered principles may be seen to function in communicative contexts having more advanced and somewhat more complex dimensions. This functional application will require a heavier experiential involvement on your part, and a more direct commitment to participate than has been required heretofore.

We have frequently cited as our general paradigm for speech communication the image of "two persons conversing," proposing it as the archetype of all communicative contexts. In Chapter 8, we ask that you again project yourself into that setting as we make close and specific scrutiny of some practical ways in which one agent can achieve interaction *with one other agent.* We stress the *patterning* of that interpersonalizing and try to show how your awareness of the patterns can facilitate your interaction with a fellow communicator. We endeavor to extend this facility by laying out some guidelines to help you discover the requirements of dyadic context, to define status and role relationships, and to seek mutually advantageous bases for one-to-one interaction.

In Chapter 9, we move to the broader and somewhat more inclusive context in which one communication agent strives to interact *with a few others.* In small group discussion we look at some of the distinctive uses and advantages; we emphasize (1) planning for task functions—especially as they relate to the problem-solving sequence, and (2) planning for social-emotional functions. And, relative to these tasks and functions, we attempt to provide some practical direction for phrasing the discussion question, organizing materials, establishing an agenda, and handling certain communication problems characteristic of small group settings.

Speech making, the context in which a single agent (the speaker) attempts to achieve interaction *with many other agents* (an audience) at and during a given time, is the core of our concentration in the concluding chapter of this volume. There, our concern is the quite specific task of the individual agent as he presents sustained and fairly formal discourse to a comparatively large number of listeners whose immediate feedback is chiefly nonverbal and silent. Our explorations and instructions center upon three phases of the act of "public communication": (1) planning, (2) practicing, and (3) evaluating the speech-making process.

Throughout these concluding chapters we maintain, as we have throughout, that the essential principles of effective speech communication are applicable in all three of these interactive contexts. The precepts noted and advice offered for any one of the contexts should apply also to each of the others. In Part V we attempt to develop quite fully that the differences among the converser and the discussant and the public speaker are in fact mainly matters of *degree* and that no sharp line can be drawn to separate them. The range of those differences, the special uses customarily made of each context, and the particular requirements imposed by each are matters we shall attempt to highlight in these remaining pages. You are urged, therefore, to study these three concluding chapters as a *unified whole:* you will not have finished the first until you have read the last.

One caution we feel impelled to make. The fact that individuals are unique makes it inevitable that a specific procedure which "works" for one may not be at all helpful for another. Accordingly, our intention here is not to provide "formulas for success" in any given instance. General guidelines are offered only with the hope that they will assist—not enslave —you; they are presented as your servant—not your master. In all your study and practice, regardless of the directions you may take, you will need to work assiduously to cultivate the individual style which works best for *you* as you try to engage effectively in interaction with your fellow beings.

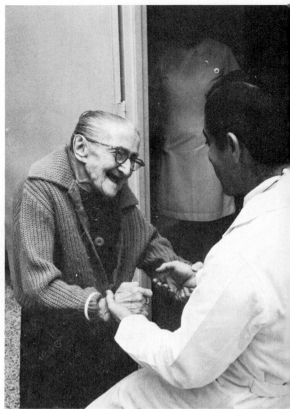

In seeking interaction, an agent will do well always
to be sensitive to the demands of the communication context
and try to determine the status and role relations
between himself and the other.

Chapter 8
Achieving Interaction with One: Interpersonal Speech Communication

The image of *two persons conversing* was presented in Chapter 2 as a general paradigm for speech communication. The two-person situation contains all the essential elements of the speech communication process, and the principles applicable in that setting apply as well to all other communication forms and settings.

Two-person interpersonal communication is the form of direct speech involvement you most frequently experience. As we noted earlier (pages 46–47), even in a small group discussion, interaction occurs most often between two participants. And it is two-person communication that allows for maximally direct interaction and involvement.

In Chapter 3 we introduced the basic principles for participating effectively in this and in other forms of speech communication, and we stressed the necessity for understanding the communication agents and the context, and for achieving interaction by the appropriate concerns for feedforward and feedback.

We return now to the topic of two persons conversing, in order to suggest additional, specific ways for achieving interaction in an interpersonal setting. Some of the general principles of Chapter 3, as they apply especially to the two-person setting, will be amplified here.

We must recognize at the beginning that in some instances communicative interaction between two agents may be unattainable. One agent, or both, may refuse to meet the other, or one or both may withdraw totally from the context. However, such cases are not entirely hopeless. An intermediary, or second-level communicator (X), may be enlisted to intercede between non-interacting agents (A) and (B), so that two-person interaction occurs between X and A, and X and B. It is even possible that the intermediary X may be able eventually to induce agents A and B to resume direct interaction.

STUDY PROBE 1

Examining the Role of the Intermediary
in Interpersonal Communication

Consider the values and problems inherent in the use of intermediaries in interpersonal relationships. Describe any experience you have had with the use of an intermediary in an interpersonal dealing—perhaps the arrangement of a blind date or an agreement to purchase something "through a friend who can get a better price." Cite some of the values and problems evident in your experience.

Outline a serious argument which could be presented for both sides of the proposition that marriages should be arranged by matchmakers rather than the couple involved. In what ways would a matchmaker be similar to an arbitrator in a labor-management dispute? How would a matchmaker differ from a marriage counselor?

Rarely are the channels between communication agents completely open. In extraordinary circumstances (a natural catastrophe such as an earthquake, or a man-made catastrophe such as an urban riot), an agent may have communicative channels fully opened to receive as many informative cues as possible. In strange environments (travel in foreign countries) we may be more open than usual in pursuing friendships, once the acquaintanceship is initiated. Children typically maintain open channels; and until or unless they are taught that strangers may be dangerous, they will talk with almost anyone.

STUDY PROBE 2

Exploring the Openness of Communication Channels

Discuss with another student some emergency situations which each of you has encountered. Compare how receptive both of you were to communicative stimuli at those times. What were the chief channels of communication that you used?

In ordinary interpersonal situations, neither of the extremes of completely closed or completely opened channels is usual. Most often the available channels will be only *partially* open because of the demands of the particular situation, status differences between agents, personality characteristics of the agents, and other dissimilarities. In this chapter we will avoid the extremes, and consider only cases in which the communicative agents are willing at least to entertain possibilities for interaction and are open to mutual efforts in that direction.

The professional interviewer is typically adept at keeping communicative channels open. As depicted in this illustration, he looks closely at the interviewee for all possible feedback. And the latter, in the process of answering, may look away from time to time as if to better concentrate on the idea he is expressing. Relevant to this interaction pattern is the finding through research studies that people use more direct eye contact when they listen than they do when they speak.

Interpersonal Speech as Patterned Communication

STUDY PROBE 3
Studying a Greeting Ritual

Consider the following communicative exchange:

John: Hi.
Bill: Hi. How are you?
John: Great. And you?
Bill: Just fine.
John: Good. See you around.
Bill: Right. So long.

Would you judge this conversation to be typical of that which might occur during a brief encounter between friends? Do you perceive anything in an exchange of this kind other than a typical greeting ritual? Explain.

When two acquaintances meet one another on the street, they invariably exchange a few routine remarks in passing. A casual observer might say that they are simply following social custom—that their conversation is a standard greeting ritual and nothing more. The content of what is said in such an exchange means little. The frequently asked question "How are you?" does not really call for—or even want—a full answer.

As with other rituals, the behavior in a greeting ritual is obviously patterned and very predictable. After all, we learn communicative rituals early in life and play them over with little variation thousands of times. But to conclude that communication rituals are casual and routine would be a serious mistake. On the contrary, such rituals have *considerable significance.* The significance of these learned patterns for interaction is not in their content, but in the fact that they occur—in the fact that the ritual is performed, and performed according to the "rules," or expectations.

Much of our interpersonal communication operates according to unstated but well-accepted rules. These rules, and the resulting behavioral patterns, are learned much as are the rules for grammar: we tend to follow the specific rule even though we may not be able to describe or state it explicitly. This is probably because we have internalized rules of this order by constant practice and imitation of others when we were very young—long before they were taught to us in school.

One rule of interpersonal communication is that we "take turns" when speaking. One person speaks, then the other, and so on. If one person were to speak all the time, some communication might occur; but obviously the act could not be called a conversation. We also learn, as a rule, about how *long* such a ritualistic communication should be—about how much interaction time is appropriate. The duration of the greeting ritual must be fitting for the agents interacting within the given circumstance or context. Although we cannot know with any real exactitude how much is "too brief" or "too much" time, we do develop a feeling for or sensing of such matters. If the exchange is unusually brief, it may signify something about a changing relationship between agents. If, on the other hand, one agent who has had only a nodding acquaintance with a second agent stops to talk for an extended period of time, the breaking of the pattern may signify an overture for closer friendship. Whenever one agent violates the rules or does not meet the expectations of a situation, the deviation from the norm will likely be interpreted by the other agent as a statement about their relationship. One may break an expected pattern of communication, but not without implicitly calling for a restructuring of the situation. Any change from expected communication patterns can be interpreted as being meaningful and significant.

STUDY PROBE 4

Identifying Communication Patterns

What are some other patterns and rules that you follow when speaking with another person? How far apart do you stand or sit? Do you orient yourselves face-to-face? Do you each speak an equal amount of the time? Do you observe different patterns and rules with different people? You might follow up this analysis by reading Erving Goffman's *Interaction Ritual* (Garden City, N.Y.: Doubleday & Company, Inc., Anchor Books, 1967).

Identify three communicative patterns you dare not break with a close friend lest he or she think "there's something wrong." Explain why this is so.

Virginia Satir, among many other scholars, has suggested that any communication from an individual has two levels: the *denotative* level—the literal content; and the *metacommunicative* level—a comment on the literal content, as well as on the relationship between the communicative agents.[1] This concept is described as a *metacommunication*.

Suppose, for example, that one person—while smiling—directs an insulting comment to another. The smile is metacommunication. It says that the literal comment can be ignored because the remark is not intended seriously. The smile also says that the relationship between the agents is such that bantering of this type is permissible.

STUDY PROBE 5

Exploring Metacommunication

Observe a conversation between two persons on a television "talk show." Pay particular attention to their communicative exchange with reference to the denotative and metacommunicative levels just described. Are you able to detect both levels of communication in both agents? Elaborate on your answer, citing specific examples of metacommunication.

Describe some of the ways you have used metacommunication to modify the meaning of verbal messages in communicating with friends.

---

[1] Virginia Satir, *Conjoint Family Therapy*, rev. ed. (Palo Alto, Calif.: Science & Behavior Books, Inc., 1967).

Communication rituals serve, in part, what has been called a "metacommunicative" function in defining the relationship between interacting agents. Violations of communication rituals and the expectations deriving from them —although not significant in literal content—may have profound effects because of what they signify regarding an interpersonal relationship.

Communication rituals evolve, and they eventually define our behavioral norms. They embody prescribed patterns of what is "normal" and what can be expected. Following the pattern of a communication ritual becomes somewhat akin to following the rules of a card game. Rules and procedures become settled first. If we know and follow the "rules," everyone else who knows what the "rules" are also knows what's going on. If we violate the "rules," those familiar with the accepted patterns become perplexed. Communication rituals maintain order and allow for efficiency in communication as long as they are accepted by the participating parties. If they are followed, the communicative interaction can proceed—the game can be played out. But if they are rejected or broken by either party, then the interpersonal relationship and the context must be restructured or terminated.

In sum, one factor contributing to efficient and effective interaction is the mutual acceptance of unstated rules for communicative conduct. The mutual following of such rules can most often be observed in patterned, relatively predictable, and reliable behavior in communication contexts. In such situations, the expectations of one agent about behaviors of the other agent tend to be confirmed, and a ground for trust and further interaction is possible.

Let us turn now to practices which a communicative agent can follow in determining what expectations are likely to be directed toward him.

Determining Contextual Requirements:
Criterial Questions

A communication agent should seek first to discover the demands of the specific context in which he finds himself. What does the situation require? We might begin by listing some of the possible contexts in which two persons converse and the demands these contexts impose upon communicators. The following are a few examples:

1. *Loving relationship.* The individuals may proclaim trust, affection, and concern for one another—for example, husband and wife.

2. *Therapeutic association.* One agent may attempt to help the other to resolve a personal crisis or emotional difficulty—for example, a doctor and patient, or a counselor and client.

3. *Social conversation.* Two persons may exchange views, reinforce one another's beliefs and evaluations, or engage in "grooming" talk—for example, two close friends.

4. *Becoming acquainted.* Strangers may meet and interact while getting to know one another—for example, new neighbors.

5. *Instruction.* One agent may hope to enlighten the other by presenting evidence, facts, and/or acceptable new beliefs—for example, professor and student.

6. *Interview.* One agent may assess the qualifications of another for a certain task—for example, personnel director and prospective employee.

7. *Bargaining.* The agents may try to negotiate a difference in position and resolve a conflict between themselves—for example, agents in a labor-management contract dispute.

8. *Persuasion.* One agent may attempt to change the Belief-Evaluation clusters of the other—for example, insurance salesman and customer.

9. *Combat.* The agents may engage in verbal battling in the hope of destroying each other's position—often while aiming at the persuasion of a third party who is observing the encounter—for example, opponents in a political debate.

10. *Coercion.* One agent may attempt to force compliance by the other by the use of threats—for example, college official and student demonstration leader.

This brief listing will illustrate the wide range of experiences which can be subsumed under the heading of interpersonal communication. For each of the many possible contexts in which two persons converse, we should have some guide as to what is expected—what the rules are—what will facilitate interaction.

INTERPERSONAL COMMUNICATION-SITUATION ASSESSMENT SCALES

The scales which follow are similar in some respects to those you completed in Chapter 3 (pages 56–59). They are designed to help you assess your reactions in the ten interpersonal communication contexts just described.

Mark the scales just as you did those in Chapter 3. First, try to imagine yourself in the situation described in the title. Then, for each of the five listed responses (a, b, c, d, e) circle the number (7, 6, 5, 4, 3, 2, 1) in the response-continuum range which best describes how you think you would feel in the designated situation.

If, for example, the descriptive term at the left end of the scale (Relaxed) *describes your feelings completely*, then circle the number 7; if the descriptive term at the right end of the scale (Tense) describes your feelings most accurately, circle the number 1.

If one of the terms *describes your feelings fairly well*, but not completely, then circle the number 6 or 2, one range position away from the term.

If one of the terms *describes your feelings only somewhat*, but better than does the other term, then circle the number 5 or 3, two scale positions away from the appropriate term.

If neither term at the ends of the response-continuum scale seems appropriate, or if both terms *describe your feelings equally*, then circle the number 4.

Using two colored pencils, respond *twice* to the scales given here. First, complete each scale according to *how you believe you would feel* in the given contexts. Then complete the scales according to *how you believe the other person in that context would feel.* Compare the two sets of reactions or predictions. Then compare your scales with those of your classmates. (See pages 367–372 for extra copies.)

INTERPERSONAL COMMUNICATION-SITUATION ASSESSMENT SCALES

1. COMMUNICATING IN A LOVING RELATIONSHIP

a.	Relaxed	7	6	5	4	3	2	1	Tense
b.	Pleasant	7	6	5	4	3	2	1	Unpleasant
c.	Informative	7	6	5	4	3	2	1	Not Informative
d.	Stimulating	7	6	5	4	3	2	1	Boring
e.	Self-fulfilling	7	6	5	4	3	2	1	Not Self-fulfilling

2. COMMUNICATING IN A THERAPEUTIC SETTING

a.	Relaxed	7	6	5	4	3	2	1	Tense
b.	Pleasant	7	6	5	4	3	2	1	Unpleasant
c.	Informative	7	6	5	4	3	2	1	Not Informative
d.	Stimulating	7	6	5	4	3	2	1	Boring
e.	Self-fulfilling	7	6	5	4	3	2	1	Not Self-fulfilling

3. COMMUNICATING IN A SOCIAL CONVERSATION

a.	Relaxed	7	6	5	4	3	2	1	Tense
b.	Pleasant	7	6	5	4	3	2	1	Unpleasant
c.	Informative	7	6	5	4	3	2	1	Not Informative
d.	Stimulating	7	6	5	4	3	2	1	Boring
e.	Self-fulfilling	7	6	5	4	3	2	1	Not Self-fulfilling

4. COMMUNICATING WHILE BECOMING ACQUAINTED

a.	Relaxed	7	6	5	4	3	2	1	Tense
b.	Pleasant	7	6	5	4	3	2	1	Unpleasant
c.	Informative	7	6	5	4	3	2	1	Not Informative
d.	Stimulating	7	6	5	4	3	2	1	Boring
e.	Self-fulfilling	7	6	5	4	3	2	1	Not Self-fulfilling

5. COMMUNICATING IN AN INSTRUCTIONAL SETTING

a.	Relaxed	7	6	5	4	3	2	1	Tense
b.	Pleasant	7	6	5	4	3	2	1	Unpleasant
c.	Informative	7	6	5	4	3	2	1	Not Informative
d.	Stimulating	7	6	5	4	3	2	1	Boring
e.	Self-fulfilling	7	6	5	4	3	2	1	Not Self-fulfilling

The appropriate and expected communicative behaviors will vary along several dimensions, and they can be determined, in part, by answering such questions as those in the series beginning at the bottom of the facing page and on the pages immediately following it.

6. COMMUNICATING IN AN INTERVIEW SETTING

a.	Relaxed	7	6	5	4	3	2	1	Tense
b.	Pleasant	7	6	5	4	3	2	1	Unpleasant
c.	Informative	7	6	5	4	3	2	1	Not Informative
d.	Stimulating	7	6	5	4	3	2	1	Boring
e.	Self-fulfilling	7	6	5	4	3	2	1	Not Self-fulfilling

7. COMMUNICATING IN A BARGAINING SETTING

a.	Relaxed	7	6	5	4	3	2	1	Tense
b.	Pleasant	7	6	5	4	3	2	1	Unpleasant
c.	Informative	7	6	5	4	3	2	1	Not Informative
d.	Stimulating	7	6	5	4	3	2	1	Boring
e.	Self-fulfilling	7	6	5	4	3	2	1	Not Self-fulfilling

8. COMMUNICATING IN A PERSUASIVE SETTING

a.	Relaxed	7	6	5	4	3	2	1	Tense
b.	Pleasant	7	6	5	4	3	2	1	Unpleasant
c.	Informative	7	6	5	4	3	2	1	Not Informative
d.	Stimulating	7	6	5	4	3	2	1	Boring
e.	Self-fulfilling	7	6	5	4	3	2	1	Not Self-fulfilling

9. COMMUNICATING IN A COMBATIVE SETTING

a.	Relaxed	7	6	5	4	3	2	1	Tense
b.	Pleasant	7	6	5	4	3	2	1	Unpleasant
c.	Informative	7	6	5	4	3	2	1	Not Informative
d.	Stimulating	7	6	5	4	3	2	1	Boring
e.	Self-fulfilling	7	6	5	4	3	2	1	Not Self-fulfilling

10. COMMUNICATING IN A COERCIVE SETTING

a.	Relaxed	7	6	5	4	3	2	1	Tense
b.	Pleasant	7	6	5	4	3	2	1	Unpleasant
c.	Informative	7	6	5	4	3	2	1	Not Informative
d.	Stimulating	7	6	5	4	3	2	1	Boring
e.	Self-fulfilling	7	6	5	4	3	2	1	Not Self-fulfilling

Does the Context Call for Cooperation or Conflict?

In determining the order in which to present the ten contexts of the succession of scales, we attempted to begin with those requiring the most cooperation and to conclude with those likely to produce the most conflict.

STUDY PROBE 6
Analyzing Cooperation and Conflict in Communication Contexts

Would you agree with our rank ordering of communication contexts on the basis of cooperation and conflict? If not, what modifications would you make in the listing? In your judgment, what level of cooperation and what level of conflict exist in Contexts 5 and 6?

We can easily see the relationship in the contrasting cases. Conflict is not a typical, expected behavior in a loving relationship, nor is cooperation typical of a coercive context. Of course, some contexts may call for a measure of *both* cooperation and conflict. In an interview, for example, the agents may—at one and the same time—have cooperative desires and conflicting interests. You must assess carefully the degree of cooperation and/or conflict expected in a given setting, for you will be more successful as an agent if you employ behaviors that are generally expected in that setting (unless, of course, you wish to attempt a restructuring of the entire situation).

However, we should be alert to the possibility that behaviors may turn out to be entirely *unexpected.* We may encounter instances in debates during which one agent treats the issue in a manner appropriate for a bargaining context by attempting to compromise on the issue. The other agent may then refuse to restructure the combative situation, catch his opponent off balance, and thereby make the position of his opponent appear weaker. We will suggest later a procedure for safely initiating changes such as this.

Does the Context Call for Symmetrical or Complementary Behaviors?

Watzlawick, Beavin, and Jackson, in their *Pragmatics of Human Communiciation,* suggest that all communicative interchanges are either symmetrical or complementary, depending on whether they are based on equality or difference.[2] Symmetrical behavior, they say, means that the agents behave similarly—from the same motives, and for the same ends. Complementary behaviors appear in situations in which the behaviors, motives, and aims of the agents differ. Yet, differing behaviors need not indicate conflict. The behavior of one may fill out or complete the behavior of the other. Hence, it is complementary. Communicative behaviors of two agents may be termed complementary if their actions mutually supply each other's lack.

STUDY PROBE 7
Comparing Behavioral Dimensions

Rank order the ten Interpersonal Communication Situations (pages 246–247) according to whether they call for symmetrical or complementary behaviors. Compare this ordering with that which you determined for the Cooperation/ Conflict continuum in Study Probe 6.

[2] Paul Watzlawick, Janet Beavin, and Don Jackson, *Pragmatics of Human Communication* (New York: W. W. Norton & Company, Inc., 1967), pp. 67–71.

A loving relationship is symmetrical: the agents act alike, for the same reasons, and for the same ends. In conflict situations, the agents may also act much alike, for the same reasons, and for the same ends. So the conflict setting may also involve symmetrical behaviors. Therapeutic and instructional contexts, on the other hand, are more likely to involve complementary behaviors. The behaviors of the agents in these settings differ from one another, but mesh together in accomplishing the agents' shared goals. The Cooperation/Conflict and the Symmetrical/Complementary behavioral dimensions of interpersonal communication are not perfectly correlated. The rank ordering of our contexts on these two dimensions would not be identical.

STUDY PROBE 8

Determining Symmetrical and Complementary Behaviors

Consider the classroom settings in which you are interacting this term. In what ways are your behaviors and the behaviors of your instructors symmetrical and/ or complementary?

To summarize, then, in answering this question, the agent must ask whether the context calls for him to "mirror" the behaviors of the other agent (symmetrical behavior) or whether his behaviors should be the counterpart of or the "other side of the coin" (complementary behavior) with respect to the behaviors of the other agent.

Does the Context Call for the Presenting of Self or the Sharing of Self?

Some research scholars have distinguished between "presentational encounters" and "sharing encounters."[3] In "presenting" the self, an agent attempts to project (or "present") an image of his choosing, and to protect the self. In "sharing" the self, the agent's goal is an openness and an overlapping of his "self-system" with that of the agent with whom he wishes to interact. These scholars believe that a relationship of this kind is continually being developed in the interaction process.

In *The Presentation of Self in Everyday Life,* Erving Goffman views human interaction as though it were action in the sense of the theatre. He discusses the actions of an agent as being "on stage" and "off stage." He suggests that a waitress, for example, is "on stage" when waiting on customers, and "off stage" when in the kitchen picking up orders.[4] She may be quite natural and open (sharing) with the kitchen help, but may wear a "smiling" mask when presenting her image to the customers. A communication agent must determine in every setting what type of image and how much image-projection is expected of him.

[3] J. Watson and R. Potter, "An Analytic Unit for the Study of Interaction," *Human Relations,* XIV (1961): 245–263.

[4] Erving Goffman, *The Presentation of Self in Everyday Life* (Garden City, N.Y.: Doubleday & Company, Inc., Anchor Books, 1959).

STUDY PROBE 9
STUDY PROBE 9
Ranking Contexts on the Self-Presentation/Self-Sharing Dimension

Again, rank order the ten Interpersonal Communication Situations (pages 246–247) on a continuum with presentation of self at one end and sharing of self at the other. How does this ordering compare with those you have made for the Cooperation/Conflict dimensions and the Symmetrical/Complementary dimensions? Was this ordering more difficult or less difficult to make than the others? How might you explain your answer?

Does the Context Call for Movement Toward, Against, or Away from the Other Agent?

Psychiatrist Karen Horney classifies interpersonal relations as indicating movement by each agent toward, against, or away from the other agent.[5] Movement *toward* shows affiliative and affectionate desires; movement *against* reveals combative tendencies; and movement *away* indicates a desire not to be involved with and influenced by the other. "I like you," "Let's fight," and "I'm sorry, but I don't want to get involved" are verbal illustrations of these three directions in which interpersonal interaction may move.

STUDY PROBE 10
*Ranking Communication Contexts on Movement
Toward, Against, or Away from Other Agents*

Again refer to the ten Interpersonal Communication Contexts, examine them for these directional movements, and rank order the contexts accordingly.

In a loving relationship, the expected movement would be toward; in combat, the movement would be against. What of the instruction and interview contexts? Possibly the movements in the latter settings could be either toward or against, but more probably there would be an ambivalence or balancing caused by tendencies toward and tendencies against. In any of the contexts we have discussed, the relationship could deteriorate for one reason or another so that one or both agents would decide to move away and withdraw from the interaction.

Does the Context Call for a Continuing or Temporary Association?

Referring again to our ten Interpersonal Communication Situations, those that we found at or near the "loving relationship" end of the continuum would tend to be continuing relationships also, while those at the opposite end would tend to be more temporary and short-lived.

[5] Karen Horney, *Our Inner Conflicts* (New York: W. W. Norton & Company, Inc., 1945).

STUDY PROBE 11
Developing Continuing Associations

Consider some current interpersonal relationship which you now anticipate to be temporary but which you enjoy—perhaps with a member of the class or an instructor. What might you do to make this a more continuing and enduring association?

In your work with the Interpersonal Communication-Situation Assessment Scales, you have no doubt observed that we have placed at the left-hand end of the continua descriptive terms which suggest the more favorable or "positive" conditions in a communicative relationship; and at the opposite end we have positioned the less favorable or "negative" conditions. Quite probably, too, you have observed that continuing relationships seem generally to be associated with the factors at the positive ends of the continua: Relaxed, Pleasant, Informative, Stimulating, Self-fulfilling. A wide range of research studies—especially those based on observations and reports having to do with gaming settings, community-conflict situations, and international relations—support the validity of such an association and conclusion.[6] From this research, it appears that with extended interaction, one agent tends to reciprocate the actions of the other, and both come to behave similarly. Of course, keeping in mind our comments regarding causal analysis in Chapter 6 (pages 187–191), we must be wary of drawing a necessary causal inference and stating that continuing relationships *cause* harmonious relationships. It might be the other way around. If such relationships do indeed exist, their harmoniousness may be so satisfying and rewarding that they cause continuing relationships. Or, possibly, both conditions may derive from some other common cause.

We do find, however, that continuous relationships and harmonious relationships are positively correlated. And this in itself should be sufficient reason for anyone who desires either condition to strive for both.

We have been insisting that an agent should always seek to determine the contextual demands and—from them—the expectations which the other agent will have concerning their impending communicative interaction. But how shall he do that? For one thing, he can try to concentrate his efforts upon finding useful answers to the five questions which he can ask about the context to assist him in determining what patterns of behavior will be expected of him; specifically:

1. Does this particular context appear to call for *cooperation* or *conflict?*

2. Does the context appear to call for *symmetrical* or *complementary behaviors?*

3. Does the context appear to call for *self-presentation* or *self-sharing?*

[6] Kenneth W. Terhune, "The Effects of Personality in Cooperation and Conflict," *The Structure of Conflict*, ed. Paul Swingle (New York: Academic Press, Inc., 1970).

4. Does the context seem to call for movement *toward, against,* or *away from* the other agent?

5. Does the context appear to call for a *continuing* association or only a *temporary* one?

In an interpersonal relationship, you should know that if you meet the expectations of the other agent, you will be seen by him as "playing according to the rules," and the interaction can proceed as is normal in that specific type of context. If, on the other hand, you "break the rules" and *deviate* greatly from the other's expectations, then the normal relationship will be violated and must undergo a complete restructuring. Unfortunately, you can never be certain of the outcome of such a restructuring. The consequence of such a period of uncertainty and even chaos could eventually, of course, be a more honest and productive relationship. On the other hand, the outcome could be to destroy the relationship utterly. In either case the stakes may be very high, and you or the other agent—or both of you—could prefer not to take the necessary gamble.

Clearly, then, what we need is a helpful means for changing the interpersonal relationship for the better *within the existing context.* And there is such a means.

Changing the Nature of a Context: Gradual Reciprocal Increments

As you are aware, one of the central and continuing themes of this textbook has been that speech communication is a dynamic, ongoing process, a process which is constantly undergoing change and development. Within such a process, we believe, *a carefully guided change* in interpersonal, communicative relationships is possible. This change, we think, can be effected by means of what might be described as *gradual reciprocal increments.*[7] By following such a give-and-take, reciprocal arrangement, an agent can effect controlled change and improvement in an interpersonal relationship.

Simply put, this incremental procedure calls for a series of small changes gradually initiated by one agent and reciprocated by the other. You, as the first agent, must begin by modifying—by a small amount at least—your attitudinal, communicative behavior (perhaps becoming more cooperative, or more self-sharing), but at the same time making sure that you modify it enough so that it may be easily detected by the other agent. You then wait to see if your movement is reciprocated. If it is, you may make another small attitudinal/behavioral change in the same direction, wait for reciprocation, and—if it is forthcoming—continue to repeat the procedure. If, following your initial effort, your partner chooses not to reciprocate or elects to change to a different relationship, you stand to lose very little. The risk taken with your first small change is not great.

[7] David Braybrooke and Charles E. Lindblom, *A Strategy of Decision* (New York: The Free Press, 1963), especially Chapters 5 and 6.

STUDY PROBE 12

Learning to Use Gradual Reciprocal Increments

For each of the five major questions considered for speech contexts, and summarized on page 251, discuss with another person some specific ways in which communication agents desiring to improve a particular interpersonal relationship could attempt to do so by gradual reciprocal increments. Compare your conclusions with others who will be discussing the same procedure and problem.

Together with a classmate, role play the following situation (or devise one of your own), using gradual reciprocal increments to improve the conflictive nature of the context. Before the experiment begins, expand on each agent's role so that the discussion will be as realistic as possible. *Situation:* A college administrator meets with the leader of a group of militant students to discuss the students' demands for a greater voice in policy-making decisions, curriculum changes, hiring and firing of faculty members, etc.

If handled with care and genuine concern, a change by means of gradual reciprocal increments can help appreciably to avoid the confusion of a drastically altered relationship and can, at the same time, provide a practical path for the growth of a more mutually satisfying and useful relationship between agents. Some sensitive selectivity is required, and some careful decision making is in order here. An individual will have to choose and decide upon the small behavioral changes which, by metacommunication, he can use to signify his aims and intentions. He must *say* that he desires change, but he must also be able to *show* it.

STUDY PROBE 13

Applying Gradual Reciprocal Increments to a Personal Problem

In an interpersonal relationship in which you may now be experiencing some difficulty, attempt a modification of the situation by the use of gradual reciprocal increments. Prepare a report describing your efforts in some detail and indicating the extent to which they appeared to be reciprocated and successful.

Defining Status and Role Positions

In the preceding pages we have been concerned with determining some of the contextual requirements of interpersonal communication. We asked what particular situations require and what expected behaviors derive from those situational demands. Here, our purpose will be to ascertain what the status and role position of *another* agent require and to examine the behavioral expectations created by those requirements. From the standpoint of the communicative agents, the latter concern is closely related to the former and in some ways overlaps it, for the other agent is—as we know—always a part of the total, interactive context.

Status and Roles

Status can be thought of as a collection of rights and duties assigned to and expected of an individual. Differences in ability, position, control over others, age, and wealth are some of the factors which may create status differences between agents. Other status differences often are decreed by social organizations and social conventions. For example, most organizations have an assigned hierarchy of leadership which establishes status differences within and sometimes outside of the organization. In groups without prescribed order, such status differences usually develop as time passes.

Status levels, whether formally or informally created, are always somewhat like the "pecking orders" among animals: to be operative the ordering must be accepted by all the parties involved. Such acceptance is clearly evident in a number of research studies of the effects of status upon communication in small groups. These studies have found that quite without regard for the actual situation itself, perception of status differences alone will lead to changed behaviors.[8]

Status differences are often revealed by the manner in which one individual addresses another. If two men address one another as George and Mr. Brown, we recognize their status differences immediately. As you know, in many languages a distinction is made between a formal and an informal word for the person "you"; one "you-word" is far more formal than an alternative "you-word." In languages where this is the case, status differences are revealed when two agents address one another with different forms of *you*.

STUDY PROBE 14

Identifying Status Differences

Refer again to the ten interpersonal contexts we have employed for analysis in this chapter (pages 246–247). In the most typical instances of each context, specify the status differences that usually exist between the agents involved. Under what circumstances might the hierarchical order change? In what ways would the status differences between the persons affect their interpersonal communication?

We expect a person of high status to make more *pivotal* comments, to initiate more interaction, and to control and direct interaction. This does not mean, of course, that he necessarily talks more; he may or he may not. A person of lower status is expected generally to show deference in his communicative behavior—regardless of how much or how often he speaks. These expectations would apply to what is said, how it is said, and when it is said.

---

[8] Floyd L. Ruch and Philip G. Zimbardo, *Psychology and Life,* 8th ed. (Glenview, Ill.: Scott, Foresman and Company, 1971), pp. 105–106.

STUDY PROBE 15
Exploring Status Differences

We usually associate higher status with persons who occupy space in the front of a group, room, or at the head of a table. What are some other physical, non-verbal factors you associate with high status? Consider physical appearance, speaking mannerisms, dress, and voice.

Using the two floor-plan diagrams of the business office shown below, arrange a desk, chair, table, three side chairs, and two file cabinets so as to (1) maximize, and (2) minimize status differences between the occupant and a visitor.

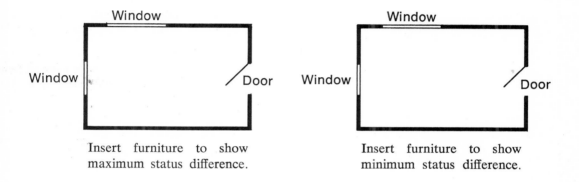

Insert furniture to show maximum status difference.

Insert furniture to show minimum status difference.

Role play each of the following situations twice—once in the office arranged for maximum status difference, then again in the office arranged for minimum status difference: (1) executive interviewing prospective employee, and (2) executive meeting with his assistant to review progress on an important project.

Whenever two agents interact, each one will be playing or acting out some kind of role. A role, as we define it here, is a unified pattern of behavior that reveals only a part of an individual's total nature. Psychiatrist Carl Jung has pointed out that an individual can never meet his fellow man with the totality of his personality. He can never, in fact, have all the facets of his personality even under his own control at one time. In a particular social context we develop —or at least "present"—only specific *parts* of our personality, according to the communication context and the other agent with whom we are trying to interact. An individual is a child to his parents, a student to his teacher, an employee to his job supervisor. Jung wrote of these roles as the *persona,* a Latin word meaning "masks."[9] A role that we play or a mask that we wear in a given situation will depend largely upon and reveal something of our relationship with the other communicator. As with status differences, if the agents mutually understand and accept the masks being presented, they can proceed with the interaction.

[9] See summary of Jung's views in Ira Progoff, *Jung's Psychology and Its Social Meaning* (New York: Grove Press, Inc., 1955), especially Chapter 3.

Interaction with Status and Role Differences

Although status and role differences may exist, it is nevertheless possible to achieve effective interaction. To do so, you will of course have to strive for sensitivity to the needs of the other agent. And you cannot hope to achieve this sensitivity unless you have some way of predicting what those needs are likely to be.

William Schutz has presented a useful analysis of three interpersonal needs.[10] In developing this threefold system of needs, Schutz contends that each of us has:

1. *Need for Inclusion.* The need to establish and maintain a psychologically satisfactory interaction and association with others. The need to be "in" and involved. The need for esteem in the eyes of the other agent.

2. *Need for Control.* The need to establish and maintain a degree of control and power over the other agent. The need to feel personally competent and responsible.

3. *Need for Affection.* The need to establish and maintain a relationship of love and affection with another. The need to be close to another. The need to feel that the self is lovable.

In every instance, as a communicative agent desiring to develop sensitivity you should consider these needs of the other agent and how the satisfaction of these needs relates to his status and roles. While you cannot always do what is necessary and appropriate to fulfill these satisfactions, by being aware of them you will at least better understand what impels him to think and behave as he does.

Complementary, rather than conflicting, status and role positions will be most productive. Eric Berne emphasized this point in *Games People Play*.[11] He observed that in every social setting an individual exhibits the ego states of Parent, Adult, or Child. (Berne distinguished ego states from roles, but that distinction is not pertinent to this point.) He argued that communication can proceed smoothly as long as transactions between the agents are complementary: if, for example, A and B address each other as adults, or if A addresses B as parent-to-child and B reciprocates by addressing A as child-to-parent. If the transactions are crossed, however, the communication will break down.

STUDY PROBE 16
Evaluating Communication Transactions

Refer to the Speech Communication Assessment Scales which you completed in Chapter 3, pages 56–59. Using Berne's concept of complementary or crossed transactions, analyze your interaction in each of those contexts. Note any specific ways in which this analysis helps to explain the anxieties and frustrations which you may have experienced in certain of those settings.

---

[10] William C. Schutz, *FIRO: A Three-Dimensional Theory of Interpersonal Behavior* (New York: Holt, Rinehart & Winston, Inc., 1960).

[11] Eric Berne, *Games People Play* (New York: Grove Press, Inc., 1964), especially pp. 29–34. *Note:* The diagrams on the facing page are adapted from Berne, ibid., pp. 30–31. Copyright © 1964 by Eric Berne.

An example of a crossed transaction would be a situation in which A addresses B as parent-to-child, while B addresses A as adult-to-adult. Thus:

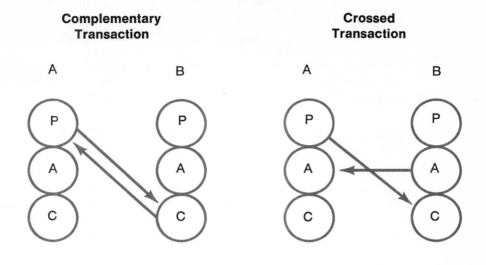

Complementary Transaction   **Crossed Transaction**

STUDY PROBE 17
Discovering Crossed Transactions

Carefully observe some of the speech interaction in classes you are currently attending. Discover instances where an instructor and a student are having difficulties in communicating interpersonally. Can you trace the problems to apparent crossed transactions? Be prepared to discuss this in class, or to deliver a written report on your findings.

Whether he views his co-communicator's needs as Schutz suggests or sees his role relations as Berne proposes, the communicating agent is sensitizing himself to the status and role differences of his "other" and to what this human relationship demands. Again, because of the patterned and role-like nature of communication and the efficiency which can result from following accepted patterns for interaction, a sensitive communicating agent will attempt to choose the role and status positions he will exhibit during interpersonal interaction, and will try to assess the positions he anticipates his colleague will exhibit. His next task is to compare the expectations of the two agents, himself and his "other," to see whether they are in harmony. If so, the interaction may proceed. If not, he should probably seek a better balancing, if that is at all possible. One of the procedures by which he could strive for such a balance is by gradual reciprocal increments, which we have previously discussed. In addition, as we shall outline in the ensuing section, there are some other procedures which may be profitably pursued by agents who seek improved interaction.

Seeking Mutuality and Bases for Interaction

Alienation is a word commonly used to describe the feelings of remoteness being experienced by significant numbers of individuals in our contemporary society. The frequency with which the word is heard suggests that many of us may have lost our grasp on the fundamental touchstones of social interaction. Family and church play a less central role in our time than in previous eras. Often, increasing technology and population are singled out as factors which have diminished our potential and our significance as individual human beings. Today, many of us are searching seriously for new and better roadways to group identification and community awareness.

What possible actions in the interpersonal context may help to mend and heal these feelings of alienation? We suggest the following additional procedures as meaningful and practical approaches to improved interpersonal interaction.

Seek Experience with Widest Possible Range of Communication Contexts and Agents

One means by which a communicative agent can better prepare himself for successful speech communication interaction is to gain experience in as many differing communication settings and with as many different individuals as possible. The more varied the situations we encounter and learn to adjust to, the more flexible and able we should be to adapt to any still newer situation in which we may become involved. The more we tend to confine our interaction to a single group of similar people in the same setting and with the same purpose, the greater will be our difficulties in facing new and different situations.

STUDY PROBE 18
Assessing the Heterogeneity/Similarity Ranges of Other Agents

List all the persons with whom you have talked in two-person settings for periods of longer than five minutes during the past week. What is the range of ages, occupations, beliefs, values, and experiences of the persons on this list? Would you say these persons, as a group, are heterogeneous and varied, or are they generally like one another?

Our counsel to you as a student of speech communication is that you should not close off near-at-hand opportunities for speech interaction. Too many students, for example, search for materials for assigned papers only in libraries, and neglect to interview professors and others who may be experts on the subject and who may be easily accessible on campus. Don't overlook such an opportunity to widen the scope of your interpersonal speaking experiences. Some citizens, both old and young, complain about the actions of the city council, but they only talk *about* councilmen—rather than *to* them. Aside from the limited effects which "talking about" can induce, you will be missing a chance to take direct action and widen your communicative contacts—an opportunity which any alert person ought always to cultivate.

Search for Possible Common Ground

The character of each individual has many facets. These facets often prompt one individual to clash with another on certain limited levels and to interact as antagonists. Quite possibly, however, if both would pause to reflect, they would realize that in their many-faceted characters they *could* find certain similarities and points in common—likenesses which could serve to establish a common ground and produce positive, productive interaction. Unavoidably, you will find it necessary from time to time to interact with others on matters of dispute. In such circumstances, begin by trying to search out *mutuality* and lines of *commonality*. As a strategy for interpersonal relations, almost invariably you will find it easier to interact with another in controversial matters if you make a real effort to find common ground.

Giffin and Patton describe a technique used by R. D. DuBois in promoting better relations among representatives from disparate groups.[12] Instead of having these persons come together and talk about intergroup differences and conflicts, they are asked to talk about their most pleasant childhood memories. (A contemporary instance of this practice might involve representatives from such dissimilar groups as black militants and policemen.) What appears to happen is that, after a time, members of these essentially different groups find that many of their childhood happinesses, feelings, and experiences were similar. This gives the participants a common ground.

STUDY PROBE 19
Seeking Common Ground

Enumerate five or six discussion topics other than childhood memories which may enable disparate individuals to discover some degree of common ground. Describe a number of other experiences which could also contribute to this end.

Some might argue that a discussion of pleasant childhood memories is time-consuming and irrelevant to the problem. These objections must of course be taken into consideration. Yet, as we pointed out in Chapter 4, there are many reasons why a man speaks. Before the basic communicative purpose can be effectively pursued, it may be necessary for the involved agents to prepare the psychological climate of the context with techniques such as those suggested here.

STUDY PROBE 20
*Testing Your Abilities to Listen to Other Agents
and Restate Their Views*

Carry out the following experiment as a test of your critical listening abilities. In a conversation in which you and another agent are advancing opposing positions, listen carefully to his statement of his proposition and then try to restate his views in terms that he will accept. If, at first, you cannot restate the point or proposition so that he will agree that you understand his position, try again.

---

[12] Kim Giffin and Bobby R. Patton, *Fundamentals of Interpersonal Communication* (New York: Harper & Row, Publishers, 1971), pp. 183–184.

Maintain Continuing Involvement with the Other Agent

A communication agent should strive to sustain interaction and involvement with the other agent over as long a period as is practical and appropriate for their mutual purposes. In our discussion of continuing contexts (pages 250–251), we pointed out that those settings that maintain the mutual association of the agents tend to have certain positive ends. Those communicators who interact frequently tend to like one another better and gradually become more alike in their beliefs, evaluations, and values.

Practice Active Affirmation in Interaction

Consider the following pair of statements:

a. My pet is a dog.
b. My pet is not a dog.

The initial statement is an affirmation. The second statement is a negation. Aside from this obvious distinction, there are other significant differences between them. The first statement informs us (1) that the speaker has a pet and (2) that the pet is a dog. This short assertion carries a great amount of information. It eliminates any uncertainty we may have had regarding the question of whether or not the speaker has a pet. But the statement also reduces uncertainty among many more possibilities. The second statement leaves us in doubt. If the speaker has a pet, it could be any one of dozens of possible pets. The first statement reduces the possibilities by all but one when it informs us specifically that the pet is a dog. Information theorists define information as a "reduction of uncertainty." By that definition, the first statement is much more informative.

In contrast, the second statement is not nearly as informative. We may infer from the statement that the individual has a pet, but we have no idea what it may be. Of the dozens of possibilities, the statement eliminates only one. The second statement reduces much less uncertainty than the first, and is a great deal less informative.

This example reveals the nature of affirmation and its advantages over negation. Affirm a policy and we know what you support. Negate a policy and we may have no idea what you stand for. And you may not either.

STUDY PROBE 21
Differentiating Affirmation and Negation

Imagine that you are playing the game of "Twenty Questions." Suppose in one series you receive five consecutive "yes" responses. In another series you receive five consecutive "no" responses. In which instance will you probably have progressed further toward the correct answer? Devise several specific examples of questions to which a "no" response can provide as much information as a "yes" response. Try also to devise several questions requiring a "no" response which can carry more information than can a "yes" response.

There are some who speak at length about repression in our society, in the present structures in university education, and elsewhere. Often these speakers list at length what they don't like. But some of them are suddenly inarticulate when they are asked what they want—what they *do* like. Quite frequently the only "constructive" suggestion they make in such circumstances is to "get rid of the old system." But this apparent inability or unwillingness to speak positively and informatively can only frustrate the other agent, and does little to promote productive interaction. For *lack* of information, the very pattern of communication heightens rather than reduces conflict between agents.

The type of analysis we have offered for *affirmation versus negation* is applicable also for the *active-versus-passive* dimensions of behavior. Activity, like affirmation, carries a large amount of information. Passivity, on the other hand, leaves us uncertain as to just what the other person stands for.

STUDY PROBE 22

Making Interpersonal Speech Active and Affirmative in Interviews

Select a classmate as a partner and together work out two hypothetical job interviews. Alternate in your role playing between the positions of *interviewer* and *interviewee*. In one instance, as interviewee, simply respond impromptu— "off the cuff"—to the statements put to you by the interviewer. In another instance, before participating in the interview, plan carefully a summary of your abilities, experience, qualifications, and interests. Make tape recordings of the interviews so that later you can make a careful analysis of the interaction. In preparing a report on your analysis, indicate—among other things—in which of the two instances your speech behaviors were more active and affirmative.

What we have said, certainly, should not be interpreted to mean that you ought never to oppose programs or never play passive roles. What we do wish to emphasize is we can be most helpful to the other agent if we decide what actions we *do* advocate and support and then speak *for* those positions. We owe it to any other agent with whom we interact to have thought sufficiently about the subject under discussion to have formulated a clear and specific position to advance, advocate, or support.

Strive for Supportive Rather than Defensive Interaction

In a study based on observations of small group discussions in various contexts, Jack R. Gibb distinguished between communication behaviors typical of *supportive* climates and of *defensive* climates in interpersonal interaction.[13] Gibb's classification system contrasts six pairs of behaviors, as follows:

[13] Jack R. Gibb, "Defensive Communication," *The Journal of Communication,* XI (1961): 141–148.

BEHAVIORS CHARACTERISTIC OF
SUPPORTIVE AND DEFENSIVE CLIMATES

Supportive		Defensive
1. Description	vs.	Evaluation
2. Problem Orientation	vs.	Control
3. Spontaneity	vs.	Strategy
4. Empathy	vs.	Neutrality
5. Equality	vs.	Superiority
6. Provisionalism	vs.	Certainty

Gibb's system suggests that remarks which are descriptive and neutral in connotation will tend to be supportive, whereas comments that are highly evaluative in connotation may cause the other agent to become defensive. Attempts to control the other agent will create defensiveness, whereas an orientation in which attempts are made to control the problem will be supportive.

Gibb proposes that stratagems intended to manipulate will cause defensiveness, whereas open, spontaneous discussion will be supportive. In some respects, this pair of terms can create misunderstanding. We must not infer from Gibb's study that spontaneity is always "good" or that careful planning is "bad." The difference should be seen as one of manipulative strategy in contrast to open and honest discussion. It is not a difference between careful planning and unplanned remarks made on "the spur of the moment."

STUDY PROBE 23

Differentiating Supportive and Defensive Communication in Interpersonal Contexts

Join another classmate in developing a series of role-playing conversations. Build your experiment in two different contexts: (1) a social conversation context, and (2) a bargaining-and-negotiating context, with you and your partner performing and then exchanging roles for each context. Vary your role playing in each of these contexts so that in one instance you use "supportive" behaviors and in another you employ "defensive" behaviors. Again, if possible, tape record your conversations for later analysis. Prepare a report describing the results, concentrating on the differences among the various communicative climates arising from the alternating contexts and contrasting behaviors.

Neutral comments directed toward the other agent might be interpreted as signifying a lack of concern and lack of desire for involvement, whereas empathic remarks show a sensitivity toward the other person and the ability to see the matter from his view. In an interpersonal context, if your comments show that you consider the other as an equal rather than as an inferior, you are clearly being more supportive. And finally, statements that are absolute and un-compromising may create a defensive response, whereas a provisional or tentative approach will be likely to evoke a more supportive response.

We have suggested in this chapter that interpersonal speech communication is patterned. To achieve the highest levels of interaction, a communication agent should be aware generally of the usefulness of following and occasionally of re-shaping the expectations deriving from these patterns. An agent will do well al-ways to be sensitive to the demands of the communication context in which he finds himself. He should determine the status and role relations between himself and the other. With this knowledge in mind, he should seek the closest possible interaction. An efficient principle in this quest is the modification of behavior by gradual reciprocal increments. In seeking bases for interpersonal interaction, one seeks empathy, affinity, and harmony with another. The behaviors suggested throughout this chapter are all intended as means to those ends.

Suggested Readings

Erving Goffman, *The Presentation of Self in Everyday Life* (Garden City, N.Y.: Doubleday & Company, Inc., Anchor Books, 1959). This paperback de-velops the dramatistic theme in which the individual is seen as playing roles and presenting himself in all his speech communication interactions.

Paul Watzlawick, Janet Beavin, and Don Jackson, *Pragmatics of Human Com-munication* (New York: W. W. Norton & Company, Inc., 1967). This work presents interesting material about patterns and problems in com-munication interaction.

Kim Giffin and Bobby R. Patton, eds., *Basic Readings in Interpersonal Com-munication* (New York: Harper & Row, Publishers, 1971). This paper-back contains many interesting selections from varied sources relating to interpersonal communication. It permits the reader to sample widely and follow up on those references he finds most interesting.

Chapter 9
Achieving Interaction with a Few: Small Group Discussion

While the discussion task provides the purpose and the goal
for a problem-solving discussion group,
task functions are not the only important acts in group process;
clearly, social-emotional behaviors also play a major role.

The small, communicating group is an ubiquitous feature of modern society. Most organizations, ranging from whole societies, governments, giant business concerns, and educational systems, to local civic clubs, activity groups, and often families, rely on small group interaction for their existence and maintenance. While some persons may shy away from speech making to larger audiences (even at their own personal loss), it is nearly impossible for any of us to avoid participation in small group communication. As students and practitioners of speech, therefore, we ought to give careful attention to this context for interaction.

The Usefulness of Small Group Discussion

Purposes

The small group discussion setting can serve a wide range of purposes. Most extensively, probably, it is used for *problem solving* and *decision making*. An organization is faced with a problem and the need for some course of action. A small group of individuals come together to discuss the situation and arrive at a decision regarding the best solution to their common problem. Such a group can meet at the highest or the lowest levels of the organization. The problem may be profoundly significant or of lesser importance. Yet the communication problems may be much alike. Most of our emphasis in this chapter will be upon this decision-making or problem-solving function of group discussion.

Another important purpose for group communication is *information sharing*. Sometimes a group does not have as its goal the determining and implementing of policy. It may be that it is not qualified or authorized to make decisions. Or that particular goal may not be the desire of the group. For example, subcommittees in the League of Women Voters are frequently formed to survey problems and assemble and organize pertinent information. The information is usually intended for distribution to the League members prior to their formulation of a decision as an entire group. The task within the subcommittee, then, is to gather and share information. In a slightly different way a meeting of a Great Books group has the primary purpose of information sharing. However, since information sharing through group effort also occurs as one of the phases of problem-solving discussions, our emphasis upon problem solving will still ensure coverage of the way in which information is shared within small groups.

A further purpose for group communication can be to provide *mutual support* for the participants. For example, group therapy is now widely practiced.[1] Organizations such as Alcoholics Anonymous serve the primary function of providing mutual support to their members. It is also true, however, that while some group meetings emphasize this goal in their activity, *every* group discussion contributes somewhat to this end. Although it may not be so pronounced, mutual support among participants—each for the other—is a function and, ideally, a result of every problem-solving discussion as well. We can therefore treat these supporting functions of groups as we consider the major functions of problem-solving groups.

---

[1] Irvin D. Yalom, *The Theory and Practice of Group Psychotherapy* (New York: Basic Books, Inc., Publishers, 1970). See Suggested Readings at the end of this chapter.

Advantages

Why bother with communication in groups? Why not let single individuals, at every level within an organization, make all policy decisions?

STUDY PROBE 1

Comparing Individual Versus Group Decision Making

List the task groups of which you have been a member—that is, those groups which were oriented toward a specific goal. Evaluate the productive efforts of each group. What decisions were made by each group? Could one person have made the decisions as well as the group? If one person had been given the decision-making responsibility, would the resulting decision have been the same? Would it have been as satisfactory to the group members? Could one person have implemented the decisions as well as the group? Substantiate your answers with possible reasons.

Research studies have shown a number of ways in which group decision making can be superior to that of individuals.[2] First, the group can usually assemble more resource material than any one person can. If the task in any way permits a division of labor, then the group will collect more information. Group processes are also superior in that random errors can be eliminated as the data of a number of individuals are pooled. One person may get sidetracked because of a simple mistake, or fail to see an obvious alternative solution. A group of people can correct these temporary oversights of individuals.

Professor Dean Barnlund compared decision making by individuals, by group-majority rule, and by group discussion. His study revealed that discussion was significantly better.[3] He found that membership in the discussion group produced a higher level of interest in the successful completion of the task. Group members knew their views were being weighed by others and were more careful and deliberate in their thinking. Group members also recognized a wider range of issues inherent in the topic than did individuals working alone. The studies further revealed that the competition among the private prejudices of the group members resulted, finally, in a more objective view of the problem.

Group work is also beneficial because it provides social motivation and rewards. People often seem to enjoy working together in groups and are stimulated by that setting. Any researcher using groups for a study is always aware of what is called the "Hawthorne effect," so termed because of some early studies in industrial settings of the Western Electric Company plant by that name. The most important finding of these studies was that when persons perceived themselves as members of a special group working on a special task, their morale improved and their productivity increased.[4]

[2] Marvin E. Shaw, *Group Dynamics: The Psychology of Small Group Behavior* (New York: McGraw-Hill Book Company, 1971), pp. 59–67.

[3] Dean C. Barnlund, "A Comparative Study of Individual, Majority, and Group Judgment," *Journal of Abnormal and Social Psychology,* LVIII (1959): 55–60.

[4] F. J. Roethlisberger and W. J. Dickson, *Management and the Worker* (Cambridge, Mass.: Harvard University Press, 1939).

Another related advantage of group work is the increased commitment which the individual feels to his group's decision. Some studies have indicated that if an individual has participated in and has been able to express his view during decision making by a group, he will then be more committed to the group's final decision, even if it does not represent his personal or original view. Other studies show that participation in group discussion of a topic is more likely than individual reflection to produce behavioral changes. In these cases, the public commitment to a course of action and the feeling of having had a fair hearing probably contribute to the result noted.[5]

Disadvantages

Group problem solving is not all profit, however; there is some cost. Before discussing these "costs," you will probably find it useful to probe some of your personal experiences and try to recall some of the deficiencies and drawbacks which may have frustrated various discussion groups as they attempted to accomplish their purposes.

STUDY PROBE 2

Examining Some Impediments to Group Progress

Consider again the groups in which you have participated. What problems were most apparent in your experience with each group? Attempt to categorize these problems (1) as being related to the task or goals of the group, or (2) as being primarily social-emotional in nature. Can you make any generalizations about the relation between the purpose of a group and the factors which hindered or impeded its work?

The major limitation of group discussion is that it takes so much time. *Time* must be available, and well used, if the benefits of this form of communication are to be realized. There are problems and cases for which there is not adequate time for group processes to be employed. A second limitation has to do with the nature of the participants—namely *people*. All the human weaknesses and problems characteristic of human communication will be apparent in group discussion. A number of these will be discussed later in this chapter. The student of speech must be prepared for these limitations and be tolerant of them. In most instances involving social problems, the benefits to be gained from this form of communication far outweigh the disadvantages.

Concepts of Leadership

For years the topic of leadership has been a dominant concern in the theory, research, and teaching about group communication. Let us now discuss that concept, and organize our application of communicative principles around it.

Early studies of leadership attempted to determine the underlying *traits* of leaders. The idea was to identify leaders, to see what they had in common, and

[5] Floyd L. Ruch and Philip G. Zimbardo, *Psychology and Life,* 8th ed. (Glenview, Ill.: Scott, Foresman and Company, 1971), pp. 492–493.

to ascertain how they differed from non-leaders. Measurements of intelligence, information, and even height and weight were sought. Some positive findings did appear from these studies, but on the whole they were disappointing. The findings of one study seemed to contradict the conclusions of another. Eventually the trait-index approach to leadership analysis largely faded away.[6]

Another hope has been to learn about leadership by looking for general leadership *styles.* Some early studies compared "autocratic," "democratic," and "laissez-faire" styles of leadership. In the "autocratic" approach the leader remained aloof from the group and dictated procedures. In the "democratic" situation the leader took an active role in guiding the group's activity, but allowed the group to determine policies through discussion. In the "laissez-faire" style the leader played a passive and aloof role, available only if called upon. Generally in these studies the "democratic" style has proved superior.[7] Rarely, however, is leadership in real life so stereotyped and consistent.

Psychologist Floyd Ruch summarizes some of this research with the general observation that:

> . . . *it has been found that leaders in most situations are distinguished by three important characteristics: their awareness of group attitudes (social perception), their ability in abstract thinking, and their good emotional adjustment. Personal popularity may also play a part.*[8]

Ruch also observes that *good leaders and good followers have much in common.* This point begins to get to the heart of the matter.

Robert Bales has suggested that leadership is not a unidimensional concept. His studies indicate that there is "task" leadership in which a person focuses upon the work or task confronting the group and guides the discussion toward the goal. There is also a "social-emotional" leader who functions primarily to prevent conflicts, resolve tensions, and promote group unity.[9]

Many studies on leadership end with "it all depends . . ." It all depends on the situation, the persons involved, the topic, the setting. One person may emerge as a "leader" in certain cases, but not in others. In any discussion, one individual may "lead" at one time, but not at another. And one person may lead primarily on task matters, while others lead mainly on social-emotional matters.

STUDY PROBE 3
Analyzing Yourself in a Leadership Role

Recall your association with task groups in which you have served in a position of leadership. Describe your performance in terms of "style." Would you char-

[6] Cecil A. Gibb, "Leadership," in *The Handbook of Social Psychology,* 2nd ed., ed. Gardner Lindzey and Elliot Aronson (Reading, Mass.: Addison-Wesley Publishing Co., Inc., 1969), v. IV, pp. 205–282.

[7] Marvin E. Shaw, *Group Dynamics: The Psychology of Small Group Behavior* (New York: McGraw-Hill Book Company, 1971), pp. 270–274.

[8] Floyd L. Ruch, *Psychology and Life,* 7th ed. (Glenview, Ill.: Scott, Foresman and Company, 1967), p. 566.

[9] Robert F. Bales, "In Conference," in *Basic Readings in Interpersonal Communication,* ed. Kim Giffin and Bobby R. Patton (New York: Harper & Row, Publishers, 1971), pp. 418–431.

acterize your behavior as "autocratic," "democratic," or "laissez-faire"? Would you categorize your leadership functions as primarily oriented toward the group's task or toward the social-emotional needs of the group and its participants? In which leadership roles have you felt most comfortable? most successful? Verify your analysis by asking a friend, who was a member of one of the groups for which you served as leader, to answer these same questions about you.

The concept of leadership should not be viewed as a static concept. We should not search for the leader or the act of leadership. Rather, we should consider *leadership functions: the actions which influence group members in positive ways toward the achievement of their group goal.* Any one, or all, of the members in group discussion can serve as leaders. Some will lead at certain times and in certain ways. At other times and in still other ways, others may lead. Leadership occurs whenever an individual expresses a comment that exerts a positive influence on the group's interaction. Any person doing this is fulfilling a leadership role and serving a leadership function.

But you may say that a person is often assigned—by a teacher or an executive—to be "the leader." In reality, however, that person is assigned to serve as *chairman,* as coordinator and guide for the discussion. He will, it is to be hoped, lead at some times and in some ways during the discussion. But so should all the other participants. We expect a chairman to serve as guide during the meeting; but we hope every participant will serve, along with the chairman, in fulfilling the necessary and helpful leadership functions. This is the kind of shared leadership that makes groups function most productively.

With this concept of the nature of leadership in mind, let us consider the essential principles for effective speaking in the small group communication setting. Whether you are acting as assigned chairman or as discussion participant, you will need to observe some practical guidelines in planning for task functions and for social-emotional functions in group communication.

Planning for Task Functions

Let us consider first the discussion task. What is essential in order to accomplish the group's goal? What steps should be followed? We will suggest here one possible means of developing thought and talk in a small group problem-solving discussion. We will attempt to cover fully the problem-solving discussion, although occasional comments will deal with discussion forms having more limited goals. Whatever has bearing upon the larger case should also fit the more limited one.

The Problem-Solving Sequence

Assume that the members of a small group are given a problem to discuss, and are asked to arrive at the best possible solution. How can they proceed most effectively from problem to solution? There are *many alternative approaches* that could be suggested. One could consider an "incrementalist" strategy, related in some ways to the gradual reciprocal increments proposal of Chapter 8.[10] The

---

[10] David Braybrooke and Charles E. Lindblom, *A Strategy of Decision* (New York: The Free Press, 1963), especially Chapters 5 and 6.

"mixed-scanning" approach of Amitai Etzioni is another possible strategy for solving problems.[11] Our proposal here, however, will be a more traditional Problem-Solving Sequence derived from John Dewey's description of the steps of thinking (Chapter 7, page 200) and adapted by several scholars over many years. Our suggested procedure is rigorous in that it demands a high level of effective interpersonal communication, perhaps more than some other approaches. Yet we believe it is potentially the most effective problem-solving system.

The Problem-Solving Sequence is composed of the five steps listed below. In following this sequence, the group progresses through the five steps, completing each step to the satisfaction of the majority of the group members before moving on to the next, and building one step upon the other; thus:

1. Analyze the Problem (Symptoms).
2. Determine Causes.
3. Establish Standards for Judgment.
4. Consider Possible Actions.
5. Settle on the Best Solution.

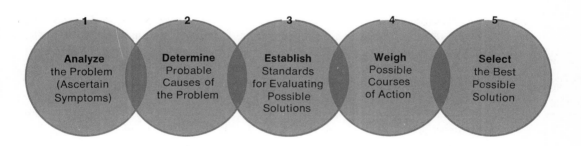

A Problem-Solving Sequence

1. Analyze and Detect Symptoms of the Problem

The first step calls for an analysis of the problem—a diagnosis of the symptoms. How do we know that we have a problem? We usually become aware of a problem because we can see its *symptoms,* the *signs* of a problem. How do we know that we are physically ill? We have a headache, feel weak, and have an above-normal temperature which can be easily measured. These are symptoms or signs of illness. How do we know that there is an urban-center problem in a certain city? Because there is rioting, looting, destruction of property, and even

---

[11] Amitai Etzioni, *The Active Society* (New York: The Free Press, 1958), especially Chapters 11 and 12.

loss of life. All these events are definite and real, and they are easy to observe, measure, and count. They are the symptoms, or the signs, of the problem. How do we know that we have a water-pollution problem? Because a beach is condemned as physically unsafe for swimming; fish and fowl die and can no longer live in and on the water; plant growth spreads throughout the underwater area. These easily observable, measurable phenomena are the symptoms or the signs of a problem.

The first step, then, in a problem-solving discussion should be to consider and assess the symptoms or signs of the problem. If there are no symptoms, there is little use in further discussion; if there are symptoms, the group should *list and evaluate them.* Just what has happened and what is happening? How widespread is the problem? How significant is it? Do the symptoms matter—can we live with them? The group should also attempt to assess the *trends* of the symptoms. Is the scope or size of the symptoms increasing? If we do nothing about the symptoms, will they simply fade away? Are any present attempts being made to meet the problem? If so, what are they, and what effects are they having upon the symptoms? What actions, if any, have been taken to reduce the symptoms, and what are the current trends? In this first step the group should present, consider, evaluate, and come to some clear conclusions about the evidence indicating symptoms or signs of a problem. The point here is for *all* communicative agents to come to the fullest possible understanding of the observable effects of the problem and their probable consequences if the problem is not solved.

2. Determine the Causes of the Problem

The second step, and a most crucial one, is for the group to ascertain the causes of the problem. This is a very difficult step and a stumbling block to the solution of many human social dilemmas. Much of the difficulty lies in our analysis of causation and in the confusions pointed out in Chapter 5 (pages 147–149) and Chapter 6 (pages 187–191). We must realize first that the *symptoms of a problem are not usually the causes of the problem.* Symptoms are observable effects, or results, or signs. Causes are usually complex and often not observable, but they are the forces that produce the problem.

The headache lets us know we have a problem. But the headache results from our having "a cold"; the headache does not cause the cold. An unseen virus is the cause of the problem. So how do we treat a cold? Sometimes we take aspirin and in a few days the cold is gone. But it is important for us to realize what we have done here: we have followed a course of action to eliminate a symptom temporarily. We have done nothing about the cause. Our body fights off the real cause of the cold for us, and we soon become well—quite without any help from the aspirin. If our body did not wage the real battle against the cause, we could take aspirins continually and never be rid of the affliction.

STUDY PROBE 4

Distinguishing Between Symptoms and Causes of a Problem

Discuss several contemporary issues with your classmates in small group settings. In each case try to distinguish between the *symptoms* of the problem and the *causes* of the problem. For example, cases you might consider are: (1) the rising crime rates, (2) pollution of the environment, and (3) diminished U.S. prestige abroad.

Just as anyone who is suffering from a cold must bear in mind the difference between the symptoms and the causes of the illness, so a discussion group must distinguish with equal clarity between symptoms and causes, and know which is going to be treated. Social ills, unlike physical disorders such as the common cold, have no intrinsic defenses or mechanisms to search out and eliminate the cause of the problem. They require intervention from "outside." If the problems are to be cured, intensified group efforts will be necessary. Too often, in dealing with social problems, we make the "mistake of the common cold": we attempt to eliminate problems by treating symptoms only. Most often this is unsuccessful. Even if we eliminate a symptom but allow the cause to remain unchecked, that cause can produce other symptoms. At times it may be necessary to treat the symptoms of social problems, as in instances of riots and wars. To effect genuine and lasting improvement, however, we must search out and treat the causes.

Consider some social problems. Rioting and looting are not the causes of urban problems; they are the results. The impulse of many members of society is to say, "Let us end rioting and looting—let us stop crime—let us strike at the symptoms." If we use sufficient armed power, rioting and looting can usually be temporarily stopped. But if the underlying causes go untreated, the urban problem may appear in other forms, perhaps with different symptoms. By treating only the symptoms of the urban problem, we may be committing ourselves to a permanent armed-camp life. Or, a different consequence may occur from treating only symptoms: temporary answers to problems may become permanent. Dead fish and a condemned beach are, as we have said, symptoms and not causes. We may continue to restock streams and clean up beaches regularly, but if the water remains polluted, the fish will continue to die and the beaches will be periodically unsafe. A wiser course would be to seek the cause and try to eliminate the pollutants.

There are understandable reasons why individuals and groups are so prone to attack symptoms only. Causes are elusive because they are most often unseen, even unseeable. Frequently they are psychological rather than physical. They are usually complex. Usually they can be viewed not only as causes of certain effects but also as effects of even more remote causes. They are often multi-faceted, so that they have a different appearance if viewed from different angles. Consider an example. Why is person X a criminal? One may view him and his situation from an external standpoint and attribute his criminal behavior to an undesirable childhood environment, a broken home, erratic discipline, and so on. Another look, taken from inside, may suggest that his criminality is due to feelings of rejection, a lack of love, and so on. A different view, still from inside, will suggest that a chromosome abnormality is really the cause. All views yield answers that agree that the man is a criminal, and they agree on what he has done. But the understandings of the causes differ widely. This example might shed some light on the tendency—which all of us exhibit—to treat only the symptoms of problems. It is a far simpler course of action.

In the cause-determination phase of group problem solving, you and your colleagues in discussion must consider alternative points of view from which problems (signified by symptoms) can be inspected and their causes discovered. You must realize that framing causes is like setting the boundaries of a concept prior to verbal labeling. The boundaries must be arbitrarily established by your group. In all of this you should be guided by an awareness of your goal, and you should choose an approach to the examination of causes which will facilitate the remainder of the discussion. If a broader social view of the causes rather than a narrower psychological perspective will make it easier to arrive at a workable solution, then the former should be used.

After proposing, considering, and weighing the causes as they see them, members of a discussion group should eventually arrive at a list of causes *with some judgments as to their relative strengths*. Which are the primary causes, which the secondary? Which causes must be treated if any progress is to be made? Which are less crucial? These are decisions group members must make at this stage in their efforts, or else they cannot know what to solve.

3. Establish Standards for Evaluation of Possible Solutions

As their third step the discussion participants need to decide on the standards by which they will judge possible solutions. Consider an analogy. If you planned to buy a car, you would not merely walk into an automobile agency and say, "I want to buy one of your cars"—period. If your mind were no better settled than this remark suggests, you would have to consider every automobile the dealer had, or buy whatever he offered you. The chances of your purchase being a "good" one *for you* would be limited. Your actual practice would be to determine in advance *standards* for your selection. You would arrive at the dealer's showroom knowing you were interested in a certain model, a certain size, a certain price range, and so on. No doubt you would have additional requirements —engine horsepower, trunk space, gas mileage, ease of maintenance, and possibly more. You would give such information to a salesman who would then select from all possible choices only those that fit the standards you have established. Time would not be wasted in considering unacceptable choices. This is the efficient way to proceed, unless one is just "window shopping" and doesn't mind impulse buying. Our car-buying situation illustrates several reasons why we need early determination of "standards," either as individuals or as members of groups.

Most social problems are far too important and pressing for us to proceed in any such "window-shopping" manner. As we mentioned at the outset of our discussion, time limitations are a big factor in group decision making, so everything possible should be done to keep the work of the group orderly and efficient. By establishing definite standards for an acceptable solution, we greatly improve efficiency. But groups often omit this step unknowingly, and move directly from causes to solution, if not from problem to solution.

If it is to function efficiently and with genuine knowledge of what it is doing, a problem-solving group needs to pause after completing its view of the problem (symptoms and causes) to take stock of what kinds of answers are even *worthy* of consideration. Is there really *need* for solutions at all? If there is, then *just what* needs solving and what does not? What *special requirements* must be met? What *limits* choices among solutions? These are among the questions participants in problem solving need to ask themselves before rushing headlong in search of answers.

One of the most practical standards any acceptable solution will have to meet is that it must fit within the limits of your resources—financial, manpower, etc. To toy hopefully with a $1000 solution if your group can raise only $100 is wasteful of time and effort and is foolish. To speculate about the merits of a solution that will require the work of more people than you have available to work is equally wasteful and frustrating.

There are other kinds of "standards" that also need to be explored. *Which* causes should you or can you attack? In what order? Or to what degree would a solution be acceptable if it could only reduce symptoms? And if symptoms are to be reduced, which ones, and in what order? Only after considering such questions as these about the "standards" that acceptable solutions have to meet are the participants in a discussion prepared to move into consideration of possible courses of action.

STUDY PROBE 5
Establishing and Applying Evaluative Criteria

Plan to meet with a small group of classmates for two sessions. At the first session select something to be judged, and determine the standards by which this "something" could be evaluated. Be specific, and try to consider all of the ramifications of the criteria which you are establishing. At the second session, apply these standards to something specific, and make a judgment accordingly. For example, you could set up standards for judging political speeches, television commercials, summer jobs, or restaurants; then subsequently, you could evaluate a particular speech, a televised commercial, a summer job, or a restaurant by using the stated criteria as your basis for judgment.

---

4. Consider Possible Courses of Action

As a fourth step in problem solving, your group should locate and consider the possible courses of action available to you within the limits of your established standards. Initially, you can assemble a listing of all possible solutions which you and your colleagues have found or developed, including only those which *fit the major, limiting standards*. Once this list has been assembled in as complete a form as possible, you and the other participants can focus upon each possibility in turn and judge it against the full set of standards, as well as against each of the alternative solutions in your list. Probably, few proposed solutions will attack the specific causes of your problem and meet the established standards for judgment to your complete satisfaction. You will usually find it necessary, therefore, to make comparative judgments and compromises. In this way you can determine the relative effectiveness of the proposals or, perhaps alter and combine plans to make them more satisfactory.

STUDY PROBE 6
Brainstorming

In a small group setting, choose a problem for consideration by the group, and then try to "brainstorm" for possible courses of action or solutions to the problem. Bear in mind the following guidelines to be heeded in this technique: (1) Present as many different possibilities as you can. (2) Do not expand or develop any suggestion when it is made; just note it and move on. (3) Do not criticize any idea which is suggested, or any person suggesting an idea. See how many possible solutions the group can list in ten minutes.

In evaluating the proposed solutions, members of a discussion group must do more than weigh one solution against another and against the standards. Each solution must also be considered in terms of its consequences. Where would this proposal lead? What side effects might it produce, and how would we like those side effects? Most changes introduced in a system will have far-reaching effects, and those effects should be predicted and assessed.

Perhaps an example will help to clarify this step of the sequence. As we battle the causes of disease and mortality, we increase population, with its attendant effects. So, in a way, the widespread use of penicillin and other "miracle drugs" is a remote cause of water pollution and city parking problems. Some ramifications, perhaps less dramatic, are inherent in many solutions you will deal with. Some solutions may effectively counter the cause of a problem, but they may have so many undesirable side effects as to be impractical and unwise.

During this—the fourth—phase in problem solving, then, a group lists possible solutions, considers their probable consequences, and judges them against the standards for evaluation. With this knowledge clear to everyone, group members are then ready to make a decision as to the "best" action or solution.

5. Select the Best Possible Solution

In the fifth and final step in problem solving, the group endeavors to settle upon the best possible solution—the original and climactic objective and one which follows quite naturally from the work of the fourth step. The best possible solution may be among those proposed earlier, or it may be made up of parts or combinations of several proposed solutions. It may have long-range as well as short-range components. The solution may entail the steps for its own implementation and later re-evaluation.

As a general rule, if the group elects to employ the Problem-Solving Sequence each of the five steps should be completed in turn. As we have emphasized, a group should stay with each of the consecutive phases of the sequence until all questions related to that phase have been defined, determined, and/or resolved; only then should the participants move on to the next phase. Each step should be built upon the preceding stages. The causes should be causes of the problem discussed. The standards for evaluation should fit the ascertainable causes. The possible solutions considered should conform to the standards selected. The entire process should demonstrate coherence and progress from problem to final solution. If followed carefully, this sequence can do much to provide order and efficiency to group decision making. In applying this sequence, however, the participants must be flexible. The proposed steps may have to be modified in some cases. This system must *serve* the discussants rather than master them.

The Problem-Solving Discussion Question

With the general problem-solving sequence in mind, we can turn next to the *chronology* of planning for the discussion task functions. The first task is to decide upon the *wording* for the problem-solving question.

The framing of a discussable question must be considered carefully because the way a question is phrased usually provides some direction for its answer. The group members have to *see* clearly, and *agree on* the point of discussion and on the terms of the discussion. Without this prior agreement, the discussion may not "get off the ground." Susanne Langer presents one such case.[12] Suppose one person asks the question, "Who created the earth?" and another person replies, "No one created it!" Langer says the second person has not really answered the question at all; he has *rejected* the question. This can happen in discussions of social problems. A group may meet to answer the question, "How can we best improve our mathematics program in X Junior High School?" Suppose one or more participants begin by saying, "We don't see anything wrong with the program." These participants are rejecting the question. A comment such as this could start an argument that is really apart from the question itself. The question *assumes* the improvement is necessary, desirable, and possible. Only participants who are willing to make these assumptions can profitably discuss the question. Perhaps the members of the group should discuss first whether there is anything wrong with the present program.

The point here must not be mistaken. We are not arguing that everyone must always agree that problems exist, or that participants must accept every question. We are suggesting simply that everyone should begin with a mutual basic assumption—should "start off on the same foot." If one person comes prepared to suggest new programs and another is set only to defend the present system, there will be difficulties. Remember the "status of the question." If the "status" is not similar for all participants, the discussion cannot begin smoothly. It is the function of phrasing discussion questions to identify the "status" at which *this* group can and will begin problem solving. A good discussion question must be so framed that the participants will agree with the assumptions inherent in it. The question must ask for precisely the kinds of answers which all participants are seeking.

A discussion question should be stated in interrogative form, simple and clearly put; and the meaning of essential terms should be agreed upon by the participants. If, for instance, a discussion is to focus on water pollution, *what* we want to know about it must be clearly asked and the meaning of the terms must be settled before attention is turned to analyzing "the problem."

Beyond these requirements a problem-solving question should call for the entire Problem-Solving Sequence. "What should constitute our foreign-aid program to country X?" asks for consideration of symptoms, causes, standards, possible actions, and solution. If we were to ask the question "What is wrong with our foreign-aid program to country X?" a simple listing of the ills of the present program would probably suffice as an answer. This question in no way asks for a solution. "What has caused the pollution in lake X?" does not call for a solution. If you desire only a listing of problems, or difficulties, or causes, you may ask a question leading to such a listing. But *if you want a solution, you should ask for it.*

A good problem-solving discussion question will usually limit the scope of the topic, but not limit the consideration of potential solutions. "How can we best improve our educational system?" is much too broad. It could at least be narrowed to "How can we best improve our educational system in the United States?" Better still might be "How can we best improve our secondary education system in Madison?" or "How can we best improve our mathematics program in X Junior High School?"

[12] Susanne K. Langer, *Philosophy in a New Key* (New York: The New American Library Inc., 1942), p. 15.

Most discussion groups attempt to answer questions that are too broad. There are several reasons why the consideration of very broad questions is inadvisable. The problems, in these instances, are often seen as too complex; sufficient materials are not readily available for a thorough and satisfactory analysis; and the discussion tends to be carried on at such a general level as to be of little value. The topic should be qualified and limited in scope to a subject-area that the group can conceivably cover. As with our education problem, questions usually can be limited to certain levels, to certain geographical locations, or to specific subjects.

On the other hand, the wording of discussion questions should not arbitrarily rule out the consideration of any possible solution. A topic should be open to the evaluation of all possible solutions. For this reason it is never good practice to frame a problem-solving discussion question that can be answered with "yes" or "no." "Should this state legalize abortion?" is a question that can be discussed, but it is not a problem-solving question. It proposes a specific course of action and asks, "Do we want this particular solution—yes or no?" It is a question that could well occur in the latter steps of the Problem-Solving Sequence, when the group is evaluating several alternative courses of action and attempting to arrive at an overall solution. It could occur under problem-solving questions such as "How can we best meet the problem of overpopulation?" But, in itself, it is a question that begins with one possible solution to be evaluated rather than a problem to be solved. Under the topic of "birth control," abortion could be evaluated in conjunction with many other possible solutions. Hopefully, the interplay and joint evaluation of several possible solutions will lead to a better answer to the problem-solving question.

In sum, it is usually desirable for problem-solving questions to be simply and clearly stated, to call for the consideration of all the steps of the Problem-Solving Sequence, to limit the scope of the topic, and not to restrict the solutions which the group may consider. The assumptions underlying the question should be agreed upon or tacitly accepted by all the participants before they proceed to consider the problem.

STUDY PROBE 7

Evaluating Problem-Solving Discussion Questions

Evaluate the suitability of the following six questions for problem-solving discussions:

a. In what ways would more government planning help?

b. What steps, if any, should be taken to end tensions in the Middle East?

c. How can we best cope with increasing technology?

d. How can we best improve the mathematics program in X High School?

e. Should student automobiles be prohibited on campus?

f. What are the problems with drugs?

In instances where you feel the example is not a good problem-solving discussion question, modify it so that it becomes acceptable.

Materials and Agenda

Whether you serve as the assigned chairman or as a participant in a group discussion, you will need to know the topic well. Every group member should assemble as much material as possible on all aspects of the problem. As a participant you will probably have to refer to your research materials during the discussion; therefore, those materials should be abstracted or copied on note cards, organized for easy reference, and brought to the meeting. This is simply a precaution against becoming confused about the facts or your own ideas during the give-and-take of discussion in a group.

The *agenda* for a meeting is the order of topics to be considered. These topics should be coordinate and related to one another. During the discussion, the participants will discuss these topics in the sequence suggested by the agenda. Included in it, of course, are those topics that must be covered if the group is to answer the discussion question. For a problem-solving question the agenda most often will be the five steps of the Problem-Solving Sequence adapted to the proposed content of the discussion.

A group should settle on its general agenda as early as possible, preferably before the first working session. This will enable the participants then to use the items in it as reference points for research on the topic for the ordering of their materials. This will be true even if the task is not one of problem solving. If a book-review group is planning a discussion, it will likely be more effective if a tentative agenda is determined before the participants begin preparing. For problem-solving questions a participant can safely use the steps of the sequence as headings for the organization of his research materials.

STUDY PROBE 8
Preparing and Following an Agenda

With the other members of your class, try the following group experiment. Agree on a problem-solving discussion question to be considered. Then divide the class into groups of five or six persons each. Let each group set up a different agenda to follow in consideration of the question. Some possible agendas might be:

Group 1   a. Symptoms
           b. Causes
           c. Evaluative criteria
           d. Possible solutions
           e. Best solution

Group 2   a. Survey of the facts
           b. Possible solutions
           c. Criteria for judging
           d. Best solution

Group 3   a. Possible solutions (by "brainstorming")
           b. Best solution

Following the discussions, each group should report its progress to the class as a whole. Compare the solutions arrived at by the various groups. In what ways did each group's agenda influence the end result of the discussion?

As we have previously suggested, the chairman has additional responsibilities for task functions and must plan for them. If you are to be the chairman, you should prepare your outline for the agenda, listing the main headings and subordinate points which must be taken up. You should plan a *series of questions* that you can pose to ensure that the group will keep moving along at each step in the agenda. You may anticipate some points where *transitional remarks* must be made and at which *summaries* might be helpful. You should attempt to gauge very roughly how much *time* can be allotted to each step so that you can keep the group moving toward the goal. You should give some thought to procedures for *ending the discussion*. Is a final summary enough? Must there be a written report? Is any follow-up meeting or other action needed?

At the outset of the meeting, before the main discussion begins, the chairman and participants ought to *agree on goals and procedure or agenda*. Often, groups tend to omit or overlook this step; instead, they "take off" in several directions at once. It is much simpler and certainly more efficient to spend a few moments to review and agree on the agenda and procedure before moving to explore the problem posed in the discussion question.

Necessary Attitudes for Task Functions

Task functions, or goal-related speech behaviors, also have an attitudinal component. No task should be pursued without *motivation* and *feeling*. What are some of the desirable attitudes which contribute to effective group work on a task? We suggest that the discussion participant should (1) be goal oriented, (2) show a sense of inquiry, (3) be a good listener, (4) be patient, and (5) be willing to share leadership functions.

Being Goal Oriented

If group members keep in mind their immediate task, the time available and their ultimate goal, their solution will probably be found sooner and be of greater usefulness. Of course, goal-oriented discussion is hard work. It is much easier to ramble aimlessly in a "bull-session" manner. If the group does go astray, the chairman or any one of the participants can attempt to get it back on the track by presenting a summary of the group's progress up to the point of the digression, and then by asking a question to get the discussion moving again, away from the tangent and in a more productive direction.

STUDY PROBE 9

Helping Group Discussion to Remain Goal Oriented

We have discussed the tendency of the participants in task groups to wander away from the central issue onto related but somewhat tangential subjects. The next time you are part of a group and this occurs, as it almost inevitably does, try the technique just described. Summarize the progress of the group to the point at which the digressive comments began; check to be sure that you have the group's agreement with your summary. Then ask a question aimed at getting the group discussion going again, but in the direction indicated by the agenda.

How successful was your attempt to keep the discussion goal-oriented? What was the reaction of the group to your efforts?

Showing a Sense of Inquiry

A second desirable attitude is a sense of *inquiry*. We may assume that, before the discussion begins, all group members have certain beliefs and evaluations about the topic. This is only natural. But the task will be made easier if the participants are open to new and additional information, to the opinions of others, and if they desire to learn more about the topic. In fact, without this sense of inquiry, the group can settle nothing. The use of the *question,* a subject we considered in some detail in Chapter 5 (pages 148–149), is most helpful as a tool for such inquiry.

We may note also that the question is a helpful way of raising an objection. Suppose someone says something with which you disagree. If you say, "Well, I don't agree with that," you only create a conflict. The other person has no idea *why* you disagree. Suppose you say, "I don't agree with that because . . . ." In this case, he does know your grounds for disagreement; but in your first five words you are flatly inviting a clash. It may be better to ask, "What about the chances that . . . ?" and proceed to phrase the essence of the objection in question form. This calls upon the other person to answer your objection without your having introduced any personal conflict into the issue. Then, too, if you ask a question, you are calling for an answer; and you yourself may be more interested in the answer than if you had merely declared your disagreement. Clearly, the manner in which an issue is raised will influence the matter of the answer. Task functions motivated by and revealing a desire for inquiry will usually be more productive. But the motives must be positive. If the question form is used out of a sense of manipulative strategy and not a sense of inquiry, the positive effect may be lost.

Being a Good Listener

A related motive is the intention of being a *good listener*. Good listening consists of attending carefully to another, understanding his meaning, thinking about what he said, and being able to rephrase it in your words to his satisfaction. Descriptive studies have pointed out that a time differential exists between our usual listening rate and our thinking rate. Although a speaker normally will utter 125–150 words per minute, most of us are able to listen to oral communication if it comes to us three times that fast without losing much comprehension. This is due, in part, to a natural redundancy in our speech. Thoughts are repeated, and standard phrases are used; many elements in any spoken message could be omitted without greatly reducing comprehension.

Because of this rate differential and redundancy, as a discussion participant you will necessarily spend much of your time in listening. How, then, will you use that time? A good listener will use this time to reflect on messages, rephrase them in his own words, and associate them to other related elements he knows in order to understand and evaluate them. Accordingly, it is a useful exercise occasionally to ask another, "Are you saying . . . ?" or "Is your point that . . . ?" See if you can state *his* point in *your* language to *his* satisfaction. Thus, you will be checking on your own spare-time thinking. Try this when you seem to be in disagreement with another. If you can do this successfully, you are probably doing a good job of listening, and you will certainly be engaging in the clarification of ideas for yourself and others. Another aid to listening and memory is the taking of notes. During a discussion, all group members—and especially the chairman—should periodically make notes of the major lines of development and accomplishment that might be especially helpful for recall later in the discussion.

Being Patient

Another helpful attitude for task functions is *patience*. As we have stressed, the most efficient procedure in problem solving is to take up points one at a time and resolve each before moving to the next point. However, some participants have little patience. Once a problem is mentioned, and before it or its causes or anything else has been discussed, the impatient participant will offer a solution. Such comments offered prematurely can frequently do more harm than good to group progress. As we pointed out in Chapter 5 (pages 144–145), the natural human impulse is to meet every problem head-on with a quick solution, but good group discussants must try to curb this impulse. You must be patient enough to assist others in understanding the issues as you see them; and, further, you must be patient enough to take the time to understand their positions with reference to those issues.

Sharing Leadership Functions

A final desirable attitude is a willingness to share leadership functions with all group members. It is especially important that an assigned chairman not be so jealous of this position that he tries to dominate the group-guidance chores. A chairman should encourage other group members to assist with all task functions—and they should cooperate. It should not always be the duty of the chairman to make internal summaries, or to ask the questions that get the group back on the right track, or to note that the group must soon move on to the next topic. Everyone should be ready to do these things when they are needed. Concern for the task shows goal orientation. As we discussed earlier in this chapter, every group member should be motivated by this attitude, and it should be apparent as all shoulder the responsibilities for group task functions.

STUDY PROBE 10

Experimenting with Small Group Discussion

Plan to experiment in class with small group discussion. Four or five students in the class should discuss the question "How can we improve academic grading procedures within our college or university?" Following their discussion, the entire class should conduct a complete evaluation of their efforts. Then, using the evaluation as a guide, another group of four or five class members should discuss the same question. Again, the class evaluates their performance. What differences can be noted between the first and the second discussions? In the second discussion observe in particular the structure that emerges, the group's attention to productive procedure, the way the participants cooperate to build ideas, their willingness to consider and evaluate possible solutions, etc.

A Sample Case for Discussion

Some of these problems of task-oriented groups may be seen more easily in an example. On the first day in a discussion class, I often give four or five members of the class a case for discussion—without any advanced warning, preparation, or instruction. The point is to see how the discussion "naturally" progresses, what weaknesses are most common, and what some of the points are on which we must concentrate. What follows is a sample case for discussion, and a transcript of actual student comments about the case. Remember there is no warning, no preparation, no instruction other than to arrive at a group decision on the question, and no chairman is assigned.

DICK AND JANE

It is Christmas vacation time at college, and Dick and Jane are planning to talk again to their parents about marriage plans. They are hoping to be married in June. They have gone steady for the past three months since meeting early this fall.

Dick is twenty years old and in his third year in engineering—a five-year program. He has slightly better than a B average. He must attend at least one summer session to finish on schedule in two and one-half years. Jane is nineteen, a sophomore in history, with nearly an A average. She has considered graduate school because of encouragement by two of her professors.

About 80% of their college expenses thus far have been paid by their parents. Dick and Jane have made up the other 20% by work during summers, he for a construction company and she typing in an office.

Jane's parents oppose their marriage so soon. Dick's parents say they are willing to go along and would continue to give the couple the same support they now give Dick.

What do you believe the couple should do about marriage plans?

(The discussion usually begins after several moments of awkward silence.)

1-A: Well, I don't think they should be married so soon.

2-B: It's not a good idea to rely so much on parents for money. They may become psychologically dependent on them, too.

3-C: Well, I don't know.

4-A: She could become pregnant. Then where would they be?

5-B: Right.

6-D: They are very young. How old—or how mature—should one be before he gets married?

7-C: Well, it all depends.

8-E: Won't they just be frustrated if they don't get married? It could interfere with their studies.

9-B: I just don't believe in taking money from parents. When people get married, they should be independent. Or at least nearly independent.

10-C: What will happen to Jane's plans for graduate school?

11-E: Still, it's their business. I don't see why they can't do whatever they like. Who are we to tell them what to do?

12-D: Maybe we should look at the other side—why should they get married?

(and so on)

This portion of a discussion, typical of this situation, reveals a number of problems: The opening comment of A is common. The discussion begins with a personal, immediate, and unqualified answer to the group question. It is as if the speaker intends to end the discussion rather than begin it. There are also many comments such as 3 and 7 by participant C which offer very little to the group. They are just self-expressive statements of perplexity. One major difficulty is revealed in comment 11 by E. These group members have not *discussed* their purpose or goal. Comment 11 really asks whether there should be a discussion; the reason for the discussion is not clear. Why is the group meeting? Why are they taking up the question? Are they to give advice or not? If comment 11 has a point, then the discussion has not. But this would not be the case had the group begun by considering whether they had a discussable problem.

Rarely are any procedural plans made initially in these impromptu discussions. Only occasionally does a group member suggest an agenda which could be followed, or suggest that the group might pick a chairman to guide the discussion. As a result, these experimental discussions usually drift aimlessly, touching

STUDY PROBE 11
Analyzing Discussion Participation—Personal Interaction

Observe a small group discussion and tally each comment made by each participant. Using a chart like the one below, indicate to whom each comment was made. Distinguish between comments made to other individuals and those addressed to the group as a whole.

CHARTING DISCUSSANTS' INTERACTION

Person Making Comment	Person to Whom Comment Is Directed						Total Comments
	A	B	C	D	E	Group	
A	—						
B		—					
C			—				
D				—			
E					—		

Who made the most comments? Who made the fewest comments? Who most often addressed the group as a whole? Can you identify cliques by finding persons who speak most often to one another? In your opinion who was the task leader, and who was the social-emotional leader? Compare their profiles on the chart. What other pertinent information can be gleaned from this kind of an analysis? (Continued on facing page) on many points but settling few. There are periodic comments, such as 2 and 9 by B, which raise issues basic to the central question. But they are never systematically considered by all group members at one time, and they are not resolved. Seldom does one discussant build on or react to the comments of another.

In sum, these class-exercise discussions usually lack just about every attitudinal quality we have specified for accomplishing task functions. Rarely is a clear procedural pattern agreed upon and followed. There is no organized and complete consideration of standards for judgment. In the "Dick and Jane" Sample Case cited on pages 282–284, there are many points that could be important in weighing a final decision. What about the ages of the couple? Parental support? Continuing their education? Chances of the unexpected, such as the girl's becoming pregnant or the boy's being drafted? Some of these points are mentioned in hit-or-miss fashion during the quoted discussion, but none is examined for its significance or its bearing on a final decision.

The many possible alternative courses of action are seldom mentioned. The question is usually treated as if it were: "To marry in June—yes or no?" But several other possibilities could readily be taken into account: they could be married later this summer, or next summer, or the next—when both have their college degrees. The consequences and likely results from following a specific solution are seldom pursued. For any decision affecting our lives, we should want all reasonable solutions to be considered, but the many different possi-

STUDY PROBE 11 (continued)
Analyzing Discussion Participation—Nature of Comments

Observe a small task group, and analyze their discussion-participation according to the types of comments which are made by the members. Using a chart like the one below, tally and categorize each comment made by each participant.

CHARTING TYPES OF DISCUSSANTS' COMMENTS

Type of comment / Person	Initiating new ideas	Clarifying ideas	Substantiating ideas	Developing ideas	Summarizing ideas	Agreeing	Disagreeing	Asking questions	Making procedural comments
A									
B									
C									
D									
E									

Who would you judge to be the task leader and the social-emotional leader of the group? Compare their profiles. What other conclusions can you draw from an analysis of this kind? (For extra Charts, see Appendix B, pages 373 and 375.)

bilities are infrequently listed and weighed against carefully derived standards for judging. There is little of the problem-solving sequence, and there are few of the suggested task-function attitudes apparent in these discussions. Fortunately, once the task functions of discussion have been examined in class and practiced during the semester, there is usually noticeable improvement.

Our example is a fair representation of what you and your colleagues are likely to do with a group task unless you turn your minds sharply toward *methods* of discussing a topic. Whenever several people sit down together, the invitation to wandering, desultory conversation is strong. Some degree of self-discipline in communication is needed even in one-to-one discourse, as we showed earlier; self- and group-discipline become more and more important as the numbers of communicative agents are increased. This is why we have urged that you learn and generally follow the stages of the Problem-Solving Sequence. Not only does the sequence present an efficient way of proceeding; if agreed upon and followed by a group, it helps keep digressive, chaotic talk to a minimum.

Planning for Social-Emotional Functions

While the discussion task provides the purpose and the goal for a problem-solving discussion group, task functions are not the only important acts in group process. There are also certain significant non-task functions which involve social-emotional behaviors and which are needed to produce maximally effective interaction within groups.

The Scope and Value of Non-Task Functions

Research studies have found that fewer than half of the comments in discussion are strictly essential to the task. Much of the time is (usefully, in most cases) taken up with exploratory comments, comments affirming agreement among participants, comments elaborating and clarifying ideas already before the group, humorous comments, and so on.[13]

Clearly, such social-emotional behaviors also play a major role in group discussion. It may well be that these functions contribute to or even are essential to the accomplishment of task functions. The author's research into the discussion process suggests that the movement toward the final solution is not a steady, uniform, linear development. Rather, the development of an idea seems to occur in phases: Participants carry an idea forward for a time; then there is a pause, followed by more forward movement, followed by another period of pausing. These recurring plateaus are occupied by social-emotional comments. They are intervals during which groups consolidate their gains, relax for a moment, and confirm mutual agreement and support. These are times, also, when speech communication serves purposes (as discussed in Chapter 4, pages 107–110) other than the basic communicative purpose.

Probably, many of the values deriving from group work are the results of social-emotional functions. Task efforts can provide the solution to problems, but social-emotional responses are probably responsible for the group spirit and

[13] Thomas M. Scheidel and Laura Crowell, "Idea Development in Small Discussion Groups," *Quarterly Journal of Speech,* L (1964): 140–145.

rapport, the solidarity, and the group loyalty to the solution that are often observed in small discussion groups. The increased likelihood for behavioral change might very well find its motivation in social-emotional activity.

Social-emotional functions—like task functions—should be the concern of every group member. As with task functions, better results can usually be attained if all group members are responsible for and contribute to these efforts. The "strength in numbers" comes from united action. If most group members work together on task and social-emotional leadership functions, the chances for productive group meetings are much improved.

For effective small group communication, as for all oral interaction, each individual will want to learn as much as possible about the other agents and about the communicative context. He should try to anticipate the communication problems that may develop during the meetings. Beyond the general aim of contributing to the establishment of a pleasant, relaxed, lively atmosphere for the occasion, every participant should also aim to cope with the inherent difficulties. Just as he plans beforehand for speech making and for discussion task functions, so should he plan in advance to meet social-emotional communication problems.

Communication Problems in Small Group Discussion

There are, of course, many communication problems which may arise during a small group meeting. We will treat some of the more frequently occurring problems here and suggest some approaches for handling them. Specifically, we shall consider (1) the *withdrawing participant,* (2) the *too-talkative participant,* (3) *participant defensiveness,* (4) *tendency to conformity,* and (5) *interpersonal conflict.*

The Reluctant Participant

A group needs all of its resources and cannot afford to let a member sit silently if he has something to offer. If one or two members of the group are saying very little, what should a chairman or the other participants do? Often, the advice given is that the chairman or other discussant ask the withdrawing participant a direct question in order to get him involved. But there are cases where somewhat shy participants are driven even deeper into their shells by direct questions. The first step should probably be to *ask yourself why this person is withdrawing.* This suggestion underscores the need for knowledge of the other agents and for planning. Perhaps the person is failing to interact because he knows nothing about the topic and has not made much effort in preparation. In such case, pleasantly invite participation, but make no insistent efforts to get the person involved. His best contribution to the group (and if only ill-prepared persons could realize this) may be to sit quietly.

Suppose you, as a discussant, know that a quiet colleague does have a contribution to make, but is shy. If possible, you should talk to him before the meeting and make opportunities for other group members also to talk with him. This will make it easier for him to speak up during the meeting. Try to find out what aspects of the problem interest him most, or on which topics he has the most information. Then during the meeting you may try to involve him primarily in the discussion of those topics. If you are chairman and can make the seating arrangements, be sure he is not allowed to place himself on the periphery of the group. If the shy or withdrawing member is allowed to sit where he likes, he is likely to seek out that position. By placing him in a seat near the center of the group, or elsewhere so you can see him easily and direct talk toward him, you will ensure that he will not be excluded from the group for "geographical" reasons alone. Moreover, once discussion is under way—especially on those topics you know to be of most interest to him—you may ask the timid or withdrawn member an *indirect* rather than a direct question. Say, for instance, "Does anyone have information about . . . ?" and look at him. This puts some pressure upon him, but not as much as if you were to ask, "Do you know anything about this, George?"

STUDY PROBE 12
Improving Participation in Small Group Discussion

Identify a shy or retiring member of some group to which you presently belong. Attempt to talk with this person outside of the group meeting and determine, if you can, the reason for his lack of participation. Try to establish sufficient rapport with this person so that at the next meeting you might bring him more into the mainstream of the group's discussion. Describe and evaluate your efforts in this regard.

Repeatedly, we have stressed the importance of getting all participants in a group discussion involved early in the meeting. As a matter of principle, we should know *why* a certain person may be withdrawing from the group discussion and meet the problem on its own terms. Whether you are chairman or a participant, if a potentially valuable group member is not contributing to the discussion, the situation deserves countering efforts on your part.

The Too-Talkative Participant

Another difficulty (and, on the surface, opposite from the former) is the member who wants to talk *too* much and too frequently. Not all participants normally speak for an equal amount of time. Some naturally talk more than others. When we discuss here the "too-talkative" participant, we mean that person whose talk exceeds the normally expected range, and thereby calls undue or excessive attention to himself and prevents the normal participation of others.

Again, the admonition is: ask why this person is talking so much. If you have met him prior to the discussion meeting, you may have some insight into his personality. Perhaps he has an especially strong background on this topic and has made extraordinary efforts in his preparation. If so, you may decide that his talking so much is really helpful for the group efforts, and you may elect to take no countermeasures.

Unfortunately, there are other reasons why people talk too much. Some are verbose and avoid one word where two will do. For this person you might occasionally interrupt with "Your position, then, is . . ." and proceed to provide a concise summary. Be ready to draw in other members, too. If the talkative participant agrees with your summary, you can move on to another person, having seemingly "closed" the long talker's point. Some people talk simply to hear themselves. You may need to interrupt these people occasionally. Or you may redirect attention by comments such as "We haven't heard from X about this," or "I wonder if anyone else has a comment on this point?" Again, there is the device of asking a general question and *looking* at some other person for an answer. If you know the too-talkative person well enough, and have established good rapport with him, you might even be able to be more pointed in turning off his flow of words. The values of knowing your fellow discussants can be considerable. If you are responsible for the seating arrangements, you may place the too-talkative discussant *away* from the center of the group, nearer the periphery. If you are chairman, place him next to you so your glances will not encourage him unintentionally. Obviously, it would be tactless and probably pointless to try to silence anyone, but reasonable attempts to limit the comments of some can contribute to group achievement.

Participant Defensiveness

Few normal people enjoy criticism and rejection, and for this reason the actions of group members sometimes betray caution and conservatism due to fear of taking a public stand and thus subjecting themselves to possible rejection. If a discussant feels that his ideas are rejected by a group, he may react (1) by withdrawing from the discussion and offering fewer ideas, or (2) by becoming openly antagonistic and negative. One of the best ways of countering this tendency is to try to keep personalities out of the discussion as much as possible. Ideas should be separated from persons. Once an idea is presented for consideration, it is better to label it the group's idea than to identify it by its sponsor's name. Then if the idea is later rejected, it will not be so necessary for any one member to feel personally rejected.

Another procedure for limiting defensiveness is the process we have called "brainstorming." Here the group tries to present as many different ideas on a topic as possible. Criticism is ruled out when the ideas are presented. The more ideas presented and the wider their range, the better. All group activity could profit from a little of the spirit of brainstorming. All participants should try to make it easy for the others to offer suggestions without fears of immediate and undue criticism or ridicule. Even when "brainstorming" ends and the group returns to evaluating, any limits on ideas presented should derive from considerations of the task and not from social-emotional concerns.

Conformative Tendency

Another communication problem in discussion work is the *tendency to conformity*. A classic study by Asch found that about one third of his subjects would conform in judgment of the lengths of lines even when their own perceptions differed from the stated majority opinion.[14] Similar conformity is sometimes observed in discussion groups.

People become tired, or impatient, or less concerned, and so are "willing to go along" uncritically even with doubtful views that are advanced in groups. Indifference of this sort should be guarded against. Sometimes, when the moment arrives for a transition from one agenda topic to another, the chairman may summarize by saying, "Well, we seem to have agreed that . . ." and the participants all indicate their concurrence. If you have listened to the discussion and know that the chairman's statement is not what really happened, or that it could

[14] Solomon E. Asch, "Effects of Group Pressure Upon the Modification and Distortion of Judgments," *Groups, Leadership, and Men,* ed. H. Guetzkow (Pittsburgh: Carnegie Press Publishers, 1951), pp. 177–190.

hardly be acceptable to all in view of the discussion, you should ask *why* there is no challenge to the summary. If you suspect that some members of the group are going along out of frustration or desperation, you may want to seek the reasons for those feelings. Genuine settlement of issues can only be accomplished by open discussion. Bypassing issues only delays the trouble. Of course, if the main reason for undue conformity by participants is fatigue, perhaps the time has come to adjourn the meeting.

Conformity has its value and, to some degree, is essential to productive group work. In any game one must be willing to conform to the rules. In group discussion, as we have emphasized, the individual must conform to the norms and goals and procedures decided upon by the group. He must also conform to certain expectations about group conduct. But if members begin pointlessly conforming and become willing to go along with anything, then the communication act has broken down, and this problem must be confronted. The difficulty itself should be raised and discussed.

Interpersonal Conflict

A certain amount of clash and conflict between ideas and points of view is almost inevitable in the group communication process. Sometimes these conflicts represent differences of opinion which must be settled before a group can move on. At other times they may reveal genuine personality conflicts or significant differences in the basic value systems of the participants.

When such conflict arises, all group members should be aware of it and should promptly attempt to assess its cause. As we have seen, it is always wise to keep the interplay of ideas as objective as possible. This can be done if you use questions to probe the conflict of views. You and your colleagues need to understand fully each other's positions. "Are you saying that . . . ?" "Is it your view that . . . ?" "What about the problem that . . . ?" Look first to see where the conflict rests. Is it merely a semantic difference—similar positions being stated in different words? Or is there a difference in sources or materials that leads to the conflicting views? If so, the sources of materials can be compared. In all cases it is wise to keep ideas and personalities separated. Ideas, language, sources, and even values can be dissected without danger to group productiveness, but personalities cannot.

Sometimes a group has a genuine, full-blown personality conflict in its midst. In these cases, about all that can be done is to remain calm, and try—to the extent that may be possible—to keep the antagonists from interacting too directly and too emotionally with one another. If you are the chairman, seat them in such a way that it is difficult for them to challenge each other. Keep emphasizing the group task and goal so that it remains uppermost in the minds of everyone. Let the ideas of the pair in conflict interact through you rather than directly. This is equivalent to stepping between two people who are fighting, but with much less danger of being hurt yourself.

STUDY PROBE 13
Understanding Small Group Interaction Through Role Playing

Conduct the following role-playing experiment in class. Have the instructor choose some issues for discussion by four- or five-member groups. School grading policies or dormitory problems are two possible topics. One member of the group should act as chairman. One or two other members of the group should play a special "problem role" (for example, a domineering advocate, a joker, a reluctant participant, a person who wants to rush to a solution); but the chairman and the other participants in the experiment should not be aware of these "special roles." As the discussion proceeds, observe how the chairman and other members of the group react to and resolve the problems that arise. Conduct this experiment several times, with different issues, different groups, and different "special roles." How skillful were the group members in handling the "problem participants"? How successful were they in their consideration of the issue?

With any communication problem, your practice should be to search for what lies behind it, and to do whatever you can to alleviate the difficulty without hindering the forward progress of your group. Knowing the members of the group beforehand and anticipating likely communication problems will enable you to avoid surprises and to plan ahead for these difficulties.

In this chapter we have attempted briefly to point out some of the special advantages and procedural problems of speech interaction in a small group setting. We have emphasized the values of encouraging leadership behavior from all participants. We have tried to offer a number of specific suggestions to facilitate effective group interaction on task and social-emotional functions.

Suggested Readings

Marvin E. Shaw, *Group Dynamics: The Psychology of Small Group Behavior* (New York: McGraw-Hill Book Company, 1971). This current textbook summarizes the psychological sources in which small group research is available. The treatment covers the nature and origin of groups. Findings relevant to the physical environment, the personal environment, the social environment, and the task environment of groups are presented.

Robert F. Bales, *Personality and Interpersonal Behavior* (New York: Holt, Rinehart & Winston, Inc., 1970). This important work brings together the research of twenty years by Professor Bales and his colleagues. It presents his latest revision of Interaction Process Analysis, a procedure for the study of small group interaction comments. It also presents detailed studies of types of group participants—their personality characteristics, their contributions and behaviors in groups, their personal values.

Irving D. Yalom, *The Theory and Practice of Group Psychotherapy* (New York: Basic Books, Inc., Publishers, 1970). This source provides another approach to small groups. While our interest has not been on the goal of therapy in group interaction, Yalom's work is interesting reading, and it provides texture to our special interests by overlapping in some places and contrasting in others.

Every speech
is something like a symphony
with higher and lower moments,
recurring
but differently developed themes,
calculated simultaneously
to give and to require
audience involvement.

Chapter 10

Achieving Interaction with Many: Speech Making

In this final chapter of our textbook the emphasis is upon the special consider-ations necessary when one agent uses sustained discourse to address others. Oc-casions for such communication are numerous. An individual may be asked to speak to a PTA meeting or to a civic organization or at a political rally. While a public meeting is in progress, he may decide to comment on a current item of business; or he may be called upon to voice his opinion. Every such occasion requires one agent to achieve interaction with many others.

STUDY PROBE 1

Comparing Images of Speech Making and of Listening

a. Interview an older friend or a teacher; or, if time permits, write a letter to your parents or grandparents to learn what they remember about listening to speeches as children. What speakers, topics, and contexts do they remember? What behaviors were expected of them as listeners? Do their recollections con-tain both pleasant and unpleasant elements?

b. Ask a few elementary school teachers in your community to find out what their pupils think a speech is and what they think they are supposed to do during a speech. Report your findings to your class. How do the elementary stu-dents' perceptions compare with your own, and with those you gathered in Item (a) above?

All of the general principles for effective communicative interaction that we have discussed in previous chapters are also applicable in one-to-many speech contexts. It is as necessary in this context as in the others for the agent to under-stand the contextual elements and to try to achieve interaction with the other agents. The basic principles of adaptation to feedback operate here as they do in the one-to-one and one-to-few settings. The unique feature of the one-to-many context lies in the special preparation usually undertaken for it. Accordingly, what we shall consider in this chapter are procedures for (1) *speech planning* and (2) *speech practice* which you will need to follow when preparing for the presentation of consecutive, extended discourse in any of its traditional forms, before large or small audiences, and for any speech purpose.

The Roman rhetorician Quintilian, warning against the use of absolute and rigid rules for speech making, asserted:

> *The art of speaking can only be attained by hard work and assiduity of study, by a variety of exercises and repeated trial, the highest prudence and unfailing quickness of judgement. But rules are helpful all the same so long as they indicate the direct road and do not restrict us absolutely to the ruts made by others.*[1]

The guidelines of this chapter should be seen, as Quintilian proposed, as sug-gestions rather than rigid directives. As we have emphasized before, you should

[1] Quintilian, *Institutio Oratoria*, trans. H. E. Butler, 4 vols. (Cambridge, Mass.: Har-vard University Press, 1963 printing of Loeb Classical Library), v. I, p. 297.

be seeking always those variations and special procedures that work best and most easily for you.

As an aid to you in reading this chapter, a model speech is included in Appendix A. It is "The Dimensions of a Complete Life," given by Martin Luther King, Jr. (1929–1968), on November 13, 1960, at Ithaca, New York, in a non-denominational service in Sage Chapel on the Cornell University campus. In the pages to follow we shall draw on this speech for illustrations of certain concepts and procedures we shall discuss. In choosing this speech for our purposes, we were influenced by three considerations. Our aim was to avoid "showcase" speeches and use a *real speech* with vitality—one which reflected qualities of immediate communicative interaction. We sought also a speech that was primarily the *work of a single man and mind*—one that was not the product of a ghost-writing committee or advertising agency. And finally, the content and manner of the speech had to be *worthy of consideration* for its own sake and illustrative of skilled communication with many. Dr. King's speech meets these specifications.

Speech Planning

Suggestions made in Chapter 3 concerning self-assessment and the collection of speech materials are continuously pertinent in the first steps in the preparation for a speech occasion. You should always gather more material than you will be able to use in the speech. If you collect just the minimum materials necessary to carry you through your communication, you will have narrowed the range of your choices; you cannot choose the *best* example, the *most telling* statistic, the *most persuasive* testimony, because you have not gathered any alternative materials. This is the limitation of the person who merely reads one magazine article for a speech. He can only imitate—parrot—the viewpoint of someone else; he himself is not selecting the materials, determining their organization, couching his own ideas in his own language, or aiming for the effect *he* wants and which *his* context invites. He is a mere marionette, bereft of originality and capable of revealing very little of himself.

In selecting material for a speech, you should make all the choices yourself. Speech planning can be a very creative task. Classical rhetoricians recognized this fact in labeling the preparation process *inventio*—invention. We will be highlighting later a number of the creative tasks of the speaker.

The second reason for gathering more material than you will actually use in a given speech is the frequent need to make rapid adjustments to audience feedback. Suppose at one point the audience appears puzzled. What do you do? If your speech is fully determined beforehand and you have no other information, you can only react to this feedback by doing nothing (which is bad), or by merely repeating what you have already said (which is only a little better). But if you have made an ample selection of materials and if you have more background resources than you could include in the speech as you prepared it, you will be able to respond to the puzzled expressions of your audience by citing another example or additional data which you hadn't planned to use originally, but which may now turn out to be useful in meeting the needs of your listeners.

| Desire to interrupt | Defensiveness or frustration | Concern over a decision | Doubt |

BODY LANGUAGE—HOW DO YOU READ IT?

Those conversant with the study of body language maintain that human interaction is greatly facilitated through recognition of and sensitivity to messages conveyed, however covertly or unintentionally, via that medium. To be at all reliable, interpretation of such nonverbal feedback presupposes an understanding of the persons involved and of the communication context; also, more reliance can be placed on a "cluster" of signs—or an overall body positioning or movement—than on an isolated sign. These principles are stated in Gerard I. Nierenberg and Henry H. Calero, *How to Read a Person Like a Book* (New York: Hawthorn Books, Inc., 1971), copyright © 1971 by Gerard I. Nierenberg and Henry H. Calero—the source from which these illustrations have also been adapted. Included here are four separate signs and their possible meanings (top row), as well as three significant clusters (lower row).

| Rejection | Cooperation | Critical evaluation |

Determining the Specific Purpose

Once a sizeable part of the necessary information is assembled, you must settle on the specific purpose for your speech. What is it, in a sentence or two, that you want to accomplish with your communication? Determining the specific purpose is one of the creative tasks facing any effective speaker. Since it is the cornerstone of a speech, it will be useful to you to write your purpose at the heading of a page on which you will next begin to outline your speech. The statement can then stand as a note to you, reminding you of the scope and limits of your intentions. At any moment, it will serve as a ready reference. You can refer back to the specific purpose and ask whether the material you are now developing is directly related and necessary to it.

A statement of specific purpose should indicate what you will discuss and with what intended effect. Examples are:

> It will be the specific purpose of this speech to analyze three of Picasso's paintings in order to create greater appreciation for his work.

> It will be the specific purpose of this speech to summarize the major scientific theories advanced to explain the origin of the moon in order to provide better understanding of the conflicting viewpoints.

STUDY PROBE 2

Identifying Specific Communicative Purposes

Select a number of editorials from current daily newspapers. Determine the specific purpose of each editorial. Give the editorial to a friend to check your judgment. Is the specific purpose always stated explicitly? Is it repeated within the editorial? If neither, can you see "behind" the editorial to discover the purpose the writer actually had in mind? If so, how do you think his specific purpose might be stated in words?

A statement of the specific purpose, as such, may or may not appear in the actual speech. Whether it does or not depends upon your plans for the development of the outline. Examine the public address by Martin Luther King, Jr., in Appendix A (pages 345–352), and write out the specific statement which you think most accurately describes the speaker's intentions. Then look through the speech to see how he revealed his purpose. Is the specific purpose ever stated completely and explicitly? Is it stated only once, or is it repeated in different wordings?

Speech Organization: General Concerns

Once you have assembled ample materials and have determined your specific purpose, you are ready to begin organizing your speech: selecting, arranging, and developing those materials which will be presented in it. Plato wrote that a speech should have a beginning, middle, and end. We defer to that position and will consider the *introduction,* the *body,* and the *conclusion* as basic to speech organization. These three parts of a speech should be considered first as you begin to plan your outline.

There are differing views regarding satisfactory outline forms. Some people prefer complete-sentence outlines in which every thought is phrased as a complete syntactical statement. Others use key-word or phrase outlines in which thoughts are listed in elliptical or abbreviated form. The "best" method is a matter for each speaker to settle for himself, but it is important that you not opt immediately for what seems the easiest system. Try several approaches and then settle on the one which helps you most.

STUDY PROBE 3

Practice in Outlining a Speech

Outline the first point of the model speech in Appendix A (paragraphs 5–8) using (1) a complete-sentence outline and (2) a key-word or phrase outline. Compare your outlines with others. Which do you find most helpful? In what ways? Is your key-word outline too sketchy with reference to any of the subpoints?

The Body of a Speech: Determining and Arranging Main Heads

Suppose that you have a sheet of paper headed by a statement of specific purpose and have some notion of how to write outlines. What next? At this point you should move directly into planning the body of your speech: that portion of the talk which develops, supports, and aims to accomplish your specific purpose. You can work out the introduction later; only then will you know what you are introducing. The body is, of course, the longest portion of the speech and contains the main points of the presentation in a given order and suggests the materials for their development.

STUDY PROBE 4

Determining the Limits of the Introduction, Body, and Conclusion

The divisions between introduction, body, and conclusion are never absolute. Examine the speech of Martin Luther King, Jr. In your opinion, which paragraphs contain the body of this speech? You will find one possible answer on the following page.* Compare it with yours. What case can be made for each of these judgments if they are not identical?

Look for similar division-points in lectures and speeches you hear.

As a speaker you must determine first what main points you wish to develop. To determine the main points, you must ask yourself: "What is needed to accomplish my specific purpose?" The essential items should be limited in number. Some students attempt to cover ten coordinate main points in a six-minute presentation. This is too many thoughts to develop adequately in a brief speech, and too many for an audience to remember. Two to six coordinate main headings are probably enough for any outline.

When you are satisfied that you have determined what your main points or headings are to be, set them down on the sheet of paper headed by the statement of your specific purpose. Reexamine this purpose in terms of the list of your main points, asking yourself: "If these main points were to be clearly established, would my specific purpose be accomplished? Have I omitted any necessary heading from this list—are there any gaps? Have I listed any point that is *not* essential to accomplishing the specific purpose?" (Remember, of course, that it is possible at this time for you to change the specific purpose itself.)

STUDY PROBE 5
Developing Main Headings for a Speech Outline

Develop some appropriate main headings for these statements of specific purpose:

a. It will be the purpose of this speech to describe some of the views I saw from a plane window on my trip from New York to Los Angeles, in order to provide a greater appreciation of U.S. geography.

b. It will be the purpose of this speech to convince the listeners of the need for reforming our federal and state prisons in order to change the listeners' existing apathetic attitudes.

Once the main points have been listed and tested, you should determine how they will be worded. In wording main points, it is often helpful to create parallel phrasings, in order to emphasize for listeners the coordination and equal weighting of the points. For example, in a speech on types of taxation you might create the headings:

Income tax—the tax on what we earn.
Sales tax—the tax on what we buy.
Property tax—the tax on what we own.
And so on.

In Dr. King's speech you will find this parallelism:

The length of life.
The breadth of life.
The height of life.

Your next creative task is to determine a *pattern* or sequence in which to arrange the main points or headings. Frequently used are:

The chronological pattern.

The spatial pattern.

The causal pattern.

The topical pattern.

* The author's answer to the question in Study Probe 4 would be paragraphs 5–31.

This list, of course, is not exhaustive. There are other less familiar but equally effective patterns. Moreover, you can always combine patterns or elements of patterns. The four patterns listed above are used frequently and should be considered as *possibilities* at this stage in your planning. Their characteristics are discussed below.

Chronological Pattern

The pattern of following a *time* sequence in listing main heads is the chronological pattern. In describing processes which occur over time (the building of a house, a body-conditioning program, the diffusion of information throughout an organization or country, revolutions in society), one can look at stages of the process in consecutive sequence, outlining main heads according to what occurs first in time, what next, and so on.

Spatial Pattern

Occasionally the significant relationship among main headings for a speech lies in their differing geographical or spatial locations. One may then talk about spaces or places as headings. For example, in discussing election results, you might find it helpful to use headings such as Northeast, South, Midwest, Far West. In discussing the assembling of some product, you might make the process clear by using a spatial pattern, following the product through the plant along the assembly line.

Causal Pattern

Main headings sometimes are interrelated as causes and effects of one another, a subject we explored in some depth in Chapters 5 and 6. In discussing water pollution, we might find it possible to discuss causes first and then effects. Or we could discuss effects first and then develop the causes. This arrangement is closely related to what we have described as a "problem-solution" pattern in which a speaker first surveys the problem and then proposes a solution to it.

Topical Pattern

Another suggested arrangement for organizing main headings is the topical pattern. When a speaker employs this pattern, he first looks for the natural divisions of his subject. Then he attempts to arrange the main topics in such a way as to stimulate the natural and usual patterns of thought of his audience. For example, a speaker discussing the governmental power structure of the United States would most likely use the natural divisions of executive, legislative, and judicial branches as his main headings.

STUDY PROBE 6
Experimenting with Patterns for Speech Organization

a. Try to think of a few speech topics which could be developed usefully according to several of the patterns discussed. For example, the "Building of a Moon Rocket" might be developed with a chronological, or a spatial (no pun intended), or a topical outline.

b. See if you can conceive of sets of circumstances (particular agents and/or contexts) for which each of the patterns would be most appropriate and desirable. For the topic "Building of a Moon Rocket," can you think of a set of circumstances in which a chronological outline would be most appropriate? Can you devise another set in which a topical outline would be better? Illustrate.

Most important in giving a pattern to main headings is that you choose some arrangement which fits your subject and which will contribute to accomplishing your specific purpose. This, at the same time, will facilitate your listeners' understanding. The patterns mentioned above can be helpful because they are all usual ways of thinking about things and so are keyed to improve audience understanding. Western man thinks often in terms of temporal, spatial, causal, and topical relationships. At this moment you are probably wearing a watch, and there is probably a larger clock in the room. Within the last hour you have probably looked at one of them to check the time. Clocks direct much of our activity. We are quite the servants of time. Consider how often you think in spatial terms —going uptown, turning left, traveling north. In addition, much of our thought is dominated by causes and effects. Given any occurrence, we look for the cause. If shown something with power, we ask what it does (the effects of it). These habits and procedures of thought are basic to us. If we were computers, we would say these habits of thought are "wired in." This is the reason a speaker assists his listeners when he structures his talk in one of these ways.

When a speaker chooses one of these forms, he is adapting material to a usual—and useful—pattern of human thinking, putting his materials in an arrangement that is meaningful for his listeners and that will make the reception and recall of those materials easier for them. As he moves chronologically from one point to another, the listeners "experience" a passage of time. When he speaks of the East, his listeners become prepared for the South and the West. As he concludes a discussion of the problem, his listeners anticipate some comment about a solution. Clearly, if one of these common patterns fits a speaker's topic and specific purpose, he should use it.

In the model speech in the Appendix (pages 345–352), Dr. King discusses three aspects of life: *length, breadth,* and *height.* These are three dimensions so much a part of our common experience that we can anticipate "breadth" and "height" as soon as "length" is mentioned, and we cannot fail to feel the "completeness" of a treatment that covers all three. These, then, are a set of familiar spatial headings.

Consider their arrangement. Moving from length to breadth to height, Dr. King associates these dimensions with man's concern for himself, for others, and for God. *Do not* misjudge this order by calling it simply climactic; the movement of the speech is from within outward, from the inner self outward. This is a familiar direction of thought in religion. Dr. King, a religious man, uses this religious conception, along with the basic spatial pattern, in developing his speech. Thus, the very organization of his materials contributes to his advocacy of the completeness of the continually expanding religious view.

As a speaker you, too, must search for an arrangement of main headings that will strike an understanding chord in the minds of your listeners. The pattern you choose should facilitate your listeners' receptions and ease of recall of the main points.

The Body of a Speech: Selecting Developmental Materials

When you have determined your specific purpose, and properly phrased and patterned the main points of the body of your speech, you will be ready to move on to the next step: filling out the main headings with *developmental materials*. This is another significant creative task for a speaker. Main headings must be explicated, completed, developed, emphasized, and made clear, understandable, and interesting. There are numerous types of materials useful in this development, namely:

Definitions

Examples

Comparisons and Contrasts

Narratives

Testimony

Quantitative Data

Some materials, it is true, may have more than one of the attributes suggested by these terms; but, for purposes of examining the kinds of developmental resources more closely, we will treat them singly.

Definitions

Occasionally a speaker will introduce or use a term or concept which requires definition. The term or concept may be new to the audience, or the speaker may wish to provide the audience with a fuller or different understanding of it. Definition is helpful whenever there is likely to be uncertainty about the nature of a concept—what is included in it and what is excluded from it.

When defining speech communication in Chapter 1 (pages 6–13), we described three means of definition: (1) definition by *example,* in which specific instances of the object are presented along with the defining label; (2) definition by *genus* and *difference,* in which the object defined is related to the classes and subclasses to which it belongs; and (3) definition by *stipulation,* in which the definer specifies what the term means to him and how he will use it.

STUDY PROBE 7

Exploring Definitions for Communicative Occasions

Define each of these terms first by *stipulation,* then by *genus* and *difference,* and finally by *example:*

racism	The Establishment
hippie	responsibility
love	life

For what types of communicative occasions might these different forms of definition be most appropriate?

You should search through your general topic and the main heads of your outline to determine whether there are terms which will require definition. If only a quick reference seems needed, you may elect definition by example; if the matter is more complicated, you may attempt definition by genus and difference; if you hope to use a term in a somewhat unusual manner, you can probably best employ a definition by stipulation. As you incorporate later developmental materials, you should be on the lookout for additional terms and concepts that might need to be defined.

Examples

Examples are probably the most widely used developmental materials. These are the specific, elaborated instances—the actual or hypothetical cases presented and described verbally to show the character of all the related cases in a category. An instance of what is being talked about is singled out for consideration. From the instance, the speaker and listener may generalize to all related cases.

An example may be mentioned only briefly or may be developed at some length. In either case the purpose for using an example is the same: to add concreteness, exactness, definiteness, and often realism and liveliness to audience understanding. Hence, Dr. King does not simply assert that poverty exists in the world; he takes the matter out of the abstract by citing examples of what he saw in India. This way he provides both "proof" and visual imagery.

In planning a speech you, too, should consider all the examples that are available to you, and then *choose* those that will best fit your purpose, audience, and context.

Comparisons and Contrasts

A speaker will often attempt to reveal the nature of a topic by showing how it compares and contrasts with other topics that are better known to his audience, or to which they have more ready access. One might use a model engine, for example, to illustrate a function because the model is easier to see and manipulate than is the actual object. Or one might compare a rare and unfamiliar bird to a familiar one.

Comparisons include *literal analogies,* in which two objects from the same class and level are compared; and *figurative analogies,* in which objects from different classes are related. Malcolm X once argued that in those African countries that had been granted independence without a fight, good will toward the former colonizer prevailed; in countries where independence had to be won by battle, the same good will was not apparent. He argued from these known and fairly clear cases to the situation in the United States.[2] Although the situations referred to were certainly not alike in all details, there were enough similarities so Malcolm could make a fairly effective literal analogy. He was pointing to similar attributes in each situation.

Leonard Bernstein used a figurative analogy to describe "syncopation":

A good way to understand syncopation might be to think of a heartbeat that goes along steadily and, at a moment of shock, misses a beat. It is that much of a physical reaction.[3]

[2] For a good sampling of the speeches of Malcolm X, see *Malcolm X Speaks,* ed. Bruce Breitman (New York: Grove Press, Inc., 1965).

[3] The text of Leonard Bernstein's television lecture, "The World of Jazz," is available in Leonard Bernstein, *The Joy of Music* (New York: Simon and Schuster, Inc., 1959). The text is also available in Carroll C. Arnold, Douglas Ehninger, and John C. Gerber, *The Speaker's Resource Book* (Glenview, Ill.: Scott, Foresman and Company, 1966), pp. 67–76.

Contrast is simply the other side of comparison. The speaker sets two objects or concepts side by side and singles out for attention a *difference* or differences. In using comparisons and contrasts, you should be certain that the materials you chose make clear and meaningful points pertaining to whatever subject is being discussed. The relationship must not be obscure or strained.

Narratives

A speaker may use a story or narrative to develop a point. Narratives and anecdotes are used most often to illustrate points in interesting and indirect ways—to show ideas from a fresh vantage, to illuminate them, or to make them easier to see.

The indirect quality of narratives can be most useful. They often *imply* as well as tell. Throughout history men have used stories as vehicles with which to voice their admonitions for the practical reason that people may be more willing to accept advice through the indirectness of a story. Similarly, in situations where authoritarian governments will tolerate no open criticism of the system, it is sometimes possible for a speaker or a writer to make a criticism indirectly or obliquely—and get it across—in the guise of a narrative.

Narratives may take the form of *anecdotes*. An anecdote is a brief story, humorous or serious, which usually deals with true-to-life characters. It is often useful in illustrating a point. Another form of narrative is the *fable,* a fictitious story enforcing some point and often using animals as characters. We all know the moral about the fox and the "sour grapes" from Aesop's fables. The *parable* is still another form of narrative in which a fictitious, illustrative story is presented and from which a moral is drawn. Much of Jesus's teaching was by parable.

Dr. King, in his speech, drew upon the parable of the Good Samaritan to develop much of his argument about the breadth of life. Reread those portions of King's speech in which he used this ancient parable (paragraphs 10–14, pages 348–349) and see again how he associated the story with modern experiences and interpretations to make his point a little more directly and fully.

The beginning speech student tends to use comparatively few narratives but many examples and literal comparisons. As you look over the main divisions of your speech plans and search for the best means of developing these main points, you should consider the possible usefulness of anecdotes or longer narratives. If you have opportunity to use a narrative, it must be filled with sufficient detail and suspense to build and maintain some degree of interest. Such factors as action and pictorialization grip attention especially well. And while a narrative is usually only indirectly related to a topic within a speech, the *point* of the story must bear clearly and directly upon it, and be appropriate for the listeners and the speech context.

Testimony

Much of what we know and believe has come to us from the testimony of others. There are such great limits to what we can learn through direct, personal experience that we come to accept much of the experience of others. As we pointed out in Chapter 5, the voices of our parents, friends, and teachers join with what we read and hear from other respected sources to provide much of the data upon which our beliefs, evaluations, and motives are founded.

A speaker will frequently call upon some personality other than himself or his listeners for testimony. He may seek and cite an expert opinion so that his statements will seem more authoritative than they would seem if he alone had said them. Or he may use the statement of someone else simply because it happens to be especially well expressed.

Martin Luther King, Jr., referred to a number of religious scholars and literary figures in his speech. While the character of the men cited undoubtedly added to the weight of his case, Dr. King seemed also to use some of these sources for the aptness of their phrasings. This is surely true of his references to Donne and Keats.

In use, all testimony has this double edge. A speaker is able to present statements which have special authority, or perhaps more agreeable and memorable phrasings, while he is associating the *ethos* of the personalities cited with his position and thereby gaining the strength that lies in numbers.

As a student speaker you will probably have use for some testimony in almost every speech. So far, your knowledge and experience with many matters is limited, and your listeners know that you will therefore often have need to look for statements of authority figures which can be useful. The important point is that the authority be respected and judged to be authoritative by your listeners. But occasionally you will also want to present the views of experts who are not generally known. You should then introduce the material with a few words asserting or describing the expertness of the source. Dr. King did this by saying ". . . a brilliant Jewish rabbi, the late Joshua Liebman . . . ."

STUDY PROBE 8
Using Authorities for Testimony

a. Make a list of authorities whose testimony you would accept on these topics:

wages	marijuana
college education	dormitory regulations
air pollution	communes
life insurance	guitars

Compare your list of authorities with those of your classmates. Are any authorities on the lists acceptable on *more* than one topic? If so, what makes them so?

b. After consulting several standard biographical reference books in the library, write out a brief statement indicating the topics on which these individuals could provide expert testimony:

Abbie Hoffman	Ralph Nader
Eric Hoffer	Herb Alpert
Dean Rusk	Muhammed Ali
William Kunstler	Barry Goldwater

One problem with the use of expert testimony is the possible bias of the expert. A speaker who cites an authority should be aware of possible biases of that authority and adjust them to his listeners' biases if necessary. If significant to the case at hand, the biases of a cited authority should be discussed and discounted; otherwise, that source probably should not be used. Another way for a speaker to adjust bias is to use an authority figure whose testimony goes counter to his own best interests. That authority's view, presumably reluctantly arrived at by the speaker, is usually all the more acceptable to listeners.

Sometimes a speaker will find it necessary to quote an anonymous source, as when referring to a wire-service clipping or an editorial in a newspaper or an unsigned article in a magazine. If you find yourself in such a circumstance, you should provide an exact citation: source, issue, date, page number, etc. To a challenging audience, nothing is less persuasive than a feeble "Well, *they* say . . . ."

Quantitative Data

Numerical data, numbers and figures, seem to have a magic about them. Statistics can be very illuminating and tremendously influential in a speech. Every speaker should consider the use of quantitative data, and every communicative agent must have some facility with this type of developmental material.

Quantitative materials are most useful for two purposes: (1) for precise description and illumination of data and (2) for comparison of objects. The chief virtue of this type of material is that it is specific, definite, and concrete. Forty-two percent, $77.20, 3.62 are exact quantitative descriptions.

Martin Luther King, Jr., could have stopped with his question: "How can one avoid being concerned when he sees with his own eyes millions of people sleeping on the sidewalks at night?" But notice how he developed the point further with the use of quantitative description:

> *In Calcutta alone, more than a million people sleep on the sidewalks at night. In Bombay more than six hundred thousand people sleep on the sidewalks every night. How can one avoid being concerned when he discovers that out of India's population of almost 400 million people, more than 325 million of these people make an annual income of less than $50 a year? Most of them have never seen a doctor or dentist.*

This development provided specificity and definiteness to his hypothetical question. It makes the problem easier for us to visualize and feel.

Paradoxically, there are times when a number may be more exact than is desirable. Attention may be directed too intently to the exactness of the number itself, as when it is used primarily to illustrate or corroborate another point. In these instances it may be better to round the numbers off so they will be easier to comprehend and remember. For these reasons King spoke of "more than a million," "almost 400 million," and "less than $50 a year." For his purposes these less exact figures gave an ample impression of the great and small quantities he wanted listeners to perceive.

Greater care must be exercised when numbers are used for comparison or when inferences are to be based on numerical data. In these circumstances some common-sense standards must be applied. You must ask: Exactly how are these data being used, and is such use appropriate and proper? Whence are the figures derived? Are they based on a large enough sample to be representative, and were they measured at the appropriate time? Was the comparison made at the appropriate time? Was the comparison made appropriate for what is claimed?

You must be careful, too, with averages. The "average" man, after all, doesn't really exist. Suppose you are discussing average income. What do you mean by average? Are you speaking about *mean* income, which is what is usually meant by "average": the sum of all the values tested in the sample divided by the number of values in the sample? Or are you speaking of *median* income, the midpoint (or "middle case"), which has half the values above it and the other half below it?

The difference is important because with income the mean—except in purely theoretical cases—is always greater than the median. The reason for this can be shown with just a few cases, as in Figures 1 and 2 below. Only if income were distributed in fairly regular, even steps—as indicated in Figure 1—could the mean and the median values be identical.

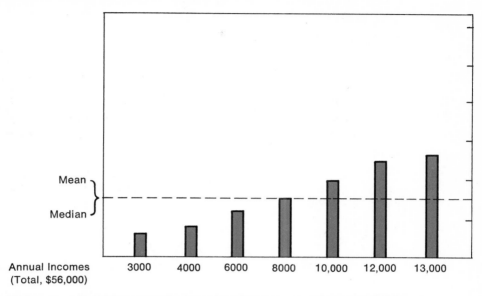

Annual Incomes (Total, $56,000)

Figure 1.   Hypothetical Case in Which Mean and Medium Incomes Coincide ($8000)

Actually, however, there is a great difference between the levels where most incomes cluster and the incomes at higher levels. The effect of these higher incomes is to pull the mean upward and away from the median, as illustrated in Figure 2. For this reason, when we are dealing with incomes the mean is always greater than the median.

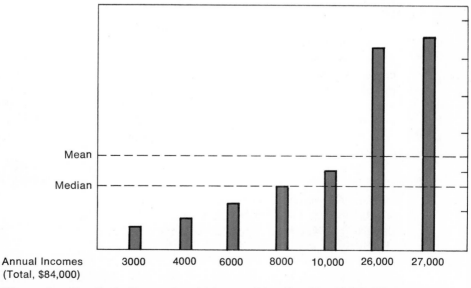

Annual Incomes (Total, $84,000)

Figure 2.   Realistic Example of Income Distribution, in Which Mean ($12,000) Is Greater Than the Median ($8000)

To take an extreme case, if we "average" the incomes of a millionaire and a man on welfare, the result would *seem* to indicate two very rich men. We must be careful, therefore, in citing or accepting averages. For a true picture, we should look at the range of values (the difference between the highest and the lowest ones) and at the way the values are distributed within the sample being considered.

STUDY PROBE 9

Using Quantitative Data in Communication

a. Ask a local bank for a copy of their most recent financial report. What descriptive and comparative statements can you make about the bank's success or failure based on the statistics indicated in the report?

b. Select two or three current magazines and study the ways in which statistics are used (or misused) in the advertisements. Report your findings to the class.

Quantitative comparisons can also be troublesome. Suppose that you are interested in comparing morbidity rates of several nations. You must carefully consider (1) the living conditions, (2) the cultural attitudes toward diseases and reporting them, (3) the quality of medical care in the countries, including the quality of diagnostic procedures, and (5) the thoroughness of health surveys taken.

Suppose one country had a higher morbidity rate than another country last year. You must look to the trends. Was the past year typical or exceptional? If one nation had a lower *increase* in morbidity than another, you must look to the base levels on which the increases were judged. The nation with the lower increase may have had a much higher initial ratio of illnesses per thousand persons.

Suppose, in another case, that as the amount of A increases, the amount of B also increases. One cannot infer from this correlation that there is a causal relation between A and B. It *may* be that A causes B. Or it *may* be that B causes A. There could also be an unknown factor or factors that contribute to the cause of both A and B. The relationship observed between the two could even be coincidental. As a speaker you must be cautious about the assertions you make with regard to causation, lest your listeners become confused or find your reasoning faulty. Your protection when analyzing and discussing causation was developed in Chapters 5 and 6.

As a speaker you should also be sure of the accuracy and the relevancy of your figures: They must be correct, and they must bear on the point being discussed. You must be sure that they are appropriate for the main heading to which they are to be applied, and the figures must be exactly what you claim them to be. Numbers appear as absolutes; and when they are wrong, they are absolutely wrong.

Definitions, examples, comparisons and *contrasts, narratives, testimony,* and *quantitative data*—these, then, are the developmental materials which become the texture of the body of the speech.

Using Developmental Materials in a Speech

Plan and present to your class a short speech in which you use at least one example of each of the six types of developmental material we have discussed in the section above.

The Body of a Speech: Checking Final Requirements

At this point in the planning of your speech, you should have the statement of your specific purpose; you should have the main points for the body of the speech properly phrased and arranged; and you should have selected the necessary materials for developing each of these main points or heads. You need now to reassess all that you have developed.

Reviewing and Rechecking the Outline for Purpose and Validity

At this juncture, you should reexamine and, if necessary, reshape your outline; also you should attempt to judge, considering your listeners and the speech context, whether what you have assembled will be likely to accomplish your specific purpose. You should, for example, analyze the reasoning and its validity against the various tests discussed in Chapters 6 and 7, especially causality, the syllogistic model, and the Toulmin pattern.

Generally, every idea planned for a speech should appear in the outline, even if only briefly noted. Again, we can use Dr. King's speech for illustrative purposes. One possible working outline of the important second point of his speech (pages 347–350, paragraphs 9–23) would be as follows:

  B. The *breadth* of life.
      1. Define as "outward concern for the welfare of others."
      2. Parable of Good Samaritan.
         a. Present parable.
         b. Consider possible reasons for actions of priest and Levite.
         c. Give personal experience on Jericho road.
      3. Apply parable to racial crisis in this nation.
         a. Privileged need to add breadth to their lives.
         b. Oppressed must be concerned about the breadth of their lives.
      4. Apply parable to international crises.
         a. Personal experiences in India.
         b. Situation in Africa and South America.
      5. Conclude with quotation by John Donne.

Applying Tests of Reasoning to the Outline

See how well you can apply the syllogistic model and the Toulmin pattern for analyzing reasoning to Dr. King's assertions in support of his third major division (paragraphs 24–31).

Having progressed this far in your speech preparation, what questions should you as a student speaker address to your own outline? You might ask first whether you have made an adequately varied selection of supporting materials. We have already pointed out that *stimulus change* is crucial to sensation. No listener cares to hear point after point developed in the same way. Then, too, some people are more attuned to certain types of support than to others. Some prefer numbers. Others identify quickly with narration. Still others are caught up most easily by visual aids. By using a variety of supportive or developmental materials, you are more likely to be including something for all tastes.

Checking for Coordination and Subordination

Another question to ask about an outline is: Are the levels of coordination and subordination properly maintained? Every speech has points that are coordinate: points at the same level and equally vital to the topic. Some of these may be developed in more detail than the others, but still the coordinate points are of equal logical importance to the whole of what is to be said. The *main headings* in the body of a speech should be *coordinate*. Subordinate materials lie beneath them in the outline, at lower levels. Supporting materials should be subordinate to the main point, and a useful outline should show this clearly. You should ask: Is the main heading prominent and predominant? Does it stand out? Is the subordinate material really subordinate to it and supportive of it?

STUDY PROBE 12
Relating Subordinate and Supportive Materials

Consider the parable of the Good Samaritan in the Martin Luther King, Jr., speech. Do you remember what major point was supported by the use of the parable? If one was impressed by the use of the parable and remembered it, but did not remember the main point it was used to support, then the parable did not function as subordinately and supportively as it should have—for that listener or reader.

Providing Internal Summaries and Transitions

To ensure a smooth flow or movement of ideas in a speech, a speaker should use *internal summaries* and *transitions*. Internal summaries and transitions are statements that stand as signposts throughout a speech, informing the listeners, as the talk proceeds, where they have been and where they are going, intellectually and substantively. Internal summaries remind listeners of what has been covered to that point. Transitions prepare listeners for what is coming directly ahead. So that these elements can be meaningful and yet be unobtrusive in your speeches, you should plan for and use them appropriately. As you develop speaking skill through practice, you will learn a number of general patterns for summaries and transitions and will be able to call upon these varied resources in appropriate places. In a sense, they can become part of your "style."

Using Restatement and Repetition

Another advantage of internal summaries is that they allow a speaker to repeat and restate points previously covered. Repetition is one of the most important aids to listeners' memories, and to the degree that you want portions of your speech remembered, you must plan to include some repetition and restatement. It is important that repetition of major ideas be distributed throughout your speech in order to help listeners keep the *whole* of your message in mind. Repetition is also used for dramatic effect. For a striking example of this, see the text of the speech Martin Luther King, Jr., gave to climax the Civil Rights March in Washington, D.C., August 28, 1963, with its thematic and memorably recurring phrase, "I have a dream . . . ."

When you have satisfied yourself on the above matters, you can take a broader view of planning for the speech body. What of the *overall* pacing and development of your thoughts? From the standpoint of a listener, does the speech go anywhere? Is there movement in it? Does it build to some point, and then back off a bit to begin building to another point? Or does it move steadily forward? Every speech is something like a symphony with higher and lower moments, recurring but differently developed themes, calculated simultaneously to give and to require audience involvement. Try to look upon your speech as a unity-in-process rather than simply as a collection of discrete parts. If a speech is ever to have this quality, it must be developed and instilled at this stage in a speaker's planning.

The Introduction of a Speech

With the planning for the body of a speech completed, you should next turn your efforts to introducing the message you have developed. This introduction, although necessarily shorter than the body, should be similarly outlined. The first question always is: "How long should the introduction be?" And the answer always is: "Just long enough to accomplish the goals of an introduction." Depending upon the topic, the audience, and the context, an introduction for a two-hour speech might take half an hour; for a brief speech, the introduction might require only a single sentence.

The goals for the introduction of a speech are:

1. To develop attention and interest for the topic.
2. To relate the topic to the concerns of the listeners.
3. To provide a bridge to the body of the speech.

Let us see how each of these objectives can be accomplished.

Developing Interest and Attention for the Topic

In the introduction proper, a speaker must develop attention and interest for his topic. We must stress here that the first step is to get attention *for the speech topic as such,* and not simply to gain attention for the speaker.

In discussing developmental materials, we singled out most of the means for gaining interest. An anecdote, a single example, the development of conflicting or contrasting positions, a quotation from some respected source, an unexpected and slightly startling statement—*so long as they are relevant to the topic*—all can be effective ways to begin a speech.

Occasionally I have had students in class who, when opening speeches, thought primarily about attention for its own sake. One day a student whipped out a bell from beneath his sport jacket and rang it. Another student speaker secretly lighted a firecracker behind the lectern. Still another, speaking against pep pills, hurled a bottle of them against the wall, shattering the bottle and scattering little round pills all over the room. In each case the speaker got attention. But, also in each case, the speaker's *ethos* plummeted; all of the listeners were very distracted as they wondered during the early part of the speech whether this speaker had cracked under some pressure or other. Those in the front rows sat noticeably erect throughout these speeches, as if ready to bolt from the spot if a final disintegration should occur. The attention these speakers gained was *not* attention to their topics but attention to their startling *behaviors* as speakers.

Relating the Topic to the Concerns of the Listeners

In introducing your speech, plan ways to relate your topic to the special concerns of the audience. Carefully consider these typical questions: Why should they care? What do they have to gain from this topic? You must often dispel listeners' doubts, resistance, and apathy toward a topic. You must try to show how the aspects of the topic bear upon beliefs, evaluations, and values known to be held by the audience. Apathy is not easily combatted, so you must try to relate your position or proposal to the self-interests of your audience, and you must begin this process in your introduction.

Providing a Bridge to the Body of the Speech

A successful introduction should provide a bridge to the body of a speech. You should not begin with "My first point is . . . ." This consideration for your audience must, of course, be reflected in your outline: What will be needed to gain your listeners' interests, to develop their concern for the topic, to prepare them for the body of the speech?

Dr. King begins his speech with a few kind words about his audience and their institution. He then presents the Biblical passage which he will use as a base for his speech. Next he turns quickly from the text itself to his first main heading (paragraph 4). In this way, he moves smoothly from introduction to body.

The Conclusion of a Speech

In preparing an outline of a conclusion, you should be seeking the most effective means for reinforcing your specific purpose and for bringing your speech to a close. A conclusion will frequently contain some drawing together of the main points of the speech and/or some final appeal. You should seek a strong closing, as well as a strong beginning, so that the speech doesn't just taper off or fade away. Dr. King's summary (paragraph 32) draws together his three major points in brief statements—as commandments—in his final appeal. His specific purpose is also emphasized in his excellent closing remarks.

Depending upon your specific purpose, of course, the following objectives are some which you will do well to keep in mind as you conclude your one-to-many communications:

1. Summarize the major points of your speech.
2. Reiterate your contention(s) and solidify your position.
3. Appeal skillfully and strongly for listeners' acceptance of your ideas and/or the action you have proposed.

4. Clearly affirm your own personal intentions regarding the action you are seeking or the proposition you are advancing.

5. Develop a sense of climax and conclusiveness or finality in the thinking and feeling of your hearers. If your speech has been successful, presumably you will have re-balanced their cognitions—at least to a certain extent.

Remember, above all, that the conclusion of a speech should never be—or appear to be—a mere tacked-on statement or an anticlimactic afterthought. The conclusion is what you have been building toward from the very beginning. Having presented your proposal or plan of action in the body of the speech, the ending is the place where you "drive the final nail home and clinch it." To use a somewhat different analogy, you might think of the introduction of your speech as the act of pulling the trigger to fire the bullet—the central idea of your speech—the body of the speech as the bullet's trajectory, and the conclusion as the bull's-eye of the speech target.

Facilitative Factors in Structuring Speeches

With your full outline prepared, you may well give some attention and planning to special approaches which may facilitate the eventual presentational flow of your materials in the speaking context. These approaches are best considered carefully at this point in speech planning, rather than neglected until you begin oral practice for your speech presentation. We shall focus upon two of these facilitators, particularly: (1) the use of *visual and auditory aids* and (2) the use of *humor*.

Visual and Auditory Aids

The use of exhibits, visual aids, and auditory aids will contribute to the effectiveness of many speeches. A speaker does well always to consider whether use of such aids as charts, drawings, flannel boards, pictures, slides, films, tape and disk recordings, and the like, can help him communicate his meanings. The availability of such materials and the appropriateness of their use in the specific context should be the standards for determining whether they will be used.

This group is evaluating data in a vertical bar chart, projected onto a screen for easy viewing by an overhead projector. The speaker, who stands to the side of the screen and faces his listeners as he speaks, demonstrates proper use of this kind of visual aid.

These aids to speaking are especially helpful because they can add to the total information provided for the listeners. By employing them, a speaker expands the visual and auditory response-experience of his listeners; thereby, he increases their attention to and retention of material basic to his message. Accordingly, a speaker will find these aids especially useful in those speeches in which his specific purpose is to present a somewhat complex concept or process in a simple, concise form.

Helpful aids are not always available; at other times they can be produced only with unwarranted difficulty or expense. In such cases speakers may still be tempted to use materials that, unless reinforced visually, are neither very interesting nor very informative. The temptation to use them should probably be resisted, for there is little evidence that a poor aid is better than none. There may also be occasions in which the audience does not expect the speaker to use visual or auditory aids, or occasions in which they would feel uncomfortable if he did so. For instance, during a *formal* church sermon it would seem inappropriate to use flip-chart visual aids.

STUDY PROBE 13

Influencing Listeners by Visual Impressions

a. Study carefully the window displays in several of the large clothing stores in your city. What "messages" do these visual displays seem to transmit?

b. Visit an automobile dealer's showroom and ask for one of his company's brochures describing the new cars for the year. Report to the class how visuals are used in these brochures.

Whenever visual or auditory reinforcement is used, it (1) *must fit the topic well,* (2) *must be appropriate to the level of the audience,* and (3) *must serve as an aid to the speech rather than become the point of the speech or a hindrance to it.* This third requirement, in particular, cannot be overemphasized. Too often aids dominate the speaker's presentation; they then appear to be his reason for giving the speech. Or aids may interrupt the smooth flow of the speech. The speaker may, for instance, be moving forward smoothly in the development of his message; suddenly, with a jarring change of pace and much confusion, he interrupts himself and diverts attention to a visual aid; then he turns too abruptly from the aid and resumes speaking about the next point.

A cardinal rule in using visual aids is that they must be carefully planned and prepared for use as you develop a speech as a whole. You should determine very early what points will benefit most from reinforcement, and then decide upon the type of aid likely to be most helpful. Situational considerations are important, too. How large will the audience be, what will be the seating arrangement, and what facilities (blackboard, flannel board, supports for charts, etc.) will be available? The aids used must not be too many or too complex, and they must be large enough for all to see.

A commonly raised question asks whether it is better to use a blackboard or to prepare diagrams or drawings beforehand. The answer, again, depends on the situation. If the drawing is to be quite simple, you may decide to produce it on the board during the moments of presentation. The board may also be preferable if your drawing involves some "development" of an idea or process that can best be shown by putting up a representation of part of the idea, discussing that, and then adding other parts. This can be done equally well with a flannel-board exhibit. Whatever aids you decide on, the basic admonition still holds: *Carefully prepare ahead of time for every visual or auditory aid you will want to use.* Without prior preparation and planning, you must gamble that all will be at hand and in order. How many speakers, for example, have you seen who have reached for chalk that wasn't there or have searched for a nonexistent electrical outlet into which to plug a tangled extension cord?

If aids are small—a scale model, a mimeographed diagram, or even the object itself—you may elect to pass it around to the members of the audience. There are difficulties in doing this, however, and generally it is preferable to retain control over your visual and auditory reinforcements. You can then refer to them when and as you like—at the most crucial or desirable moments. The advantages of this are elemental: Once an object or item is in the hands of someone else, attention tends to be focused on the object and away from the speaker. For this reason it is certainly never a good practice to pass aids around in the audience while you continue speaking. When this is done, one can usually observe very clearly the wave of inattention to the speaker as the aid is examined by one member of the audience after another.

STUDY PROBE 14
Evaluating the Use of Visual Aids

Keep a log of all the uses of visual aids you see in lectures and speeches during one week. What types of aids are employed? Are any types overused? Are the aids used at appropriate points in the presentation? Cite instances where the aids were used either in especially helpful ways or in undesirable ways.

Pool the observations of all in the class. Were your experiences similar?

We can summarize the advice thus far given by saying:

1. In preparing aids, you should make them large and simple enough to be seen and understood by everyone in your audience.
2. You should make certain that any facilities needed for your aids will be available.
3. You should plan to integrate the aids smoothly into your speech presentation.
4. You should maintain control over your auditory and visual reinforcements and use them *only as aids* to your speech.

Humor

A lively sense of humor is a genuine advantage for any speaker, and student speakers should consider some use of humor as they select and determine how they will develop the materials of speeches. Material of a light nature, oc-

John F. Kennedy's use of humor, oftentimes impromptu, created innumerable lighter moments in serious discussions; it is perhaps one of the best-remembered qualities of his public utterances. Here the camera records an amiable exchange between the President and members of the press.

curring from time to time throughout the presentation, can help to gain and sustain attention and interest. It provides a desirable change of pace and variety. If properly handled, humor can create amiability and good will which are especially valuable assets if a speaker finds himself facing an unsympathetic or hostile audience.

Use of humor can backfire, however, and speakers must be wary of its possible negative effects. Most of us are familiar with the graceless speaker who, in attempting to prove what a "regular guy" he is, tells a hoary joke, pauses in the wrong places—for too long—then laughs too heartily, waits while his listeners laugh politely and feebly, then waits a bit longer during that awkward silence, and finally goes on with his speech.

It is, perhaps, easiest to say what *not* to do with humor. So many community service-club speakers begin with:

A funny thing happened to me on the way here.

I want to tell a story I heard.

Here's a good one. There were these two Irishmen . . .

And then, following two or three "jokes," the speaker stiffens as he announces, "And now for my speech . . ." or "But turning now to more serious matters . . . ." *Then* the *audience* stiffens.

The fact that an audience laughs at a story is not the most important criterion for effective humor; most audiences are polite and know how to play their role accordingly. The first time we heard about the politician whose "entire personal library was burned—both books—and he hadn't a chance to color in one of them yet," we thought the story was funny. But now, years later, when someone repeats it, we wonder where he has been.

The best humor for any occasion derives from the speech context or is closely adapted to it. As you plan a speech you should look for sources of amusement in the context. But they must meet the critical test: Does the humor help to make a relevant point? A further test is: When the listener recalls to mind the humorous remark or incident, will he also recall the point with which it was associated? If a witticism or anecdote is recalled for itself only, then it was not highly effective in serving the purpose of communication.

The use of humorous material must not be restricted to the opening of a speech. Actually, either in terms of point-development or of capturing attention, it may be needed *less* in the introduction than elsewhere in the speech. Almost any speaker is granted a fair amount of attention when he begins his speech. The audience's natural curiosity ensures that. It is later, in the body of the speech, that attention will more likely lag. Humor in the introduction can often help a speaker, for it can suggest that warmth and good will are a part of his personality. But it certainly makes no sense to use humor in the introduction to a speech and nowhere else. In fact, this is one sign of a poor speaker. He reproduces a hackneyed formula without any real thought for what he is doing.

The first requirement of humor is that it be humorous. This doesn't mean that every light turn in a speech should cause the listeners to double up in laughter. A remark can serve the function of humor if it simply creates a feeling of amusement, of ease and relaxation in the audience—if it gives listeners a moment to shift in their seats or to glance about at fellow listeners. Good humor serves the special function of establishing rapport among all the agents in a speech context: speaker and listener, and listener and listener. Being amusing and amused is usually a relaxed and noncombative activity, an interaction which allows the expression of mutual good will.

We often find humor in the unexpected. We tend to laugh at what surprises us. This is one of the reasons why little children laugh at the minor accidents of others around them. We stub a toe, and they laugh. Later, they learn to distinguish surprises of that type from surprises created and controlled by an agent, and they learn to laugh openly only at the latter. The unexpected remark, an exaggeration, an understatement, a double meaning of a pun, the incongruous—all can produce responses of amusement. Hopefully, their use will be intentional.

When Fabia, the wife of Dolabella, asserted that she was thirty years old, Cicero remarked that he knew this was true for he had "heard it for the last twenty years." A widower, lamenting the loss of his wife who had hanged herself upon a fig tree, was asked by his friend: "Would you give me some shoots from that tree so that I may plant them in my yard?" Concerning a rival, a politician inquired: "What does this candidate for public office lack except personal wealth —(pause)—and virtue?" And then there is Cicero's memorable remark about the man caught in the act of adultery (for this you must see *De Oratore,* Book II, Section 68). Note how these jests, all 2000 years old, surprise and amuse by taking the unexpected turn.

In sum, if it is in harmony with your self-conception and experience, and with the requirements of the specific context of your speech, you may—and should—plan to use humor in treating the developmental material for supporting main points.

Making a Final Check of the Speech Organization

At this stage of the development of a speech, you should have before you, perhaps on several sheets of paper, a complete speech outline. The outline should be headed with a statement of specific purpose. It should have interestingly and well-developed sections for the *introduction, body,* and *conclusion;* the main points of the speech should be fully developed with supporting materials. Visual reinforcements, if there are to be any, should be listed or sketched out. You should now look on the product of your efforts as the "blueprint" for your speech. Once more you should step back (figuratively) and look at the larger context. You should consider your audience and the specific occasion as you reevaluate your planning. If changes seem desirable, or if new thoughts occur to you, they can easily be introduced into the speech at this time.

STUDY PROBE 15
Analyzing a Sample Speech: Materials and Development

Read again the speech by Martin Luther King, Jr., in Appendix A. Write a critique of his speech using as your evaluative criteria the sufficiency of:

> interest-maintaining factors
>
> coordination and subordination
>
> summaries and transitions
>
> restatements
>
> pacing
>
> the introduction and conclusion

You should now examine your outline for evidences of that well-known triad: *unity, coherence,* and *emphasis.* A speech must have unity or "oneness." This means essentially that every point in the outline should bear on the specific purpose. One reason for a specific-purpose statement is to provide unity to a speech, thus allowing speaker and listener to focus on exactly what the whole communication "adds up to." Judge every item in the outline against it. The speech should have coherence; the parts should "stick together." Throughout, the transitions and movement from one part of the speech to the next should be smooth. No succeeding point should ever come as a surprise or jar audience expectations. The speech should have emphasis; the main headings should "stand out" above others.

STUDY PROBE 16
Analyzing a Sample Speech: Unity, Coherence, and Emphasis

Using the criteria of unity, coherence, and emphasis, write a three- or four-page paper in which you evaluate Dr. King's speech as it appears in Appendix A. In making your analysis, also consider his use of language, the development of his ideas, and the manner in which he apparently adapted them to his audience.

Speech Practice

With a completed, reviewed, and evaluated outline, you are ready to move to the second phase of your preparation for a speech occasion. The fully shaped speech and all the materials needed for your presentation are at hand. You are now ready to begin practicing the presentation of your speech. Hopefully, this practice can be distributed over several days. A few hours practice spaced throughout a week will do more to give you command of a speech than several hours in one "cramming" session the evening before. In Chapter 5 (page 134), where we discussed speech skills as patterned behavior, we defined some of the basic components of effective oral practice. Before you begin to practice your speech presentation, you may find it advantageous to review the nature of those components.

Practicing to Communicate Orally

You should begin practice by standing up and delivering your speech aloud, from your outline, in an empty room. Too many students sit at a desk and mumble through a speech for practice. This is like practicing a tennis stroke in a chair. It misses the whole "feeling" of the activity. You should try to practice in conditions that are as nearly like the actual situation as possible, for you cannot expect to feel comfortable speaking out before an audience if your only practice has been to mumble to yourself.

In the early stages of practice you should try to "talk through" your entire speech several times without stopping. Referring to the outline when necessary, you should begin to set the sequence of main ideas and developmental materials clearly in your mind. Given one point, you should have a feeling for what comes next. When we have listened many times to a long-playing record with several selections, we can anticipate what will come next. You should develop much the same kind of anticipation for the sequence of main ideas in your speeches, and oral practice is one of the most productive ways to accomplish this.

When the sequence of main ideas is established in your mind, you should settle on the type of notes you will use while giving the speech. You might possibly use a full-speech manuscript. Or you might decide to use an outline—or no notes at all. Most likely, however, you will use a few note cards containing some of the material from your initial outline, now in abbreviated form. These notes can be put on 3 x 5 or 4 x 6 cards, or even on a sheet or two of 8½ x 11 paper. Notes for shorter speeches of ten minutes or so in length ordinarily can be contained on a single sheet of paper. The smaller the space you allot to such notes (retaining an easy-to-read quality), the more easily you will be able to handle and refer to them while talking.

As a speaker you ought to use whatever type of notes is most helpful to you. The important point is that they contain enough needed information in

Not a bridge but a barrier: Notes from which a speaker cannot liberate himself obviously come between him and his listeners, and minimize whatever communicative contact he might have achieved.

easy-to-read form. You should rely on these aids *only* to the extent that they are necessary to help you move smoothly through your planned speech without undue hesitations and without worry that you may forget some of the material. If you have practiced thoroughly, you will need to refer to your notes only for those materials that are so detailed you cannot easily remember them.

The chief objection to the use of notes in formal speaking is that ordinarily they are badly used. In fact, this criticism can apply to the use of almost every form of presentational aid. Give most speakers a manuscript, and they will stare at it and read it word-by-word with all the liveliness and communicative interaction they would achieve if they were reading a telephone directory. There are also speakers who, throughout their speeches, stare down at notes even when they don't need such reminders, thereby losing all communicative contact with their audiences.

As a speaker, you should keep your notes at hand for *emergency purposes only* and should address your audience—not your note cards. Notes can become a crutch, and a speaker often looks at them in order not to face his audience. But this destroys the human interaction which is a necessary part of speech communication. In practicing speeches, you will ordinarily make frequent references to your notes at the beginning; but each time you repeat the speech, you must endeavor to become more independent of them. The less you need to concentrate on your notes, the more you can concentrate on feedback from your listeners.

"Well, then," you may ask, "am I to memorize my speech?" Many would quickly answer, "Of course not!" There are a number of misconceptions about what we mean by "memorize." Probably no one should be advised to try to memorize a speech word for word and then try to present it. In the limited time available, one probably could not master it completely enough to communicate it with a conversational quality. Successful speakers, however, usually memorize *portions* of their speeches. You, too, should learn the sequence of your main ideas and the development of your materials so well that they come to mind quickly and in the planned order. And you may even want to memorize *some* of the wording or phrasing you consider especially important and effective. This does not mean that you cannot make changes while speaking or that you are unable to adapt to the ever-changing context of the communication process. On the contrary, the fact that a sequence of supporting materials is memorized should make it all the easier for you to shift materials into an order *different* from the one you planned. *If* a shift is needed, you will know precisely what segment or materials you are shifting.

Making Language Meaningful

Language usage, or "style" (the choice of words and the arrangement of words), was among the topics most seriously considered by classical rhetoricians. Aristotle, Cicero, and Quintilian each devoted substantial portions of their works on rhetoric to discussions of oral style. Some rhetoricians devoted whole treatises to the subject. Contemporary rhetoricians still emphasize the significance of language in rhetorical acts for the good reason that it is through the symbols we call language that people make some of their most important communicative contacts with one another.[4]

[4] The significance of language in the view of contemporary rhetoricians is evident in *The Prospect of Rhetoric,* ed. Lloyd F. Bitzer and Edwin Black (Englewood Cliffs, N.J.: Prentice-Hall, Inc., 1971).

As a speaker you, too, should give special consideration to your use of language when you practice a speech. Especially, you should make a conscious effort to use language that is *clear, appropriate,* and *vivid.*

Be Clear

Clarity of language increases the likelihood that your intent will become immediately obvious to your listeners. Clarity is achieved by choosing words and expressions that convey your meaning in such a way as to require the minimum of translation and transformation by listening agents.

In striving for clarity, you should try to use concrete and specific terms rather than abstract and general ones. Use familiar words. If unfamiliar technical language or jargon must be used, it should be defined or explained as you use it. In a speech, statements should be fairly brief, though you should avoid overcondensation. A single "yes" is sometimes not enough to provide listeners with a full answer to a question. If it is not, we have an instance of brevity but not clarity.

Be Appropriate

A second important quality of language that works as intended is appropriateness. The language you use has to be appropriate to you as speaker, to the audience, to the context, and to the subject. One cannot use the same language everywhere. Some occasions are more formal than others. Some audiences expect more elegance in speech. Others appreciate a down-to-earth—even an earthy—approach. It is a good exercise sometimes to practice a speech with one type of audience and occasion in mind, and then practice it later with another hypothetical context and group of listeners in mind. This kind of exercise can help you develop some variety of stylistic approaches to a subject and in that way also increase your total fund of verbal resources. As you gain command over a wider range of speaking styles, you gain the ability to adapt to a wider range of speaking situations.

STUDY PROBE 17

Adapting a Speech to Different Audiences

Review the portion of Dr. King's speech found in paragraphs 5 through 8. Rewrite that section of the speech as *you* would present it to (1) a college audience today and (2) an audience of thirteen-year-old students in a public school.

Be Vivid

To be effective, language must also be vivid—lively, intense, sharp, and colorful. There are so many devices for making a speech vivid that it is difficult to select only a few; one is forced to omit so many other possibilities. Yet the topic is important, and we must consider at least some of the means we may use to vivify our communications.

One useful vivifying device is the *metaphor,* in which a word or phrase that literally denotes a certain object or concept is applied to another for the purpose of suggesting a likeness or similarity. Bernstein said that the improvising jazz player uses a popular song "as a kind of dummy to hang his notes on. He dresses it up in his own way, and it comes out an original." Notice that the "dummy" metaphor allowed Bernstein to present a *visual* image of what the musician actually does melodically.

The use of metaphor can easily add this quality of visualization and concreteness to an otherwise abstract thought. At the grave of his brother, Robert G. Ingersoll visualized and softened the concept of a premature death by this means:

> *Yet, after all, it may be best, just in the happiest, sunniest hour of all the voyage, while eager winds are kissing every sail, to dash against the unseen rock, and in an instant hear the billows roar above a sunken ship. For, whether in midsea or 'mong the breakers of the farther shore, a wreck at last must mark the end of each and all. And every life, no matter if its every hour is rich with love and every moment jeweled with a joy, will, at its close, become a tragedy as sad and deep and dark as can be woven of the warp and woof of mystery and death.*[5]

Another device often used to add vividness is *hyperbole,* an obvious and deliberate overstatement or understatement: Her "fair skin is whiter than snow"; he moves "slower than a snail." These statements claim more than is really meant; we grasp the emphasis intended from the exaggeration itself. But you must be wary of hyperbole. Consider the sports announcer who labels every minor incident in a game "a tragedy," "a momentous play," "the greatest pass in history!" When overused, hyperbole soon becomes dull—and often incongruous—losing its ability to clarify, emphasize, or vivify. Further, figures of speech which employ such extravagance tend to become trite rather quickly.

A speaker may use *irony,* in which his true meaning is contrary to his words. The incongruity between the words and the vocal inflection in Mark Antony's "For Brutus is an honorable man" reveals heavy irony when read aloud. Irony is a resource of language that often allows a speaker to use humor as a cutting edge with persuasive effect. And the contrast between what is really meant and the literal words gives vividness and liveliness to ironic language.

Rhetorical questions create audience involvement by calling for implicit audience responses. William Wirt's account of Patrick Henry's speech to the Virginia House of Burgesses contains this series of questions:

"But when shall we be stronger?

Shall we gather strength by irresolution and inaction?

Why stand we here idle?

What is it that gentlemen wish?

Is life so dear, and peace so sweet, as to be purchased at the price of chains and slavery?"

Can you imagine an audience unmoved by such questioning? Dr. King used rhetorical questions in his speech (see Appendix) when he asked gently, "How can one avoid being depressed? . . . How can one avoid being concerned?"

[5] Robert G. Ingersoll's "Oration at His Brother's Grave" is available in *The World's Great Speeches,* ed. Lewis Copeland (Garden City, N.Y.: Garden City Publishing Co., Inc., 1942), pp. 324–325.

A speaker may also make use of *antithesis,* in which he brings opposites together verbally. The clashing of cognitions makes the point and lends vividness to what is said. All of us are acquainted with the statement, "Ask not what your country can do for you, but what you can do for your country." Some of the memorable quality of this line comes from the balanced rhythms of the clauses, but much of it comes from the *opposed* sentiments so expressed.

A widely used and effective device is displayed in the *parallel and balanced phrases* used in the antithesis just quoted. As we have seen earlier, parallels and balanced phrases may occur in main headings or in supporting material, together or separated in a speech, with similarity in whole or only in part. You know many, such as these:

> The length of life
> The breadth of life
> The height of life
>
> I came, I saw, I conquered.
>
> Of the people, by the people, for the people . . .

These are merely a few of the devices you may draw upon to add vividness to your speeches. Used correctly, these vivifiers will help to dramatize your points and thereby aid the audience in taking note of the important issues of the speech.

STUDY PROBE 18
Analyzing Word Usage

List the *words* you can find in Dr. King's speech that have all three qualities we recommended—clarity, appropriateness, and vividness. How long is your list? Compare your list with lists prepared by others. Is it likely that some of your classmates evaluated word meanings differently from the way you did? What is the explanation? You may want to refer back to Chapter 6 for possible answers.

We have just explained *what* can be done to make language usage effective. Now *how* can you, as a speaker, incorporate this knowledge into your own speech habits and styles in such a way as to ensure that such usage will become almost automatic? It will require effort. You should probably start with an assessment of your own use of language in speaking. You must begin to pay more attention to how you speak; you must listen to yourself. This will be difficult, for our speaking style soon becomes habitual, and we perform the acts without being very conscious of them or paying attention to them.

You should attempt to judge how ample and varied your spoken expression is *now*. Do you often struggle to find the right word—and then give up? Do you overuse any expressions so that they become distracting to a listener? The language of some speakers is sprinkled with expressions such as "you know," "you see," "and so," and similar overworked phrases. To such speakers, these are "fillers"; to listeners, they become grating repetitions.

The most helpful, positive aid to language improvement probably results from careful reading of models of good language. Try to read good speeches such as those available in the collections of famous speeches. Above all, you should read some of these models *aloud* so that the sound and the sense of the language will combine in your memory. Oral language is meant to be heard, and you need to *hear* it to receive full influence from it. Moreover, reading aloud can be of great general benefit to any student of speech. For comparison, you ought to listen to yourself on tape recordings in order to evaluate and refine your own oral language.

STUDY PROBE 19
Practicing the Use of Vivid Language

a. When describing an event which had great emotional impact on us, we tend naturally to use vivid language. Select an event from your experiences when you were embarrassed, or overjoyed, or angered, or exhausted, or saddened, or frightened, or ashamed. Write a short, descriptive essay about this event, using as many vivifying devices as you can. Exchange your descriptive essay with a classmate and, in the margins, label the devices he has used.

b. In small group-research teams, examine a number of essays written by war correspondents, or sports editors, or automobile advertisers, or auto test drivers, or similar people. Copy the better instances of their vivifying devices, e.g., metaphor, hyperbole, etc.

c. Try to describe in vivid language several commonplace scenes, e.g., a traffic intersection, a dorm room on a Saturday morning, an interstate highway at night, etc.

Making the Delivery of a Speech Effective

Demosthenes once was asked what is the most important element in speaking, and he quickly replied, "Delivery." When asked what is second most important, he again replied, "Delivery." And third most important—"Delivery." Cicero agreed: "Delivery, I say, has the sole and supreme power in oratory."[6] While the factors that make up speech are probably too interrelated to allow any such rank ordering to be very meaningful, there can be little question that a well-delivered speech has much greater chances for being effective. Delivery is, therefore, another factor you should pay special attention to when practicing speeches. As with language and style, you should attempt to hear and visualize yourself in the role of speaker and should work, among your other goals, for improved speech delivery.

Delivery, as a speech concept, involves the auditory and visual channels through which symbols are transmitted during the speech act. A speaker's delivery makes up the sights and sounds of communication insofar as his listeners are concerned, and it is from these sights and sounds that they infer and interpret his meanings. In the ensuing pages we will concern ourselves with the audi-

---

[6] Cicero, *De Oratore,* trans. H. Rackham, 2 vols. (Cambridge, Mass.: Harvard University Press, 1960 printing of Loeb Classical Library), v. II, p. 169.

tory and visual channels, providing some analyses of and suggestions regarding each; and we will also devote attention to some useful things which a speaker can do to improve his speech-delivery skills.

Auditory Factors

Auditory stimuli are what the listener hears. The essential vocal dimensions are pitch, intensity or loudness, rate, and quality. *Pitch* is the perception of the frequency of the transmitted sound waves. The greater the frequency of cycles per second, the higher the pitch. Some studies have shown that what is judged effective speaking is associated not so much with a certain pitch level (a high-pitched voice or a low-pitched voice) but with *variety* in pitch. We have all heard the speaker who drones along in a monotone. Nothing stands out in his speech, and the total effect induces uneasiness or sleep. All of our experiences indicate clearly that such speech tends to diminish listeners' comprehension and retention of what is said. Variety in pitch level is, therefore, something you should strive for if you don't already have it naturally. And, of course, the vocal variations must be meaningful. Emphasis in intensity should correspond with emphasis in thought.

Loudness is the perception of *vocal intensity*. Some speakers speak so softly they can hardly be heard, yet a speaker ought to be certain that he can be heard easily by all his listeners. Other speakers shout their entire speeches, seeking in this way to give emphasis to what they say. But if *every* thought is emphasized through loudness, no single idea stands out from the others, and nothing is emphasized. However, if such a speaker were to drop his voice and present a point in a low and calm manner, he would give it a far greater emphasis because of the *change* in the strength of the stimulus. *Vocal contrast* is imperative in making a succession of ideas stand out—each from the other.

Speech rate has to do with timing and pace. Words on a printed page stand more or less equidistant from one another, and follow along uniformly. This is not true in oral discourse. What appear as words on paper are combined in utterance, so oral pace becomes a matter of spacing "bursts" of sound that are in fact word-clusters. You should determine your own pattern for spacing words by varying your rate of presentation and judging in what way you communicate *all* your oral meanings best—by being deliberate, rapid, or varied in rate.

Voice quality, as we can readily observe from the "qualities" of musical instruments, is a complex trait. Two musical instruments may play a tone at the same pitch level and intensity level. Yet they "sound" different. This special sound of any tone producer is its quality. It results from a combination of the other basic elements. Because of differences in resonators, overtones appear in resonated sound with different intensity levels, and this interaction of pitches and intensities is what is perceived as quality. A pleasant vocal quality is helpful for speech communication. Some less pleasant vocal qualities may be described as breathiness, shrillness, hoarseness, and nasality. Each occurs as the result of some inefficient functioning of sound producer-resonator control, and each interferes to a greater or lesser extent with oral interaction.

Articulation has to do with the production of distinguishable speech sounds. English has about forty-five distinctive groups of speech sounds, or phonemes. These sounds are produced when the articulators of speech—tongue, teeth, lips, and palate—function together in close coordination to modify the breath stream as it passes them. Some cases of faulty articulation are severe enough to warrant a visit with a speech therapist. Your speech teacher will know when this is the case. But even among so-called "normal" speakers, certain problems of articulation often occur. Because of bad speech habits a speaker may mumble his words. The articulation is not sharp and precise, and because of a "mushy" quality all the sounds are not easy to distinguish. A tape recording of your speech will provide an objective sample of your articulation; if minor changes are needed, your speech teacher should be able to advise you.

Pronunciation has to do with the choice of sounds. Sometimes a speaker will leave a sound out of a word, or he will substitute an incorrect one, or add one. When a speaker drops the "g" in "ing" endings, as in "goin' " and "doin'," he is really substituting sounds, using [n] for [ŋ] as written with phonetic symbols. Some eastern speakers frequently drop [r] sounds except as a link between vowels, where they may add it. Some New Yorkers will say something like "fa" and "fam" for "far" and "farm," but will add [r] in "the idear of it."

Standards of pronunciation differ from area to area. If adaptation is easy, perhaps you should adapt. There is no virtue in refusing to go along with the way a person pronounces the name of his home town. When in Cairo, Illinois, you might as well give it the local pronunciation. If you move from one region of the country to another, however, you may always be an outsider because of the dialect you learned elsewhere. This is like moving from one particular language community to another. If it is important to you, or necessary for your career, you may decide to learn the new language. Usually, however, if you speak clearly and carefully, your dialect will not cause you great hardship. But slovenly articulation and pronunciation in any language or dialect will diminish your speaker *ethos* for most listeners.

Pausing and *phrasing* are also very important elements in vocal delivery. We write in sentences, using commas, semicolons, periods, and the like for punctuation. As we have mentioned before, we speak in *phrases* or *word-clusters,* using pauses of varying lengths as punctuation. The phrase or word-cluster is a word or group of words spoken as one single breath unit and/or thought unit. Speakers too frequently fight this characteristic of oral communication, and instead try to pause only at those places where they probably would find a comma or period in written discourse. This practice usually produces too much material within a single thought unit; it makes communication difficult for the audience to follow because listeners are used to the phrasing patterns of *speech*. Other speakers may pause too frequently, uttering only two or three words per phrase. Often this can be traced to nervousness, which causes rapid, shallow breathing that cannot give enough support for the longer phrases in which speech patterns normally fall.

Try speaking the first sentence of the Gettysburg Address as indicated below. In each version, pause and breathe at each point where there is a dash (—), and *only* where there is a dash.

> "—Fourscore and seven years ago our fathers brought forth on this continent a new nation conceived in liberty and dedicated to the proposition that all men are created equal—"

Did you make it? How meaningful was the statement? Try again.

"—Fourscore—and seven years—ago—our fathers—brought forth—on this—continent—a new—nation—conceived—in liberty—and—dedicated —to the—proposition—that—all men—are created—equal—"

This could be the phrasing of an extremely nervous speaker. It is not very communicative. What about the following?

"—Fourscore and seven years ago—our fathers—brought forth on this continent—a new nation—conceived in liberty—and dedicated to the proposition—that all men are created equal—"

It is not necessary—or even possible—of course, to breathe every time you pause. Go back over these three samples, making sure you pause at each (—), but breathing only when necessary. The pauses can be of different durations also. Finally, determine how you would phrase the sentence for the best possible effect. Where would you pause, and for how long? Where would you take a breath? After comparing the above versions, perhaps you can better understand why pausing and phrasing are so important to effective speech communication.

"Twinkle, twinkle, little star, how I wonder . . . ." Say this well-known rhyme to yourself a few times and also have someone else try it. It will very probably be phrased the same each time. The delivery may be varied, but it will also be *patterned*. The variation is always the same; that is, the variation *itself* becomes a pattern—a pattern almost indistinguishable regardless of who utters it. We all tend to use the same melody—the same pattern. When we say delivery should be varied, we mean varied *and* variable, with variation determined by meaning. In our old rhyme, the melody is as important as the meaning. We know the rhyme linked with the melody, almost as we know a song.

Whenever a speech is presented with a patterned phrasing so obvious or evident that any audience member could produce the phrasing for the next sentence, we say the speaker has a "sing-song" delivery. This means that the *pattern* has attracted audience attention, and audience members are distracted from the meaning. When reading quotations from written material, many beginning speakers use a "sing-song" delivery. Often when speaking the words of another, unless you take time to consider the meaning of the material, you will tend to adopt a patterned presentation. The way to avoid this is simple: Always keep the meaning of a thought central in your speaking, and never heedlessly repeat a thought until you have a sense of its meaning.

Before concluding this section, we must consider another nemesis of speech delivery: the *vocalized pause*. James Winans accepted the old proverb that "Speech is silver; silence is golden" and pointed out that silence is never more golden than in the midst of speech. Unfortunately, pauses always seem much longer to a speaker than they do to a listener. But pauses can be most helpful. Let us look more closely at some of the reasons this is so:

1. Pauses provide *punctuation* to a speaker's thoughts; they can give to utterance the "commas," "semicolons," "exclamation marks," "question marks," "quotation marks," "periods," and "ellipses" needed by listeners.

2. Pauses can serve well to establish *transitional intervals* between developmental thoughts.

3. Pauses allow the listeners to relax and reflect on what they have heard, to associate it with other aspects of the topic.

4. Pauses provide moments for the speaker to reflect on his next thought and get it clearly in mind before beginning to utter it.

5. Pauses, especially longer ones which precede or follow a point, give the strongest possible *emphasis* to the point.

Many speakers are afraid to be silent, even momentarily, during speech presentations. This may be due to the deep-seated fear of silence that we mentioned in Chapter 4, or it may be simply a bad habit. But most beginning speakers, unless they work against it, will fill many of the needed "silent" periods in their speeches with noisy, distracting, vocalized "um's," "er's," "ah's," and "uh's." Sometimes these vocalized pauses are uttered more loudly than the rest of the speech. They may, in fact, be the most emphasized parts of the speech event. Again, read the following passage aloud:

> "Fourscore and—uh—seven years ago—er—our fathers brought forth—ah—on this—um—continent a new nation conceived in—ah—liberty and dedicated to—ah—the proposition that all—er—er—men are created—um—equal."

With conscientious effort, any speaker can eliminate vocalized pauses. Do you believe it is worth the effort?

We encourage you, as a speaker, to practice your speeches with an ear to self-hearing. Listen for weaknesses in delivery and attempt to eliminate them *in practice.* You should work for a generally fluent delivery with adequately precise (but never overprecise) articulation and pronunciation, vocal variety determined by the meaning of what you say, appropriate pausing and phrasing, and elimination of vocalized pauses. The usefulness of a tape recorder for this self-assessment should be self-evident.

STUDY PROBE 20
Listening to Yourself Speak

Daily newspapers and news magazines frequently print long advertisements for consumer products. Locate an advertisement that impresses you as well written and use this material as the basis for an oral reading. Exaggerate your delivery. That is, overarticulate, use lengthy pauses, and vary your intensity and rate of speech. The effect should be entertaining—and should provide you with an opportunity to "hear yourself."

Visual Factors

The second aspect of delivery is that which the audience will *see.* Much of the meaning in speech communication is transmitted through the visual channel. You have only to consider the performance of a mime to know the large amounts of meaning that can be transmitted by visual cues alone. Demosthenes reportedly used a large mirror to gain a sense of the visual impression he made upon his audience. However you do it, you should assess your visual presentation and work for improvement through practice. You should give some attention to *posture, physical movement, gesture,* and *visual directness.*

Your *posture* should be erect, poised, and relaxed. You "look better" that way; but, more importantly, this is the posture from which it is always easiest to *move* in order to express ideas and thought-variations. You should feel comfortable and free to move or gesture as you like. What is to be avoided is conflict between the information received by the listener from the visual and the auditory channels. This conflict occurs, for example, when a speaker says his topic is of the greatest importance, but slouches over the speaker's stand as he says it.

General *physical movement* is also important. Some degree of movement will help to reduce bodily tensions. Movement can also provide visual transitions. If, in concluding a main point, you pause and take a step or two away from the position you have been holding, the action harmonizes and is consistent with the shift of thought, and it emphasizes that shift in the perceptions of the listeners. But, for the reasons mentioned above, if you try to make a serious point and at the same time pace back and forth, or shuffle your feet noisily, or stand with your shoulders swaying back and forth like a little child caught stealing cookies, the incongruity between what you say and how you present it will work against your general effectiveness.

Gestures are an important part of visual information received by listeners. Doubtless, you have observed many different types of hand gestures. A "locative" gesture may be used to point to a particular section of a visual aid in order to direct attention to it. An "illustrative" gesture may be used to describe the curves of a model or the dimensions of an object. The most common gestures are the "emphatic" gestures used to give added emphasis to a point. These gestures are usually made with a pointed finger, a clenched fist, or the edge of a flat hand.

Like all other aspects of delivery, gestures should be in harmony and in time with the thoughts being spoken. Some speakers never gesture and, as a consequence, appear reserved and a bit stiff. Some speakers gesture too much. They flail away incessantly at the air about them. The impulse to gesture is for most people a natural one, especially if the speaker is at ease. You will be well advised, then, to view your attempts at developing gestural communication in terms of *growth,* avoiding frequent, aimless gesturing or gesturing in a mechanical or patterned manner. You need also to be relaxed and free to gesture so that if the impetus to gesture occurs or an idea requires it, you can respond freely— something you cannot do if you are leaning on your elbows or have your hands in your pockets.

Hand gestures are only a part of the communicative, gestural resources at your command. Equally important are head gestures and facial expressions. The expressionless "deadpan" may be fine for a game of poker, but a speaker is supposed to be giving us clues to how he feels about his "cards." His interest in his topic is usually revealed by lively facial expressions and head movement.

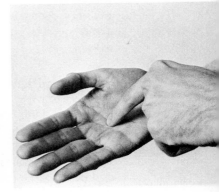

A speaker demonstrates some commonly used gestures. At left, in an illustrative gesture he may be showing the shape of an object, direction, or spatial relationships between two objects. Left to right below are a locative pointing gesture and two emphatic gestures—the clenched fist striking the palm and the finger positioned against the other hand to stress the importance of a point being made.

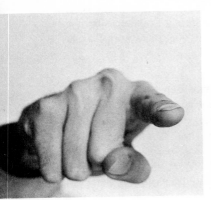

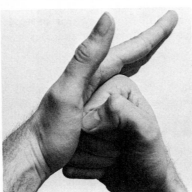

Possibly, one of the reasons why some people dislike and distrust individuals who wear beards is simply that the unaccustomed mass of facial hair obscures facial expressions which they have habitually come to depend upon in judging the veracity of others.

STUDY PROBE 21

Studying Facial Expressions as Symbolic Cues

Recite the sentences below to a classroom partner. Try to express the thoughts with the same tone and inflection that you would use if talking to a good friend. As you make each statement, have your partner write down a description of your facial expression.

"I can't hear you."

"I don't understand what you mean."

"I'm bored with what you are saying."

"I agree with what you are saying."

"I'm interested in what you are saying."

Follow that same procedure with your partner speaking the sentences.

When you have finished writing down your descriptions, compare notes with your partner and the rest of your classmates. You will probably discover that most people use similar facial expressions for each type of statement. To the degree that this is true, such expressions can serve as symbolic carriers of meaning. Although a speaker cannot read the minds of his listeners, he can read their facial expressions and bodily attitudes (see page 296) which reflect with considerable validity what is going on in those minds.

As a speaker genuinely interested in what you have to say and in its effect upon your listeners, you must sustain a *visual directness*. If you refuse to look at your audience, you have no gauge by which to judge their reactions—no feedback to your message. And if you are oblivious or indifferent to feedback, you cannot possibly make any adjustment to it. When members of an audience see a speaker looking intently at the floor, at the ceiling, or out the window, they sense immediately that he is either ill at ease and/or unconcerned; it is at this point that real, productive interaction is seriously negated.

Learn to talk warmly and directly with the people in your audience. Like you, they are living, breathing personalities; and they will appreciate your treating them as such, rather than as empty chairs or as faceless objects on the periphery of your consciousness. Remember, too, that visual directness is not just a perfunctory turning of your head from side to side, a mere mechanical sweeping back and forth of your glance as if you were watching a tennis match in slow motion. Obviously, you will probably look most closely and frequently at the faces directly before you, but make sure also that from time to time you look into the countenances of those seated toward the back and at the sides of the room. Try always to look at your audience—see them, see their reactions, and respond!

Your listeners are more likely to respond favorably if you speak to them as living personalities rather than as a group of empty chairs.

STUDY PROBE 22
Interpreting Nonverbal Messages

To sharpen your ability to detect and interpret nonverbal messages:

a. Invite a few drama students from your school to your class. Ask them to demonstrate how they would physically portray these emotions on stage: anger, interest, curiosity, disbelief, confusion, etc. Discuss what they do and why you do or don't "read them" as they intend you should.

b. Attend a campus lecture and sit near one side of the audience. Take notes on the audience reactions you observe while the speaker is speaking.

c. While they are working, observe a cashier in a bank, a bartender, a traffic policeman, a lifeguard, or a football coach. Present to your class a discussion of the nonverbal messages they transmit.

If interested in readings on this topic, you could see:

Haig Bosmajian, ed., *The Rhetoric of Nonverbal Communication* (Glenview, Ill.: Scott, Foresman and Company, 1971).

We commented earlier on the preparation of visual aids. When practicing a speech, you should also practice using any visual aids you plan for the speech so you will become accustomed to them. You should learn not to draw on a blackboard while the audience sits looking at your back. You must learn that a good visual aid can be very helpful at one point in a speech, but can be distracting at another. Practice setting up visual aids unobtrusively at the point in the speech where you will need to refer to them, and practice putting them away with a minimum of distraction as you move on.

In practice for formal speaking, then, you should be (1) gaining control over the ideas and the materials of your speech; (2) settling upon and mastering firmly the sequence and coherence of thoughts, points of emphasis, and the meaningfulness of your message; (3) becoming free of reliance upon your manuscript or notes; (4) attempting to instill clarity and vitality in your presentation; and finally, (5) working for a delivery which is not patterned and mechanical but lively and appropriate and reinforced with relevant nonverbal clues.

The Speaker's *Ethos* and the Audience

Having considered the elements and processes of speech planning and speech delivery, let us turn our attention now to *ethos,* an aspect of communication which is involved in and grows out of all of the available choices open to you in assembling a speech. In commenting on *ethos,* or the "character" of the speaker, Aristotle declared:

> *Persuasion is achieved by the speaker's personal character when the speech is so spoken as to make us think him credible. We believe good men more readily than others: this is true generally whatever the question is, and*

absolutely true where exact certainty is impossible and opinions are divided. This kind of persuasion, like the others, should be achieved by what the speaker says, not by what people think of his character before he begins to speak. It is not true, as some writers assume in their treatises on rhetoric, that the personal goodness revealed by the speaker contributes nothing to the power of persuasion; on the contrary, his character may almost be called the most effective means of persuasion he possesses.[7]

Aristotle believed that behaviors exhibited by a speaker, during speaking, were interpreted by listeners as indicating "data" about the speaker's character, intelligence, and good will. He contended that the listeners' "readings" of this "evidence" strongly affected persuasive influence.

Contemporary studies of *ethos* have frequently used the following elements in defining this concept operationally:

Expertness

Trustworthiness

Personal dynamism[8]

Many studies have demonstrated the persuasive influence of credibility, but in most of them credibility was studied as it existed *prior* to the speech event rather than as it was developed *within* and *during* the speech. Prestige is a name for whatever positive or favorable feeling an audience holds toward a speaker *before* he begins to speak. To the degree that a speaker enjoys prestige, he begins his speech with a natural advantage.

But what of the *ethos* of the student speaker who has yet won no special awards and who does not enjoy the advantages of high prestige? Is there any way that he can establish *ethos* during the speaking occasion? What can he do, and begin to do, in his introduction that will cause the listeners to see him as a person who is knowledgeable, trustworthy, and dynamic?

If a speaker has prepared well, if he knows his topic and has chosen material only after much research, if he has organized his speech carefully and practiced it, if he has adapted his speech to his audience and has correctly anticipated audience responses, he is almost sure to demonstrate considerable expertise. If he is well prepared, his materials should be more suitable for the occasion. He should be more confident and at ease, and better able to adapt to audience feedback. With more confidence in himself and his speech, a speaker will be more dynamic in his presentation. He will have greater self-control. A speaker who approaches his research effort and preparation with an open mind can contribute to his topic a more balanced and fairer interpretation—a quality which, in turn, significantly increases audience confidence in his good will and trustworthiness. Full and careful preparation will thus result in a speech and in speech presentation that will do more to establish a speaker's *ethos* than anything else he can do.

There are still other means for developing *ethos*. Frequently, one speaker is introduced by another. The person introducing the speaker should at least have the background information which will be helpful for the audience to know.

[7] Aristotle, *Rhetorica*, trans. W. Rhys Roberts, in *The Basic Works of Aristotle*, ed. Richard McKeon (New York: Random House, Inc., 1941), p. 1329.

[8] David K. Berlo, James B. Lemert, and Robert J. Mertz, "Dimensions for Evaluating the Acceptability of Message Sources," *Public Opinion Quarterly*, XXXIII (1969): 563–576.

(In fact, this is a matter a speaker had better check on if his being introduced is an important part of the speech context.) The speaker can also inject into his own remarks additional information which will help to strengthen the audience's impression of his qualifications and personal attributes. He can do this obliquely or directly, but he should always do it with the proper degree of objectivity. If he has taken the trouble to correspond with the head of some state office about his speech topic, or to interview a professor who is an authority on the subject of his speech, a student speaker can lead into this information with such a remark as:

> In personal correspondence from the State Department X, I found that . . .

> In a personal interview with Professor X, I learned . . .

Remarks such as these provide two kinds of information to an audience. First, they can attach more than the usual significance to a statement. That is, the material being presented derives from a respected authority already established as trustworthy. Second, the statement suggests that the speaker was sufficiently interested in learning about his subject to make an extra effort to locate substantive, reliable information.

STUDY PROBE 23
Establishing Ethos

a. Certain professions tend to suffer from negative stereotypes. Encyclopedia salesmen, automobile salesmen, real-estate promoters—to name but a few —often encounter resistance because people tend to distrust them. In teams of two in front of the class, role play an encounter between one of these salesmen and a potential but distrusting client. Discuss what the role-players did to establish trust. What are the implications for a student speaker? How would you describe this situation in the terms of B-E clusters developed in Chapters 5 and 7?

b. Assume that one of your classmates intends to speak on the subject of "motorcycles." Also assume that you tend generally to trust that classmate already. What would he necessarily need to say to convince you that he is an expert? Suppose the subject were drugs, suicide, abortion, or capitalism. Are there differences among your responses?

In this chapter it has been our intent not to proclaim rigid rules or an inflexible system but to lay out broad, flexible formulations and guidelines to assist you as you go about the tasks of selecting and structuring materials for a speech, incorporating facilitative aids, and practicing your speech in order to effect the most desirable and maximal interaction with your co-agents in the communication context. We have attempted to provide, in some detail, a general approach to the preparation for speech making that has proved helpful to many; we hope that it will prove useful for you as you extend your efforts and experiences in various public communication settings.

These suggestions should be applicable to speech making in almost any of its forms; before large audiences, small audiences, a radio microphone, or a television camera; to a long speech or a short speech. Although they represent the best counsel we can now give, we must emphasize that, in the final application, the speaker-agent must always adapt any system to his own special situation, his own particular abilities, his own judgment.

STUDY PROBE 24
Speech-Making Exercises

Among the speech-making experiences in which you might beneficially engage, consider the following:

a. Write a general topic on a note card and turn it in to your instructor to shuffle with similar cards received from your classmates. Then pick a random card from the "deck" and immediately give a short impromptu speech on the topic noted on the card.

b. Present a short persuasive speech to your class. Have one or two classmates appointed as hecklers. Try not to become involved in lengthy arguments with your hecklers, but do answer any significant objections they may raise—at least to the satisfaction of your other listeners.

c. Plan, practice, and present a twelve-minute speech on some aspect of a contemporary social problem. Arrange a schedule with your instructor during which you discuss your statement of specific purpose, your outline, and any facilitative aids you plan to use.

EVALUATING PUBLIC SPEECH COMMUNICATION: A CHECKLIST

From time to time in the foregoing pages—usually in the Study Probes—we have suggested that you prepare, practice, present, and analyze various kinds of public speeches in class-room settings and elsewhere. Invariably, a twofold task has been stated or implied: speaking *and* listening. In these communicative activities you will at times be functioning as a speaking agent and at other times as a listening agent. Fundamental to these functions—if growth, discernment, and improvement are to be made—is careful *evaluation*. To assist you in making your evaluations we have prepared and class-tested the "Checklist" shown below.

Instructions for Using the Speech Evaluation Checklist

In particular, as you listen and respond to the public speeches of your classmates and others, you will find that the eight component-factors of the Checklist—*Specific Purpose, Introduction, Body, Conclusion, Facilitative Materials, Language Usage, Delivery,* and *Ethos Development* (and their several subelements) can serve usefully as guides to deriving your estimate of the *Overall Effectiveness* of the speech and the interaction which it is intended to create.

In the "Evaluations" column, use ratings from 1 to 7 along a continuum from "needs improvement" (1) to "well done" (7) to indicate your evaluation of the successive component-factors. In the "Comments" column, you should write brief explanatory notes that reflect and amplify the reasons for your ratings. The following marked Sample Checklist will serve to illustrate the way to use this evaluative device and to suggest the types of "Comments" which may prove productive for your analytical purpose. *Unmarked* copies of the Checklist are included in Appendix B, pages 377–384.

SPEECH EVALUATION CHECKLIST

Factors	Evaluations	Comments
1. Specific Purpose		Specific purpose was too broad for a short speech.
Clear and to the point	2	
Appropriately narrowed in scope	2	
Appropriate for listener-agents	6	
Appropriate for context	6	
2. Introduction		Introduction was very effective. It got my interest.
Attention of listener-agents secured	6	
Interest of listener-agents developed	7	
Specific purpose related to listener-agents	7	
3. Body		Too many main points. Except for third point, they were not adequately developed. More examples and illustrations needed.
Main points fulfilled specific purpose	4	
Main points appropriately patterned	6	
Main points emphasized	2	
Main points unified and coherent	3	
Developmental materials varied and helpful	1	
Transitions effective	5	
Internal summaries helpful	5	
4. Conclusion		Conclusion was fairly effective.
Final summary effective	5	
Final appeal appropriate	5	

Factors	Evaluations	Comments
5. Facilitative Materials		*Use of visual aids would have helped speech.*
Visual aids helpful to purpose	1	
Visual aids used effectively	1	
Humor used effectively	5	
6. Language Usage		*Language was generally effective.*
Language clear	6	
Language appropriate to listener-agents	6	*Easy to understand, and appropriate.*
Language appropriate to context	6	
Language vivid	4	
7. Delivery		*Delivery was somewhat monotonous.*
Vocal variety utilized	2	
Pronunciation and articulation appropriate	5	*Try to eliminate vocalized pauses.*
Phrasing and pausing effective	5	*You slumped over lectern and therefore were unable to move freely or use gestures effectively.*
Vocalized pauses avoided	2	
Good posture practiced	2	
Ease of movement demonstrated	2	
Gestures natural	2	
Facial expressiveness varied	6	
8. Ethos Development		*You needed to demonstrate greater expertness and concern for your topic.*
Knowledge demonstrated	2	
Trustworthiness shown	5	
Dynamism/Magnetism shown	2	
OVERALL EFFECTIVENESS	4	*Next speech: Limit main ideas. Prepare developmental materials more carefully. Improve posture by practice.*

Suggested Readings

For more detailed treatments of public speaking the following excellent textbooks are recommended:

Alan H. Monroe and Douglas Ehninger, *Principles and Types of Speech,* 6th ed. (Glenview, Ill.: Scott, Foresman and Company, 1967).

John F. Wilson and Carroll C. Arnold, *Public Speaking as a Liberal Art,* 2nd ed. (Boston: Allyn and Bacon, Inc., 1968).

Donald C. Bryant and Karl Wallace, *Fundamentals of Public Speaking,* 4th ed. (New York: Appleton-Century-Crofts, 1969).

Speech Communication: Projections and Prospects

Throughout this textbook we have pointed to the process of speech communication as the chief available means for achieving cooperative and productive interaction. We defined speech communication, early in Chapter 1, as

> . . . *the socially learned process occurring when two or more persons are interacting by transmitting and receiving visual and auditory stimuli which are treated as symbolic cues to which meaning is attached*

and we closed the chapter by challenging you to seek out and take an active role as a speech communication agent.

Implicitly and explicitly, our definition and our challenge reflect clearly *the unique duality of principle and practice*. We have tried to explicate this duality (1) by presenting and developing theoretical concepts and constructs and (2) by providing practical suggestions for the improvement of your everyday communicative capabilities. We wish now to conclude our considerations by restating within a somewhat eclectic frame of reference the essential duality of principle/practice, and then to reiterate with a slightly different thrust the participatory challenge laid down in our initial chapter.

The Principle/Practice Duality: Some Implications and Extensions

In the tradition of public address there has been a long-standing distinction between "rhetoric" and "oratory." Rhetoric, usually, was defined as the body of *principles* inherent in and applicable to public speaking, whereas oratory was the term given to the *practice* of public speaking. In this tradition Aristotle, for instance, is remembered most as a rhetorician, a "thinker" about principles, who observed and taught the precepts of speaking. Demosthenes, in contrast, is remembered as a "doer"—a practicing speaker or orator. A limited few—Cicero, for example—traveled both paths: writing about the principles and also engaging in the actual practice of speech making as leading spokesmen of their particular eras.

The significance of the principle/practice duality is by no means limited to public speaking. When we are thinking about speech communication of any kind, these multidimensional facets have far-reaching ramifications. Indeed, the necessity of distinguishing between analysis and understanding on the one hand and between activity and performance on the other extends to realms far beyond oral communication. To cite but a few instances, we can draw useful and often necessary distinctions between the study of music theory and the practice of piano playing, between theoretical physics and applied physics, between studying oceanography and catching fish, between the science of agronomy and the practice of farming.

Regardless of the discipline or subject-area involved, the natural division between "thinking about" and "doing" creates certain unavoidable difficulties when anyone attempts to discuss or comprehend both theory and practice in a single presentation—as in this textbook, for instance. Theory and practice are two *aspects* of the same thing; they are like the two sides of a coin. Looking at one necessarily puts the other momentarily out of sight. To depict the "two sides" simultaneously, we would need something like a Picasso portrait to present two aspects of a face on a single plane. Yet principles and practice are probably most clearly comprehended when the understanding of one is tempered by an understanding of the other. Oratory is most genuine when it is influenced by rhetoric, and rhetoric is most meaningful when its postulates are weighed in the light of prevailing practice in oratory.

This textbook has attempted to invite attention to *both* principle and practice. We have tried to interrelate and integrate the two as much as possible. Organizationally, we have tried to accomplish some of this by balancing Part II, primarily an "action/analysis" section, against Part I, a process-and-conceptualizing section; and, further, by balancing Part II and Part V, both centering upon performative/practice concerns, against Parts III and IV, which explore in largely theoretical and conceptual terms the purposes and effects of speaking and the processes of thinking, reasoning, language-labeling, and decision making as they bear upon communicative behavior.

Even so, however, we are constrained by the limitations of one-dimensional *print*. Much of the interrelating of principle and practice can be presented only by suggestion and implication. For example, a careful study of Chapter 7, "Decision Making," should give added import and impact to Chapter 9, "Small Group Discussion." Similar interrelationships abound, but by no means may all of the possible connections be spelled out verbally. If the materials we have presented here are to be most meaningfully integrated, that integration must occur in the one place where it is most likely to have effect—namely, *in the mind and thought processes of the reader.*

Now let us examine the previously reiterated challenge in terms of the principle/practice duality. In contemplating the future of speech communication and projecting our thinking *beyond* the immediate confines of this volume, we may see the challenge to the scholar/practitioner as taking two parallel trajectories: (1) a challenge to locate and learn more about oral communication activity by means of scientific methodology and (2) a challenge to motivate and energize personal, performative skills which will, in turn, ensure communicative participation in and involvement with significant social problems.

A Challenge to Locate and Learn More About General Principles

Much of what we know about speech communication we have tried to present in the foregoing pages of this textbook. If you have read discerningly, you must be well aware that there is still much that is *not* known. How are we to learn more? That is part of the challenge. Thoughtful introspection and general observation will, in part, help us meet it. Most of the Study Probes in the successive chapters invite you to learn more by these means. But to study speech communication scientifically—applying scientific attitudes, values, and methods in *research*—is of pressing importance if we are to avoid carrying on too much of our communication by intuition, mere guesswork, or superficial judgment. Over the past three or four decades, the application of what may be called "social science" or "behavioral science" to speech communication has provided us with some highly useful and productive ways of gaining understandings of human communicative activity.

This method of scientific inquiry is characterized by three essential phases:

1. Observation and description.

2. Explanation.

3. Testing.

The first phase involves the careful observation and description of the particular phenomena under study. The second phase, explanation by means of hypothesis and theory, follows closely upon the first and is developed from it. The third and final phase involves the testing of the proposed hypothesis and theory.

As we apply the successive steps of this methodology to our knowledge about speech communication, we can readily see that much investigation is still to be made. We need, for instance, many carefully *descrip-*

tive studies of speech communication phenomena: How can we observe and perceptively describe what occurs when two people converse? What indicators do we have that their interaction is really meaningful and mutually influencing rather than being solely ritualized social behavior? What variables are important in such engagement? How do we describe and categorize them?

Further, when we have learned how to observe keenly and to describe accurately the results of such observations, how can we best formulate consistent and valid *theoretical explanations* for them? What general explanations will account for what we "know" about speech communication and, at the same time, lead us to an awareness of previously untapped nuances of our subject? And finally, of course, we need extensive, thoroughgoing research to *test* the explanations that are being generated by research—and which will continue to be generated.

Although this textbook is aimed primarily at improving and enlarging your understanding of the principles of speech communication and their practical application, an *additional* development greatly to be desired is that at least a few of you will feel sufficiently challenged to want to involve yourselves in the kind of research we have been describing. By reason of such involvement, we believe, you might well contribute improved descriptions of the speech process, more accurate explanations of communicative effects, and more painstaking testing of theoretical approaches to human interaction. There is much to be done, and room for many to do it.

A Challenge to Personal, Performative Involvement

Much of what we have included in these pages has been intended to motivate, encourage, and enable you to become a more active and skillful communication agent. There are of course those who, when they consider the influential uses of speech, think first of public speech making. In these ten chapters we have attempted to modify that somewhat restricted conception by stressing the importance of what one agent may accomplish by working in interpersonal and small group contexts. We have also stressed the general necessity for thoughtful analysis, positive activity, and acquiring knowledge about other agents and contexts as we find them in all kinds of orally communicative endeavors. To be effective as both listeners and speakers we must understand and be sensitive to these necessities in every speech encounter.

Some individuals refrain from speaking because they fear that their contribution will not be considered helpful or that the effects of their speaking will be minimal at best. William James wrote about a man stranded on a mountainside during a blizzard. Alternative pathways are occasionally visible to him through the swirling snow—some leading to possible safety in the valley below, others continuing along the precipitous, ice-covered ledge and leading to almost certain death. The choice, clearly, is an urgent and fateful one. In it we can find an important analogy for ourselves: Which path should we take when we cannot be sure of the outcome? As individuals we may, of course, refuse to make a choice: we may stand still. But, as James points out, inaction *in itself* represents a decision—a choice which, in the case of the mountain climber, would also lead to death. What we are saying here is that as human beings and as communicators we must be prepared always to accept the consequences of our *inactions* as well as of our actions.

We hope that as a result of your working through this volume you will be somewhat better prepared to make useful and informed decisions and that you will have greater ability, awareness, and confidence as you try actively to exert positive influence upon your fellow beings and interact with them in an ever widening range of speech communication contexts. This is our challenge to you.

THE DIMENSIONS OF A COMPLETE LIFE

*A speech given by Martin Luther King, Jr.,
on November 13, 1960, in Sage Chapel
at Cornell University, Ithaca, New York**

Martin Luther King, Jr.

THE DIMENSIONS OF A COMPLETE LIFE

I need not pause to say how very delighted I am to be here today and to be on the campus of this historic institution. I have looked forward to the opportunity of coming to Cornell for a long, long time, and I can assure you that it is a great privilege and pleasure for me to be here. I only regret that an extremely crowded schedule makes it necessary for me to make my visit rather brief. But I do hope that in this brief period I will have the opportunity of meeting many of you.   /1

I would like to use as the subject from which to preach this morning "The Dimensions of a Complete Life." Many, many centuries ago a man by the name of John was in prison out on a lonely, obscure island called Patmos. While in this situation John imagined that he saw the New Jerusalem descending out of heaven from God. One of the greatest glories of this new city of God that John saw was its completeness. It was not partial and one-sided, but it was complete in all three of its dimensions. So, in describing the city John says—in the Book of Revelation—"The length and the breadth and the height of it are equal." In other words, this new city of God, this city of ideal humanity, is not an unbalanced entity, but it is complete on all sides.   /2

Now, John is saying something quite significant here. For so many of us the Book of Revelation is a difficult book, puzzling to decode. We see it as something of an enigma, wrapped in mystery. Certainly, if we accept everything in the Book of Revelation as actually true or if we accept this as the record of actual historical occurrences, it is a difficult book, shrouded with impenetrable mysteries. But if we will look beneath the peculiar jargon of the author, beneath what Biblical theologians would call the prevailing apocalyptic symbolism, we will find in that book many eternal truths which forever challenge us.   /3

And one such truth is the truth of this text. For what John is saying is really this: that life at its best—and life as it should be—is a life that is complete on all sides. So there are three dimensions of any complete life to which we can fittingly give the words of this text: *length, breadth,* and *height.*   /4

Now, the *length* of life as we shall use it here is not its duration, not its longevity. It is rather the push of a life forward to achieve its ambitions and personal ends. This is the inward concern for one's welfare. The *breadth* of life as we shall use it here is the outward concern for the welfare of others, and the *height* of life is the upward reach for God. These are the three dimensions of life which must be coordinated if the life is to be complete. On the one hand, there is the individual person; on the other hand, there are other persons; and there is the infinite, supreme person—God. And these three must be incorporated in every life if that life is to be complete, because complete life is the three-dimensional life.   **/5**

Let us begin with the first dimension; namely, the length of life. I have said this is the dimension in which the individual is concerned with developing his inner powers. To a degree, this is the selfish dimension of life. There is such a thing as rational and healthy self-interest, even moral self-interest; for if an individual is not concerned about himself, he cannot be really concerned about other selves. Some years ago a brilliant Jewish rabbi, the late Joshua Liebman, wrote a book entitled *Peace of Mind*. He has a chapter in that book entitled "Love Thyself Properly." He says, in substance, in that chapter that before we can love other selves adequately, we must love our own selves properly; and many individuals have been plunged into the abyss of emotional fatalism because they didn't love themselves properly. So we have a legitimate right to start out in life with healthy and moral self-interest.   **/6**

This dimension of length means that we must be concerned about ourselves to the point that we set out to discover what we are made for, what we are called to do; and after discovering that life's work, we set out to do it with all of the power and all of the strength and dedication that we can muster up. There is within all of us something of a center of creativity, and we have the responsibility of discovering that center of creativity. And once we discover it, we must set out to do it so well that the living, the dead, or the unborn couldn't do it better. Man should seek to do his life's work as if God Almighty called him at this particular moment in history to do it.   **/7**

To carry this to one extreme, if it falls your lot to be a street sweeper, you should seek to sweep streets like Raphael painted pictures or like Michelangelo carved marble. You should seek to sweep streets like Shakespeare wrote poetry, or like Beethoven composed music. Sweep streets so well that all the hosts of heaven and earth will have to pause and say "Here lived a great street sweeper who swept his job well." This is what Douglas Malloch meant when he said:

> *If you can't be a pine on the top of a hill,*
> *Be a shrub in the valley,*
> *But be the best little shrub on the side of the rill;*
> *Be a bush, if you can't be a tree.*
>
> *If you can't be a highway, just be a trail.*
> *If you can't be the sun, be a star;*
> *For it isn't by size that you win or fail.*
> *Be the best of whatever you are.*

This inner discovery—this determined push to the end of self-realization and self-fulfillment—is the length of one's life.   **/8**

But we must not stop here. Some people never get beyond the length of life. They discover early the basic bent of their lives in terms of their professions or their vocations. They develop these to a brilliant extent, but they live as if nobody else lives in the world but themselves. And there is nothing more tragic than to find an individual bogged down in the length of life, but devoid of the breadth. For when the individual does this, he uses other persons as means to his end. Other persons become mere steps by which he climbs to his inner ambitions and personal ends. If life is to be complete, it must move on; not only must it have length, but it must have breadth. The breadth of life is the outward concern for the welfare of others. And I submit to you this morning that an individual hasn't begun to live unless he can rise above the narrow confines of his individualistic concerns to the broader concerns of all humanity. **/9**

One day a man went to Jesus. He raised some very interesting questions. He was concerned about eternal life. Finally he got around to the question, "Who is my neighbor?" This question could have very easily ended in the abstract, could have very easily ended in a philosophical debate. Jesus immediately pulled that question out of midair and placed it on a dangerous curve between Jerusalem and Jericho. He talked about a certain man who fell among thieves. We all know the story. It is a familiar parable. Three men passed; two of them passed by on the other side— the priest and the Levite. Finally, the man of another race came by, and he stopped and helped the man and administered first aid. Jesus said, in substance, that this was the good man. This Samaritan was a great man because he had the capacity to project the "I" into the "Thou." **/10**

So often in reading this parable, realizing that it is a parable, we use the imagination a bit and try to think of reasons why the priest and the Levite passed on the other side. Sometimes we say that they were busy carrying out ecclesiastical responsibilities and they had to hurry; they didn't have time to stop because they had heavy schedules. And so they might have felt that the responsibilities ahead were much greater than the responsibility of stopping for the moment to help this man on the Jericho road. It is even possible that they were going down to Jericho to organize a Jericho-Road-Improvement Association. That's a real possibility. **/11**

There's another thing that I think about when I think of this Jericho-road experience. It's possible that they passed by on the other side and failed to stop to help the man because they were *afraid*. This is a real possibility. You see, the Jericho road is a dangerous road. A few months ago Mrs. King and I were in Jerusalem, and we rented a car and drove down to Jericho, and I never will forget the experience of riding around this meandering road, this road full of curves. And I said to myself, I can see why Jesus used this road as the occasion, or rather the setting, for his parable because it's a dangerous road. It's very conducive for robbery. Here is Jerusalem some twenty-six hundred feet above sea level; and here is Jericho more than twelve hundred feet below sea level. And you go this distance within about fifteen or sixteen miles around this meandering, dangerous road. It's certainly possible that the robbers were still around; and if the priest and the Levite stopped, the robbers could have done something to them. Or maybe the man on the ground was faking, and he was just there to fool them over, and then would— in turn—rob them. **/12**

These are things that we think about on the various Jericho roads of life. Sometime when you're driving your car at night and someone seeks to stop you, the first thing that you think about is that this may be a person to do me harm, and the tendency is to keep going. Well, this is a real possibility—that the priest and the Levite found themselves in a state of fear. In other words, the first question that the Levite raised and the first question that the priest raised was this: "If I stop to help this man, what will happen to me?" Then the good Samaritan came by, and by the nature of his concern reversed the question, "If I do not stop to help this man, what will happen to him?" **/13**

And so this was a good man because he had the mental equipment and the moral capacity for a dangerous altruism. He was a great man because he could surround the length of his life with the breadth of life. He was great not only because he had ascended to the heights of economic security, but because he could condescend to the depth of human need. This is always a challenging opportunity of life—that of adding breadth to length.   /14

I think this text has a great deal of bearing on the racial crisis which we confront in our nation today. I'm convinced that many of the problems that we face in the Southland today are due to the fact that there are some white brothers among us who are concerned merely about the length of life—their preferred, privileged economic positions, their political power, their social status, their so-called "way of life." If only they would add breadth to length, the other-regarding dimension to the self-regarding dimension, we would be able to transform the jangling discords of the South into a beautiful symphony of spiritual harmony.   /15

Now, this also applies to those who are seeking to break loose from the yoke of oppression. They, too, must incorporate breadth. Those who have been on the oppressed end of the old order must be concerned with more than length. Because if they are concerned only about length, they will seek merely to gain their rights—and seek to gain their rights at any cost. And this is why I believe so firmly in nonviolence, because nonviolence takes under consideration the other person also. It takes under consideration the fact that you do not seek to annihilate the opponent, but to convert him. Therefore, as the Negro struggles for his rights in the United States, as colored people struggle for freedom and human dignity all over the world, it is necessary to add breadth to length.   /16

So the aim of oppressed groups must not be to defeat or humiliate the white man, but to win his friendship and understanding. Yes, we must work passionately and unrelentingly for first-class citizenship. We must never use second-class methods to gain it. And, therefore, we must never seek to rise from a position of disadvantage to one of advantage, thus subverting justice. So we will realize that a philosophy of Black Supremacy is as dangerous as White Supremacy. For God is not interested merely in the freedom of black men and brown men and yellow men, but in the interests of freedom of the whole human race. And so one day we will discover that we must seek to create a society of white men and black men, Jews and gentiles, Protestants and Catholics, where all men live together as brothers, and where every man will respect the dignity and worth of all human personality. This is essentially what the breadth of life tells us.   /17

Now, not only does this text apply in our particular situation in the United States, but it also has a great deal of bearing on the international crisis. I am convinced that colonialism came into being because some nations were concerned only about their self-interests—the length of life. So they ended up dominating people politically, exploiting them economically, segregating and humiliating them. And so many of the problems which we face in the world today we face because some nations have been concerned about length and not about breadth. Now, this dimension of breadth is reminding us that we must be concerned about all nations, and every nation must come to see now that it is dependent upon every other nation and that we must learn to live together.   /18

It was my good fortune some few months ago to journey to that great country in the Far East known as India. Mrs. King and I went over together, and we will never forget the great and lasting experience of going to that great country, talking with the leaders of government and with the people all over in the villages and cities of India. And certainly I will remember this experience as long as the chords of memory shall lengthen.   /19

I must also say that there were those depressing moments. For how can one avoid being depressed when he sees with his own eyes millions of people going to bed hungry at night? How can one avoid being concerned when he sees with his own eyes millions of people sleeping on the sidewalks at night? In Calcutta alone, more than a million people sleep on the sidewalks at night. In Bombay more than 600 thousand people sleep on the sidewalks every night. How can one avoid being concerned when he discovers that out of India's population of almost 400 million people, more than 325 million of these people make an annual income of less than $50 a year? Most of them have never seen a doctor or a dentist. Many of these conditions exist because these people have been dominated politically and exploited economically across the years.   **/20**

And as I watched these conditions and as I watched other conditions of poverty in Africa and South America this past summer, I found myself saying, "Can we in America stand idly by and not be concerned?" And something within me cried out, "Oh, no! Because the destiny of the United States is tied up with the destiny of India, with the destiny of Africa, with the destiny of South America!" And I had to think about the fact that we in the United States spend millions of dollars a day to store surplus food, and I found myself saying, "I know where we can store that food free of charge—in the wrinkled stomachs of the hungry people all over this world." We must use our vast resources and wealth to aid these undeveloped countries. And maybe in the United States we've spent too much of our money establishing military bases around the world, rather than bases of genuine concern and understanding.   **/21**

All I'm saying is simply this: All life is interrelated, and we are caught in an inescapable network of mutuality, tied in a single garment of destiny. And so whatever affects one individual directly, affects all indirectly. Whatever affects one nation directly, affects every nation indirectly. So long as there is poverty in this world, and millions of people go to bed hungry at night, you can never be totally rich even if you have a billion dollars. As long as diseases are rampant, and millions of people cannot expect to live more than twenty-eight, or thirty, or thirty-two years, you can never be totally healthy even if you have just got a perfect bill of health from Mayo Clinic or Johns Hopkins Hospital, or what have you.   **/22**

I can never be what I ought to be until you are what you ought to be. This is the way the world is made. John Donne caught this idea years ago and placed it in graphic terms: "No man is an island, entire of itself. Every man is a piece of the continent, a part of the main." And then he goes on—toward the end—to say: "Any man's death diminishes me because I am involved in mankind. Therefore, never send to know for whom the bell tolls; it tolls for thee." When one recognizes this—lives by this principle—that individual has mastered the second dimension of life.   **/23**

Again, however, we must not stop here. There is another dimension. Some people never get beyond the first two dimensions. They master their inner powers; they are often brilliant people. They go to the point of developing a real concern for humanity, a real love for humanity. But they stop right here. They seek to live life without a sky. It seems to me that if life is to be complete, one must reach up beyond his self-interests. One must reach up beyond humanity and discover God, the *height* of life.   **/24**

In our modern world we have neglected this third dimension of life a great deal. For many reasons, we have sought to live on the horizontal plane without any concern for the vertical plane. There are many reasons why we have neglected this third dimension. Sometimes people have done it honestly; they've had honest doubts. They have often looked out in life. They've noticed the glaring, colossal reality of evil—that something that the poet Keats calls "the giant agony of the world." They have found themselves asking, "How can an all-powerful God who is at the same time a concerned, a loving, a good God allow all of this evil to exist?" Sometimes they have found it difficult to square their intellectual world views with the often crude and primitive ideas of God that exist, and the sometimes unscientific dogmas of religion.   /25

Then there are others who have watched people who say they believe in God. They've watched organized religion, and they've seen organized religion—as something to crystallize the status quo. And so, because so many people who claim they believe in God live so far contrary to the will of God, they have lost interest in even cultivating a belief in God. So there are those people who for honest, intellectual reasons have neglected this third dimension.   /26

But I imagine that most people fit into another category altogether. They have not denied God's existence theoretically. I would imagine that most people have just done it from a practical point of view. They have lived as if there is no God. They have become so involved in the things of life, they have become so involved in the man-made things about them, that they have unconsciously come to believe that only *things* have reality. So we find ourselves at once living in what Professor Sorokin, formerly of Harvard University, called "sensate civilization"—believing that only those things that we can see and touch and apply our five senses to have existence.   /27

In spite of our doubts, we still feel another order constantly impinging upon us. In spite of our theoretical denials, we continue to have spiritual experiences in life: sometimes—in the aesthetic realm—the beauty of great music, the beauty of nature, the love for a child, and many other things. We continue having these spiritual experiences that cannot be explained in materialistic terms.   /28

In spite of our inordinate worship of things, something constantly reminds us that the unseen is real. We go out at night and look up at the beautiful stars as they bedeck the heavens like swinging lanterns of eternity. At once we think we see all, but then something comes to remind us that we don't see all. We can never see the law of gravitation that holds them there. We come on this beautiful campus, and we look at this beautiful chapel and these beautiful buildings around, and we think we see all at once. But, oh no, we can never see the mind of the architect who drew the blueprint, and never see the love and the faith and the hope of the individuals who made these buildings possible. Well, I'm sure you're saying this morning, "We see Martin Luther King because he's preaching to us." Well, I hate to disappoint you. You see my body, but you don't see my mind; you don't see my personality; you can never see the "me" which makes me *me*.   /29

So, in a sense, everything that we see is a shadow cast by that which we do not see. Maybe Plato was right: "The visible is a shadow cast by the invisible." Even though we can't see God, He may still be around. And all of our new knowledge—and we must seek to gain it at every point—all of our new knowledge can banish God neither from the microcosmic compass of the atom, nor from the vast, unfathomable ranges of interstellar space. Living in a universe in which we are forced to measure stellar distance in light years, confronted with the illimitable expanse of the solar system, in which stars are five-hundred-million million miles from the earth, in which heavenly bodies travel at incredible speed, and in which the ages of planets are reckoned in terms of billions of years, modern man is forced to cry out with the psalmists of old: "When I behold the heavens, the moon and the stars, and all that Thou has created, what is man that Thou art mindful of him, and the son of man that Thou remember him?" And so maybe the height of life is still a reality in our scientific age. And, therefore, I say that we must seek to cultivate this dimension. When an individual discovers the power that comes with this, he moves through life with new meaning.   **/30**

There is something in this universe—a creative power—call it what you may. Maybe you would prefer, with Whitehead, to call it a "principle of concretion." Maybe, with Paul Tillich, you would call it "being itself"; maybe, with Henry Nelson Wyman, "a process of integration"; maybe, with Jan Smuts, "a principle of wholism." Whatever you call it, there is a power—a creative force—in this universe working at every moment to bring low prodigious hilltops of evil and to pull down gigantic mountains of opposition. And so as we work for righteousness, as we work for goodness—yes, as we work for integration in the United States—we do not struggle alone. We have cosmic companionship. For there is something in the universe which justifies Carlyle in saying, "No lie can live forever." There is something in this universe which justifies William Cullen Bryant in saying, "Truth crushed to earth will rise again." And there is something in this universe which justifies James Russell Lowell in saying, "Truth forever on the scaffold/ Wrong forever on the throne/ Yet that scaffold sways the future/ And behind the dim unknown/ Standeth God within the shadow/ Keeping watch above his own." And so this is it. This is the power; this is the faith that can keep us going. Saint Augustine was right: "We were made for God, and we will be restless until we find rest in Him."   **/31**

Love yourselves. That means rational and healthy self-interest. You are commanded to do that. And that is the length of life. Love your neighbor as you love yourself. You are commanded to do that. That is the breadth of life. But never forget that there is the first and even greater commandment, "Love the Lord thy God with all thy heart and with all thy soul and with all thy mind." This is the height of life. And when you achieve these three, you have developed a complete life.   **/32**

Thank God for John, who centuries ago caught a vision of the New Jerusalem, and grant that we will catch a vision of this and decide to move forward to that city of complete life in which the length and the breadth and the height are equal. Whenever we decide to do this collectively, figuratively speaking, the morning stars will sing together, and the sons of God will shout for joy.   **/33**

Eternal God, our Father, we thank Thee for the inspiration of the ages. We thank Thee for Jesus who came to show us the way, for the prophets of the ages, for the saints of the ages; and grant that we will follow their insights, and seek to develop this three-fold integration: Integration with ourselves, integration with our neighbors, and integration with Thee, so that our lives will be complete. In the name and Spirit of Jesus we pray. Amen.   **/34**

Appendix B
Self-Assessment Scales and Evaluative Forms

(Note: *All forms in the ensuing section are perforated to facilitate removal, exchange, and/or handing them in to the course instructor.*)

SPEECH COMMUNICATION ASSESSMENT SCALES

The following scales are designed to help you assess your probable reactions in various speech communication settings. The desired method of marking the scales and the procedure by which to make your assessment are demonstrated in the sample scale immediately below and in the explanation which follows it.

SPEAKING WITH A SMALL CHILD

a.	Relaxed	(7)	6	5	4	3	2	1	Tense
b.	Pleasant	7	6	5	4	(3)	2	1	Unpleasant
c.	Informative	7	6	5	(4)	3	2	1	Not Informative
d.	Stimulating	7	6	(5)	4	3	2	1	Boring
e.	Self-fulfilling	7	6	5	4	3	(2)	1	Not Self-fulfilling

First, try to imagine yourself in the situation described in the title (in the sample scale, "Speaking with a Small Child"). Then, for each of the five listed responses (a, b, c, d, e) circle the number (7, 6, 5, 4, 3, 2, 1) in the response-continuum range which best describes how you think you would feel in the designated speech communication situation.

If, for example, the descriptive term at the left end of the scale (Relaxed) *describes your feelings completely,* then circle the number 7; if the descriptive term at the right end of the scale (Tense) describes your feelings most accurately, circle the number 1.

If one of the terms *describes your feelings fairly well,* but not completely, then circle the number 6 or 2, one scale position away from the term.

If one of the terms *describes your feelings only somewhat,* but better than does the other term, then circle the number 5 or 3, two scale positions away from the appropriate term.

If neither term at the ends of the response-continuum scale seems appropriate, or if both terms *describe your feelings equally,* then circle the number 4.

In the sample scale above, the respondent would describe his experience in speaking with a small child as completely relaxing, somewhat stimulating, somewhat unpleasant, for the most part not self-fulfilling, and neither especially informative nor especially uninformative.

Now try to imagine yourself in each of the twenty-four speech communication situations listed below. For each of the items (a, b, c, d, e) in each of the twenty-four situations, indicate on the response-continuum range (7, 6, 5, 4, 3, 2, 1) your numerical assessment, as explained above, of the feelings that you believe you would experience in the designated situation.

There are no correct or incorrect responses. Try only to estimate in each instance how you believe you would feel in the given circumstance. After you have filled out these scales, you will score them on the basis of your numerical responses, and in accordance with the instructions on page 60. From this score you will be able to appraise your expected performance in each of the areas covered. This can provide a positive first step toward "knowing yourself" as a communicative agent.

1. TALKING WITH YOUR FATHER ABOUT YOUR FUTURE PLANS

a.	Relaxed	7	6	5	4	3	2	1	Tense
b.	Pleasant	7	6	5	4	3	2	1	Unpleasant
c.	Informative	7	6	5	4	3	2	1	Not Informative
d.	Stimulating	7	6	5	4	3	2	1	Boring
e.	Self-fulfilling	7	6	5	4	3	2	1	Not Self-fulfilling

2. RECEIVING A CRITICISM FROM YOUR MOTHER

a.	Relaxed	7	6	5	4	3	2	1	Tense
b.	Pleasant	7	6	5	4	3	2	1	Unpleasant
c.	Informative	7	6	5	4	3	2	1	Not Informative
d.	Stimulating	7	6	5	4	3	2	1	Boring
e.	Self-fulfilling	7	6	5	4	3	2	1	Not Self-fulfilling

3. DISCUSSING CURRENT WORLD EVENTS WITH A CLOSE FRIEND OF THE SAME SEX

a.	Relaxed	7	6	5	4	3	2	1	Tense
b.	Pleasant	7	6	5	4	3	2	1	Unpleasant
c.	Informative	7	6	5	4	3	2	1	Not Informative
d.	Stimulating	7	6	5	4	3	2	1	Boring
e.	Self-fulfilling	7	6	5	4	3	2	1	Not Self-fulfilling

4. CONVERSING WITH A CLOSE FRIEND OF THE OPPOSITE SEX AT A SOCIAL AFFAIR

a.	Relaxed	7	6	5	4	3	2	1	Tense
b.	Pleasant	7	6	5	4	3	2	1	Unpleasant
c.	Informative	7	6	5	4	3	2	1	Not Informative
d.	Stimulating	7	6	5	4	3	2	1	Boring
e.	Self-fulfilling	7	6	5	4	3	2	1	Not Self-fulfilling

5. TALKING WITH A CLOSE FRIEND OF THE OPPOSITE SEX ABOUT YOUR FUTURE PLANS

a.	Relaxed	7	6	5	4	3	2	1	Tense
b.	Pleasant	7	6	5	4	3	2	1	Unpleasant
c.	Informative	7	6	5	4	3	2	1	Not Informative
d.	Stimulating	7	6	5	4	3	2	1	Boring
e.	Self-fulfilling	7	6	5	4	3	2	1	Not Self-fulfilling

name_____

6. RECEIVING A CRITICISM FROM A CLOSE FRIEND
OF THE OPPOSITE SEX

a.	Relaxed	7	6	5	4	3	2	1	Tense
b.	Pleasant	7	6	5	4	3	2	1	Unpleasant
c.	Informative	7	6	5	4	3	2	1	Not Informative
d.	Stimulating	7	6	5	4	3	2	1	Boring
e.	Self-fulfilling	7	6	5	4	3	2	1	Not Self-fulfilling

7. DISCUSSING CURRENT WORLD EVENTS WITH A JOB SUPERVISOR

a.	Relaxed	7	6	5	4	3	2	1	Tense
b.	Pleasant	7	6	5	4	3	2	1	Unpleasant
c.	Informative	7	6	5	4	3	2	1	Not Informative
d.	Stimulating	7	6	5	4	3	2	1	Boring
e.	Self-fulfilling	7	6	5	4	3	2	1	Not Self-fulfilling

8. CONVERSING WITH A TEACHER AT A SOCIAL AFFAIR

a.	Relaxed	7	6	5	4	3	2	1	Tense
b.	Pleasant	7	6	5	4	3	2	1	Unpleasant
c.	Informative	7	6	5	4	3	2	1	Not Informative
d.	Stimulating	7	6	5	4	3	2	1	Boring
e.	Self-fulfilling	7	6	5	4	3	2	1	Not Self-fulfilling

9. TALKING WITH YOUR MOTHER ABOUT YOUR FUTURE PLANS

a.	Relaxed	7	6	5	4	3	2	1	Tense
b.	Pleasant	7	6	5	4	3	2	1	Unpleasant
c.	Informative	7	6	5	4	3	2	1	Not Informative
d.	Stimulating	7	6	5	4	3	2	1	Boring
e.	Self-fulfilling	7	6	5	4	3	2	1	Not Self-fulfilling

10. RECEIVING A CRITICISM FROM A TEACHER

a.	Relaxed	7	6	5	4	3	2	1	Tense
b.	Pleasant	7	6	5	4	3	2	1	Unpleasant
c.	Informative	7	6	5	4	3	2	1	Not Informative
d.	Stimulating	7	6	5	4	3	2	1	Boring
e.	Self-fulfilling	7	6	5	4	3	2	1	Not Self-fulfilling

11. DISCUSSING CURRENT WORLD EVENTS WITH YOUR FATHER

a.	Relaxed	7	6	5	4	3	2	1	Tense
b.	Pleasant	7	6	5	4	3	2	1	Unpleasant
c.	Informative	7	6	5	4	3	2	1	Not Informative
d.	Stimulating	7	6	5	4	3	2	1	Boring
e.	Self-fulfilling	7	6	5	4	3	2	1	Not Self-fulfilling

12. CONVERSING WITH YOUR MOTHER AT A SOCIAL AFFAIR

a.	Relaxed	7	6	5	4	3	2	1	Tense
b.	Pleasant	7	6	5	4	3	2	1	Unpleasant
c.	Informative	7	6	5	4	3	2	1	Not Informative
d.	Stimulating	7	6	5	4	3	2	1	Boring
e.	Self-fulfilling	7	6	5	4	3	2	1	Not Self-fulfilling

13. TALKING WITH A CLOSE FRIEND OF THE SAME SEX ABOUT YOUR FUTURE PLANS

a.	Relaxed	7	6	5	4	3	2	1	Tense.
b.	Pleasant	7	6	5	4	3	2	1	Unpleasant
c.	Informative	7	6	5	4	3	2	1	Not Informative
d.	Stimulating	7	6	5	4	3	2	1	Boring
e.	Self-fulfilling	7	6	5	4	3	2	1	Not Self-fulfilling

14. RECEIVING A CRITICISM FROM YOUR FATHER

a.	Relaxed	7	6	5	4	3	2	1	Tense
b.	Pleasant	7	6	5	4	3	2	1	Unpleasant
c.	Informative	7	6	5	4	3	2	1	Not Informative
d.	Stimulating	7	6	5	4	3	2	1	Boring
e.	Self-fulfilling	7	6	5	4	3	2	1	Not Self-fulfilling

15. DISCUSSING CURRENT WORLD EVENTS WITH A TEACHER

a.	Relaxed	7	6	5	4	3	2	1	Tense
b.	Pleasant	7	6	5	4	3	2	1	Unpleasant
c.	Informative	7	6	5	4	3	2	1	Not Informative
d.	Stimulating	7	6	5	4	3	2	1	Boring
e.	Self-fulfilling	7	6	5	4	3	2	1	Not Self-fulfilling

16. CONVERSING WITH A CLOSE FRIEND OF THE SAME SEX AT A SOCIAL AFFAIR

a.	Relaxed	7	6	5	4	3	2	1	Tense
b.	Pleasant	7	6	5	4	3	2	1	Unpleasant
c.	Informative	7	6	5	4	3	2	1	Not Informative
d.	Stimulating	7	6	5	4	3	2	1	Boring
e.	Self-fulfilling	7	6	5	4	3	2	1	Not Self-fulfilling

17. TALKING WITH A JOB SUPERVISOR ABOUT YOUR FUTURE PLANS

a.	Relaxed	7	6	5	4	3	2	1	Tense
b.	Pleasant	7	6	5	4	3	2	1	Unpleasant
c.	Informative	7	6	5	4	3	2	1	Not Informative
d.	Stimulating	7	6	5	4	3	2	1	Boring
e.	Self-fulfilling	7	6	5	4	3	2	1	Not Self-fulfilling

18. RECEIVING A CRITICISM FROM A JOB SUPERVISOR

a.	Relaxed	7	6	5	4	3	2	1	Tense
b.	Pleasant	7	6	5	4	3	2	1	Unpleasant
c.	Informative	7	6	5	4	3	2	1	Not Informative
d.	Stimulating	7	6	5	4	3	2	1	Boring
e.	Self-fulfilling	7	6	5	4	3	2	1	Not Self-fulfilling

19. DISCUSSING CURRENT WORLD EVENTS WITH YOUR MOTHER

a.	Relaxed	7	6	5	4	3	2	1	Tense
b.	Pleasant	7	6	5	4	3	2	1	Unpleasant
c.	Informative	7	6	5	4	3	2	1	Not Informative
d.	Stimulating	7	6	5	4	3	2	1	Boring
e.	Self-fulfilling	7	6	5	4	3	2	1	Not Self-fulfilling

20. CONVERSING WITH A JOB SUPERVISOR AT A SOCIAL AFFAIR

a.	Relaxed	7	6	5	4	3	2	1	Tense
b.	Pleasant	7	6	5	4	3	2	1	Unpleasant
c.	Informative	7	6	5	4	3	2	1	Not Informative
d.	Stimulating	7	6	5	4	3	2	1	Boring
e.	Self-fulfilling	7	6	5	4	3	2	1	Not Self-fulfilling

21. TALKING WITH A TEACHER ABOUT YOUR FUTURE PLANS

a.	Relaxed	7	6	5	4	3	2	1	Tense
b.	Pleasant	7	6	5	4	3	2	1	Unpleasant
c.	Informative	7	6	5	4	3	2	1	Not Informative
d.	Stimulating	7	6	5	4	3	2	1	Boring
e.	Self-fulfilling	7	6	5	4	3	2	1	Not Self-fulfilling

22. RECEIVING A CRITICISM FROM A CLOSE FRIEND OF THE SAME SEX

a.	Relaxed	7	6	5	4	3	2	1	Tense
b.	Pleasant	7	6	5	4	3	2	1	Unpleasant
c.	Informative	7	6	5	4	3	2	1	Not Informative
d.	Stimulating	7	6	5	4	3	2	1	Boring
e.	Self-fulfilling	7	6	5	4	3	2	1	Not Self-fulfilling

23. DISCUSSING CURRENT WORLD EVENTS WITH A CLOSE FRIEND OF THE OPPOSITE SEX

a.	Relaxed	7	6	5	4	3	2	1	Tense
b.	Pleasant	7	6	5	4	3	2	1	Unpleasant
c.	Informative	7	6	5	4	3	2	1	Not Informative
d.	Stimulating	7	6	5	4	3	2	1	Boring
e.	Self-fulfilling	7	6	5	4	3	2	1	Not Self-fulfilling

24. CONVERSING WITH YOUR FATHER AT A SOCIAL AFFAIR

a.	Relaxed	7	6	5	4	3	2	1	Tense
b.	Pleasant	7	6	5	4	3	2	1	Unpleasant
c.	Informative	7	6	5	4	3	2	1	Not Informative
d.	Stimulating	7	6	5	4	3	2	1	Boring
e.	Self-fulfilling	7	6	5	4	3	2	1	Not Self-fulfilling

1. TALKING WITH YOUR FATHER ABOUT YOUR FUTURE PLANS

a.	Relaxed	7	6	5	4	3	2	1	Tense
b.	Pleasant	7	6	5	4	3	2	1	Unpleasant
c.	Informative	7	6	5	4	3	2	1	Not Informative
d.	Stimulating	7	6	5	4	3	2	1	Boring
e.	Self-fulfilling	7	6	5	4	3	2	1	Not Self-fulfilling

2. RECEIVING A CRITICISM FROM YOUR MOTHER

a.	Relaxed	7	6	5	4	3	2	1	Tense
b.	Pleasant	7	6	5	4	3	2	1	Unpleasant
c.	Informative	7	6	5	4	3	2	1	Not Informative
d.	Stimulating	7	6	5	4	3	2	1	Boring
e.	Self-fulfilling	7	6	5	4	3	2	1	Not Self-fulfilling

3. DISCUSSING CURRENT WORLD EVENTS WITH A CLOSE FRIEND OF THE SAME SEX

a.	Relaxed	7	6	5	4	3	2	1	Tense
b.	Pleasant	7	6	5	4	3	2	1	Unpleasant
c.	Informative	7	6	5	4	3	2	1	Not Informative
d.	Stimulating	7	6	5	4	3	2	1	Boring
e.	Self-fulfilling	7	6	5	4	3	2	1	Not Self-fulfilling

4. CONVERSING WITH A CLOSE FRIEND OF THE OPPOSITE SEX AT A SOCIAL AFFAIR

a.	Relaxed	7	6	5	4	3	2	1	Tense
b.	Pleasant	7	6	5	4	3	2	1	Unpleasant
c.	Informative	7	6	5	4	3	2	1	Not Informative
d.	Stimulating	7	6	5	4	3	2	1	Boring
e.	Self-fulfilling	7	6	5	4	3	2	1	Not Self-fulfilling

5. TALKING WITH A CLOSE FRIEND OF THE OPPOSITE SEX ABOUT YOUR FUTURE PLANS

a.	Relaxed	7	6	5	4	3	2	1	Tense
b.	Pleasant	7	6	5	4	3	2	1	Unpleasant
c.	Informative	7	6	5	4	3	2	1	Not Informative
d.	Stimulating	7	6	5	4	3	2	1	Boring
e.	Self-fulfilling	7	6	5	4	3	2	1	Not Self-fulfilling

*name*_____

6. RECEIVING A CRITICISM FROM A CLOSE FRIEND OF THE OPPOSITE SEX

a.	Relaxed	7	6	5	4	3	2	1	Tense
b.	Pleasant	7	6	5	4	3	2	1	Unpleasant
c.	Informative	7	6	5	4	3	2	1	Not Informative
d.	Stimulating	7	6	5	4	3	2	1	Boring
e.	Self-fulfilling	7	6	5	4	3	2	1	Not Self-fulfilling

7. DISCUSSING CURRENT WORLD EVENTS WITH A JOB SUPERVISOR

a.	Relaxed	7	6	5	4	3	2	1	Tense
b.	Pleasant	7	6	5	4	3	2	1	Unpleasant
c.	Informative	7	6	5	4	3	2	1	Not Informative
d.	Stimulating	7	6	5	4	3	2	1	Boring
e.	Self-fulfilling	7	6	5	4	3	2	1	Not Self-fulfilling

8. CONVERSING WITH A TEACHER AT A SOCIAL AFFAIR

a.	Relaxed	7	6	5	4	3	2	1	Tense
b.	Pleasant	7	6	5	4	3	2	1	Unpleasant
c.	Informative	7	6	5	4	3	2	1	Not Informative
d.	Stimulating	7	6	5	4	3	2	1	Boring
e.	Self-fulfilling	7	6	5	4	3	2	1	Not Self-fulfilling

9. TALKING WITH YOUR MOTHER ABOUT YOUR FUTURE PLANS

a.	Relaxed	7	6	5	4	3	2	1	Tense
b.	Pleasant	7	6	5	4	3	2	1	Unpleasant
c.	Informative	7	6	5	4	3	2	1	Not Informative
d.	Stimulating	7	6	5	4	3	2	1	Boring
e.	Self-fulfilling	7	6	5	4	3	2	1	Not Self-fulfilling

10. RECEIVING A CRITICISM FROM A TEACHER

a.	Relaxed	7	6	5	4	3	2	1	Tense
b.	Pleasant	7	6	5	4	3	2	1	Unpleasant
c.	Informative	7	6	5	4	3	2	1	Not Informative
d.	Stimulating	7	6	5	4	3	2	1	Boring
e.	Self-fulfilling	7	6	5	4	3	2	1	Not Self-fulfilling

11. DISCUSSING CURRENT WORLD EVENTS WITH YOUR FATHER

a.	Relaxed	7	6	5	4	3	2	1	Tense
b.	Pleasant	7	6	5	4	3	2	1	Unpleasant
c.	Informative	7	6	5	4	3	2	1	Not Informative
d.	Stimulating	7	6	5	4	3	2	1	Boring
e.	Self-fulfilling	7	6	5	4	3	2	1	Not Self-fulfilling

12. CONVERSING WITH YOUR MOTHER AT A SOCIAL AFFAIR

a.	Relaxed	7	6	5	4	3	2	1	Tense
b.	Pleasant	7	6	5	4	3	2	1	Unpleasant
c.	Informative	7	6	5	4	3	2	1	Not Informative
d.	Stimulating	7	6	5	4	3	2	1	Boring
e.	Self-fulfilling	7	6	5	4	3	2	1	Not Self-fulfilling

13. TALKING WITH A CLOSE FRIEND OF THE SAME SEX ABOUT YOUR FUTURE PLANS

a.	Relaxed	7	6	5	4	3	2	1	Tense
b.	Pleasant	7	6	5	4	3	2	1	Unpleasant
c.	Informative	7	6	5	4	3	2	1	Not Informative
d.	Stimulating	7	6	5	4	3	2	1	Boring
e.	Self-fulfilling	7	6	5	4	3	2	1	Not Self-fulfilling

14. RECEIVING A CRITICISM FROM YOUR FATHER

a.	Relaxed	7	6	5	4	3	2	1	Tense
b.	Pleasant	7	6	5	4	3	2	1	Unpleasant
c.	Informative	7	6	5	4	3	2	1	Not Informative
d.	Stimulating	7	6	5	4	3	2	1	Boring
e.	Self-fulfilling	7	6	5	4	3	2	1	Not Self-fulfilling

15. DISCUSSING CURRENT WORLD EVENTS WITH A TEACHER

a.	Relaxed	7	6	5	4	3	2	1	Tense
b.	Pleasant	7	6	5	4	3	2	1	Unpleasant
c.	Informative	7	6	5	4	3	2	1	Not Informative
d.	Stimulating	7	6	5	4	3	2	1	Boring
e.	Self-fulfilling	7	6	5	4	3	2	1	Not Self-fulfilling

16. CONVERSING WITH A CLOSE FRIEND OF THE SAME SEX AT A SOCIAL AFFAIR

a.	Relaxed	7	6	5	4	3	2	1	Tense
b.	Pleasant	7	6	5	4	3	2	1	Unpleasant
c.	Informative	7	6	5	4	3	2	1	Not Informative
d.	Stimulating	7	6	5	4	3	2	1	Boring
e.	Self-fulfilling	7	6	5	4	3	2	1	Not Self-fulfilling

17. TALKING WITH A JOB SUPERVISOR ABOUT YOUR FUTURE PLANS

a.	Relaxed	7	6	5	4	3	2	1	Tense
b.	Pleasant	7	6	5	4	3	2	1	Unpleasant
c.	Informative	7	6	5	4	3	2	1	Not Informative
d.	Stimulating	7	6	5	4	3	2	1	Boring
e.	Self-fulfilling	7	6	5	4	3	2	1	Not Self-fulfilling

18. RECEIVING A CRITICISM FROM A JOB SUPERVISOR

a.	Relaxed	7	6	5	4	3	2	1	Tense
b.	Pleasant	7	6	5	4	3	2	1	Unpleasant
c.	Informative	7	6	5	4	3	2	1	Not Informative
d.	Stimulating	7	6	5	4	3	2	1	Boring
e.	Self-fulfilling	7	6	5	4	3	2	1	Not Self-fulfilling

19. DISCUSSING CURRENT WORLD EVENTS WITH YOUR MOTHER

a.	Relaxed	7	6	5	4	3	2	1	Tense
b.	Pleasant	7	6	5	4	3	2	1	Unpleasant
c.	Informative	7	6	5	4	3	2	1	Not Informative
d.	Stimulating	7	6	5	4	3	2	1	Boring
e.	Self-fulfilling	7	6	5	4	3	2	1	Not Self-fulfilling

20. CONVERSING WITH A JOB SUPERVISOR AT A SOCIAL AFFAIR

a.	Relaxed	7	6	5	4	3	2	1	Tense
b.	Pleasant	7	6	5	4	3	2	1	Unpleasant
c.	Informative	7	6	5	4	3	2	1	Not Informative
d.	Stimulating	7	6	5	4	3	2	1	Boring
e.	Self-fulfilling	7	6	5	4	3	2	1	Not Self-fulfilling

21. TALKING WITH A TEACHER ABOUT YOUR FUTURE PLANS

a.	Relaxed	7	6	5	4	3	2	1	Tense
b.	Pleasant	7	6	5	4	3	2	1	Unpleasant
c.	Informative	7	6	5	4	3	2	1	Not Informative
d.	Stimulating	7	6	5	4	3	2	1	Boring
e.	Self-fulfilling	7	6	5	4	3	2	1	Not Self-fulfilling

22. RECEIVING A CRITICISM FROM A CLOSE FRIEND OF THE SAME SEX

a.	Relaxed	7	6	5	4	3	2	1	Tense
b.	Pleasant	7	6	5	4	3	2	1	Unpleasant
c.	Informative	7	6	5	4	3	2	1	Not Informative
d.	Stimulating	7	6	5	4	3	2	1	Boring
e.	Self-fulfilling	7	6	5	4	3	2	1	Not Self-fulfilling

23. DISCUSSING CURRENT WORLD EVENTS WITH A CLOSE FRIEND OF THE OPPOSITE SEX

a.	Relaxed	7	6	5	4	3	2	1	Tense
b.	Pleasant	7	6	5	4	3	2	1	Unpleasant
c.	Informative	7	6	5	4	3	2	1	Not Informative
d.	Stimulating	7	6	5	4	3	2	1	Boring
e.	Self-fulfilling	7	6	5	4	3	2	1	Not Self-fulfilling

24. CONVERSING WITH YOUR FATHER AT A SOCIAL AFFAIR

a.	Relaxed	7	6	5	4	3	2	1	Tense
b.	Pleasant	7	6	5	4	3	2	1	Unpleasant
c.	Informative	7	6	5	4	3	2	1	Not Informative
d.	Stimulating	7	6	5	4	3	2	1	Boring
e.	Self-fulfilling	7	6	5	4	3	2	1	Not Self-fulfilling

INTERPERSONAL COMMUNICATION-SITUATION ASSESSMENT SCALES

The scales which follow are designed to help you assess your reactions in the ten interpersonal communication contexts in the respective titles.

Mark the scales just as you did those in Chapter 8. First, try to imagine yourself in the situation described in the title. Then, for each of the five listed responses (a, b, c, d, e) circle the number (7, 6, 5, 4, 3, 2, 1) in the response-continuum range which best describes how you think you would feel in the designated situation.

If, for example, the descriptive term at the left end of the scale (Relaxed) *describes your feelings completely*, then circle the number 7; if the descriptive term at the right end of the scale (Tense) describes your feelings most accurately, circle the number 1.

If one of the terms *describes your feelings fairly well*, but not completely, then circle the number 6 or 2, one scale position away from the term.

If one of the terms *describes your feelings only somewhat*, but better than does the other term, then circle the number 5 or 3, two scale positions away from the appropriate term.

If neither term at the ends of the response-continuum scale seems appropriate, or if both terms *describe your feelings equally*, then circle the number 4.

Using two colored pencils, respond *twice* to the scales given here. First, complete each scale according to *how you believe you would feel* in the given contexts. Then complete the scales according to *how you believe the other person in that context would feel*. Compare the two sets of reactions or predictions. Then compare your completed scales with those of your classmates.

1. COMMUNICATING IN A LOVING RELATIONSHIP

a.	Relaxed	7	6	5	4	3	2	1	Tense
b.	Pleasant	7	6	5	4	3	2	1	Unpleasant
c.	Informative	7	6	5	4	3	2	1	Not Informative
d.	Stimulating	7	6	5	4	3	2	1	Boring
e.	Self-fulfilling	7	6	5	4	3	2	1	Not Self-fulfilling

2. COMMUNICATING IN A THERAPEUTIC SETTING

a.	Relaxed	7	6	5	4	3	2	1	Tense
b.	Pleasant	7	6	5	4	3	2	1	Unpleasant
c.	Informative	7	6	5	4	3	2	1	Not Informative
d.	Stimulating	7	6	5	4	3	2	1	Boring
e.	Self-fulfilling	7	6	5	4	3	2	1	Not Self-fulfilling

3. COMMUNICATING IN A SOCIAL CONVERSATION

a.	Relaxed	7	6	5	4	3	2	1	Tense
b.	Pleasant	7	6	5	4	3	2	1	Unpleasant
c.	Informative	7	6	5	4	3	2	1	Not Informative
d.	Stimulating	7	6	5	4	3	2	1	Boring
e.	Self-fulfilling	7	6	5	4	3	2	1	Not Self-fulfilling

4. COMMUNICATING WHILE BECOMING ACQUAINTED

a.	Relaxed	7	6	5	4	3	2	1	Tense
b.	Pleasant	7	6	5	4	3	2	1	Unpleasant
c.	Informative	7	6	5	4	3	2	1	Not Informative
d.	Stimulating	7	6	5	4	3	2	1	Boring
e.	Self-fulfilling	7	6	5	4	3	2	1	Not Self-fulfilling

5. COMMUNICATING IN AN INSTRUCTIONAL SETTING

a.	Relaxed	7	6	5	4	3	2	1	Tense
b.	Pleasant	7	6	5	4	3	2	1	Unpleasant
c.	Informative	7	6	5	4	3	2	1	Not Informative
d.	Stimulating	7	6	5	4	3	2	1	Boring
e.	Self-fulfilling	7	6	5	4	3	2	1	Not Self-fulfilling

*name*_____

6. COMMUNICATING IN AN INTERVIEW SETTING

a.	Relaxed	7	6	5	4	3	2	1	Tense
b.	Pleasant	7	6	5	4	3	2	1	Unpleasant
c.	Informative	7	6	5	4	3	2	1	Not Informative
d.	Stimulating	7	6	5	4	3	2	1	Boring
e.	Self-fulfilling	7	6	5	4	3	2	1	Not Self-fulfilling

7. COMMUNICATING IN A BARGAINING SETTING

a.	Relaxed	7	6	5	4	3	2	1	Tense
b.	Pleasant	7	6	5	4	3	2	1	Unpleasant
c.	Informative	7	6	5	4	3	2	1	Not Informative
d.	Stimulating	7	6	5	4	3	2	1	Boring
e.	Self-fulfilling	7	6	5	4	3	2	1	Not Self-fulfilling

8. COMMUNICATING IN A PERSUASIVE SETTING

a.	Relaxed	7	6	5	4	3	2	1	Tense
b.	Pleasant	7	6	5	4	3	2	1	Unpleasant
c.	Informative	7	6	5	4	3	2	1	Not Informative
d.	Stimulating	7	6	5	4	3	2	1	Boring
e.	Self-fulfilling	7	6	5	4	3	2	1	Not Self-fulfilling

9. COMMUNICATING IN A COMBATIVE SETTING

a.	Relaxed	7	6	5	4	3	2	1	Tense
b.	Pleasant	7	6	5	4	3	2	1	Unpleasant
c.	Informative	7	6	5	4	3	2	1	Not Informative
d.	Stimulating	7	6	5	4	3	2	1	Boring
e.	Self-fulfilling	7	6	5	4	3	2	1	Not Self-fulfilling

10. COMMUNICATING IN A COERCIVE SETTING

a.	Relaxed	7	6	5	4	3	2	1	Tense
b.	Pleasant	7	6	5	4	3	2	1	Unpleasant
c.	Informative	7	6	5	4	3	2	1	Not Informative
d.	Stimulating	7	6	5	4	3	2	1	Boring
e.	Self-fulfilling	7	6	5	4	3	2	1	Not Self-fulfilling

1. COMMUNICATING IN A LOVING RELATIONSHIP

		7	6	5	4	3	2	1	
a.	Relaxed	7	6	5	4	3	2	1	Tense
b.	Pleasant	7	6	5	4	3	2	1	Unpleasant
c.	Informative	7	6	5	4	3	2	1	Not Informative
d.	Stimulating	7	6	5	4	3	2	1	Boring
e.	Self-fulfilling	7	6	5	4	3	2	1	Not Self-fulfilling

2. COMMUNICATING IN A THERAPEUTIC SETTING

a.	Relaxed	7	6	5	4	3	2	1	Tense
b.	Pleasant	7	6	5	4	3	2	1	Unpleasant
c.	Informative	7	6	5	4	3	2	1	Not Informative
d.	Stimulating	7	6	5	4	3	2	1	Boring
e.	Self-fulfilling	7	6	5	4	3	2	1	Not Self-fulfilling

3. COMMUNICATING IN A SOCIAL CONVERSATION

a.	Relaxed	7	6	5	4	3	2	1	Tense
b.	Pleasant	7	6	5	4	3	2	1	Unpleasant
c.	Informative	7	6	5	4	3	2	1	Not Informative
d.	Stimulating	7	6	5	4	3	2	1	Boring
e.	Self-fulfilling	7	6	5	4	3	2	1	Not Self-fulfilling

4. COMMUNICATING WHILE BECOMING ACQUAINTED

a.	Relaxed	7	6	5	4	3	2	1	Tense
b.	Pleasant	7	6	5	4	3	2	1	Unpleasant
c.	Informative	7	6	5	4	3	2	1	Not Informative
d.	Stimulating	7	6	5	4	3	2	1	Boring
e.	Self-fulfilling	7	6	5	4	3	2	1	Not Self-fulfilling

5. COMMUNICATING IN AN INSTRUCTIONAL SETTING

a.	Relaxed	7	6	5	4	3	2	1	Tense
b.	Pleasant	7	6	5	4	3	2	1	Unpleasant
c.	Informative	7	6	5	4	3	2	1	Not Informative
d.	Stimulating	7	6	5	4	3	2	1	Boring
e.	Self-fulfilling	7	6	5	4	3	2	1	Not Self-fulfilling

*name*_____

6. COMMUNICATING IN AN INTERVIEW SETTING

a.	Relaxed	7	6	5	4	3	2	1	Tense
b.	Pleasant	7	6	5	4	3	2	1	Unpleasant
c.	Informative	7	6	5	4	3	2	1	Not Informative
d.	Stimulating	7	6	5	4	3	2	1	Boring
e.	Self-fulfilling	7	6	5	4	3	2	1	Not Self-fulfilling

7. COMMUNICATING IN A BARGAINING SETTING

a.	Relaxed	7	6	5	4	3	2	1	Tense
b.	Pleasant	7	6	5	4	3	2	1	Unpleasant
c.	Informative	7	6	5	4	3	2	1	Not Informative
d.	Stimulating	7	6	5	4	3	2	1	Boring
e.	Self-fulfilling	7	6	5	4	3	2	1	Not Self-fulfilling

8. COMMUNICATING IN A PERSUASIVE SETTING

a.	Relaxed	7	6	5	4	3	2	1	Tense
b.	Pleasant	7	6	5	4	3	2	1	Unpleasant
c.	Informative	7	6	5	4	3	2	1	Not Informative
d.	Stimulating	7	6	5	4	3	2	1	Boring
e.	Self-fulfilling	7	6	5	4	3	2	1	Not Self-fulfilling

9. COMMUNICATING IN A COMBATIVE SETTING

a.	Relaxed	7	6	5	4	3	2	1	Tense
b.	Pleasant	7	6	5	4	3	2	1	Unpleasant
c.	Informative	7	6	5	4	3	2	1	Not Informative
d.	Stimulating	7	6	5	4	3	2	1	Boring
e.	Self-fulfilling	7	6	5	4	3	2	1	Not Self-fulfilling

10. COMMUNICATING IN A COERCIVE SETTING

a.	Relaxed	7	6	5	4	3	2	1	Tense
b.	Pleasant	7	6	5	4	3	2	1	Unpleasant
c.	Informative	7	6	5	4	3	2	1	Not Informative
d.	Stimulating	7	6	5	4	3	2	1	Boring
e.	Self-fulfilling	7	6	5	4	3	2	1	Not Self-fulfilling

ANALYZING DISCUSSION PARTICIPATION: SMALL GROUP INTERACTION

Observe a small group discussion and tally each comment made by each participant. Using a chart like the one below, indicate to whom each comment was made. Distinguish between comments made to other individuals and those addressed to the group as a whole.

CHARTING DISCUSSANTS' INTERACTION

Person Making Comment	Person to Whom Comment Is Directed						Total Comments
	A	B	C	D	E	Group	
A	—						
B		—					
C			—				
D				—			
E					—		

Who made the most comments? Who made the fewest comments? Who most often addressed the group as a whole? Can you identify cliques by finding persons who speak most often to one another? In your opinion who was the task leader, and who was the social-emotional leader? Compare their profiles on the chart. What other pertinent information can be gleaned from this kind of analysis?

SMALL GROUP INTERACTION—ANALYSIS OF COMMENTS

Observe a small task group, and analyze their discussion participation according to the types of comments which are made by the members. Using a chart like the one below, tally and categorize each comment made by each participant.

CHARTING TYPES OF DISCUSSANTS' COMMENTS

Person	Initiating new ideas	Clarifying ideas	Substantiating ideas	Developing ideas	Summarizing ideas	Agreeing	Disagreeing	Asking questions	Making procedural comments
A									
B									
C									
D									
E									

Who would you judge to be the task leader and the social-emotional leader of the group? Compare their profiles. What other conclusions can you draw from an analysis of this kind?

name

ANALYZING DISCUSSION PARTICIPATION:
SMALL GROUP INTERACTION

Observe a small group discussion and tally each comment made by each participant. Using a chart like the one below, indicate to whom each comment was made. Distinguish between comments made to other individuals and those addressed to the group as a whole.

CHARTING DISCUSSANTS' INTERACTION

Person Making Comment	Person to Whom Comment Is Directed						Total Comments
	A	B	C	D	E	Group	
A	—						
B		—					
C			—				
D				—			
E					—		

Who made the most comments? Who made the fewest comments? Who most often addressed the group as a whole? Can you identify cliques by finding persons who speak most often to one another? In your opinion who was the task leader, and who was the social-emotional leader? Compare their profiles on the chart. What other pertinent information can be gleaned from this kind of analysis?

SMALL GROUP INTERACTION—ANALYSIS OF COMMENTS

Observe a small task group, and analyze their discussion participation according to the types of comments which are made by the members. Using a chart like the one below, tally and categorize each comment made by each participant.

CHARTING TYPES OF DISCUSSANTS' COMMENTS

Person	Initiating new ideas	Clarifying ideas	Substantiating ideas	Developing ideas	Summarizing ideas	Agreeing	Disagreeing	Asking questions	Making procedural comments
A									
B									
C									
D									
E									

Who would you judge to be the task leader and the social-emotional leader of the group? Compare their profiles. What other conclusions can you draw from an analysis of this kind?

name_____

EVALUATING PUBLIC SPEECH COMMUNICATION: A CHECKLIST

Instructions for Using the Speech Evaluation Checklist

In the "Evaluations" column, use ratings from 1 to 7 along a continuum from "needs improvement" (1) to "well done" (7) to indicate your evaluation of the successive component-factors. In the "Comments" column, you should write brief explanatory notes that reflect and amplify the reasons for your ratings. The marked Sample Checklist in Chapter 10, pages 336–337, further explains the use of this evaluative form and suggests some types of "Comments" which may be useful for your analytical purposes.

SPEECH EVALUATION CHECKLIST

Factors	Evaluations	Comments
1. Specific Purpose		
Clear and to the point		
Appropriately narrowed in scope		
Appropriate for listener-agents		
Appropriate for context		
2. Introduction		
Attention of listener-agents secured		
Interest of listener-agents developed		
Specific purpose related to listener-agents		
3. Body		
Main points fulfilled specific purpose		
Main points appropriately patterned		
Main points emphasized		
Main points unified and coherent		
Developmental materials varied and helpful		
Transitions effective		
Internal summaries helpful		
4. Conclusion		
Final summary effective		
Final appeal appropriate		
5. Facilitative Materials		
Visual aids helpful to purpose		
Visual aids used effectively		
Humor used effectively		

*name*_____

Factors	Evaluations	Comments
6. Language Usage		
Language clear		
Language appropriate to listener-agents		
Language appropriate to context		
Language vivid		
7. Delivery		
Vocal variety utilized		
Pronunciation and articulation appropriate		
Phrasing and pausing effective		
Vocalized pauses avoided		
Good posture practiced		
Ease of movement demonstrated		
Gestures natural		
Facial expressiveness varied		
8. Ethos Development		
Knowledge demonstrated		
Trustworthiness shown		
Dynamism / Magnetism shown		
OVERALL EFFECTIVENESS		

SPEECH EVALUATION CHECKLIST

Factors	Evaluations	Comments
1. Specific Purpose		
Clear and to the point		
Appropriately narrowed in scope		
Appropriate for listener-agents		
Appropriate for context		
2. Introduction		
Attention of listener-agents secured		
Interest of listener-agents developed		
Specific purpose related to listener-agents		
3. Body		
Main points fulfilled specific purpose		
Main points appropriately patterned		
Main points emphasized		
Main points unified and coherent		
Developmental materials varied and helpful		
Transitions effective		
Internal summaries helpful		
4. Conclusion		
Final summary effective		
Final appeal appropriate		
5. Facilitative Materials		
Visual aids helpful to purpose		
Visual aids used effectively		
Humor used effectively		

name_____

Factors	Evaluations	Comments
6. Language Usage		
Language clear		
Language appropriate to listener-agents		
Language appropriate to context		
Language vivid		
7. Delivery		
Vocal variety utilized		
Pronunciation and articulation appropriate		
Phrasing and pausing effective		
Vocalized pauses avoided		
Good posture practiced		
Ease of movement demonstrated		
Gestures natural		
Facial expressiveness varied		
8. Ethos Development		
Knowledge demonstrated		
Trustworthiness shown		
Dynamism / Magnetism shown		
OVERALL EFFECTIVENESS		

SPEECH EVALUATION CHECKLIST

Factors	Evaluations	Comments
1. Specific Purpose		
Clear and to the point		
Appropriately narrowed in scope		
Appropriate for listener-agents		
Appropriate for context		
2. Introduction		
Attention of listener-agents secured		
Interest of listener-agents developed		
Specific purpose related to listener-agents		
3. Body		
Main points fulfilled specific purpose		
Main points appropriately patterned		
Main points emphasized		
Main points unified and coherent		
Developmental materials varied and helpful		
Transitions effective		
Internal summaries helpful		
4. Conclusion		
Final summary effective		
Final appeal appropriate		
5. Facilitative Materials		
Visual aids helpful to purpose		
Visual aids used effectively		
Humor used effectively		

name_____

Factors	Evaluations	Comments
6. Language Usage		
Language clear		
Language appropriate to listener-agents		
Language appropriate to context		
Language vivid		
7. Delivery		
Vocal variety utilized		
Pronunciation and articulation appropriate		
Phrasing and pausing effective		
Vocalized pauses avoided		
Good posture practiced		
Ease of movement demonstrated		
Gestures natural		
Facial expressiveness varied		
8. Ethos Development		
Knowledge demonstrated		
Trustworthiness shown		
Dynamism / Magnetism shown		
OVERALL EFFECTIVENESS		

Study Probes

Chapter 6   Speech Communication: Sensation, Perception, Language, and Reasoning

Chapter 7   Decision Making

Chapter 10   Achieving Interaction with Many: Speech Making

Index